Communications
in Computer and Information Science 726

Commenced Publication in 2007
Founding and Former Series Editors:
Alfredo Cuzzocrea, Dominik Ślęzak, and Xiaokang Yang

More information about this series at http://www.springer.com/series/7899

Luca Longo · M. Chiara Leva (Eds.)

Human Mental Workload

Models and Applications

First International Symposium, H-WORKLOAD 2017
Dublin, Ireland, June 28–30, 2017
Revised Selected Papers

 Springer

Editors
Luca Longo ⓘ
Dublin Institute of Technology
Dublin
Ireland

M. Chiara Leva
Dublin Institute of Technology
Dublin
Ireland

ISSN 1865-0929   ISSN 1865-0937 (electronic)
Communications in Computer and Information Science
ISBN 978-3-319-61060-3   ISBN 978-3-319-61061-0 (eBook)
DOI 10.1007/978-3-319-61061-0

Library of Congress Control Number: 2017943071

Printed on acid-free paper

This Springer imprint is published by Springer Nature
The registered company is Springer International Publishing AG
The registered company address is: Gewerbestrasse 11, 6330 Cham, Switzerland

Preface

The pervasive use of technologies in daily activities and working environments in the last decade is defining a changed environment where the requirement for cognitive resources seems to be increasing while the level of physical effort seems to be decreasing. The rapid developments in the Internet of Things (IoT) and its novel automation archetypes in cyber-physical systems as well as the upscaling of big data analytical requirements are a few examples of underpinning elements marking an increased cognitive demand on individuals to perform control tasks and achieve an overview of the distributed systems we are required to monitor. The principal reason for measuring mental workload is to quantify the mental cost of performing tasks and its implications on human performance. The modeling of human mental workload (MWL) can be used to inform the design of interfaces, technologies, and information-processing activities better aligned to the human mental limited capacities. Understanding the mechanisms of MWL, its main drivers, and how MWL affects human performance is an open fundamental problem. Research on mental workload can be traced back to the early 1960s; since then there have been hundreds of studies on the measurement of mental workload. However, as pointed out by Wickens in this volume, the scientific and industrial communities still need to be provided with a validated set of models and metrics for MWL. There are many operational definitions of MWL from various fields but they often disagree about its main contributing factors, its dimensions, and the mechanism to aggregate these dimensions and their impact on human performance. This trend is also confirmed by the best papers selected in this book from the proceedings of H-WORKLOAD 2017: the First International Symposium on Human Mental Workload. The selected papers went through a strict review process, with an average of four reviews for each paper. Some authors considered task-specific dimensions, while others chose a combination of task- and user-specific dimensions. Primary researchers have mainly employed self-reporting measurements or a combination of psychophysiological techniques. However, the development of a generally applicable model that manages to incorporate task, user, and context-specific dimensions is yet to be achieved.

As pointed out by Hancock in one of the chapter in this volume, the development of new models should consider subjective, task-objective, and physiological measures together and not in an isolated way, so as to address the scope of cross validation. Brookhuis's contribution at the symposium recommended further efforts in the area of convergence of various measurement techniques for MWL. Past and present research on MWL modeling has had a tendency to focus on complex safety-critical systems generating a plethora of simulations and applications that seems to be rather "ad hoc" and specific to the domain or area of application (such as the models and measures adopted in the rail, aviation, and nuclear industry etc.). However, various researchers in other fields are now highlighting the need for robust and transferable MWL models for predicting human performance employable for design purposes in everyday activities and in domains like manufacturing of electronic goods, human–device interaction, teaching, learning, and training, which are significantly different from the original safety-critical ones.

This book endeavors to stimulate and encourage further discussion on mental workload, its measures, dimensions, models, applications, and consequences. We believe this discussion should be multidisciplinary, and not only confined to ergonomics. It should be at the intersection of the fields of human factor, computer science, psychology, neuroscience, and statistics. This book presents recent developments in the context of theoretical models of MWL and practical applications aimed at task support and MWL management in operations. Thus, the contributions have been organized in two sections: models of MWL and applications.

The idea for the book and its central theme arose in the context of the First International Symposium on Mental Workload, Models and Applications (H-WORKLOAD 2017. We wish to thank all the people who helped in the Organizing Committee of the First International Symposium on Mental Workload, Models and Applications (H-WORKLOAD 2017), in particular Dr. Nora Balfe, Dr. Dervla Horgan, Dr. Sarah Sharples, Dr. Bridget Kane, Ms. Paula Hicks, Mr. Rory Carrick, Dr. Leonard O'Sullivan, Dr. Matjaz Galicic, Mr. Maurice Wilkins, Ms. Alison Kay, Ms. Eileen Murphy, and many more of the members of the Scientific Committee. We want to also thank the sponsors of the event, the Irish Ergonomics Society, The ADAPT Center (Global Center for Excellence in Digital Content and Media Innovation), without whom neither the conference nor the book would have been realized. Our gratitude is extended to the Chartered Institute of Ergonomics and Human Factors, the Dublin Institute of Technology, Science Foundation Ireland, as well as all the reviewers of the Program Committee who provided constructive feedback. A special thanks goes to the researchers and practitioners who submitted their work and attended the event allowing us to meet and share our experiences on this fascinating topic.

May 2017   Luca Longo
                                                                            M. Chiara Leva

Organization

Organizing Committee

General Chairs and Editors

Luca Longo	Dublin Institute of Technology
Chiara Leva	Dublin Institute of Technology

Program Committee and Publication Chairs

Bridget Kane	Karlstad University, Sweden
Sarah Sharples	University of Nottingham, UK

Publicity Chair

Nora Balfe	Transport Research Laboratory, UK

Finance Chair

Dervla Hogan	University College Cork, Ireland

Steering Committee

Luca Longo	Dublin Institute of Technology
Chiara Leva	Dublin Institute of Technology

Program Committee

Nora Balfe	Transport Research Laboratory, UK
Roland Barge	Rolls-Royce, UK
Emanuele Bellini	LOGOS, Italy
Ronald Boring	Idaho National Lab, USA
Karel Brookhuis	University of Groningen, The Netherlands
Aydan Byrne	Swansea University, UK
Joan Cahill	Trinity College Dublin, Ireland
Brad Cain	CAE Defence and Security, Canada
Tiziana Callari	Università di Torino, SAA School of Management, Italy
Martin Castor	The Group of Effectiveness, Interaction, Simulation, Technology and Training, Sweden
Loredana Cerrato	Eitdigital, Sweden
Michael Cooke	Trinity College Dublin, Ireland
Siobhan Corrigan	Trinity College Dublin, Ireland
António Pedro Costa	Universidade de Aveiro e Ludomedia, Portugal
Micaela Demichela	Politecnico di Torino, Italy
Dick Dewaard	University of Groningen, The Netherlands
Pierpaolo Dondio	Dublin Institute of Technology, Ireland

Contents

Models

Whither Workload? Mapping a Path for Its Future Development.   3
  P.A. Hancock

Mental Workload: Assessment, Prediction and Consequences 18
  Christopher D. Wickens

Assessment of Mental Workload: A Comparison of Machine
Learning Methods and Subjective Assessment Techniques 30
  Karim Moustafa, Saturnino Luz, and Luca Longo

Elasticity and Rigidity Constructs and Ratings of Subjective Workload
for Individuals and Groups. 51
  Stephen J. Guastello, David E. Marra, Anthony N. Correro II,
  Maura Michels, and Henry Schimmel

Observations and Issues in the Application of Cognitive Workload
Modelling for Decision Making in Complex Time-Critical Environments 77
  K. Tara Smith

The Impact of Workload and Fatigue on Performance 90
  Jialin Fan and Andrew P. Smith

Estimation of Train Driver Workload: Extracting Taskload Measures
from On-Train-Data-Recorders 106
  Nora Balfe, Katie Crowley, Brendan Smith, and Luca Longo

The Relationship Between Workload and Performance in Air Traffic
Control: Exploring the Influence of Levels of Automation and Variation
in Task Demand 120
  Tamsyn Edwards, Lynne Martin, Nancy Bienert, and Joey Mercer

Applications

The WASCAL-Tool: Prediction of Staffing for Train Dispatching
as Part of the Design Process of Track Yards 143
  Melcher Zeilstra, Alfred van Wincoop, and Jouke Rypkema

Adaptive Automation and the Third Pilot: Managing Teamwork
and Workload in an Airline Cockpit 161
    Joan Cahill, Tiziana C. Callari, Florian Fortmann, Stefan Suck,
    Denis Javaux, Andreas Hasselberg, Sybert H. Stoeve,
    and Bas A. van Doorn

Quantification of Rail Signaller Demand Through Simulation 174
    Lise Delamare, David Golightly, Graham Goswell, and Peter Treble

Mental Workload as an Outcome in Medical Education 187
    Aidan Byrne

Effect of Control-Display Compatibility on the Mental Workload
of Submarine Helmsmen 198
    Philippe Rauffet, Christine Chauvin, Chiara Nistico, Samantha Judas,
    and Norbert Toumelin

Neuroergonomics Method for Measuring the Influence of Mental Workload
Modulation on Cognitive State of Manual Assembly Worker 213
    Pavle Mijović, Miloš Milovanović, Vanja Ković, Ivan Gligorijević,
    Bogdan Mijović, and Ivan Mačužić

The Benefits of Task and Cognitive Workload Support for Operators
in Ground Handling 225
    M. Chiara Leva and Yilmar Builes

Workload Differences Between On-road and Off-road Manoeuvres
for Motorcyclists. 239
    Simon Tong, Shaun Helman, Nora Balfe, Camila Fowler,
    Emma Delmonte, and R. Hutchins

Workload, Fatigue and Performance in the Rail Industry 251
    Andrew P. Smith and Hugo N. Smith

Author Index 265

Models

Whither Workload? Mapping a Path for Its Future Development

P.A. Hancock[(⊠)]

Department of Psychology, and Institute for Simulation and Training,
University of Central Florida, Orlando, FL 32816, USA
Peter.Hancock@ucf.edu

Abstract. I present a number of looming barriers to a smooth path of progress
for cognitive workload assessment. The first of these is the AID's of workload
(i.e., association, indifference, and dissociation) between its various reflections
(i.e., subjective, physiological, and performance measures). The second is the
manner in which the time-varying change in imposed task demand links to the
workload response, and what specific characteristics of the former drive the
latter. The third is the persistent but largely unaddressed issue of the mean-
ingfulness of the work undertaken. Thus, does interesting and involving work
result in lower workload and vice-versa? If these foregoing and predominantly
methodological concerns can be overcome, then the utility of the workload
construct can continue to grow. If they cannot be resolved then workload
assessment threatens to be ineffective in a world which desperately requires a
valid and reliable way to index cognitive achievement.

Keywords: Cognitive workload · Neuropsychological assessment · Future
challenges

1 Introduction

From a radical materialist perspective, cognitive workload is an emergent property of
the active brain which is tasked with a mission of survival in an incompletely specified
and under-explained world. While I do not share such a philosophical stance completely (Hancock 2015),[1] I am persuaded that this is the most promising foundation
from which to take our next pragmatic steps along the path of workload's journey. And
of course, this voyage is not one simply of philosophical dispute and debate. Rather,
there are many, much more practical everyday issues involved here in solving the
problems of cognitive workload assessment. Consider only two examples. First, how
do we measure and remunerate cognitive work? We generally accept that in our
modern world the cognitive dimensions of work have grown and continue to grow
across the global society. We also know that for an economic system to flourish we

---

[1] I am, rather, a real illusionist. That is, I subscribe to the existence of matter but believe all perceived
patterns in such matter are iatrogenic illusion. Such illusions are embedded in the standard narrative
of living existence, the final illusion of which is time. As a tool, time can be a useful servant but a
poor master.

© Springer International Publishing AG 2017
L. Longo and M.C. Leva (Eds.): H-WORKLOAD 2017, CCIS 726, pp. 3–17, 2017.
DOI: 10.1007/978-3-319-61061-0_1

have to be able to specify what connotes value. So how we measure, index and reward cognitive achievement is not a question simply for the hallowed halls of academe. Actually, it is front and center on the Wall Streets and Main Streets around the world. A second example of such practical concerns revolves around the issue as to how much cognitive load can one individual, or team of individuals sustain before they become incapacitated and/or unable to respond effectively. Such a concern is central to many systems which inevitably have to place high demands on these operators in both normal and emergency situations. Knowing these thresholds and 'redlines' may well help in alleviating incipient disaster. So, while we behavioral scientists research and discourse about the fundamental nature of cognitive workload, the world awaits. Whether it realizes it or not, or acknowledges this dependence explicitly or not, greater society needs reliable and valid methods to assessment workload.

As an emergent brain state, workload does not stand alone. It has a number of closely related conceptual cousins. Stress, anxiety, and fatigue among many others are each socially recognized cognitive attributes about which sufficient people express sufficient agreement so that we persist in considering them concepts of interest and even states of objective reality. Alongside these 'energetic' descriptors sit allied terms such as (i) attention (e.g., Wickens 2002), (ii) situation awareness (e.g., Endsley 1995) and (iii) consciousness (e.g., Smith and Hancock 1995) each of which similarly describe specific, discrete aspects of emergent states of mind. It is one of the central conundrums of all psychology to distill how each of these concepts relate one to another, and which possess precedence in the materialist cause and effect phenomenology. Questions intrinsic to this multi-dimensional Venn diagram populate our own particular area of scientific discourse since, as a group, we are primarily concerned with understanding human behavior. Thus, questions like, do you have to be conscious to possess situation awareness? Can we pay attention to our own stress to the exclusion of the demands of the greater environment? And most trenchantly for the present discussion, to what degree does attention mediate and/or moderate the experience of workload? Such puzzles tend to concern us particularly. We can all generate potential answers to the foregoing interrogatories, but the degree to which they apply to one single individual (such as yourself for example) and can then be expressed across the whole human population, is one of the primary intellectual challenges that fuels our specific scientific enterprise. And again, the world is watching, as evidenced by almost any of the contemporary, lurid newscasts which tragically revel in the most recent and noteworthy systemic failure in which shortfalls to human response capacities are invoked as the primary causal mechanism (e.g., the ubiquitous, human error).

Conceptual foundations are important of course. However, in the present work I want to explore three very specific and very practical issues which represents barriers to our immediate road to understanding. The first is concerned with what happens when we witness divergent information from our various workload measurement techniques and sources. That is, what happens when differing reflections of cognitive workload disagree with each other. Here, the empirical picture can quickly become very confused and confusing. Thus, I look to bring some order to counteract this confusion and offer a descriptive taxonomy which provides an initial parsing of the panoply of the differing possible patterns that may be observed. Second, I want to offer up some potential reasons for these problematic association-insensitivity-dissociation patterns and some avenues of potential progress by which we might recognize systematic resolutions. Finally, I want to consider the thorny issue of the meaning of work (and see Hancock 1997). With respect to the latter concern, we have to date, in large part, treated task demand as some rather antiseptic and sterile conception. Either we choose prototypical 'psychological' tasks (e.g., a Sternberg memory task) and then claim that results derived from such experiments somehow generalize to actual work contexts, or we explore some specific, complex (often military) mission whose generality is highly limited. Even for these two putative 'testbeds,' the value and meaning of the work itself can vary wildly. The source of motivation in such research investigations is often extrinsic to the task (e.g., course credit, TDY completion). The nature of the work undertaken, whether adverse and imposed, or pleasant and sought by the individual, is rarely factored into workload assessment. Here, I want to argue for the important, if daunting, inclusion of this dimension of meaning into our future deliberations. I conclude with some observations concerning specific future avenues of progress and remarks about the continuing importance of workload, even in a world that is threatened to be overrun with automation and autonomy (Hancock 2014; 2017).

2 Associations, Insensitivities and Dissociations: The AID's of Workload

One of the greatest challenges to be faced by the evolving workload domain concerns the degree of convergence, and/or divergence, and/or insensitivity across the multiple approaches that have been employed to measure it. The three primary reflections of workload have traditionally been couched in terms of (1) primary task performance (2) subjective perceptions and (3) physiological responses (Hancock and Meshkati 1988; Meshkati et al. 1989; Moray 1979). Each of these respective categories has, contained within it numerous possible elements (i.e., specific methods such as, TLX, fNIR, Error Rate, etc.). Thus, primary tasks are typically indexed by representations of Efficiency, Error, Time, etc. We have extensive experience with response speed and response accuracy and have reason to believe that we have a solid foundation in such forms of assessment (see e.g., Fitts 1954; Hancock and Newell 1985). Similarly, we have some decades or more experience in eliciting subjective perceptions of events. Finally, and to a degree more recent, we have vastly increased our armory of physiological assessment techniques. This increase is especially the case as new brain imaging capacities have come on line. Let us then examine the patterns that can accrue when we employ the full array of these measurement techniques to attack any particular problems to hand.

To accomplish this, let us imagine for a moment, a fairly straightforward experiment. Across a defined period of time, the imposed demand of some particular task is sequentially increased. Perhaps this is a driving task with the driver going from a quiet sub-urban backwater onto an urban arterial and then onto a crowded, multi-lane freeway. The context, pro tem, is not constrained and so you are free to imagine your own example from your own specific domain if you wish. Now we look at the outcome workload response. Here, we expect to see primary task measures show some form of systematic decline, especially as the demand progressively increases. Perhaps the variability of steering, reflected in lane positioning, goes up in the case I have cited. Perhaps response time to unexpected ambient events slows and/or exhibits greater error. Although the driver may adapt to such imposed demands, to the degree possible, we might well envisage that eventually some reflection of the progressively increasing task demand will become evident in changes in primary task response efficiency. Now imagine that we ask that driver for their subjective assessment of this same progression. We might well anticipate that on the leafy back roads they experience little perceived workload but that it would increase with the transition to the arterial roadway and then subsequently again to the freeway experience also. This direct mapping between the primary task response and the subjective assessment is an example of what I have called *association* (Hancock 1996). Now, suppose we also had the opportunity to measure certain established physiological reflections of cognitive load and that these measures also confirmed that the lowest workload occurred in the lowest demand and the highest workload in the highest demand condition. This would be an example of what I term here, *double association* (see Fig. 1). In workload terms, so far so good. However, such associations and especially these double associations do not always occur. In fact, such associations appear to be far from ubiquitous.

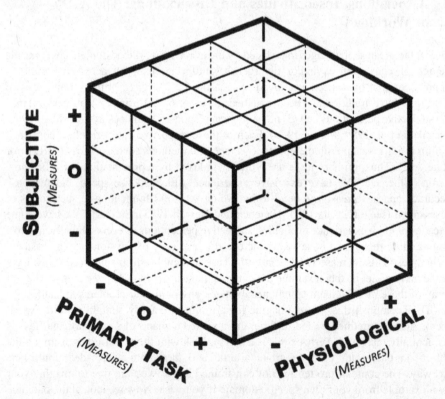

Fig. 1. The response to imposed task load by the three primary measures of workload, viz: (i) primary task performance, (ii) subjective response, and (iii) physiological processes. Patterns of association, insensitivity, and dissociation can be plotted within the identified taxonomic matrix.

So, let us now take an intermediate case. Here again, the degradation in primary performance efficiency tracks along with the increasing task demand, but now when we ask people for their subjective assessment, they report no difference between the three driving conditions. This is an example of what I have termed *insensitivity*, and to be explicit, this case specifically it refers to *subjective insensitivity* since the expectation is that both primary task performance and subjective response will track imposed task demand. While there may be, and indeed are, many reasons why the link between the task response and subjective perceptions of workload fail to agree, let us leave explanatory constructs to the side for the moment and return to them later so that we can complete the full descriptive picture. You might very well note, however, that in this latter case of subjective insensitivity we still retain that other arrow in our investigative quiver in the form of the aforementioned physiological measures. Let us further suppose here that these latter measures now accord with the pattern of primary response, but which relationship do we believe? Do we assume a form of scientific democracy and go with the majority vote? But this may not be advisable, for after all, as Gilbert (2005) has noted, in many ways it is the subjective reaction of the individual which is the principle measure of concern since they actually compose the very experiences of life. It leaves us in a methodological (and theoretical) quandary. But there are further descriptive patterns yet to consider.

The illustration in Fig. 1 shows responses to imposed task demand by the three primary measures of workload, viz: (i) primary task performance, (ii) subjective response, and (iii) physiological processes. As a result of increasing task load, primary task performance can show an improvement (+), stay the same (o), or decrease (−). Similarly, subjective responses can indicate that with increasing task load the individual can think the task is harder (−), the same (o), or even easier (+). The same pattern adheres to physiological reflections (see Fig. 1). When workload responses track to external task load we have *associations*, when reflections of workload do not change with task load we have *insensitivities*. Finally, when workload measures contradict the increase in the externally imposed task load (e.g., the task load increases but the operator reports that it is getting easier), then we have *dissociations* (see also: Yeh and Wickens 1988). Doubled associations, insensitivities and dissociations are also possible as we shall see.

Now suppose, for the sake of consistency, that primary measures still directly co-varied with what we have previously identified as increasing task demand[2]. But now, the driver reports progressively less subjective workload, even as the primary tasks measures indicate exactly the opposite. This represents an example of what I have previously termed *dissociation* (Hancock 1996; see also Yeh and Wickens 1988). It is not enough here that these differing reflections of workload do not agree (for that pattern can also include insensitivities). Rather, they must actively contradict one another. We might again choose to appeal to our suite of physiological reflections (if we have taken them) as some form of arbiter, but in this specific instance, they provide

---

[2] Of course, exactly how we determine, a priori, what represents increasing 'task demand' is itself an issue fraught with the problem of subjective assessment. For the present example, I have based the arguments on an assumption of increasing demand but need to acknowledge the potential flaws in this foundation.

no determining pattern. I refer to such collective disagreements as *double dissociations*. These cases provide very problematic outcomes for our science. Of course, they are not so prevalent in our experimental library as might be expected from pure random distributions of outcomes. Understandably, positive associations are reported much more frequently that these other patterns. However, there may well be a very considerable '*file-drawer effect*' in operation here. That is, we all have the tendency to report the positive results. We also have a tendency to report consistent results, not through some malevolent motive, but through the natural tendency to seek a coherent narrative for our immediate findings. Further, in the editorial process, we are often encouraged to provide a concise results section in which null associations (e.g., insensitivities) are often 'lost' or excised in the process.

Nor is this the worst case of dissociation or insensitivity. Imagine for a moment that you have taken several reflections of each of the three major methods. You have recorded both TLX and SWAT for subjective reflections, HRV and fNIR as physiological measures, and time and accuracy as primary task response characteristics. Now suppose that you encounter dissociations and insensitivities *within* each of these three orders of measure. What do you do? How do you pick and choose between the intra-method dissociations and insensitivities and the inter-method dissociations and insensitivities? And, of course, some of the intra-method disagreements will now negate some of the inter-method disagreements. This represents a conceptual, methodological, and even moral conundrum. As a conscientious researcher, which do you choose? It is why I refer to this whole concern as the AIDs of workload. Of course, as is clear from the foregoing observations on inter- and intra-method conflicts, the illustration in Fig. 1 underestimates the complexity of this overall issue. While it does not feature the inter- versus intra-method concern, critically, it does it illustrate the perennial and problematic issue of time. Hence, all such patterns of association, insensitivity, and dissociation are contingent upon the time-scale at which they are elicited. What are associations in one selected epoch can become dissociations in another. This is particularly the case with punctate or monetary performance measures (e.g., reaction time) compared to, for example, subjective measures which are often summed (in memory) across a much longer period. As we shall see in the coming discussion, there is strong reason to believe that each of these methods (and each of their component elements) possess their own inherent time-scale and that certain, if not many, of the associations, dissociations and insensitivities are contingent upon such temporal differences. And to pile pain upon pain, I now have to return to the vexing issue of context.

The reader will recall that, pro tem, I suspended contextual considerations. I did this so that we could consider a full (if static) taxonomic description of all the general AIDs patterns that can be experienced. However, I cannot pass over the issue of context without at least some words of caution. There are many ways in which the context of operations influence the workload response beyond the primary performance demand alone. Humans are no simple linear transducers of imposed (input) loading (Hancock and Warm 1989). Rather, their non-linear responses are complex and time-varying. Efforts to understand contextual influences, in all their diversity and profundity has, in our science, led to a more ready focus on the 'systems' approach to practical problem resolution (see e.g., Carayon et al. 2015). In respect of such 'systems' perspectives, perhaps one of the primary, proximal concerns here revolves around the adaptive capacity of the exposed individual. As I noted earlier, to a degree externally imposed cognitive task demand can be absorbed by the inherent buffering capacity of the engaged respondent with little or no overt evidence of change. To this extent, in the middle ranges of externally imposed task demand, it is reasonable, at least a priori, to hypothesize no significant change in any reflection of cognitive workload. Thus, in driving a vehicle, which is predominantly a satisficed task, we may register no extra variation in lane position, no overt change in throttle behavior, and even exhibit capacities to respond to multiple tasks at modest levels of roadway demand without any clear decrement. Drivers themselves may feel no different, and measures such as heart rate variability will also exhibit no significant change with minor variations in imposed task demand. This evidence of workload insensitivity to putative changes in objective, externally imposed task demands does not then mean the individual is oblivious to, or careless of, the task in front of them (and see Hancock and Caird 1993). It simply means that the demand is insufficient to disturb what has been traditionally identified as homeostatic balance. The simple fact here is that there is quite a large range of externally imposed demands that will not induce workload changes in our grosser measures. It may even be difficult in signal to noise terms, to pick up even minor response variations via even much more sophisticated neurophysiological techniques. Thus, the very assumption of a baseline of association is not necessarily a simple or straightforward one. Being enmeshed in this forest of methodological mysteries, can we find a systematic path forward? I think there is reason for hope that, in this case, we can.

3 Dimensions of the Workload Response

In the battle to increase our comprehension of, and use of, cognitive workload measures however, we should not seek to engage all of our forces on all fronts at the same time. We need a road map for progress, but this does not mean dawdling along the path to gorge on the putatively attractive "low hanging fruit." What we require is a principled exploration of the strengths and weaknesses of the respective tools we possess. One important step along this path can be achieved by evaluating the respective properties of the workload signal. Again, for illustrative purposes, I have shown this in Fig. 2. Here, an operator's response proves to be a combination of certain intrinsic underlying rhythms (both acute and chronic) which are then adapted to the time-varying environmental presentation of information. This compromise between internal and external states is periodically updated as the individual seeks to calibrate their response to the external demands that surround them and the goals that they themselves possess. This action-reaction synthesis forms a general picture which acts as an over-arching framework for the driving influences which are then more fully specified in Fig. 3.

Figure 2 shows the compromise then between certain intrinsic operator rhythms, which are driven by first, the internal variations and second, the imposed demands of an external environment. Each of these have been expressed as a function of information rate. Since intrinsic rhythms are overwhelmingly dealt with by implicit processes and

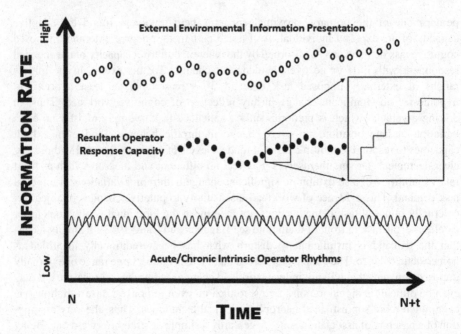

Fig. 2. Compromise between certain intrinsic operator rhythms driven by internal variations of differing intrinsic frequencies (rhythms at the bottom of the illustration), and the imposed demands of an external environment (shown at the top of the illustration). The outcome is the resultant, momentary operator capacity

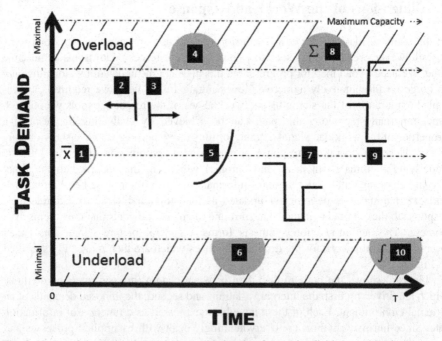

Fig. 3. Some of the major demand characteristics that feature in eliciting workload response.

are relatively regular in nature, they provide little in the way of explicit and formal information (surprise). In contrast the external environment provides constant surprise and the actions of the operator often actively seek such an important sources of novelty and process it to the limits of their own individual capacity. The window in the illustration features the step-wise nature of such up-dating processing as iterative epochs of demand are resolved and updated in memory. Based upon the forgoing general conception, we can now begin an examination of a number of potential triggers of the workload response. Each of these are contingent upon the changing nature of dynamic task demand. I have provided a limited number of examples of these triggers, sufficient to engage discussion, but not so many as to exhaust it.

3.1 Trigger 1: Standard Statistical Properties of the Overall Pattern of Demand

We can begin with the typical and traditional reflections that we have used. These are composed of the standard statistical (moment-based) representations of demand distribution. I have shown these as the mean and standard deviation, denoted by Carayon et al. (2015) in Fig. 3. It may be that cognitive workload responds to any one of these single moment of the distribution (e.g., mean, SD, skewness, kurtosis, etc.), or it may be that workload responds to a concatenation of more than one of these together (e.g., coefficient of variation) which thus prove influential. Our knowledge of these influences represent the largest body of reported understanding at the present time. But note here that each of the cited distributional moments are time dependent. That is, their absolute values co-vary with the time epoch over which they are recorded. We believe in trends such as 'regression to the mean,' indicating an assumption of stability across time or multiple observations. However, as regards to determining what specific element of each statistical moment underlies the workload response we may have to look further than such aggregated data to moment by moment response.

3.2 Trigger 2–3: Prospective of Retrospective Demand Patterns

What has begun to receive more experimental focus alongside the traditional mean and standard deviation scores are the influences of retrospection (Fitts 1954) and prospection (Flach and Voorhorst 2016). The former effect is a reflection of the influence of memory. We might take it as evident that human beings are influenced by their memory but there are powerful theories of human performance (e.g., signal detection theory) in which the effects of memory are compartmentalized. My protestation here is that both immediate (acute) experience and prolonged (chronic) memory contents each have effects on the perceived workload of the moment. Since retrospection is thought to play an important role, so prospection also exerts potential influences. Each of these effects (Fitts 1954; Flach and Voorhorst 2016), can be envisaged as reflections of hysteresis. Such hysteretic effects have been the topic of a series of recent investigations (see Jansen et al. 2016; Morgan and Hancock 2011; Prytz and Scerbo 2015). These studies demonstrate, generally, that the remembered past and prospective future, experienced by the individual, each exert significant effects upon the current level of cognitive workload. Such tendencies have been explored previously (see Hancock et al. 1995) but it is only now that a more systematic body of evidence is emerging. A strong step toward progress in workload research would be to generate a much fuller comprehension of these temporally distal influences on momentary reactions.

3.3   Trigger 4–6: Effects of Peak Experiences

If the memory of past events in general is pertinent to the momentary experience of workload, it may well be that especially meaningful memories (or prospective antici-pations for that matter) disproportionately affect the summed experience of workload across a particular interval of performance. We see evidence of this in some of Kah-neman's work on pain perception during surgical procedures involving partial anes-thetization (Kahneman 2011). By controlling incidents of peak pain, the overall experience is rated as less aversive than when some moments of excruciation are permitted. The analogy with workload, expressed in trend (Gilbert 2005), suggests that minimizing such peaks of overload could reduce the overall workload reported. Pre-cisely whether this amelioration is a good thing in relation to operator assessment in mission critical situations is open to discussion. For example, it might be misleading to underestimate exactly how arduous a particular task is solely by altering or manipu-lating these rare 'peaks' of demand. Those designing such missions or tasks in the future might then be misled into under-estimating the workload experienced. However, such minimization may be valuable for mitigating some longer-term adverse health effects of high workload. The principle here, which applies to overload, is presumed to also be reflected in epochs of underload (Hancock 1997).

3.4   Trigger 5–7: Sensitivity to Rates of Change

One of the more well-established principles that we do have in the behavioral sciences is that humans frequently prove more sensitive to change rather than the absolute level of a stimulus array. If we translate this principle to the way in which task-load and cognitive workload are linked then the rate of change in demand may be more influential on perceived load than any stable, absolute level (e.g., mean demand). This rate of change characteristic is shown as (Hancock 1996) in Fig. 3. This curve is meant to be representative of all such differentiates, including all rates of change (e.g., curve acceleration) also. Of course, many of these dimensions (Carayon et al. 2015; Fitts 1954; Flach and Voorhorst 2016; Gilbert 2005; Hancock 1996) follow or replicate descriptions of tracking behavior in motor control. However, for cognitive reactions, the association is rather less intimate since many imposed tasks are more punctate in nature. In terms of such discrete changes in demand, the step function shown in Hancock (2014) is representative of all such shifts in demand. This might, for example, be the equivalent of adding a secondary or even tertiary task in driving. Such things as answering a phone or responding to GPS instructions occur as momentary variations in task demand. In general, such demand profiles alter in the form of a square wave, rather than a continuously varying analog signal such as the primary demand of vehicle control which is, of course, a tracking task itself.

3.5   Trigger 5–7: Consciousness of Challenge and Recovery of Stability

In the same way that perceived workload may be sensitive to 'peak' demand (or of 'peak' underload) so it may be the absolute number of such memorable experiences in any one performance session (Hancock 2015) that represents the key value that ties perceived workload to imposed task load. Further, it may well also be where the level of stability is established following any demand perturbation that is of prime importance (Hancock and Ergonomics 2017). Lastly, of the present examples I have illustrated (see Fig. 3), it may be the totality of the time spent in acute underload or acute overload which proves critical for the mapping between imposed demand and experienced workload (Hancock and Caird 1993). As noted, these ten instances are examples only and do not represent an exhaustive listing (and see Longo 2015). Yet, some further comments are warranted. Firstly, the natural and intrinsic time-scale of each of the varying methods of workload assessment means that some such workload reflections will respond almost instantly. In contrast, others will possess a much longer latency between the variation in task load and the outcome workload response. Some measures, of course, are a summary of experiences across the whole task, mission, or operation. Others occur within milliseconds. Our science must distinguish these differing latencies in order to assure that dissociations are not merely categorical, time-scale errors. The illustration given in Fig. 3 shows the various characteristics that could drive the outcome workload response. On the ordinate is the time of exposure, on the abscissa is the fluctuating level of dynamic task demand. Workload may be driven by any of the moments of the task load distribution across the epoch of interest (1). It may also be sensitive to retrospective performance (2) or anticipated load (3). It may be especially sensitive to peak events (4) or rates of change (5) or calibrated to periods of acute underload (6). Workload may be driven by sudden, momentary step functions (7), the sum of overload experienced (8), or the pitch of recovery; whether within or outside stable limits (9). Workload may be sensitive to the total amount [as opposed to discrete number of 'peak' events (10)]. This is not an exhaustive listing but indicates the complexity of what can drive the workload response.

4   The Meaning of Work in Works of Meaning

In trying to understand workload as a response to task demands, we have to possess a strong grasp on what the nature of those demands are. In short, we have to understand the meaning of work (Hancock 1997). In the pragmatic aspiration to capture the 'scientific' flavor of workload, we have largely, albeit sometimes implicitly, relied upon behavioristic antecedents and engineering conceptions of work. Ever since Smith (1776), this perspective has rendered work as relatively colorless transformations of states of matter and/or information. As with Henry Ford and Frederic Taylor, it is often easy to even inadvertently 'dehumanize' work when we approach it from this stance. The unit of analysis is the level of work productivity and the degree of happiness or misery of the worker involved, within a strict interpretation of such a view, is largely superfluous. Of course, one wants to know about the health and efficiency of one's workforce, especially as it pertains to avoiding errors and failures. But the inner mental life of that working individual has about as much meaning to the production as the noise produced by moving machinery that surrounds them. In the end, however, this antiseptic view of the worker is self-defeating. For the worker is also the consumer. Like the illusory separation of church and state, one cannot dispassionately and effectively parse the totality of the human experience, however financially or pragmatically convenient it may be to do so.

The issue of meaning is bought into even more stark contrast when information is the currency of work. This is not to say that skilled physical workers cannot, and do not, find great meaning and satisfaction in some expressions of their work also. Assuredly they do. However, our modern world tends much more to be a cognitive enterprise and here the flexibility of the proximal tool. Most often the computer makes cognitive gratification all the more likely. What we have not done in workload assessment is to sufficiently value, nor sufficiently evaluate this hedonic dimension of the workload response. In the same way that we can ask whether beauty is a contributor to the optimization of design, so we can also ask whether satisfaction is a governor of perceived workload? That is, do individuals engaged in appealing, self-sought and interesting work experience different workload responses even to the same task? Put another way, can we find ways in which to make even the most rote task interesting and appealing (at least for someone)? Here, I am advocating that we can. Further, I believe we can accomplish this *by design* (and see Hancock et al. 2005). Obviously this requires that we venture from the fairly certain waters of physical workload evaluation (e.g., lifted weight, lift frequency, etc.), across the less well mapped regions of cognitive workload assessment, where we are today, to the rough and daunting passages of assessing what connotes meaning. But we will not be alone in this venture (see Flach and Voorhorst 2016).

Like the specification of beauty, the quantification of the aesthetic and the mathematics of desire, the concatenation of the hardest of hard sciences alongside the softest of soft sciences currently sounds strange in our ears. I believe it will not ring so to our progeny. I have no recipe for exactly how the full determination of meaning is to be established and this is our forthcoming challenge. I simply assert that if we do not embrace this challenge, our science will remain impoverished, incomplete, and ultimately disappointing. This is especially true for its predictions of real world behavior where, without the incorporation of such critical dimensions as meaning, it is almost certainly bound to fall short. Finally, I might ask whether had I made this narrative more interesting and involving, you would have had a lower frustration (workload) reading it? I think the case is clear, our persuasions toward a task influence how we react to its demands and even whether we perhaps choose ever to perform such work again. On an optimistic note, I do believe that we can make substantive headway in this dimension of workload assessment.

5 Summary and Conclusion

Assessing just how hard someone is working when the primary form of demand requires principally cognitive as opposed to muscular response, is an issue that remains to be resolved. This situation accrues from our knowledge that brains are more difficult to understand than muscles. The problem is a non-trivial one since such assessments underpin the very way we conceive of work and look to reward those who accomplish it. What I have chosen to address in the present chapter have been rather concrete methodological barriers that still exist which prevent us from achieving our desired state of knowledge. Emphasizing problems can be a pessimistic enterprise and so in these final remarks I want to point to a more positive perspective.

First let me say that I do not see any of the present challenges that I have raised as being insuperable. As far as I am concerned, none of the three challenges represents a 'show-stopper.' The association, insensitivity, dissociation (AIDs) issue is indeed a difficult one, but with some resolution to the intrinsic time-scale of measurement problem there is no reason to believe that we cannot conquer the methodological cohesion issue. That being so, even patterns such as double dissociations and multiple insensitivities can still prove informative. Our knowledge is not always predicated upon the positive results but the negative and null ones also. If all such patterns are context-contingent (i.e., they work in one mission scenario but are completely different in another workplace context) then we are in deep waters indeed. However, the commonalty of the human performer and the design-ability of the work environment, provides hope that such radical, situation to situation divergences will not be ubiquitous. In this respect, I offer a roadmap for future progress (see Table 1).

Table 1. A principled roadmap for future workload research

Proximal Challenges
• Distill patterns of pairwise comparisons of primary task, subjective and physiological reflections within a single, real-world performance relevant task (e.g. PVT)
• Compare the pairwise bases against three-way evaluation of the same common task
• Evaluate whether common patterns elicited from the above persist in more complex contexts
Medial Challenges
• Establish whether the patterns of association, indifference and dissociation (AIDs) map to the intrinsic frequency of the methods used to elicit them
• Compare and contrast intra-method AID observations with inter-method AID observations. Then, employ appropriate meta-analytic screening to guide targeted experimentation
• Define method-driver vs. task-driven influence. Compare and contrast different workload drivers intrinsic to the profile of imposed task demand
Distal Challenges
• Seek a validated measure of meaning
• Evaluate the affective dimensions of work in contrast to the 'objective' dimension of imposed load
• Generate a unified theory of cognitive workload. Calibrate to the spectrum of operator individual differences. Link to a context sensitive model to derive workload prediction

The meaning question is of a different order of concern. What this demands is that we become more catholic in our thinking and look to incorporate dimensions of experience that do not sit well with mathematics, computation, modelling, and the general perception of what makes things 'scientific.' Affect has always been our stock-in-trade (Hancock et al. 2002). Yet, we have often shied away from terms like affection, interest, beauty and the like. Sometimes we have sought to disguise our interest through the invention of new terms which are sufficiently ambiguous and imprecise to allow us to explore the former, meaningful terms and yet retain a sturdy veneer of scientific respectability.

We must now throw off any such need for approval from our wider peers in the academy and embrace such difficult and demanding integrations fully. Questions such as: does a beautiful task necessarily impose lower levels of cognitive demand? Can we regulate perceived workload through designed interest? While still somewhat strange to us, these question will be those that tax our progeny. I believe the challenges of cognitive workload assessment are set before us. I believe our science is mature enough to embrace these cross-disciplinary challenges. In short, I am optimistic about our future.

Acknowledgments. I am grateful to the organizers of the meeting for permitting me this opportunity and especially professor Luca Longo for his helpful and insightful suggestions on an earlier version of the present work. I am also indebted to Dr. Lauren Reinerman-Jones, and the UMPIREE Project for the support in order to consider a number of these conceptual problems.

References

Carayon, P., Hancock, P.A., Leveson, N., Noy, I., Sznalwar, L., van Hootegem, G.: Advancing a sociotechnical systems approach to workplace safety: developing the conceptual framework. Ergonomics **58**(4), 548–564 (2015)

Endsley, M.R.: Toward a theory of situation awareness in dynamic systems. Hum. Factors **37**(1), 32–64 (1995)

Fitts, P.M.: The information capacity of the human motor system in controlling the amplitude of movement. J. Exp. Psychol. **47**(6), 381–391 (1954)

Flach, J.M., Voorhorst, F.A.: What Matters: Putting Common Sense to Work. Wright State University Libraries, Dayton (2016)

Gilbert, D.: Stumbling into Happiness. Vintage, New York (2005)

Hancock, P.A.: Effect of control order, augmented feedback, input device and practice on tracking performance and perceived workload. Ergonomics **39**(9), 1146–1162 (1996)

Hancock, P.A.: On the future of work. Ergon. Des. **5**(4), 25–29 (1997)

Hancock, P.A.: Automation: How much is too much? Ergonomics **57**(3), 449–454 (2014)

Hancock, P.A.: The royal road to time: how understanding of the evolution of time in the brain addresses memory, dreaming, flow and other psychological phenomena. Am. J. Psychol. **128**(1), 1–14 (2015)

Hancock, P.A.: Imposing limits on autonomous systems. Ergonomics (2017, in press)

Hancock, P.A., Caird, J.K.: Experimental evaluation of a model of mental workload. Hum. Factors **35**(3), 413–429 (1993)

Hancock, P.A., Drury, C.G.: Does Human Factors/Ergonomics contribute to the quality of life? Theoret. Issues Ergon. Sci. **12**, 1–11 (2011)

Hancock, P.A., Meshkati, N. (eds.): Human Mental Workload. North-Holland, Amsterdam (1988)

Hancock, P.A., Newell, K.M.: The movement speed-accuracy relationship in space-time. In: Heuer, H., Kleinbeck, U., Schmidt, K.H. (eds.) Motor Behavior: Programming, Control and Acquisition, pp. 153–188. Springer, Heidelberg (1985)

Hancock, P.A., Pepe, A., Murphy, L.L.: Hedonomics: The power of positive and pleasurable ergonomics. Ergon. Des. **13**(1), 8–14 (2005)

Hancock, P.A., Warm, J.S.: A dynamic model of stress and sustained attention. Hum. Factors **31**, 519–537 (1989)

Hancock, P.A., Weaver, J.L., Parasuraman, R.: Sans subjectivity, ergonomics is engineering. Ergonomics **45**(14), 991–994 (2002)

Hancock, P.A., Williams, G., Miyake, S., Manning, C.M.: The influence of task demand characteristics on workload and performance. Int. J. Aviat. Psychol. **5**(1), 63–85 (1995)

Jansen, R.J., Sawyer, B.D., van Egmond, T., de Ridder, H., Hancock, P.A.: Hysteresis in mental workload and task performance: the influence of demand transitions and task prioritization. Hum. Factors **58**(8), 1143–1157 (2016)

Kahneman, D.: Thinking, Fast and Slow. Farrer, Strauss & Giroux, New York (2011)

Longo, L.: A defeasible reasoning framework for human mental workload representation and assessment. Behav. Inf. Technol. **34**(8), 758–786 (2015)

Meshkati, N., Hancock, P.A., Rahimi, M.: Techniques of mental workload assessment. In: Wilson, J. (ed.) Evaluation of Human Work: Practical Ergonomics Methodology. Taylor & Francis, London (1989)

Moray, N. (ed.): Mental Workload: Its Theory and Measurement. Plenum Press, New York (1979)

Morgan, J.F., Hancock, P.A.: The effect of prior task loading on mental workload: an example of hysteresis in driving. Hum. Factors **53**(1), 75–86 (2011)

Prytz, E.G., Scerbo, M.W.: Changes in stress and subjective workload over time following a workload transition. Theoret. Issues Ergon. Sci. **16**(6), 586–605 (2015)

Smith, A. (ed.): Inquiry into the Nature and Causes of the Wealth of Nations. Strahan and Cadell, London (1776)

Smith, K., Hancock, P.A.: Situation awareness is adaptive, externally directed consciousness. Hum. Factors **37**(1), 137–148 (1995)

Wickens, C.D.: Multiple resources and performance prediction. Theor. Issues Ergon. Sci. **3**(2), 159–177 (2002)

Yeh, Y.Y., Wickens, C.D.: Dissociation of performance and subjective measures of workload. Hum. Factors **30**, 111–120 (1988)

Mental Workload: Assessment, Prediction and Consequences

Christopher D. Wickens[1,2(✉)]

[1] University of Illinois at Urbana-Champaign, Chicago, USA
Wickens@colostate.edu
[2] Colorado State University, Fort Collins, USA

Abstract. I describe below the manner in which workload measurement can be used to validate models that predict workload. These models in turn can be employed to predict the decisions that are made, which select a course of action that is of lower effort or workload, but may also be of lower expected value (or higher expected cost). We then elaborate on four different contexts in which these decisions are made, with non-trivial consequences to performance and learning: switching attention, accessing information, studying material, and behaving safety. Each of these four is illustrated by a series of examples.

Keywords: Mental workload · Human performance · Effort

1 Introduction

A fatigued motorist, driving at night, along a 4-lane motorway decides to change lanes while half of his resources are diverted to a fascinating story about Brexit on BBC. A quick glance at the side view mirror suggests clear passage, but he does not rotate his head and body far enough to "check the blindspot" behind, an implicit decision, or choice of non-action, that throws his car directly into the path of the overtaking car in the next lane. It simply required too much effort to turn his head, and the accident resulted. The concept of effort or mental workload can be examined from three perspectives, those of measurement, of prediction and of consequences. We describe each of these perspectives in turn, show how they are interrelated and then focus our greatest attention on the consequences of high mental workload (MWL), particularly to decision making, as this has, I believe, been an under-represented field of research. To preview, our argument is that an underappreciated value of research on measurement of MWL is has been to provide objective criteria against which to validate predictive metrics of MWL. And the greatest value of such predictive metrics, is to be able to predict the consequences of high mental workload to performance, and particularly the decision to engage in one type of behavior (e.g., risky behavior) over another (e.g., safe behavior). There are of course a multitude of other factors that influence such choices; but the impact of effort is profound, and represents one of the most important ramifications of the MWL field of study. In the following, I will use the term "effort" and "mental workload" interchangeably.

© Springer International Publishing AG 2017
L. Longo and M.C. Leva (Eds.): H-WORKLOAD 2017, CCIS 726, pp. 18–29, 2017.
DOI: 10.1007/978-3-319-61061-0_2

2 Measurement of Workload

In the last half century, there have been hundreds of studies of the measurement of mental workload; and of the four major categories of techniques that can be used to assess the relative demands of tasks on the limited information processing capabilities of the human operator: performance of primary and secondary tasks, subjective measures and physiological measures (e.g., [1, 2]). Many of these were triggered by the foundational book edited by Moray [3]; and Fig. 1 indicates the growth of MWL studies over the last half century with the arrow signaling the acceleration of research. Certainly the recent development of new brain imaging technologies and the neuro-ergonomics approach to MWL have added to this continued growth, which shows little sign of leveling off.

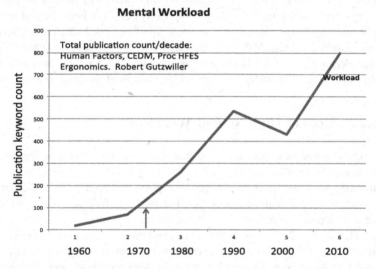

Fig. 1. Growth of the number of workload studies, as published in human factors and ergonomics journals

While I applaud this continued line of research, I cannot help but think that there may be some diminishing returns as progressively more papers appear, often repeatedly examining the same techniques (e.g., NASA-TLX). The workload research community has done a pretty good job of assessments, and it is now time to shift our efforts more toward the most critical application of assessment: the validation of models and metrics of MWL.

3 Predictive Models of Mental Workload

The value of predictive models of human performance and cognition in complex systems is realized because of the problems with systems that are fielded and then may be found out, in human-in-the-loop simulation testing or real world operations to impose excessive demands on the human operator, leading to their disuse or to workload-overload accidents. To prevent such loss of money and more tragically, the loss of life or limb, the problems above can potentially be avoided by harnessing predictive models of workload and multi-tasking capability (See Wickens and Sebok, [4] for a review of such models in aviation). Such models can be of two types: models of how multiple tasks interfere, and their performance breaksdown, such as Threaded Cognition [5] or Multiple Resources [6], and models of how the demands of individual tasks, impose on the limited resources of the performer, such as models of relational complexity [7], of working memory capacity [8], or imposed information processing bandwidth [9].

These metrics have great value because a careful tasks analysis, can reveal properties of task demand that may push performance over "the red line" of MWL where performance begins to suffer, as there is no more spare capacity remaining: the supply of cognitive effort is exhausted. Here again, as with predictive models of workload metrics, they can be implemented before complex systems are built, fielded and then found to be wanting. Their value then is to predict performance breakdowns. Naturally the models of individual task MWL can then feed directly into models of multiple task interference because such models as multiple resources have joint inputs of demand level and competition for common resources as predictors of dual task interference [6].

4   Consequences of High Mental Workload

When workload becomes excessive, three things can happen. First, over the long run, high workload can exert a toll on health and well being; thus workload is often classified, along with such factors as sleep disruption and anxiety as a stressor [10]. Second, when workload is driven over the "red line", performance can start to fail: errors begin to appear when time stress is excessive, or when digital phone numbers exceed the classic 7 ± 2 capacity limits. Third, and the focus of the remainder of this paper, because people are typically effort conserving, often wishing to avoid the stress of high MWL, they often make decisions to avoid high workload; and many of these decisions have major negative consequences to performance.

The underlying framework adopted in the following pages is the decisions that people make to choose between one of two alternatives; one of **higher value**, and the other of **lower effort**. At its most elementary level, we can think of a choice between engaging in a task, for example submitting a job application, which requires a lot of effort, or not doing so, which allows us to relax. Both options have utility. The former clearly leading to the expectancy of income (but not guaranteed, it is risky and may be wasted effort if we are not offered the job). The latter conforms to an inherent effort-conserving tendency exhibited by all species [11, 12]. Indeed this latter option should not be given the pejorative label of "laziness", because in many instances, particularly when resources are scarce, it is adaptive to conserve those resources (avoid effort). The critical influence of the metrics of mental workload, is to help predict the degree of influence of effort conservation on this choice; particularly the extent to which a high-valued option is discarded. That is, to the extent that we can predict both value (or expected value) of one option, versus the effort (saved) by the other, the choice tendency or degree of preference itself can be predicted. In the following, we consider four classes or contexts of choice, and show how they can be driven by effort conservation. These "4 Ss" are the choice:

- To **Switch** attention between tasks.
- To **Seek** information.
- To **Study** material.
- To **Safely** behave.

We consider these diverse applications in order to demonstrate the ubiquity of the concept of effort and mental workload, and the vital role that its prediction and measurement play in all aspects of human endeavor.

4.1   Switching Tasks

Two recent domains of human factors interest – interruption management [13–15] and voluntary task switching (e.g., [16, 17]) have been integrated into a multi-tasking model called STOM (Strategic Task Overload Management; [18, 19]. This is essentially a multi-attribute decision model that predicts, based on four task attributes, which task a person will choose to switch attention to (and hence, by default, which ones they will neglect or avoid), amongst a multi-task ensemble in overload situations. Such might describe the management of an off-shore oil rig disaster [20] or the aircraft pilot trying to handle an in-flight emergency in which troubleshooting, maintaining stability, navigation and emergency communications must all compete for attention. In the STOM model, the attributes of the tasks which are competing for the operators limited attentional capacity are priority, interest, salience and, most important for the current paper, task difficulty.

Two aspects of the STOM model cry out for valid predictive models of task difficulty, MWL or effort demands. First, within the four attributes, difficulty or effort demand has been found to produce a fairly robust influence on task switching: people are inclined to choose the easier of a set of tasks to switch to (assuming that all other attributes are roughly equivalent; [17, 19]. But how much of an influence does difficulty exert relative to other attributes? To determine this, it is necessary to establish a reliable metric of task difficulty, a commodity offered by a well validated predictive model of task load. Second, a fundamental component of the model is that human's have an inherent "switch resistance", or bias to keep doing what they are doing. In extreme, this can evolve into undesirable cognitive tunneling. [21] Such a bias results from the effort costs imposed by the executive functioning that underlies the very decision to switch [18]. When resources are more scarce, as when an ongoing task is more effortful, or when the operator is fatigued, the central executive is less likely to decide to switch at all. Thus the effort, or MWL of a component task in a multi-task ensemble can negatively influence the decision to switch, and if a switch is in fact chosen, what task to switch to.

4.2   Seeking and Accessing Information

As we described above, the STOM model describes the movement of *mental attention* around the "*task space*" in the brain. A model called SEEV (Salience, Effort, Expectancy, Value) is closely related to STOM because it describes the movement of *visual attention* (via some combination of scanning, head movement and body rotation) around the *visual space* in order to acquire information necessary to accomplish a specific task. That is, SEEV is a model of visual scanning [22]. As the second term in the model indicates, this too involves the role of effort in the decision of where and whether to look, in a very vital way.

These two terms, where and whether define different classes of decisions. In the first case, "where", describes an effort function, shown in Fig. 2, that approximates, roughly, the amount of effort required to move the fixation of the eyeballs from straight ahead, to various angles to the side. The function consists of three segments [23, 24] (1) an eye-field, within which there is little effort cost to move the eyes, and minimal increased costs for longer movements up to about 20°. The fact that eye movements are cheap (but not free) is because the eyeball has minimal inertia in rotation. (2) a head field, in which typical neck rotation is required, extending from 20 to about 90°. Here, because of the greater inertia of the head, and the increasing resistance to progressively larger neck rotations, there is a growing cost with increasing eccentricity relative to the forward orientation of the torso. (3) a body field, typically requiring torso rotation, and still greater muscular effort. As these effort costs grow, so does the effort conserving resistance to expending them in seeking information. Hence we can account for the

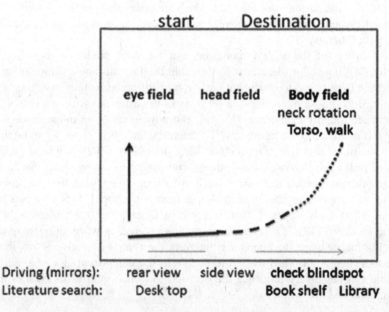

Fig. 2. Information access effort as a function of distance from the forward view: the legends on the X-axis represent the access of two different kinds of information: a view behind a vehicle (top row) and a reference citation (bottom row). From [22].

unfortunate driver's failure to decide to check the blind spot in our opening example, amplified by the added inhibition on this choice imposed when resources for peripheral information seeking were scarce (allocated to listening to BBC, and diminished by fatigue). Thus, in this case, the "where" (looking behind) influences the "whether" (the decision not to scan).

In the above example, the effort-driven decision was whether or not to seek information at all. This decision is also manifest in whether to seek information in the world, or to rely in information "in the head" (i.e., memory; [25]). As an example, I have often decided to trust my memory for the accurate date or spelling of a reference citation in a text that I am typing, rather than to take the effort to look it up, and particularly walk to the book shelf and locate the right book where I know that reference appeared in print. (Clearly the internet and computer are designed to make access to information in the world less effortful). The consequences of effort avoidance in the example of finding the book reference citation are relatively minor, a wrong citation in my text. However sometimes this effort-avoidance choice can have serious safety consequences.

As an example Yang and her colleagues [26] examined a health care professional's important decision, when communicating patient information from a departing to an arriving professional at the medical handover between shifts; this is the decision of whether to consult their memory of patient condition, or to access this information in printed medical records. The former option (knowledge in the head) is less effortful; the latter (knowledge in the world) is more valuable (i.e., more likely to be accurate). While both options were sometimes chosen by participants, a point critical to the argument here is that seeking information in the world (medical records) was signifi-cantly (4 times) less likely when those records were 5 m distant from the handover point, than when they were directly in front of the worker. This difference could have serious safety implications given that memory information was also observed to be 23% less accurate. In a second finding of the study, this tendency to sacrifice accuracy over effort conservation was further exacerbated to the extent that participants were overconfident in the accuracy of their memory, thus under-estimating the cost of the effort-reducing reliance on memory. The phenomenon of overconfidence, in biasing toward the low-effort option, will be addressed again in the following section. An important issue illustrated by the above example is the linkage it illustrates between ergonomics above the neck (decision) and below the neck (the effort of walking) [27].

4.3 Studying and Learning

Many of the choices that students make in study strategies result, in part, from the false belief that easier (less effortful) study and learning strategies signal better retention or transfer of learning; that is, higher value [28–32]. In other words, learners have a belief that cognitive ease [12] is a proxy for quality of learning. In the previous two contexts when a user decides on a low effort option, such a decision is arrived at knowing that value or accuracy may be sacrificed as a consequence. However in the case of studying, if it is believed (falsely) that the low effort option is also of higher value, the effort-avoidance tendency is likely to be particularly pernicious. In particular, Table 1

Table 1. Tradeoff of effort and value in study strategies

Lower effort and value (to retention and transfer)	Higher effort and higher value
Massed practice	Spaced practice (contextual interference)
Listening	Note taking (active response generation)
Note taking	Self quizzing (active retrieval practice)
Part task training	Whole task training

provides four examples of contrasting learning or training strategies, listed in each row. On the left is a low effort strategy that mistakenly signals better retention or transfer to the learner. On the right is a contrasting higher effort strategy that has been empirically shown to produce higher retention of studied material or transfer of training of a learned skill.

- Massed practice involves studying a given type of material (or practicing a given task) repeatedly, and doing no studying of alternative material in between trials, or periods of study of this target material. Massed practice does indeed often produce faster learning which makes it seem to the learner like retention should be better. However for longer term retention and transfer, the alternative strategy of interspersing the study/practice of other material proves superior, even though (and perhaps because) this other material provides some contextual interference with the target of study and practice [30] Learning to filter out that interference is a useful skill that can transfer beyond the learning environment.
- Pure listening or reading, even when a lecture or text is engaging and interesting, is easier than taking notes about it, which requires effort; both the physical effort of writing and the cognitive effort of deciding what to write about. Yet it is found that the active generation of responses about something lead to better retention of that material than passively experiencing it, a phenomenon known as "the generation effect" [33]. This generation effect too describes the better retention of a route followed by a driver making active navigational decisions, than that viewed passively by a passenger.
- While note taking comes out better than passive listening; it is also a poorer study strategy when compared to actively quizzing one's self about the material, following exposure to that material [34–36]. The former can be accomplished through a relatively (mental) effort-lite process of just writing down verbatim what is heard; the latter typically requires the active process of retrieving the material, a skill that will be essential when the material is used in a later context (e.g., in transfer).
- Many complex skills, such as flying an aircraft, translating speech to a different language, or playing an instrument with two hands (e.g., guitar, piano) require concurrent task performance. The easier training strategy, part task training, is to practice each task at a time, a strategy in which capacity is never overloaded. Yet empirical data indicate that despite its greater effort demands, whole task training is more effective for transfer [37, 38].

All of these examples and many more, can be characterized both by the general tendency to reduce effort (choosing the strategy on the left of Table 1), and inflating its subjective value by the simple heuristic: "if its easier to learn, I must be learning it

Table 2. Risky but low effort options (left column) versus safer but high effort options (right column)

Lower effort	Cost of compliance
No seat belt or safety helmet	Time to fasten/discomfort of helmet
Ignore safety instructions	Read safety instructions
Mind wandering while driving	Concentrate on the road
Exploit high degree of automation (of actions)	Perform manually: stay in the loop

better" [27, 28]. The role of effort here, and its measurement, is at the fundamental core of the cognitive load theory of instruction [39, 40]. This theory elaborates the single concept of effort to distinguish between three sources of effort demands (MWL) imposed in the learning environment. (1) more complex tasks intrinsically demand more effort to be performed (intrinsic load). (2) More effort can be invested into the more physically and cognitively challenging but effective strategies on the right side of Table 2: it is productive or "germane" for learning, known as germane load. (3) effort can be demanded in the learning environment that has little effectiveness, it is "extraneous load". Extraneous load might include a clunky interface in computer-based instruction; but could also include features of the learning environment that invite the investment of resources, but have little proven effectiveness in training. Examples include entertaining lecturers who tell several irrelevant jokes or anecdotes, or the introduction of distracting animation [41]. Extraneous load will always consume scarce resources in the learning environment, and hence amplify the undesirable tendency to choose the reduced-effort strategies on the left of Table 2.

4.4 Safe Behavior

We in the human factors community we are advocates for safety, and as psychologists, want to encourage or "nudge" people to make the decision to behave safely [42]. Such decisions often weight the value of safe behavior (and reducing risk) against the utility of effort reduction, or avoiding the "cost of compliance". Four examples of these, expressed in the same framework as in Table 1, are shown in Table 2.

In all of these examples, some effort cost can be attributed to the actions on the right side of the table, although these may be manifest in different ways. In the first example the "discomfort" of wearing a safety helmet is not truly a source of effort demands, but imposes the same sort of negative or unpleasant valence as expending effort, particularly if the driver is experiencing other sources of stress. In the second example, reading long safety instructions on equipment or drug labels is clearly effortful, particularly if they are not well worded and excessive in number. Safety researchers have concluded that the best technique to induce safer behavior is to reduce the cost of compliance. Like the bias to overestimate the benefits (value) of some training strategies discussed above, so also the overconfidence bias to underestimate the expected costs or risks of unsafe behavior ("it can't happen to me" [43], can further amplify the effort-reduction tendencies.

Regarding the third example of safe (or unsafe) behavior, in many boring tasks, such as driving on a straight motorway late at night, and when fatigue diminishes the capacity to mobilize effort, it is quite pleasurable, and we might say subjectively valuable, to engage in mind wandering at the expense of mobilizing effort to stay in the loop, continue to concentrate on the roadway and be vigilant for unexpected hazards; this low effort preference is clearly one factor accountable for the higher per vehicle accident risk exposure in night driving. The fourth contrast in Table 2 is directly related to the third. Higher degrees of automation facilitate the ability to engage in effort-light pleasure like mind wandering. Here "degree of automation" is defined with reference to the taxonomy of automation proposed by Parasuraman and colleagues [44], by which automation can support, and indeed replace progressively later stages of information processing, and at each stage, higher levels of automation can carry out progressively more cognitive work for the human (see also [45]). The combination of later stages and higher levels within stages defines the higher degree of automation. In particular we call attention to the distinction between earlier stage automation, that can integrate information and provide an estimate of the state of the world (supporting situation assessment), and later stage automation, that can recommend, and sometimes execute actions based on that state, supporting or replacing decision making. Since automation decision support must generally be based also on an automated assessment of the state, the lower cognitive effort availed by later stage, than by earlier stage automation is apparent. But here, explicitly, choosing to rely upon automation at all, and choosing to rely on higher rather than lower degrees of automation, is a decision that incurs progressively greater risks (lower expected value) if the automation should unexpectedly fail [46].

5 Conclusions

In all four domains above, effort or MWL imposed by a decision option is seen to negatively influence the degree of preference for, and hence the decision to avoid that option. Generally it is assumed that more effort imposes a negative weight, when balanced against the perceived or actual value of the option; and this is particularly likely when the resources are otherwise scare: depleted by fatigue, or demanded by concurrent tasks. (Of course this is not always the case, and sometimes we do gain intrinsic pleasure and value by investing more effort: the feeling of "flow" in working hard at an engaging interesting task).

Naturally there are also other factors at play to influence the decision of what tasks to attend to, where to look, what to study and whether to behave safely. Prominent among these is a miscalibrated (and often overconfident) estimation of the value of the low effort option (or under-estimation of its expected cost). We saw its operation in both the choice to access information, to study and (not) to be safe. Nonetheless effort is a vital component of all of these decisions, and if we wish to predict such choices accurately in the workplace, in the vehicle and in the schoolhouse, then validated (via assessment) and predictive quantitative metrics and models of mental workload remain of enduring importance [47, 48].

References

1. Young, M., Brookhuis, K., Wickens, C., Hancock, P.: State of science: mental workload in ergonomics. Ergonomics **58**(1), 1–17 (2015). doi:10.1080/00140139.2014.956151
2. Wickens, C.D., Tsang, P.: Workload. In: Boehm-Davis, D., Durso, F., Lee, J. (eds.) Handbook of Human-Systems Integration. American Psychological Association
3. Moray, N.: (ed.): Human Workload: Its Theory and Measurement. Plenum Press
4. Wickens, C., Sebok, A.: Flight deck models of workload and multi-tasking: an overview of validation. In: Vidulich, M., Tsang, P., Flach, J. (eds.) Advances in Aviation Psychology, vol. 1, pp. 69–84. Dorset Press, Dorset (2014)
5. Salvucci, D.D., Taatgen, N.A.: The Multi-tasking Mind. Oxford University Press, Oxford (2011)
6. Wickens, C.D.: Multiple resources and mental workload. Hum. Factors Golden Anniv. Spec. Issue **3**, 449–455 (2008)
7. Halford, G.S., Wilson, W.H., Phillips, S.: Processing capacity defined by relational complexity: implications for comparative, developmental, and cognitive psychology. Behav. Brain Sci. **21**, 803–831 (1998)
8. Engle, R.W.: Working memory capacity as executive attention. Curr. Dir. Psychol. Sci. **11**(1), 19–23 (2002)
9. Hart, S.G., Wickens, C.D.: Cognitive workload. In: NASA Human Systems Integration Handbook, chap. 6 (2010). Workload. Ergonomics **58**, 1–17
10. Hancock, P.A., Desmond, P.: Stress, Workload and Fatigue. Erlbaum, Mahwah (2001)
11. Shugan, S.M.: The cost of thinking. J. Consum. Res. **7**, 99–111 (1980)
12. Kahneman, D.: Thinking, Fast and Slow. Farrar, Straus, Giroux, New York (2011)
13. Trafton, J.G., Monk, C.: Task interruptions. Rev. Hum. Factors Ergon. **3** 111–126 (2007). http://rev.sagepub.com/content/3/1/111.short
14. Salvucci, D.: Multitasking. In: Lee, J., Kirlik, A. (eds.) The Oxford Handbook of Cognitive Engineering. Press, Oxford U (2013)
15. Dismukes, R.K.: Remembrance of things future: prospective memory in the laboratory, workplace and everyday settings. In: Harris, D. (ed.) Reviews of Human factors and Ergonomics, vol. 6. Human Factors and Ergonomics Society, Santa Monica (2010)
16. Janssen, C.P., Brumby, D.P.: Strategic adaptation to performance objectives in a dual-task setting. Cogn. Sci. **34**, 1548–1560 (2010)
17. Kool, W., McGuire, J.T., Rosen, Z.B., Botvinick, M.M.: Decision making and the avoidance of cognitive demand. J. Exp. Psychol. Gen. **139**(4), 665–682 (2010)
18. Wickens, C.D., Gutzwiller, R., Santamaria, A.: Discrete task switching in overload: a meta-analyses and a model. Int. J. Hum.-Comput. Stud. **79**, 79–84 (2015). http://doi.org/10.1016/j.ijhcs.2015.01.002
19. Wickens, C.D., Gutzwiller, R.S., Vieane, A.Z., Clegg, B.A., Sebok, A., Janes, J.: Time sharing between robotics and process control: validating a model of attention switching. Hum. Factors **58**, 322–343 (2016)
20. Flin, R., Slaven, G., Stewart, K.: Emergency dcision makig in the offshore oild and gas industry. Hum. Factors **38**, 262–277 (1996)
21. Wickens, C.D., Alexander, A.L.: Attentional tunneling and task management in synthetic vision displays. Int. J. Aviat. Psychol. **19**, 182–189 (2009)
22. Wickens, C.D.: Noticing events in the visual workplace: the SEEV and NSEEV models. In: Hoffman, R., Parasuraman, R. (eds.) Handbook of Applied Perception. Cambridge University Press, Cambridge (2014)

23. Sanders, A.F., Houtmans, M.J.M.: Perceptual processing models in the functional visual field. Acta Physiol. **58**, 251–261 (1985)
24. Wickens, C.D.: Cognitive factors in display design. J. Wash. Acad. Sci. **83**(4), 179–201 (1993)
25. Norman, D.A.: The Psychology of Everyday Things. Basic, New York (1988)
26. Yang, J., Wickens, C., Park, T., Siah, K., Fong, L.: Effects of information access cost and accountability on medical residents' information retrieval strategy and performance during prehandover preparation: evidence from interview and simulation study. Hum. Factors **57**, 1459–1471 (2015)
27. Mehta, R., Parasuraman, R.: Effects of mental fatigue on the development of physical fatigue: a neuroergonomics approach. Hum. Factors **56**, 645–656 (2014)
28. Koriat, A., Bjork, R.A.: Illusions of competence in monitoring ones own knowledge during study. J. Exp. Psychol.: Learn. Mem. Cogn. **31**, 187–194 (2005)
29. Dunlosky, J., Rawson, K., Marsh, E., Nathan, M., Willingham, D.: Improving students' learning with effective lerning techniques. Psychol. Sci. Public Interest **14**, 4–58 (2013)
30. Putnam, A., Sungkhasettee, V., Roediger, H.: Optimizing learning in college: tips from cognitive psychology. Psychol. Sci. **11**, 652–660 (2016)
31. Healy, H., Bourne, L. (eds.): Training Cognition: Optimizing Efficiency, Durability, and Generalizability. CRC Press, Boco Ratan (2012)
32. Kornell, N., Rhodes, M., Castel, A., Tasuber, S.: The ease-of-processing heuristic and stability bias. Psychol. Sci. **22**, 787 (2011)
33. Slamecka, N.J., Graf, P.: The generation effect: delineation of a phenomenon. J. Exp. Psychol.: Hum. Learn. Mem. **4**, 592–604 (1978)
34. Callender, A., McDaniel, M.: The limited benefits of rereading educational texts. Contemp. Educ. Psychol. **34**, 30–41 (2009)
35. Karpicke, J.: Retrieval based learning: active retrieval promotes meaningful learning. Curr. Dir. Psychol. Sci. **21**, 157–163 (2012)
36. Karpicke, J., Roediger, H.L.: The critical importance of retrieval for learning. Science **319**, 996–998 (2008)
37. Wickens, C.D., Hutchins, S., Carolan, T., Cummings, J.: Effectiveness of part task training and increasing difficulty training strategies: a meta-analysis approach. Hum. Factors **55**(2), 461–470 (2013)
38. Wightman, D., Lintern, G.: Part task training for tracking and manual control. Hum. Factors **27**, 267–284 (1985)
39. Paas, F., Renkl, A., Sweller, J.: Cognitive load theory and instructional design: recent developments. Educ. Psychol. **38**, 1–4 (2003)
40. Paas, F., van Gog, T.: Principles for designing effective and efficient training for complex cognitive skills. In: Durso, F. (ed.) Reviews of Human Factors and Ergonomics, vol. 5, pp. 166–194. Human Factors and Ergonomics Society, Santa Monica (2009)
41. Mayer, R.E., Griffith, I., Jurkowitz, N., Rothman, D.: Increased interestingness of extraneous details in a multimedia science presentation leads to decreased learning. J. Exp. Psychol.: Appl. **14**, 329–339 (2008)
42. Thaler, R., Sunstein, C.: Nudge: Improving Decision Making About Health, Wealth and Happiness. Yale University Press, New Haven (2012)
43. Hertwig, R., Erev, I.: The description-experience gap in risky choice. Trends Cogn. Sci. **9**, 1–7 (2009)
44. Parasuraman, R., Sheridan, T.B., Wickens, C.D.: A model for types and levels of human interaction with automation. IEEE Trans. Syst. Man Cybern. Part A Syst. Hum. **30**(3), 286–297 (2000)

45. Onnasch, L., Wickens, C., Li, H., Manzey, D.: Human performance consequences of stages and levels of automation: an integrated meta-analysis. Hum. Factors **56**(3), 476–488 (2014)
46. Sebok, A., Wickens, C.D.: Implementing lumberjacks and black swans into model-based tools to support human-automation interaction. Hum. Factors **59**, 189–202 (2017)
47. Longo, L.: A defeasible reasoning framework for human mental workload representation and assessment. Behav. Inf. Technol. **34**(8), 758–786 (2015)
48. Longo, L.: Formalising human mental workload as a defeasible computational concept. Ph. D. thesis, Trinity College Dublin (2014)

Assessment of Mental Workload: A Comparison of Machine Learning Methods and Subjective Assessment Techniques

Karim Moustafa[1], Saturnino Luz[2], and Luca Longo[1,3(✉)]

[1] School of Computing, Dublin Institute of Technology, Dublin, Ireland
luca.longo@dit.ie
[2] Usher Institute of Population Health Sciences and Informatics,
The University of Edinburgh, Edinburgh, Scotland
[3] The ADAPT Centre, Dublin, Ireland

Abstract. Mental workload (MWL) measurement is a complex multidisciplinary research field. In the last 50 years of research endeavour, MWL measurement has mainly produced theory-driven models. Some of the reasons for justifying this trend includes the omnipresent uncertainty about how to define the construct of MWL and the limited use of data-driven research methodologies. This work presents novel research focused on the investigation of the capability of a selection of supervised Machine Learning (ML) classification techniques to produce data-driven computational models of MWL for the prediction of objective performance. These are then compared to two state-of-the-art subjective techniques for the assessment of MWL, namely the NASA Task Load Index and the Workload Profile, through an analysis of their concurrent and convergent validity. Findings show that the data-driven models generally tend to outperform the two baseline selected techniques.

1 Introduction

Mental Workload (MWL) is a fundamental concept in human performance prediction. It is a complex construct that is affected by several factors measurable with various methods [38,42]. Different approaches have been proposed to aggregate these factors towards an index of MWL. However, difficulties exist in defining MWL, in understanding which factors best describe it and in building a robust model for predicting performance that have a general applicability [25,28]. State-of-the-art computational models are rather ad-hoc and their applicability is confined to specific application fields [22,23,26]. Additionally, the vast majority of these models are mainly theory-driven. This means from a set of measurable factors, theoretically related to MWL, and a computational model to aggregate these factors, an inference is made. This is usually an index of mental workload that can be theoretically related to human performance [29,30]. Not a lot has been done in the development of data-driven models of MWL, which means computational models induced by learning from a set of data that are capable of fitting human performance. One reason is that MWL

© Springer International Publishing AG 2017
L. Longo and M.C. Leva (Eds.): H-WORKLOAD 2017, CCIS 726, pp. 30–50, 2017.
DOI: 10.1007/978-3-319-61061-0_3

is still an ill-defined construct, justifying the application of deductive research methods [39]. Another reason is that MWL is a 50-year old construct, and at its origins, inductive non-linear computational methodologies were not as popular and developed as nowadays. Only in the last two decades, with the acceleration and spread of Machine Learning (ML), researchers initiated to investigate MWL using inductive data-driven research methodologies [3,12,20,43,51].

This paper is one of the few recent attempts to apply modern inductive data-driven research methodologies, namely supervised Machine Learning, to induce mental workload models from data acquired through subjective self-report measures. In particular, a unique comparison of the inferential capacity of two state-of-the-art subjective MWL measurement techniques is performed, namely the popular NASA Task Load Index and the Workload Profile instruments, against the inferential capacity of novel inductive data-driven models of MWL, built using Machine Learning.

The rest of the paper is organised as follows. Section 2 describes related work in the specific field of MWL measurement, with an emphasis on subjective self-reporting measurement methods, extracting relevant gaps and motivating the need for data-driven methods for MWL. Section 3 focuses on the design of an experiment and the description of the research methodology adopted for the development of inductive data-driven MWL models. Section 4 presents the results and critically evaluate these models through a rigorous comparison of their concurrent and convergent validity against the ones of the two selected baseline theory-driven MWL models. Finally, Sect. 5 concludes this research study highlighting the contribution to the body of knowledge and suggesting future research paths.

2 Related Work

Mental workload (MWL) is a fundamental design concept in Human-Computer Interaction (HCI) and Ergonomics (Human Factors) and it is sometimes referred to as Cognitive Load (CL), specifically in Cognitive Psychology. It is intrinsically complex and multifaceted [25,38]. There is no widely accepted definition of MWL, however, it can be intuitively described as the total cognitive load needed to accomplish a specific task under a finite period of time [5].

2.1 Mental Workload Measurement Methods

Measuring MWL is essential in predicting human performance and in turn informing the design of technologies, interfaces, information-based procedures and instructions. There are different methods that have been proposed for measuring MWL. These can be clustered in three main classes:

- *Subjective measures* - this class relies on the analysis of the subjective feedback provided by humans interacting with an underlying task and system. The feedback usually takes the form of a survey or questionnaire, often post-task. The most known methods are the NASA Task Load Index ($NASA - TLX$) [15], the Workload profile (WP) [47], and the Subjective Workload Assessment Technique (SWAT) [38];

- *Task performance measures* - this class is often referred to as primary and secondary tasks measures and it focuses on the objective performance measurement related to an underlying task. The time to complete a task, the reaction time to secondary tasks and the number of errors on the primary task are examples of measures, as well as the tracking and analysing of the different actions performed by a user during a primary task;
- *Physiological measures* - this class is based upon the analysis of physiological indicators and responses of the human body. Examples include EEG (electroencephalogram), eye tracking and heart rate measures.

2.2   Subjective Measurements Methods

This study is particularly focused on two subjective measures of MWL that have been widely employed by several researchers in the last four decades: the NASA-Task Load Index (NASA-TLX) [15] and the Workload Profile (WP) [47] based on the Multiple Resource Theory [48]. The MWL instrument developed by the NASA agency was originally conceived to support the measurement of the mental workload of pilots during aviation tasks. Subsequently, the NASA-TLX was adopted in many other fields and used as a benchmark in many research studies [39, 40]. The NASA-TLX scale is built upon six factors and their individual weights. The associated formula is shown in Eq. (1) where d_i represents the rating provided by a person after the execution of an underlying task while w_i is the weight associated with that dimension and achieved by a pairwise procedure. The questionnaire used by NASA can be found in [15].

$$NASA - TLX_{MWL} = \left(\sum_{i=1}^{6} d_i \times w_i \right) \frac{1}{15} \tag{1}$$

The Workload Profile (WP) is another subjective MWL assessment method based upon the Multiple Resource Theory (MRT) proposed by Wickens [48]. The WP index is built upon 8 dimensions: perceptual/central processing, response processing, spatial processing, verbal processing, visual processing, auditory processing, manual responses and speech responses. An operator is asked to rate the proportion of attentional resources, in the range $[0..1] \in \Re$. The final MWL index is a simple sum of the 8 factors as shown in Eq. 2.

$$WP_{MWL} = \sum_{i=1}^{8} d_i \tag{2}$$

For a further analysis of the questionnaires associated with the two aforementioned measurements methods, we refer the reader to [25].

2.3   Criteria for the Development of MWL Measurement Methods

There are different criteria that have emerged in the last few decades in the literature of mental workload for the evaluation of measurement methods and for assessing their inferential capacity [35]. A method adhering to all the criteria below is ideal, but unfortunately it is not always the case.

- *Sensitivity:* the method should be responsive to variations in task difficulties and other factors believed to influence mental workload on the task level;
- *Diagnosticity:* the method should be diagnostic and be capable of identifying the changes in workload variation and the causes of these changes;
- *Intrusiveness:* the method should not be intrusive or interfere with the primary task performance;
- *Requirements:* the method should demand minimum equipment to avoid influencing the performance of humans during primary task execution;
- *Acceptability:* the method should achieve high acceptance from humans;
- *Selectivity:* the method should be highly sensitive to MWL factors and not affected by other factors that are not related to MWL;
- *Bandwidth and reliability:* the method should be reliable during the tests and should be able to detect changes in MWL;
- *Validity:* the capacity of the method to measure MWL (sometimes referred to as reliability).

2.4   Gaps in Measurement Methods

The vast majority of the procedures for measuring MWL are theory-driven and deductive in nature. Deductive inference of mental workload follows a top-down approach. It starts with a hypothesis, or a set of hypotheses, based on existing knowledge and theories, and then it moves towards the measurement and quantification of those factors believed to influence mental workload, their aggregation and a final inference, usually an index or score. However, as in other scientific fields, inductive research methodologies can be applied to create models of mental workload from data and produce alternative inferences. An inductive data-driven inference of mental workload follows a bottom-up approach that starts with the measurement and quantification of those factors believed to influence mental workload. It then applies inductive learning classification techniques that can learn from these quantities and produce computational models capable of fitting human performance. Nowadays, one of the most popular research fields devoted to the development of inductive models is Machine learning (ML), a sub-field of Artificial Intelligence (AI). ML aims to develop algorithms and procedures that can learn from data, extract trends, patterns and make predictions.

In MWL measurement, the need to use Machine Learning arises because of the multifaceted characteristics of MWL itself, the ambiguity and uncertainty associated with the many non-linear factors shaping this construct and the difficulties associated with their aggregation and the development of computational models. Not a lot has been done in the application of ML techniques to the automatic construction of MWL models that consider subjective measures.

2.5   Machine Learning and Inductive Data-Driven Methods for MWL

Generally speaking, an inductive data-driven research approach is driven by an observation and analysis of available data toward the extraction of meaning, patterns, relationship and eventually the development of theories. From its inception, Machine Learning (ML) has gone far beyond the pattern recognition capabilities. Nowadays, ML algorithms are able to adapt, encode, decode and induce models from heterogeneous data not linearly related, with different characteristics, types, ranges and scales.

Recent studies revealed that most of the applications of Machine Learning in the field of Mental Workload focused on the processing of signals of physiological measures and as a form of benchmark for other measurement techniques [41]. For instance, [10,33,44] focused on the analysis of eye-gaze patterns of humans, while interacting with computer screens, and with other devices. Other studies focused on behavioural measures for assessing mental workload [9,13] and on modelling techniques for representing this construct [19]. Some researchers applied linguistic and keyboard dynamics for mental workload detection [34] or functional near-infrared spectroscopy for mental workload classification [16,36]. Yet, others tackled the problem of mental workload modelling through simulation, in multitask contexts [11], or in driving situations [50] employing Machine Learning.

3   Design and Methodology

This section is devoted to the design of a comparative study that consider models of mental workload, existing in the literature, and novel data-driven models developed using Machine Learning classification techniques. An existing dataset is employed for such purposes and the CRISP-DM methodology (the Cross Industry Standard Process for Data Mining) [7] is followed.

3.1   Comparative Research Design

As described in Fig. 1, the main aim of the experiment is to compare the inferential capacity of two state-of-the-art models of MWL, used as a baseline, against novel inductive models built upon an existing dataset [25]. On one hand, the baselines are the MWL subjective assessment techniques described in the previous sections: the NASA task load index (NASA-TLX) [15] (Eq. 1) and the Workload profile (WP) [47] (Eq. 2). On the other hand, the inductive data-driven models are developed employing different Machine Learning classification techniques, as described in Sect. 3.3. Baselines models and data-driven models will generate different inferences, in the form of indexes of mental workload, given the same input set, and these will be subsequently compared through an analysis of their validity.

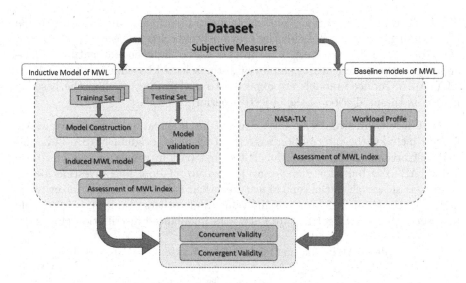

Fig. 1. Experiment Design Diagram.

3.2   Dataset

An existing dataset containing self-reporting measures, provided by users who executed a set of typical tasks over three popular web-sites, has been used [27]. The dataset contains data from more than 40 volunteers performing 9 web-based tasks of varying difficulty and contexts, and requiring different human modalities for processing information. A description of the tasks as well as the self-reporting measures collected during the experiment can be found in [25]. The participants, after each task, were asked to fill in the NASA-TLX questionnaire, the Workload Profile questionnaire and another set of questions believed to be useful for modelling mental workload. This last set of questions is not accounted for in this research study. At the end of each task, a final *objective performance class* was assigned to each volunteer:

- 0: the task was not completed as the user gave up;
- 1: the execution of the task was terminated because available time was over;
- 2: the task was completed and no answer was required by the user;
- 3: the task was completed, the user provided an answer, but it was wrong;
- 4: the task was completed and the user provided the correct.

3.3   Implementation of Machine Learning MWL Models

In order to build inductive MWL models from the chosen dataset, the Cross Industry Standard Process for Data Mining (CRISP-DM) approach was followed [7]. This process is built upon six stages; business goals, data understanding, data preparation, modelling, and eventually model evaluation and deployment.

Goals. The aim is to induce models of mental workload, from data, capable of predicting as best as possible the previously described *objective performance class* (dependent feature, Sect. 3.2) through a set of independent features. These are exactly the same features employed in the selected baseline models (NASA-TLX, WP). Induced models are expected to perform better than the baseline models in the prediction of the objective performance class.

Data Understanding. The data involved in the creation of inductive MWL models includes the information associated with the original NASA-TLX and WP instruments. Data exploration is the first part in which an Analytic Base Table (ABT) is built for discovering the nature of data and investigating its characteristics, such as the type of features, their values and ranges. Likewise, it highlights the quality of data, missing values and outliers (Table 1). It is possible to observe that the target feature follows an imbalanced distribution (Fig. 2a).

Table 1. ABT table and features (R = Range, C = Categorical)

Independent feature	type	miss	n	mean	sd	median	min	max	range	skew	kurtosis	se
Feature set 1: questions of NASA-TLX												
NASA_Mental	R	0	405	50.76	26.82	59	1	100	99	−0.25	−1.06	1.33
NASA_Temporal	R	0	405	39.54	29.8	33	1	100	99	0.34	−1.13	1.48
NASA_Stress	R	0	405	37.17	29	30	1	100	99	0.51	−0.91	1.44
NASA_Effort	R	0	405	56.38	25.75	63	1	100	99	−0.52	−0.73	1.28
NASA_Performance	R	0	405	67.95	29.41	76	1	100	99	−0.94	−0.15	1.46
Feature set 2: original pairwise comparisons of NASA-TLX												
NASA_MenTem	C	0	405	0.37	0.48	0	0	1	1	0.56	−1.69	0.02
NASA_MenPsy	C	0	405	0.3	0.46	0	0	1	1	0.89	−1.21	0.02
NASA_MenEff	C	0	405	0.63	0.48	1	0	1	1	−0.52	−1.73	0.02
NASA_MenPer	C	0	405	0.51	0.5	1	0	1	1	−0.02	−2	0.02
NASA_TemPsy	C	0	405	0.42	0.49	0	0	1	1	0.33	−1.89	0.02
NASA_TemEff	C	0	405	0.63	0.48	1	0	1	1	−0.52	−1.73	0.02
NASA_TemPer	C	0	405	0.62	0.48	1	0	1	1	−0.51	−1.74	0.02
NASA_PsyEff	C	0	405	0.73	0.45	1	0	1	1	−1.02	−0.96	0.02
NASA_PsyPer	C	0	405	0.71	0.46	1	0	1	1	−0.9	−1.19	0.02
NASA_EffPer	C	0	405	0.52	0.5	1	0	1	1	−0.07	−2	0.02
Feature set 3: total preferences of pairwise comparison (weight) for NASA-TLX												
NASA_menTotPref	R	0	405	3.2	1.13	3	1	5	4	−0.23	−0.72	0.06
NASA_TemTotPref	R	0	405	2.7	1.37	2	1	5	4	0.36	−1.12	0.07
NASA_PsychTotPref	R	0	405	2.28	1.34	2	1	5	4	0.7	−0.74	0.07
NASA_EffTotPref	R	0	405	3.46	1.1	4	1	5	4	−0.35	−0.64	0.05
NASA_PerTotPref	R	0	405	3.36	1.31	3	1	5	4	−0.27	−1.07	0.07
Feature set 4: original workload profile												
WP_CentralProcessing	R	0	405	53.02	27.36	60	0	100	100	−0.35	−0.97	1.36
WP_ResponseProcessing	R	0	405	33.92	27.14	27	0	100	100	0.48	−0.97	1.35
WP_SpatialProcessing	R	0	405	23.97	24.34	18	0	100	100	1.05	0.23	1.21
WP_VerbalProcessing	R	0	405	51.59	34.43	60	0	100	100	−0.22	−1.43	1.71
WP_VisualInput	R	0	405	62.24	27.58	68	0	100	100	−0.66	−0.5	1.37
WP_AuditoryInput	R	0	405	33.25	37.78	13	0	100	100	0.67	−1.24	1.88
WP_ManualResponse	R	0	405	30.18	26	23	0	100	100	0.62	−0.7	1.29
WP_SpeechResponse	R	0	405	12.06	18.28	3	0	100	100	1.96	3.76	0.91
Dependent feature												
Objective performance	C	15	390	3.22	1.1	4	0	4	4	−1.28	0.63	0.06

Data Preparation. The main aim of this stage is to construct the final dataset for subsequent modelling. Here, the dataset is divided into two segments: independent features and target (dependent) feature. The independent continuous features and answers of the experimental questionnaires ($[1..100] \in N$), have been normalised into a scale of unit norm $[0..1]$ *in* $\Re$ [17]. The following sets of independent features were extracted:

- *Raw-NASA* - it contains the original NASA-TLX factors excluding the physical factor as it was not part of task activities (feature set 1 of Table 1);
- *Original-NASA* - it contains all the NASA-TLX factors in addition to the binary preferences among the factors, which emerged from the pairwise comparison of the original NASA-TLX (feature sets $1 + 2$ of Table 1);
- *Weighted-NASA* - it contains the NASA-TLX factors and the calculated weight for each factor – number of times a factor has been preferred over the others, in the original NASA-TLX pairwise comparison procedure (feature sets $1 + 3$ of Table 1).
- *WP* - it includes the eight WP features (feature set 3 of Table 1).

Often, in Machine Learning, the imbalance of the target class can likely affect the creation of robust models, which will tend to be better in predicting the majority classes but not the minority classes. In order to solve this issue, an over-sampling technique has been selected and applied to restore the target class balance. In simple words, the concept of over-sampling is to reproduce relative samples for only one minority class. However, in this specific case, four minority classes exist (Fig. 2a) and hence the oversampling algorithm has been executed for all the 4 minority classes. The Density-Based SMOTE (DBSMOTE) algorithm was selected [4] among others tested in the preparation phase because of its higher capacity to avoid overfitting of data [6]. Figure 2b shows a distribution obtained using the oversampling method over the full dataset.

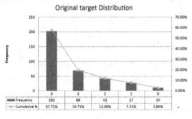
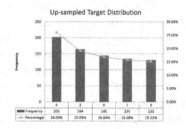

(a) Original distribution.   (b) Illustrative over-sampled distribution.

Fig. 2. Original and oversampled distribution of target using the DB-SMOTE

Data Modelling. This stage is aimed at inducing computational models by learning from data. This is a non-trivial task not only because the modelling algorithm(s) must be selected from a large number of Machine Learning algorithms, but also because an optimal configuration of these algorithms have to

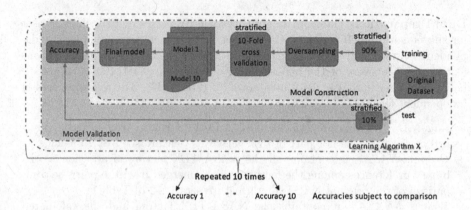

Fig. 3. Detailed design schema: model construction, validation and testing

be found. The selection of supervised learning techniques is done by type. The rationale behind selecting different types is to tackle the MWL modeling problem from different perspectives to allow subsequent triangulation of results and achieve robust findings. Four Machine Learning classification techniques have been chosen:

- Probability based: Naive Bayes
- Similarity based: K-nearest Neighbors
- Information based: Random Forest (based on Decision Trees)
- Error Based: Support Vector Machines (with Radial Basis Function Kernel)

In order to induce robust models with a higher degree of generalisability, a common way of training models is to split the original data into training and test sets (Fig. 3). Because of the limited dataset size ($|dataset| = 405\ instances$), the split ratio selected is 90% instances for training and 10% for testing. Additionally, because the original distribution of the independent feature is highly imbalanced, random stratified sampling [45] is used to perform the split. This technique allows to representatively sample even the smallest and most inaccessible subgroups both in training and test sets. Once the training set has been formed, oversampling is applied to it. Subsequently, the K-folds cross validation technique is used as the training method [1, 18, 37], always justified by the limited size of available data. This technique divides the dataset into k subsets and, for k iterations, one of the k subsets is used as the validation set and the other $k - 1$ subsets are textcolorredcombined to form the training set. Usually, the average error across all k trials is computed. In this research, k is set to 10 and the best model emerged out of 10, in term of accuracy, is selected as the final representative model. Eventually, this final model is tested against generalisability with the 10% of instances held-out originally. The overall process is eventually repeated again 10 times, shifting the test set, thus producing 10 accuracies for a given selected learning algorithm X.

Model Evaluation. This is the last stage aimed at evaluating the induced models from the previous phase and their inferential capacity and performance. Overall, 16 final models have been built (4 classifiers for 4 feature sets) each having 10 associated accuracies. The metrics selected for evaluating these final models are: prediction accuracy (observed accuracy) and the Kappa coefficient.

Accuracy is required for the overall interpretation of an induced model while the Kappa coefficient provided a more in-depth interpretation, as it is sensitive to imbalanced data. Several studies relied on the Kappa coefficient for evaluating inductive multi-class models [2,8,14]. As shown in Eqs. 3 and 4, the P_0 is the probability of overall agreement for a specific label across all classes, the P_e^C represents the sum of the proportion of the number of samples assigned to a class, times the proportion of true labels of that class. $N_{i:}$ and $N_{:i}$ are the sums of number in the i-th column and the i-th row of the confusion matrix, respectively. The Kappa statistic is a metric that compares an observed accuracy with an expected accuracy (random chance). It accounts for random chance (agreement with a random classifier), which generally means it is less misleading than simply using accuracy as a metric. An observed accuracy of 90% is less impressive with an expected accuracy of 70% versus an expected accuracy of 50%.

$$\kappa = \frac{(P_0 - P_e^C)}{(1 - P_e^C)} \tag{3}$$

$$P_e^C = \frac{\sum_{i=1}^{I} N_{i:} N_{:i}}{(N_{Total}^2)} \tag{4}$$

The criteria selected for the comparison of the inferential capacity of the baseline models (NASA-TLX, WP) and the inductive data-driven models (emerged from the previous modeling phase) are as follows.

- *Concurrent validity*: the extent to which a technique can explain objective performance measures, as in this case, the *objective performance class* [25];
- *Convergent validity*: aims at determining whether different MWL assessment techniques relate to each other [39].

4   Results and Evaluation

4.1   Concurrent Validity of Baseline MWL Models

To measure the concurrent validity of the selected baseline models (NASA-TLX, WP), the Spearman's correlation coefficient has been selected as it evaluates the monotonic relationship between the two continuous MWL indexes with the objective performance class. Table 2 depicts the correlations highlighting a weak statistically significant correlation ($P < 0.01$) between the NASA-TLX and the objective performance class and a non-significant correlation ($P = 0.72$) between the WP and the objective performance class.

Table 2. Concurrent validity: correlation of NASA-TLX, WP vs performance

*significant at the 0.01 level (2-tailed)	WP	NASA-TLX
OBJECTIVE PERFORMANCE	−.019	−.246*
Sig. (2-tailed)	.720	<0.0001

4.2 Concurrent Validity of Data-Driven MWL Models

The concurrent validity of the Machine Learning data-driven models is computed by analysing the distribution of the accuracies and the Kappa scores obtained with the 10-fold cross-validation technique used in the training phase, as highlighted in Fig. 3 (Model construction phase), across the different features sets (1, 2, 3, 4 of Table 1) and the different learning techniques (Naive Bayes, K-nearest Neighbours, Random Forest, Support Vector Machines).

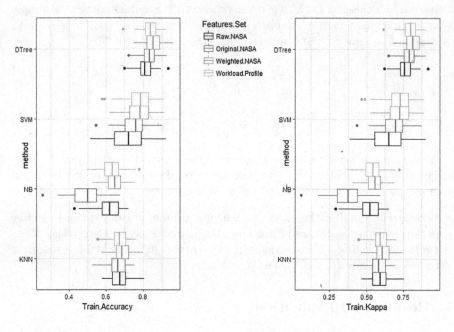

Fig. 4. Training accuracies, kappa scores grouped by Machine Learning classifier

From the boxplots of the accuracies and the kappa-scores of Fig. 4, it is possible to assess that the classification methods Random Forest and Support Vector Machines (using a radial kernel) are the most robust methods emerged from the training phase (model construction phase of Fig. 3). In details, according to the distribution of accuracies, the Random Forest method is capable of producing more accurate models of mental workload, for all the feature sets, and the distributions of the kappa scores confirm that these models are more reliable and not in agreement with a random classifier (Sect. 3.2).

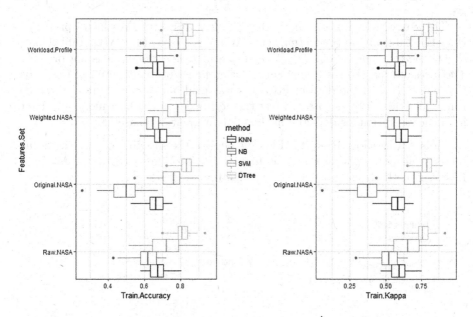

Fig. 5. Training accuracies, kappa scores grouped by independent feature set

From the boxplots of Fig. 5, a clear picture does not emerge, and it is not possible to clearly assess which feature sets are more useful in allowing the construction of inductive MWL models from data with higher accuracy. As a consequence, the models built with the Random Forest and the Support Vector Machine methods have been extracted, as depicted in Fig. 6.

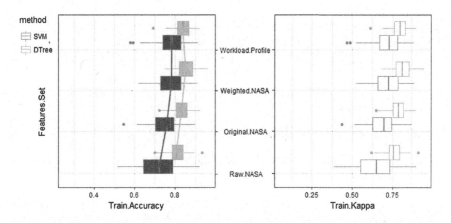

Fig. 6. Training accuracies and kappa scores grouped by independent feature set for the best models induced by Random Forest and Support Vector Machines

The boxplots of Fig. 6 suggest that the features set 4 (Workload profile of the ABT Table 1) and the feature set 3 (Weighted Nasa of the ABT Table 1) are slightly better than the others, although a statistical significance is not present. These results refer to the model construction phase of the diagram of Fig. 3. In this phase, 10% of the dataset instances was held out at each iteration, for 10 times, and this 10% was used to test the accuracies of the best model emerged from each iteration, as depicted in the model validation phase (Fig. 3).

Models Validation Results. Figure 7 depicts the distributions of the accuracies achieved by the best models (out of 10), both grouped by the Machine Learning methods used (a), and by the features sets (b).

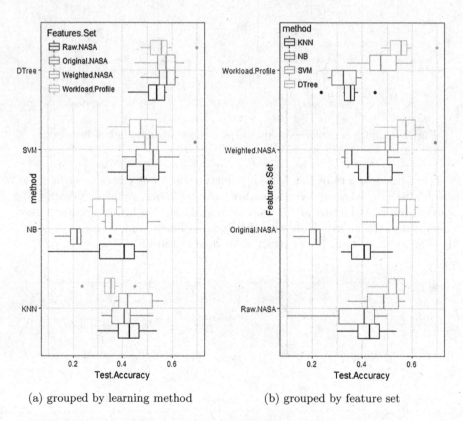

(a) grouped by learning method   (b) grouped by feature set

Fig. 7. Accuracies obtained by the best final models, emerged from the model construction phase, using the held out validation sets

The accuracies obtained (Fig. 7a) with the test sets, are on average lower than those which emerged in the model construction phase. This is reasonable given that each held out validation set contains instances of the original dataset never used in the model construction phase. However, the results show the same trends emerged during the model construction phase, confirming how

Random Forest and Support Vector machines are the most robust learning methods to build MWL models with the underlying dataset. This can be further grasped from Fig. 8(a) which plots the density distributions of all the best final models, obtained across all the features sets (4 sets × 10 iterations = 40 points per method). From Fig. 7(b), it seems that the feature set 3 (the weighted-NASA as described in Sect. 3.3) is the richest in terms of the information it carries for building MWL models when compared to the other features sets. This is also confirmed from the density plots of accuracies of Fig. 8(b) with the 'weighted NASA' feature set showing a more compact and taller curve, meaning on average superior than the other features sets. It is important to note that, even considering the best modelling methods (Random Forest and Support Vector Machines), the testing accuracies varies from 0.4 to 0.6 (40% to 60%) indicating that either more data is needed to build better MWL models or more descriptive (independent) features, carrying other information, are needed to increase their accuracies. These results are in line with current research on mental workload and the well known difficulties in predicting human performance.

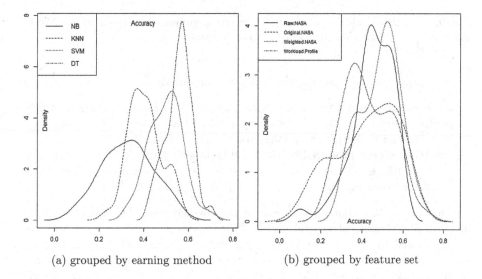

(a) grouped by earning method   (b) grouped by feature set

Fig. 8. Accuracy densities, emerged from the model construction phase, using the held out validation sets

Finally, to summarise the findings related to the concurrent validity of the inductive data-driven models produced in this study, and the baseline state-of-the-art models – namely the NASA-TLX and the Workload profile – an investigation of the correlation of their assessments against objective performance has been carried out, as depicted in Fig. 9.

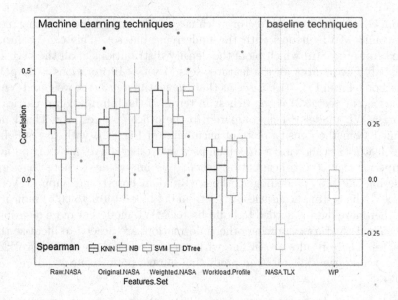

Fig. 9. Concurrent validity: distributions of the spearman correlations of the MWL inductive and deductive models against objective performance

In details, the following correlations were computed:

- the *objective performance class* (Sect. 3.2) predicted by the induced learning models against the *objective real performance class* assigned to a volunteer executing an underlying task (the ground truth, Sect. 3.2);
- the *MWL scores*, produced by the baseline models (NASA-TLX, WP, in the range $[0..100] \in N$) against the *objective real performance class* assigned to a volunteer executing an underlying task (the ground truth, Sect. 3.2).

Due to the fact that at least one of the two variables, in each correlation analysis, is always a categorical variable, the Spearman correlation method has been adopted instead of the Pearson correlation method, as the former does not require the variables being normally distributed, and the latter requires both continuous variables. From Fig. 9, it is possible to note that, on one hand, the box plots associated with the baseline models are closer to 0, suggesting that there is no real correlation between their assessment and the objective performance experienced by the volunteer in the experimental task. A similar result is achieved by the data-driven models produced using the features set 4 (containing the attributes of the original Workload Profile instrument). On the other hand, this situation is improved by the data-driven models of MWL built using the feature sets 1, 2, 3 (Sect. 3.3, containing the attributes of the original NASA-TLX). Correlations are more far away from 0, indicating that a clearer and better relationship between the predicted objective performance class, and the observed objective real performance experience by the volunteer in the experimental task can be obtained.

4.3   Convergent Validity of Baseline and Data-Driven MWL Models

The convergent validity of the Machine Learning-based induced models is computed by analysing their correlation with the original NASA Task Load Index and the Workload Profile instruments, baseline models. Figures 10 and 11 depict the correlations and, as before, the Spearman correlation coefficient has been preferred over the Pearson correlation coefficient because of the presence of categorical data and a relaxation of the assumptions of normality of variables.

The box-plots of Figs. 10 and 11 show a weak correlation between the baseline and inductive data-driven MWL models. In detail, the Machine-Learning based induced models correlate better to the assessments produced by the original NASA-TLX and have nearly null correlation with those produced by the

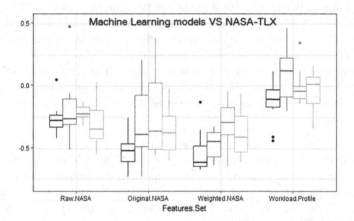

Fig. 10. Convergent validity: distributions of the spearman correlations of the MWL data-driven models against the NASA-TLX model

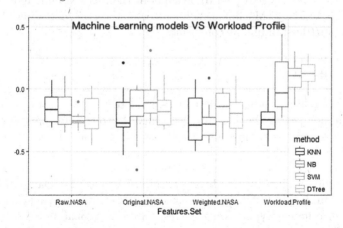

Fig. 11. Convergent validity: distributions of the Spearman correlations of the MWL data-driven models against the WP model

Workload Profile instrument. This suggests that incorporating the features of the original NASA-TLX (or their manipulation) in a data-driven model is more useful than using the features of the original Workload Profile instrument. In other words, induced models, built using Machine Learning classification techniques are closer to the NASA-TLX assessment instrument rather than the Workload Profile instrument.

4.4   Summary of Findings

The findings achieved in this empirical research showed that:

- The *concurrent validity* achieved by the inductive data-driven models of MWL, built using Machine Learning classification techniques, outperform the concurrent validity of two state-of-the-art baseline models of MWL, namely the NASA-TLX and the Workload Profile. In detail, Fig. 9 highlights the capacity of the inductive data-driven models to correlate to human performance better than the selected baseline models.
- The *convergent validity* of the inductive data-driven models, built using Machine Learning classification techniques, and the baseline models of MWL, namely the NASA-TLX and the Workload Profile assessment techniques, is rather weak.

The weak convergent validity of the inductive data-driven models and the baseline MWL models would suggest that, if the NASA-TLX and the WP instruments are taken as benchmarking, then the assessments produced by the inductive models is poorly assessing mental workload as a construct. However, the concurrent validity of the induced models better explain human performance than the NASA-TLX and WP instruments. Thus, because the main reason of assessing MWL is to predict human performance, then the inferential capacity of the inductive models is argued to be superior than the baseline models, highlighting the potential of Machine Learning as a method for modelling MWL and increasing its understanding as construct.

5   Conclusion

This unique research study, the, first of its kind to the best of our knowledge, was aimed at comparing the inferential capacity of two baseline mental workload (MWL) assessment techniques using self-reporting data – namely the NASA Task Load Index and the Workload Profile instruments – against inductive data-driven models of mental workload built using Machine Learning classification techniques. The Cross Industry Standard Process for Data Mining was followed for building inductive models using four Machine Learning classification techniques of different types: Naive Bayes, based on probability measures; the K-nearest Neighbors classifier, based on similarity measures; Random Forest, based on Decision Trees and information measures; and Support Vector Machines, based on error measures. The underlying dataset [27], used for the comparison, is part of a bigger study [24] and already used in literature [25,31,32,39]. This includes self-reporting data, obtained from human volunteers, after executing typical web-based tasks upon three popular websites. The findings confirm the original hypothesis in which MWL models, built using classification techniques, were expected to outperform baseline theory-driven models in the prediction of human performance (concurrent validity). In this context, concurrent validity was the capacity of a MWL assessment technique to predict an objective performance class (categorical variable) which was a real behavioural indicator of the performance achieved by humans on experimental tasks. Findings, although promising, cannot be generalised as only one dataset of small size has been used. Further investigations and empirical research needs to be carried out to strengthen this contribution and confirm the potential of Machine Learning as a novel methodology for building data-driven models of mental workload and increasing our understanding of this fascinating complex construct.

Future work will be devoted to collect novel data, not using only self-reporting assessment techniques, but also primary and secondary task measures as well as physiological measures. Different contexts of application will be explored, including for example virtual reality applications [21], simulation in safety critical environments [46], in educational settings [49] and clinical environments [28]. Additional Machine Learning classification techniques will be selected and further existing theory-driven models of mental workload will be considered for additional comparison.

References

1. Arlot, S., Celisse, A., et al.: A survey of cross-validation procedures for model selection. Stat. Surv. **4**, 40–79 (2010)
2. Ben-David, A.: About the relationship between ROC curves and Cohen's kappa. Eng. Appl. Artif. Intell. **21**(6), 874–882 (2008)
3. Blankertz, B., Curio, G., Müller, K.R.: Classifying single trial EEG: towards brain computer interfacing. Adv. Neural Inf. Process. Syst. **1**(c), 157–164 (2002)
4. Bunkhumpornpat, C., Sinapiromsaran, K., Lursinsap, C.: DBSMOTE: density-based synthetic minority over-sampling technique. Appl. Intell. **36**(3), 664–684 (2012)
5. Cain, B.: A review of the mental workload literature. In: Defence Research and Development Toronto (Canada), pp. 4-1–4-34 (2007)
6. Cawley, G.C., Talbot, N.L.: On over-fitting in model selection and subsequent selection bias in performance evaluation. J. Mach. Learn. Res. **11**, 2079–2107 (2010)
7. Chapman, P., Clinton, J., Khabaza, T., Reinartz, T., Wirth, R.: The CRISP-DM process model. CRIP-DM Consortium 310 (1999)
8. Choudhury, S., Bhowal, A.: Comparative analysis of machine learning algorithms along with classifiers for network intrusion detection. In: 2015 International Conference on Smart Technologies and Management for Computing, Communication, Controls, Energy and Materials (ICSTM) (May), pp. 89–95 (2015)
9. Cinaz, B., Arnrich, B., La Marca, R., Tröster, G.: Monitoring of mental workload levels during an everyday life office-work scenario. Pers. Ubiquit. Comput. **17**(2), 229–239 (2013)

10. Cortes Torres, C.C., Sampei, K., Sato, M., Raskar, R., Miki, N.: Workload assessment with eye movement monitoring aided by non-invasive and unobtrusive microfabricated optical sensors. In: Adjunct Proceedings of the 28th Annual ACM Symposium on User Interface Software and Technology, pp. 53–54 (2015)

11. Di Stasi, L.L., Marchitto, M., Antolí, A., Baccino, T., Cañas, J.J.: Approximation of on-line mental workload index in ATC simulated multitasks. J. Air Transp. Manage. **16**(6), 330–333 (2010)

12. Dornhege, G., Blankertz, B., Curio, G., Múller, K.R.: Boosting bit rates in noninvasive EEG single-trial classifications by feature combination and multiclass paradigms. IEEE Trans. Biomed. Eng. **51**(6), 993–1002 (2004)

13. Elkin-Frankston, S., Bracken, B.K., Irvin, S., Jenkins, M.: Are behavioral measures useful for detecting cognitive workload during human-computer interaction? In: Ahram, T., Karwowski, W. (eds.) Advances in Intelligent Systems and Computing, vol. 494, pp. 127–137. Springer, Cham (2017)

14. Fatourechi, M., Ward, R.K., Mason, S.G., Huggins, J., Schlógl, A., Birch, G.E.: Comparison of evaluation metrics in classification applications with imbalanced datasets. In: Proceedings - 7th International Conference on Machine Learning and Applications, ICMLA 2008, pp. 777–782 (2008)

15. Hart, S.G., Staveland, L.E.: Development of NASA-TLX (Task Load Index): results of empirical and theoretical research. Adv. Psychol. **52**(C), 139–183 (1988)

16. Hincks, S.W., Afergan, D., Jacob, R.J.K.: Using fNIRS for real-time cognitive workload assessment. In: Schmorrow, D.D.D., Fidopiastis, C.M.M. (eds.) AC 2016. LNCS, vol. 9743, pp. 198–208. Springer, Cham (2016). doi:10.1007/978-3-319-39955-3_19

17. Juszczak, P., Tax, D., Duin, R.P.: Feature scaling in support vector data description. In: Proceedings of the ASCI, pp. 95–102. Citeseer (2002)

18. Kohavi, R., et al.: A study of cross-validation and bootstrap for accuracy estimation and model selection. In: Ijcai, vol. 14, pp. 1137–1145 (1995)

19. Kumar, M., Arndt, A., Kreuzfeld, S., Thurow, K., Stoll, N., Stoll, R.: Fuzzy techniques for subjective workload-score modeling under uncertainties. IEEE Trans. Syst. Man Cybern. Part B Cybern. **38**(6), 1449–1464 (2008)

20. Lee, J.C., Tan, D.S.: Using a low-cost electroencephalograph for task classification in HCI research. In: Proceedings of the 19th ACM Symposium on User Interface Software and Technology, pp. 81–90 (2006)

21. Leva, M.C., Kay, A.M., Mattei, F., Kontogiannis, T., Ambroggi, M., Cromie, S.: A dynamic task representation method for a virtual reality application. In: Harris, D. (ed.) EPCE 2009. LNCS, vol. 5639, pp. 32–42. Springer, Heidelberg (2009). doi:10.1007/978-3-642-02728-4_4

22. Longo, L.: Human-computer interaction and human mental workload: assessing cognitive engagement in the world wide web. In: Campos, P., Graham, N., Jorge, J., Nunes, N., Palanque, P., Winckler, M. (eds.) INTERACT 2011. LNCS, vol. 6949, pp. 402–405. Springer, Heidelberg (2011). doi:10.1007/978-3-642-23768-3_43

23. Longo, L.: Formalising human mental workload as non-monotonic concept for adaptive and personalised web-design. In: Masthoff, J., Mobasher, B., Desmarais, M.C., Nkambou, R. (eds.) UMAP 2012. LNCS, vol. 7379, pp. 369–373. Springer, Heidelberg (2012). doi:10.1007/978-3-642-31454-4_38

24. Longo, L.: Formalising human mental workload as a defeasible computational concept. Ph.D. thesis, Trinity College Dublin (2014)

25. Longo, L.: A defeasible reasoning framework for human mental workload representation and assessment. Behav. Inf. Technol. **34**(8), 758–786 (2015)

26. Longo, L.: Designing medical interactive systems via assessment of human mental workload. In: International Symposium on Computer-Based Medical Systems, pp. 364–365 (2015)
27. Longo, L.: Subjective usability (system usability scale) and subjective mental workload (NASA-TLX and workload profile) of web-based tasks and interfaces (2015)
28. Longo, L.: Mental workload in medicine: Foundations, applications, open problems, challenges and future perspectives. In: 2016 IEEE 29th International Symposium on Computer-Based Medical Systems (CBMS), pp. 106–111, June 2016
29. Longo, L., Barrett, S.: A computational analysis of cognitive effort. In: Nguyen, N.T., Le, M.T., Świątek, J. (eds.) ACIIDS 2010. LNCS, vol. 5991, pp. 65–74. Springer, Heidelberg (2010). doi:10.1007/978-3-642-12101-2_8
30. Longo, L., Barrett, S.: Cognitive effort for multi-agent systems. In: Yao, Y., Sun, R., Poggio, T., Liu, J., Zhong, N., Huang, J. (eds.) BI 2010. LNCS, vol. 6334, pp. 55–66. Springer, Heidelberg (2010). doi:10.1007/978-3-642-15314-3_6
31. Longo, L., Dondio, P.: On the relationship between perception of usability and subjective mental workload of web interfaces. In: IEEE/WIC/ACM International Conference on Web Intelligence and Intelligent Agent Technology, WI-IAT 2015, Singapore, December 6–9, vol. I, pp. 345–352 (2015)
32. Longo, L., Rusconi, F., Noce, L., Barrett, S.: The importance of human mental workload in web-design. In: 8th International Conference on Web Information Systems and Technologies, pp. 403–409, April 2012
33. Mannaru, P., Balasingam, B., Pattipati, K., Sibley, C., Coyne, J.: Cognitive context detection in UAS operators using eye-gaze patterns on computer screens. In: SPIE 9851, Next-Generation Analyst IV, vol. 9851, p. 98510F (2016)
34. Ott, T., Wu, P., Paullada, A., Mayer, D., Gottlieb, J., Wall, P.: ATHENA – a zero-intrusion no contact method for workload detection using linguistics, keyboard dynamics, and computer vision. In: Stephanidis, C. (ed.) HCI 2016. CCIS, vol. 617, pp. 226–231. Springer, Cham (2016). doi:10.1007/978-3-319-40548-3_38
35. O'Donnell, R., Eggemeier, F.: Workload assessment methodology. In: Boff, K.R., Kaufman, L., Thomas, J.P. (eds.) Handbook of Perception and Human Performance, Cognitive Processes and Performance, vol. 2. Wiley, Hoboken (1986)
36. Pham, T.T., Nguyen, T.D., Vo, T.: Sparse fNIRS feature estimation via unsupervised learning for mental workload classification. In: Bassis, S., Esposito, A., Morabito, F.C., Pasero, E. (eds.) Advances in Neural Networks. SIST, vol. 54, pp. 283–292. Springer, Cham (2016). doi:10.1007/978-3-319-33747-0_28
37. Rao, R.B., Fung, G., Rosales, R.: On the dangers of cross-validation. an experimental evaluation. In: Proceedings of the 2008 SIAM International Conference on Data Mining, pp. 588–596. SIAM (2008)
38. Reid, G.B., Nygren, T.E.: The Subjective Workload Assessment Technique: A Scaling Procedure for Measuring Mental Workload, vol. 52, North-Holland (1988)
39. Rizzo, L., Dondio, P., Delany, S.J., Longo, L.: Modeling mental workload via rule-based expert system: a comparison with NASA-TLX and workload profile. In: Iliadis, L., Maglogiannis, I. (eds.) AIAI 2016. IAICT, vol. 475, pp. 215–229. Springer, Cham (2016). doi:10.1007/978-3-319-44944-9_19
40. Rubio, S., Díaz, E., Martín, J., Puente, J.M.: Evaluation of subjective mental workload: a comparison of SWAT, NASA-TLX, and workload profile methods. Appl. Psychol. **53**(1), 61–86 (2004)
41. Solovey, E., Schermerhorn, P., Scheutz, M., Sassaroli, A., Fantini, S., Jacob, R.: Brainput: Enhancing interactive systems with streaming fNIRS Brain Input. In: Proceedings of the 2012 ACM Annual Conference on Human Factors in Computing Systems - CHI 2012. p. 2193. ACM (2012)

42. Stassen, H.G., Johannsen, G., Moray, N.: Internal representation, internal model, human performance model and mental workload. Automatica **26**(4), 811–820 (1990)
43. Stevens, R., Galloway, T., Berka, C.: Integrating EEG models of cognitive load with machine learning models of scientific problem solving. In: Proceedings of 2nd Annual Augmented Cognition International Conference (September, 2006)
44. Su, J., Luz, S.: Predicting cognitive load levels from speech data. Smart Innov. Syst. Technol. **48**, 255–263 (2016)
45. Thompson, S.K.: Stratified Sampling, pp. 139–156. Wiley, Hoboken (2012)
46. Trucco, P., Leva, M.C., Sträter, O.: Human error prediction in ATM via cognitive simulation: preliminary study. In: Proceedings of the 8th International Conference on Probabilistic Safety Assessment and Management (PSAM8), pp. 1–9 (2006)
47. Tsang, P.S., Velazquez, V.L.: Diagnosticity and multidimensional subjective workload ratings. Ergonomics **39**(3), 358–381 (1996)
48. Wickens, C.D.: Multiple resources and mental workload. Hum. Factors **50**(3), 449–455 (2008)
49. Wiebe, E.N., Roberts, E., Behrend, T.S.: An examination of two mental workload measurement approaches to understanding multimedia learning. Comput. Hum. Behav. **26**(3), 474–481 (2010)
50. Yoshida, Y., Ohwada, H., Mizoguchi, F., Iwasaki, H.: Classifying cognitive load and driving situation with machine learning. Int. J. Mach. Learn. Comput. **4**(3), 210–215 (2014)
51. Zhang, Y.Z.Y., Owechko, Y., Zhang, J.Z.J.: Driver cognitive workload estimation: a data-driven perspective. In: Proceedings of the 7th International IEEE Conference on Intelligent Transportation Systems (IEEE Cat. No.04TH8749), pp. 642–647 (2004)

Elasticity and Rigidity Constructs and Ratings of Subjective Workload for Individuals and Groups

Stephen J. Guastello(✉), David E. Marra, Anthony N. Correro II,
Maura Michels, and Henry Schimmel

Marquette University, P.O. Box 1881, Milwaukee, WI 53201-1881, USA
Stephen.guastello@marquette.edu

Abstract. Differences in workload inherent in a task have indirect and non-linear relationships to performance differences because of coping strategies that people can deploy. Thus subjective ratings of workload have become commonplace for evaluating task workload. It has become apparent, however, that those ratings are affected by individual differences in personality and cognitive traits that correspond to a general theme of elasticity versus rigidity. Additionally, workload can originate from both the task and group dynamics when team work is involved. This study explored the relationship among 11 such constructs related to anxiety, coping, and fluid intelligence and ratings of individual and group workload. Participants were 360 undergraduates organized into 44 groups of different sizes who engaged in an emergency response (ER) simulation against one or two opponents. Regression analyses indicated that task conditions accounted for 7–10% of variance in individual workload ratings, and elasticity accounted for another 1–2% of the variance. Task conditions accounted for 2–4% of the variance in group-level workload ratings, and elasticity accounted for another 2–4%. Results support the continued investigation of elasticity-rigidity in the understanding of workload arising from the task and group dynamics.

1 Introduction

Widespread interest in cognitive workload problems started with Simon's [1] concept of bounded rationality and Broadbent's [2] research on cognitive capacity. In the ensuing decades two theories emerged: the fixed upper limit theory and the variable upper limit theory [3]. According to the fixed upper limit theory, a person can perform two or more tasks as long as the mental demand of the two add up to less than the upper limit. When the upper limit is exceeded, errors proliferate or response time slows. In the variable upper limit theory, the upper bound of mental capacity can stretch under conditions of high motivation, a demand for emergency action or similar demands. Later landmarks in cognitive workload theory now favour the variable upper limit interpretation. According to Hancock and Warm [4], individuals have an acceptable range of high and low workload which they attempt to maintain in order to maintain a desired level of performance. When the acceptable range exceeds those boundaries, they engage in coping strategies of various sorts to regain the desired level of

© Springer International Publishing AG 2017
L. Longo and M.C. Leva (Eds.): H-WORKLOAD 2017, CCIS 726, pp. 51–76, 2017.
DOI: 10.1007/978-3-319-61061-0_4

performance once again. When the limits of their coping strategies are reached, however, catastrophic declines in performance are likely to occur. Baddeley's [5] concept of working memory identified further degrees of flexibility. Working memory, as we now understand it, consists of an executive function and specific functionalities related to auditory and visual sensory processes. An auditory and a visual task can be performed with relative impunity because of the separate neurocognitive channels that are involved, but two tasks of the same relative size that place demand on the same channel could produce challenges to accuracy and response time once again. We have now learned since that time that the executive function of working memory recruits workspace from specific brain regions, starting with the area most closely associated with the task requirements. If there is not enough space, more workspace is recruited from adjacent areas that are probably more often dedicated to other cognitive functions, which now include psychomotor response and computational and verbal capacities [6–9]. Wickens [10, 11] expanded on the channel principle by adding that tasks involve stages of processing – perception, cognition, and action; action could also involve plural channels. If the processing stages for two tasks are not simultaneous for any of the three stages, the workload capacity is maximized, and the performance results are favorable. Otherwise, bottlenecks, errors, and slowed response times are to be expected. Following the reasoning about channel capacities and the recruitment of workspace from different cognitive areas, the effect of excessive workload can be likened to that of squeezing a balloon [12]. Pressure on one part of the system can induce breakage in another part of the system. A substantial stream of research build-up on cognitive workload [13, 14] alongside cognitive fatigue [15, 16]; the latter dates back more than century. Constructs and experiments sometimes conflated the effects of workload and fatigue on perfor-mance. The recommended remedy was to assess performance over time as workload and fatigue conditions changed using two separate mathematical models (cusp catastrophes) and designing experiments to capture the effects of both processes [17, 18]. The workload model is the primary concern here; one of its features is the principle of elasticity-rigidity, which is the primary concern in this chapter. Elasticity-rigidity is a group of variables from personality and cognitive domains that predispose a person to being more flexible with additional and varying demands. The role of elasticity-rigidity is explained further in Sects. 1.2–3.

1.1 Subjective Workload Ratings

Differences in workload that arise from various task conditions are not always apparent in task performance because individuals can employ coping strategies that buffer high and low workload levels [4, 12]. As a result subjective ratings of workload, such as the NASA Task Load Index (TLX) [19], have been valuable tools for research and system design evaluation. The TLX rating constructs are mental demands, physical demands, temporal demands, performance demands, effort required, and frustration as defined in Table 1. Although the TLX is responsive to differences in workload [20–23], additional variation in ratings have been traced to individual differences that could either be personality or cognitive in origin [24, 25]. The specific trait variables would depend on the mental resources required by the task.

Table 1. Individual and group work scales

Individual scales, NASA TLX[a]	Group workload scales[b]
MENTAL DEMAND: How mentally challenging (e.g. thinking, searching, deciding) was the task?	COORDINATION DEMAND: How much coordination activity was required (e.g., correction, adjustment)? Were the coordination demands to work as a team low or high, infrequent or frequent?
PHYSICAL DEMAND: How physically challenging (e.g. pushing, pulling) was the task?	COMMUNICATION DEMAND: How much communication activity was required (e.g. discussing, negotiating, sending and receiving messages)? Were the communication demands low or high, infrequent of frequent, simple or complex?
TEMPORAL DEMAND: How much pressure did you feel performing the task due to the pace of the task?	TIME SHARING DEMAND: How difficult was it to share and manage time between taskwork (work done individually) and teamwork (work done as a team)? Was it easy or hard to manage individual tasks and those tasks requiring work with other team members?
PERFORMANCE: How successful were you in achieving the goals of the task?	TEAM EFFECTIVENESS: How successful do you think the team was in working as a team? How satisfied were you with the team-related aspects of performance?
EFFORT: How much energy was put forth to achieve your level of performance in the task?	TEAM SUPPORT: How difficult was it to provide and receive support (providing guidance, helping team members, providing instructions, etc.) from team members? Was it easy or hard to support/guide and receive support/guidance from other team members?
FRUSTRATION: How discouraged, bothered, irritated, and annoyed were you because of the task?	TEAM DISSATISFACTION: How emotionally draining and irritating vs. emotionally rewarding and satisfying was it to work as a team?

[a]Reprinted from NASA Hart and Staveland [19]. In the public domain.
[b]Reprinted from Helton et al. [30]. In the public domain.

This study had two objectives. The first objective was to examine elasticity-rigidity variables in conjunction with subjective workload ratings. Some individual differences that influence TLX ratings are associated with skill level. Those with stronger skills would have greater automaticity in the cognitive processes and would rate a task lower in load compared to less skilled individuals [25]. Individuals with stronger skills would also be expected to have greater flexibility for coping with increases in workload. Attributes from the personality domain can also contribute to coping strategies. At this time, a roster of about a dozen such variables have been identified on the basis of their role in explaining performance differences in workload, and they are collectively known as elasticity-rigidity variables [26, 27]. Some, but not all of them, have been studied in conjunction with subjective ratings of workload.

The second objective of this study was to determine if group-level workload (GWL) ratings are also influenced by elasticity-rigidity characteristics of the participants. The widespread nature of teamwork in sociotechnical systems has attracted some new interest in group workload. The current thinking is that teamwork independently adds workload in addition to individual workload constructs due to communication and coordination demands and other group dynamics that might be involved [28, 29]. Thus, Helton et al. [30] developed a set of subjective workload ratings for GWL – coordination demand, communication demand, time sharing demand, team efficacy, team support, and team dissatisfaction – which were meant to be parallel to the TLX ratings (Table 1).

1.2   Buckling Model for Workload

The model for cognitive workload invokes the concept of Euler buckling [31, 32]. A piece of material that is subjected to sufficient amounts of stress in the form of repeated stretching will show a certain amount of deformity or strain. Rigid materials break whereas flexible materials rebound. Similarly, if we took a rigid piece of material and applied weights, nothing would happen until too much weight was placed on top of the rigid material, whereas flexible materials are pliable and can deform and often return to their original shapes.

The relationships between load, elasticity, and performance outcomes are captured by the cusp catastrophe model (Fig. 1). Changes in performance that occur in response to increasing workload can be relatively smooth and linear if bifurcation variables are low in value. They are discontinuous if bifurcation values are high. Furthermore, high bifurcation predisposes the performance to change upward or downward; thus the effect

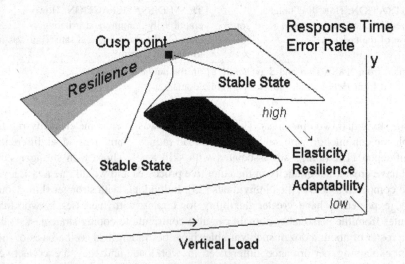

Fig. 1. Buckling model for workload.

of bifurcation variables might not be readily detected through linear modeling. This study was concerned with the psychological variables that were identified in previous research as bifurcation variables corresponding to the elasticity-rigidity construct and their relationship to subjective workload. For further background on the cusp catastrophe model, means of data analysis, and its other applications in ergonomics, see Guastello [33–35] and Guastello and Gregson [36].

The cusp model for workload has a companion cusp model for fatigue as both processes are thought to operate simultaneously in a given task situation [26, 37]. As the elasticity-rigidity principle only occurs in the workload model, the fatigue portion of the theory is not considered further here except to offer two observations. First, the relative amounts of workload and fatigue effects are traceable to the demands on the channel capacity in working memory in the case of workload and the executive function of working memory in the case of fatigue. Second, some tasks produce greater amounts of workload effects than fatigue effects, whereas the opposite can occur for other tasks.

In the case of workload effects, nearly one third of the performance variance is accounted for by the nonlinear properties of the relationships among the variables [26]. The nonlinearities explain how performance responses to workload can be sudden (high bifurcation or catastrophic), gradual and flexible (low bifurcation), or not apparent at all (see Fig. 1). The latter would occur when the workload remains below a person's threshold for sudden change [4] and elements of rigidity are relatively high. The tasks that were studied with the cusp catastrophe model were chosen to capture an array of cognitive processes that place strong demands on working memory, and to find what was generalisable about them: an episodic memory task [17], a pictorial memory task that required verbal retrieval cues [18], perceptual-motor multitasking [38], a vigilance dual task [24, 37, 39] a financial decision making task that captured both optimising and risk taking behavior [27], and an N-back task [40].

1.3   Elasticity-Rigidity Variables

Anxiety Constructs

Trait anxiety, which is an important aspect of the personality trait neuroticism, can slow response time, interfere with lucid decision making [41], and increase frustration with a task [42], but it can also focus attention on details that others might miss [43, 44]. Anxiety is operative more often when interpersonal challenges or physical hazards are present. Anxiety in this context was measured using a variation of the Taylor Manifest Anxiety Scale [45], which is centered on psychosomatic symptoms that comprise of an alternative medical diagnosis when they appear in relatively large numbers. Participants in the vigilance task who scored higher on anxiety gave higher ratings of TLX temporal demands than participants with lower anxiety scores. [24].

Emotional intelligence (EI) facilitates the understanding of one's own emotions, the emotional messages from other people, and the forming appropriate actions in response to emotions. Low EI denotes rigidity in the form of indifference, which could be a buffer against stress effects. When stress gets too high, however, the system buckles and snaps if the individual is not aware of his or her own emotional level or those of other people [46]. EI was measured in the present study with the Schutte et al. [47] scale, which favors the alexithymia construct more than it does cognitive judgment. Participants in the vigilance task scored higher on EI rated TLX temporal demands, effort, and frustration lower than participants with lower EI scores if they were working alone; if they worked with another participant, EI had the opposite effect on the same three ratings.

Empathy is usually defined with both a cognitive and an emotional component. The cognitive component is the ability of a person to take the point of view of another. The emotional component is the ability to experience vicariously the emotions of other people. The latest thinking on the empathy trait is that it might contain other facets such as self-regulation of emotion [48, 49], particularly when responding to co-workers [50]. Empathy was investigated here for the first time in conjunction with both TLX and GWL ratings.

Coping Constructs

One construct of coping flexibility is centered on emotional adjustments in the clinical sense of long-term life issues [51]. People who have a broader repertoire of coping strategies are likely to be more resilient to stress and emotional hardship. Another construct of coping is oriented towards cognitive strategies such as planning, monitoring, decisiveness, and inflexible responses to changing work situations [52]. These aspects of coping all denote contributions from the executive function of working memory. Both coping constructs were investigated here for the first time in conjunction with both TLX and GWL ratings.

Fluid Intelligence Constructs

Working memory, which is the limiting ingredient in workload tolerance, has been identified as part of the broader mental operations of fluid intelligence [53]. Field independence is a cognitive style that separates perceptions of a figure from a background. People with high field independence likely use more of their working memory capacity according to Pascual-Leone [54]. As such, field independence worked well as a bifurcation variable in studies of problem solving in chemistry [55] and financial decision making [27]. It was also associated with lower ratings of TLX physical demand and higher levels of performance demand on the financial decision making task [50].

Anagrams are one of several cognitive measures of creativity and are a part of fluid intelligence [56]. The construct played a small but consistent role in performance changes in cognitive workload or fatigue in the financial decision making task, which was an optimising task; it did not register as a significant predictor of TLX ratings [27]. Anagrams were investigated again in the present study because the emergency response (ER) task involved creative, strategic and adaptive behavior, which was the opposite of the practical and formulaic financial decision making task.

Algebra flexibility is based on the idea that, in addition to learning the rules of algebra, students should be flexible in their use of algebraic principles to solve problems [57]. It takes the form of a brief test with word problems and was an important factor in the workload model for N-back tasks [40], but algebra flexibility has not yet been studied in conjunction with TLX and GWL ratings.

Conscientiousness Constructs

Conscientiousness is a trait that predisposes a person to pay close attention to details, rules, task orientation, and a broader proclivity to focus attention. It thus implies a type of rigidity [58]. Conscientiousness has been measured as a broad trait in the sense of the five factor model of personality [59] in some of the workload experiments. In others, it was broken down into two narrower traits. One of the narrower traits measured conscientiousness in the sense of Factor G on the 16PF [24, 60], and the other measured impulsivity versus self-control, which would be similar to Factor Q3 on the 16PF. In principle, it is possible for people to be rigid in the sense of Factor G and flexible in the sense of Q3 [27]. Impulsivity was correlated with higher ratings of TLX temporal demand, and the narrower form of conscientiousness was correlated with higher ratings of TLX performance.

1.4   The Present Study

The data collection for the present study of ER teams was organised around three experimental conditions: a fixed effect for group size (3, 4, 7, or 8 individuals), a fixed effect for number of opponents (1 or 2), and a time constraint. The time constraint produced both a repeated effect and a fixed effect. The fixed effect was whether the time constraint was introduced either sooner or later in the experiment. The repeated effect was the two experimental sessions that differ in the use of the time constraint. The foregoing experimental design also afforded an opportunity to investigate changes in patterns in workload-elasticity relationships as the group matured.

A previous study [61] investigated the impact of the experimental manipulations on TLX and GWL ratings using a mixed model MANOVA analysis. Group size affected individual workload ratings but not group workload ratings. The number of opponents, however, affected most individual and group ratings. The repeated main effect of experimental session affected some individual and group ratings, indicating that workload experiences shifted as the group matured. The effect of the time constraint was assessed as an interaction between session and whether it was introduced sooner or later; the presence of the time constraint affected TLX performance and frustration scales only.

The hypotheses and analyses were structured as a hierarchical regression problem in which the objective was to determine the extent to which elasticity-rigidity affects ratings over and above that which could be accounted for by the experimental manipulation alone. Because many specific elasticity variables were involved, the regression strategy also allowed for some simplification of the experimental effects by dropping unnecessary interaction terms. Data from the two sessions were analysed separately to create a clearer picture of how workload experiences could shift over time. Another aspect of the research strategy was to analyze TLX and GLW ratings separately and not as total scores. Although there is evidence to support the use of total scores [30, 62], there is also research showing that the separate ratings can be differentially affected by experimental conditions [24, 61, 63, 64], and there was a similar amount of specificity between elasticity variables and ratings [24]. The general model for the hierarchical regression analysis is:

$$WL_i = f_1(\text{Experimental conditions}) + f_2(\text{elasticity-rigidity})$$

where WL_i is a specific workload rating, and f_1 and f_2 are weighted combinations of experimental conditions and elasticity-rigidity variables respectively. The objective is to determine whether f_2 adds anything to the prediction of workload ratings beyond what is accounted for by f_1.

The final analysis used canonical correlations to identify over-arching or emergent patterns of experimental conditions and elasticity variables on the one hand that were maximally related to weighted combinations of TLX and GWL ratings on the other:

$$f_1(\text{experimental conditions, elasticity-rigidity}) = f_2(\text{TLX}_i + \text{GWL}_i)$$

Once the calculation routine finds the first canonical variate, it searches for a second set of f_1 and f_2 that is orthogonal to the first. The maximum number of canonical variates is equal to the number of variables in the smaller of the two variable sets. The rationale behind the experimental conditions and specific hypotheses for this study are described next.

Group Size

Relatively smaller groups are more likely to be psychologically homogenous and thus more likely to be cohesive, which in turn bodes well for many types of tasks, although smaller groups might not be sufficiently equipped for creative problem solving tasks [65]. Relatively larger groups are more likely to be psychologically heterogeneous and thus more likely to produce the critical mass of ideas that are both required for creative problem solving tasks and for making the group more productive than the most competent individual [66]. However, larger groups are more prone to conflict for the same reasons [65]. Social loafing, in which some group members do more of the work than others while they all share in the same reward [67], could potentially alter workload demand on some group members. Social loafing is a potential in groups of any size but more so in larger groups. Differential work production or participation input, however, is not always a result of deliberate loafing but can be the result of poor team coordination [68]. Communication in smaller groups tends to be more equal with regard to the number of turns people take in a conversation. As groups become larger, however, larger numbers of speech turns are taken by proportionately fewer people [69]. The foregoing effects of group size could affect ratings of coordination demand, communication demand, team effectiveness, team satisfaction, and possibly team support.

Speed and Load

The two-attacker scenario should add workload for the ER teams because it creates a more challenging problem for the ER groups to overcome. Time pressure is another form of workload that was manipulated in the experiment. In one of the earliest ergonomics studies of workload, Conrad [70] showed that speed and load are important sources of demand (or stress); when multiplied together they had a strong linear correlation with task performance of individuals. Speed and load manipulations have also been studied as separate measures of workload [18, 24, 27, 39, 41, 71, 72]. Speed stress typically does not have a visible impact on performance errors until it reaches a critical point at which a speed-accuracy trade-off is observed.

Elasticity-Rigidity

Elasticity-rigidity variables were examined as correlates of the TLX and GWL ratings. The regression analyses were organised to produce competitive tests of the experimental conditions and elasticity variables for explanations of workload ratings. Individual differences were included from the anxiety, coping, and fluid intelligence groups of variables. The conscientiousness constructs were not included due to limitations on the experimental participants' time combined with the low expectation that it would be relevant to an essentially creative and adaptive task in which following rules was part of the experimental control.

Self-organisation

Self-organisation is a process in which a system that is in a high state of entropy acquires a new structure that reduces the amount of entropy, or lost energy, in carrying out its activities [73]. The new structures are often regarded as a form of *emergence* that has a visible influence on the system's continuing activities [74–76]. Human groups develop and mature over time, although not necessarily in the same temporal patterns [77, 78]. Groups engage in a variety of communication patterns, hypothetical strategies for action, and attempts to coordinate actions; as such, groups eventually establish the combination that works best for them. The specific task demands, physical workspace, and the group members themselves all contribute to the final outcome of the self-organising process. As groups evolve, their members learn coordination and effective communication patterns simultaneously while learning appropriate performance of the task; there are essentially two learning curves transpiring at once [68]. Task learning is usually regarded as explicitly learned while team coordination and related processes are implicitly learned. Furthermore, groups tend to undergo a qualitative and discontinuous shift in their internal dynamics approximately half way through their work time together; this phenomenon has been identified as *punctuated equilibrium* [79]. Both bottom-up (individual-to-group) and top-down (group-to-individual) processes are expected. They should be visible in multivariate patterns of TLX and GWL ratings, such that TLX and GWL ratings occur in combination. The alternative would be that TLX and GWL ratings remain separated and explained by different combinations of individual differences and experimental conditions.

Summary of Hypotheses

The hypotheses for the present study can be summarised as follows:

1. Increased workload in the form of number of opponents that the ER teams had to work against and speed demands would have an impact on workload ratings at the individual and group level.
2. Group size would have an impact on workload ratings. The creative problem solving nature of the task would favour lower individual ratings for larger groups. Larger groups would suggest greater demand on group-level workload, however.
3. Elasticity-rigidity variables would be correlated with workload ratings and have an effect beyond the more obvious workload conditions.

4. Patterns of elasticity, experimental conditions, and workload ratings should reflect both top-down and bottom-up dynamics.
5. There should be some changes in patterns of elasticity, experimental conditions, and workload ratings as the group matures. It is not known a priori whether the changes would be gradual or decisive.

2   Method

2.1   Participants

This study was approved by the university's Institutional Review Board with regard to all matters pertaining to the use of human research participants. Participants were 360 undergraduates who were enrolled as students in psychology courses in a Midwestern US university. Their ages ranged from 18–31 (M = 19.04, SD = 1.32). There were 102 males, 255 females, and 3 people who did not report gender. They were organised into 44 groups, who participated in three experimental sessions. The recruitment goal was to assemble four or eight participants for the ER teams (see experimental task description below), one or two to play the attackers, plus one more as a back-up in case one player did not show up for an experimental session. Attrition usually occurred after the first session. There were 252, 65, and 43 individuals participating as ER team members, attackers, and observers, respectively, who completed the simulations for data collection purposes. The breakdown of participants in the small and large group conditions with one or two attackers appears in Table 2.

Table 2. ER Team sizes by experimental condition

Attackers	Small		Large	
	No. groups	Size	No. groups	Size
1	5	3	4	7
	6	4	8	8
2	2	3	1	7
	9	4	9	8

The participants took part in three experimental sessions that were scheduled for two hours each. In the first session, they signed the consent form to participate in the experiment, completed some timed tests and an untimed questionnaire, and learned how to play the ER game. (The timed tests and questionnaire data were not analysed in the present study.) In the second and third sessions, the ER members and the attacker(s) played three games to generate data for the experimental analysis while wearing galvanic skin response (GSR) sensors, and then provided ratings of workload and teammates' participation and leadership contributions. Because of the apparent difficulty of the simulation and absence of explicit time constraints, some groups facing two attackers were only able to complete two games in session 2. GSR data were not analysed here, but there was reason to expect that simply wearing the sensors could contribute to either workload or fatigue [37, 80]. An analysis of leadership ratings from the end of the sessions was reported separately [81].

2.2 Experimental Task

The experimental medium was a board game entitled *The Creature that Ate Sheboygan* [82, 83]. For 28 of the groups, teams and attackers were given a time limit of 90 s per turn during the second experimental session although most turns required only 10 to 70 s to complete. The other 16 groups were given a time limit of 90 s during the third session only. Participants were given a 30 s warning if they took at least 60 s to make their moves. The ER teams were given five minutes at the start of a game to position their tokens on the board in any manner they thought was strategic while the attacker waited in another room out of earshot. Attackers made the first move. A turn was defined as an attacker's move followed by a team response. Attackers could burn buildings and eradicate ER teams' military, police, firefighting, and air power. The attacker, or pair of attackers, wins if it scores at least 40 points against the ER team. The ER team wins if it cuts the attacker's defense power (or each attacker's defense power in a two-attacker condition) to zero. Teams' and attackers' performance scores required data analyses at the team level, rather than the individual level, and were thus not included in this study. Of note, however, the game outcomes were close to even in the one-attacker condition with the ER teams winning 53.7% of the games; ER teams won 16.5% of the games when playing against two attackers. The median game, across all experimental conditions, lasted 11 turns (95%ile = 31 turns) and 972.5 s (95%ile = 2920.0) from the beginning of the monster's first turn to the conclusion wherein the ER teams or monsters scored enough points against the opponent to define a win.

The laboratory layout is shown in Fig. 2. When the participants arrived for the second session, they selected their own positions at the work table. After a roll of the die, the high-rolling individual was assigned the role of attacker. The back-up person was determined by another roll of the die. Participants switched places as necessary. The ER team members were then given badges that identified them as ER1 through ER4 or ER8 according to their positions shown in the diagram. Once the attackers and back-ups were identified and the ER team members were numbered by distributing name tags, they maintained those designations through the series of six games unless a participant did not show up for the third experimental session. If a no-show occurred, the back-up person replaced the missing individual. ER team members, once they were numbered, were not required to stay stationary in the seating positions shown in the diagram, but they usually did so. One research assistant (RA1) was positioned at the laptop with the GSR equipment. The GSR equipment was not used in this study; some analyses of that data were published separately [81]. The other research assistant was positioned at the location RA2. The table with the computer behind RA2 was not used in the experiment. Back-up participants who were not substituting for a player assisted the RAs with counting game points. Back-up participants were usually positioned close to RA1 but would move around to get a better view of the game board and players.

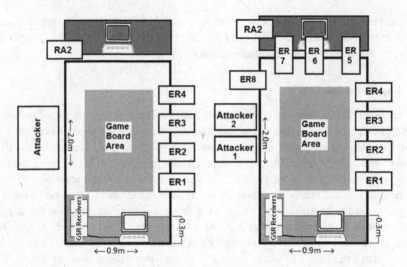

Fig. 2. Laboratory layout for the small (left) and large (right) groups.

2.3 Measurements

After the third game of each session, the participants were allowed to remove their GSR sensors, and they immediately completed the TLX and GWL ratings of workload. Both inventories (defined in Table 1) were formatted as 20-point scales (1–21) anchored as 1 = "very low" and 21 = "very high." Ratings were completed by ER team members, attackers, and observers although only the ER teams' ratings were used in some of the analyses.

2.4 Statistical Analysis

In the first series of analyses, the hierarchical regression analysis was performed using a stepwise multiple regression procedure; each of the workload ratings was evaluated as a separate dependent measure. The stepwise procedure was used instead of block entry of variables to identify the smallest number of independent variables that could account for the ratings. The independent variables were experimental control variables and elasticity-rigidity, which were tested on a competitive basis. The criterion for the F-test to add a variable was set at $p < .05$, and the criterion to remove a variable was $p > .10$. Because each rating was of interest separately, no corrections for Type I error were introduced at this stage of analysis. The error term was ordinary least squares. The analysis was performed using SPSS v.24 software. Canonical correlation was used in the second series of analyses. These analyses sought for optimal combinations of experimental conditions and elasticity-rigidity variables that correlated with configurations of TLX and GWL ratings. This multivariate procedures controls for Type 1 error in much the same way as MANOVA controls for it relative to multiple ANOVA with multiple, and probably correlated, dependent variables. Canonical correlation analysis was performed separately for sessions 2 and 3. These analyses were expected to uncover emergent patterns of experimental conditions, individual differences, and ratings. Canonical correlation is also a least squares procedure that was calculated through SPSS v.24.

3 Results

Regression results for TLX ratings appear in Table 3. Multiple R ranged from .197 for physical demands in session 3 to .439 for frustration in session 2. Higher workload ratings were consistently paired with teams having two opponents instead of one and for smaller group sizes. The time constraint condition only affected TLX Performance; ratings were lower for participants who received the time constraint earlier rather than later. Elasticity-rigidity ratings were selectively attached to the ratings. Depending on which trait was active, workload ratings were larger to the extent that EI, planning, monitoring, anxiety, or indecisiveness was higher.

The average proportions of variance associated with experimental conditions and elasticity-rigidity variables is shown in Fig. 3. The average level of prediction was 9% of the variance accounted for in session 2, which was apportioned as 7 parts from experimental conditions and 2 parts from elasticity. Each TLX rating was associated with experimental conditions. The average level or prediction increased slightly to 11% of the variance in session 3. Again all TLX ratings were associated with experimental conditions. The relative proportions were 10 parts experimental conditions and 1 part elasticity.

Regression results for GWL ratings appear in Table 4. Multiple R ranged from .00 (no variables entered the equation) for team support in session 2 and team efficacy in session 3 to .310 for communication demand in session 3. The average level of prediction for GWL ratings was generally less, accounting of an average of 6% of the variance in session 2. The apportionment in session 2 was one part experimental conditions and 2 parts elasticity. Four out of six GWL ratings were affected by experimental conditions. The active elasticity variables were coping flexibility, anxiety, EI, and inflexibility. Team support was not affected by either source of influence. The average level of prediction of GWL did not change in session 3, but the apportionment inverted to approximately two parts experimental conditions and one part elasticity. Once again four out of six GWL scales were affected by experimental conditions. The active elasticity variables were indecisiveness, empathy, and anxiety. Team efficacy was unrelated to either source of influence.

The canonical correlation analysis (Table 5) indicated that if the canonical variate contained experimental conditions their effects were exaggerated by the elasticity variables. Two canonical variates were obtained for session 2 data. In the first function (r_c = .532, p < .001), more monsters, smaller groups, and earlier time constraints produced several types of higher workload at the individual and group level and were exaggerated by anxiety. In the second function (r_c = .428, p < .10), there was a profile of elasticity variables associated with a cluster of GWL ratings. The latter p-value was high, but the model was retained because a preliminary analysis of elasticity variables without experimental conditions produced the same function at p < .05.

Table 3. Stepwise regression of experimental conditional and elasticity-rigidity variables with subjective ratings of individual workload (TLX).

Independent variable	β	t	R	Adj. R^2	(df)	F
Session 2						
Dependent: Mental Demand						
Monster condition	.204	3.255**	.196	.034	(1, 239)	9.520**
Emotional intelligence	.142	2.266*	.236	.056	(1, 238)	7.050***
Team size	−.147	−2.337*	.276	.076	(2, 237)	6.494***
Dependent: Physical Demand						
Planning	.165	2.601**	.161	.022	(1, 239)	6.382*
Monster condition	.136	2.145*	.211	.036	(2, 238)	5.540**
Dependent: Temporal Demand						
Monster condition	.190	3.015**	.190	.032	(1, 239)	8.930**
Team size	−.142	−2.251*	.237	.048	(2, 238)	7.074***
Dependent: Performance						
Monster condition	−.367	−6.092***	.367	.131	(1, 239)	37.113***
Dependent: Effort						
Monitoring	.156	2.468*	.158	.021	(1, 239)	6.114*
Team size	−.161	−2.542*	.222	.041	(2, 238)	6.168**
Dependent: Frustration						
Monster condition	.339	5.807***	.342	.114	(1, 239)	31.754***
Team size	−.221	−3.776***	.415	.165	(2, 238)	24.770***
Anxiety scale	.145	2.471*	.439	.183	(3, 237)	18.903***
Session 3						
Dependent: Mental Demand						
Monster condition	.314	5.140***	.313	.094	(1, 232)	25.188***
Team size	−.194	−3.171**	.368	.128	(2, 231)	18.113***
Dependent: Physical Demand						
Monster condition	.144	2.234*	.142	.016	(1, 232)	4.743*
Planning	.137	2.120*	.197	.030	(2, 231)	4.654**
Dependent: Temporal Demand						
Team size	−.262	−4.283***	.257	.062	(1, 231)	16.324***
Monster condition	.207	3.383***	.332	.103	(2, 230)	14.249***
Irresolute	.181	2.956**	.378	.132	(3, 229)	12.731***
Dependent: Performance						
Monster condition	−.356	−5.730***	.334	.108	(1, 232)	29.208***
Time condition	−.136	−2.191*	.360	.122	(2, 231)	17.244***
Dependent: Effort						
Team size	−.240	−3.769***	.240	.054	(1, 232)	14.205***
Dependent: Frustration						
Monster condition	.362	6.011***	.360	.126	(1, 232)	34.596***
Team size	−.185	−3.069**	.405	.157	(2, 231)	22.637***

*p < .05, **p < .01, ***p < .001

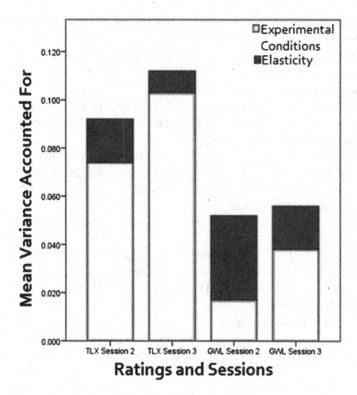

Fig. 3. Relative portions of rating variance accounted for by experimental and elasticity variables.

Two canonical variates were also obtained for session 3 data. In the first function ($r_c = .585$, $p < .001$), the experimental conditions of larger teams and only one monster resulted in higher ratings of TLX performance and lower ratings on seven other types of workload; the effect was stronger for participants with lower entropy. In the second function ($r_c = .476$, $p < .05$), the effect of time constraint was exaggerated by lower anxiety and greater flexibility; this combination of variables connected to higher ratings of temporal demand and lower ratings on three other scales.

4 Discussion

People use coping strategies of different sorts to compensate varying amounts of workload and maintain their desired performance levels. The perception and experience of workload may vary based on individual traits and, if the task involves other people, group-level factors. Individual cognitive workload is well-described by a cusp catastrophe model similar to Euler buckling for explaining the effects on performance. Increasingly, more taxing demands place pressure on cognitive processes, which can buckle once a critical point is reached and lead to suboptimal performance; however, elasticity in the form of individual characteristics, like coping flexibility, or group-level

Table 4. Stepwise regression of experimental conditional and elasticity-rigidity variables with subjective ratings of group-level workload (GWL).

Independent variable	β	t	R	Adj. R^2	(df)	F
Session 2						
Dependent: Coordination Demand						
Coping flexibility	.192	2.940**	.174	.026	(1, 224)	6.979**
Team size	−.166	−2.536*	.240	.049	(2, 223)	6.788***
Dependent: Communication Demand						
Empathy scale	.237	3.636***	.221	.040	(1, 224)	10.404***
Monster condition	.153	2.382*	.263	.061	(2, 223)	8.308***
Anxiety scale	.137	2.099*	.296	.075	(3, 222)	7.092***
Dependent: Time Sharing Demand						
Monitoring	.227	3.491***	.227	.047	(1, 224)	12.184***
Dependent: Team Efficacy						
Emotional intelligence	.231	3.489***	.193	.033	(1, 224)	8.701**
Monster condition	−.161	−2.508*	.252	.055	(2, 223)	7.568***
Monitoring	−.141	−2.131*	.287	.070	(3, 222)	6.639***
Dependent: Team Support			.000	.000		
Dependent: Team Dissatisfaction						
Inflexibility	−.178	−2.714**	.167	.024	(1, 224)	6.427*
Monster condition	.149	2.283*	.224	.042	(2, 223)	5.880**
Session 3						
Dependent: Coordination Demand						
Monster condition	.213	3.216**	.208	.039	(1, 215)	9.710*
Irresolute	−.145	−2.197*	.254	.056	(2, 214)	7.354**
Dependent: Communication Demand						
Monster condition	.240	3.687***	.231	.049	(1, 215)	12.141**
Empathy scale	.206	3.166**	.310	.087	(2, 214)	11.337***
Dependent: Time Sharing Demand						
Monster condition	.216	3.290**	.234	.051	(1. 215)	12.491***
Team size	−.180	−2.739**	.295	.078	(2, 214)	10.185***
Dependent: Team Efficacy		.000	.000			
Dependent: Team Support						
Anxiety scale	.159	2.368*	.159	.021	(1, 215)	5.608*
Dependent: Team Dissatisfaction						
Monster condition	.207	3.123**	.216	.042	(1, 214)	10.499***
Anxiety scale	.142	2.138*	.258	.058	(2, 213)	7.624***

*p < .05, **p < .01, ***p < .001

characteristics, like having more people to spread the load, can reduce task demands and enhance performance. Thus, the purposes of this study were (a) to examine elasticity-rigidity variables in conjunction with subjective workload ratings, (b) to determine if group-level ratings are also influenced by elasticity-rigidity characteristics,

Table 5. Canonical correlation analysis[a]

Experimental condition and elasticity-rigidity	Canonical loading	Subjective rating		Canonical loading
Session 2				
Canonical Variate 1: r_c = .592, Λ = .366, F(143, 1729.324) = 1.523, p < .001				
Anxiety	.283	TLX	Mental	.590
Time Condition	−.335	TLX	Temporal	.415
Team Size	−.519	TLX	Performance	−.532
Monster Condition	.526	TLX	Frustration	.760
		GWL	Coordination	.351
		GWL	Communication	.345
		GWL	Team Dissatisfaction	.257
Canonical Variate 2: r_c = .428, Λ = .511, F(120, 1590.229) = 1.198 p < .10				
Field Independence	.314	GWL	Coordination	−.318
Emotional Intelligence	−.270	GWL	Communication	−.319
Indecisiveness	.338	GWL	Time Sharing	.426
Monitoring	.596	GWL	Team Efficacy	−.624
Empathy	−.360	GWL	Team Dissatisfaction	.258
Session 3				
Canonical Variate 1: r_c = .585, Λ = .293, F(156, 1709.527) = 1.621, p < .001				
Empathy	−.297	TLX	Mental	−.690
Team Size	.426	TLX	Temporal	−.573
Monster condition	−.607	TLX	Performance	.450
		TLX	Effort	−.450
		TLX	Frustration	−.726
		GWL	Communication	−.528
		GWL	Time Sharing	−.459
		GWL	Team Support	−.427
Canonical Variate 2: r_c = .476, Λ = .446, F(132, 1590.256) = 1.243, p < .05				
Anxiety	−.298	TLX	Temporal	.512
Inflexibility	−.266	TLX	Performance	−.438
Time Condition	.651	GWL	Team Efficacy	−.305
		GWL	Team Support	−.335

Note: A criterion of 0.25 was used to interpret canonical loadings.

(c) to capture an array of cognitive processes that place (e.g., inflexible thinking) or reduce (e.g., fluid intelligence) strong demands on working memory, and (d) to investigate changes in patterns in workload-elasticity relationships as the group matured.

4.1 Task Conditions

Individual-level workload was measured by the TLX, which examines mental demand, physical demand, temporal demand, perceptions of performance requirements, effort needed to meet those requirements, and frustration. Group-level workload was measured by the GWL, which quantifies coordination demand, communication demand, time sharing demand, and perceptions of team effectiveness, support, and dissatisfaction. Several individual characteristics were investigated that had been previously identified as elasticity-rigidity variables in workload-performance studies [24, 26, 27, 37]. They were investigated here for their possible positive or negative impact on subjective ratings of workload; the list included trait anxiety, emotional intelligence, empathy, coping flexibility, planning, monitoring, decisiveness, inflexibility, field independence, creativity (anagrams), and algebra flexibility.

Hypothesis 1 stated that increased workload in the form of number of monsters and speed demands would have an impact on workload ratings at the individual and group level. This hypothesis was important because of the generally untested nature of the GWL scales, which are relatively new [30]. Our results partially confirmed this hypothesis. More monsters and greater time pressure significantly increased participants' reports of individual workload, specifically worse perceived performance in session 3. More monsters had the larger impact and predicted mental, physical, temporal demands, and frustration in sessions 2 and 3 However, the time condition did not predict workload as well. This could be explained by the fact that most turns took less than the time pressure placed on participants. Future studies will need to analyse the impact of a shorter speed demand on performance. For group workload, a similar pattern was detected. Monster conditions predicted greater demands for communication and team efficacy, and team dissatisfaction in session 2. These group-level demands were also rated more severe in session 3 as were coordination and time sharing demands.

4.2   Group Size

Hypothesis 2 stated that group size would have an impact on workload ratings. The creative problem solving nature of the task would favour lower individual ratings for larger groups. Larger groups would suggest greater demand on group-level workload, however. Greater group size predicted less individual mental and temporal demand as well as better perceived effort and less frustration in sessions 2 and 3. This is as we predicted under the reasoning that having additional resources through more team members aids creative problem solving and task performance. Our hypothesis regarding the effects of group size on group workload was inaccurate. Rather, we found that larger groups had less coordination demands in session 2 and less time sharing demands in session 3. These trends may have been due to the impact of leadership emergence or enhanced synchrony.

4.3   Elasticity-Rigidity

Hypothesis 3 stated that elasticity-rigidity variables would be correlated with workload ratings and have an effect beyond the more obvious workload conditions, which indeed happened. Individuals have unique characteristics that contribute to their perceptions of their own experiences of workload as well as their experiences of group workload. Task conditions accounted for 7–10% of variance in TLX ratings and 2–4% of the variance in GWL ratings, and elasticity accounted for another 1–2% of the variance in TLX ratings and another 2–4% in GWL ratings. The relative impact of elasticity compared to task conditions was greater for group-level workload.

The elasticity variables that appeared most frequently in the multiple regression analyses (Tables 3 and 4) were anxiety, monitoring, planning, empathy, and irresolute (indecisiveness). Anxiety is known to significantly alter cognition through difficulty concentrating; further, people with significant anxiety frequently have cognitive distortions that negatively impact their ability to monitor performance and plan effectively. Empathy and emotional intelligence (which are correlated) made a greater contribution to group workload than to individual workload. Monitoring, planning and indecisiveness were related to both individual and group workload ratings. The effect sizes for the elasticity-rigidity variables were very small, although it is important that they registered as statistically significant nonetheless. The large sample size probably helped in that regard, but the sample size was necessary because of the large number of variables and experimental conditions that were involved. It is important to remember, however, that the elasticity-rigidity variables were identified in previous studies with a *nonlinear* model for changes in *performance* in response to experimental conditions. The rigidity pole of the variables is actually associated with positive *and* negative changes in performance in the cusp catastrophe model, although linear comparison models in those studies often showed a net-positive or net-negative impact on performance for some of them. Only linear models were tested here. It is also an open question as to how subjective ratings of workload connect to performance differences within the nonlinear paradigm, given the way elasticity-rigidity variables tend to act.

The present study was concerned with individual-level measurements and their relationships to subjective workload, but the performance measures are group-level outcomes. A separate study is forthcoming that examines group-level performance in a cusp catastrophe analysis. Part of the challenge is to figure out the pathway between individual-level experiences and group-level performance with respect to both elasticity-rigidity and subjective workload ratings.

4.4   Top-Down and Bottom-Up Trends

Hypothesis 4 stated that patterns of elasticity, experimental conditions, and workload ratings should reflect both top-down and bottom-up dynamics. Such patterns were found in the canonical correlation analysis, which contained mixtures of TLX and GWL ratings on the criterion side of the functions. The predictor size of the functions contained mixtures of experimental conditions and elasticity variables, where the latter were seen to exacerbate or subdue the effects of experimental conditions. Here we also observed that field independence, and time constraints, which played little or no role in the multiple regression analyses with the single ratings as criteria, were part of the canonical functions. The four canonical functions were, in essence, emergent variables that were part of the group self-organizing process.

4.5   Group Development

Hypothesis 5 stated that there should be some changes in patterns of elasticity, experimental conditions, and workload ratings as the group matured. It was not known a priori whether the changes would be gradual or decisive. There were changes in the patterns of elasticity and experimental variables reaching significance in predicting workload over time. Arguably the smaller effects could have occurred by chance given the large number of statistical tests that needed to be made. Alternatively, however, the relative influence of elasticity versus experimental conditions reduced from session 2 to session 3 as participants presumably become more familiar with the task and each other. The canonical correlation analysis, furthermore, reflected some simplification in the arrays of active variables on both sides of the equations. Combinations of task conditions and elasticity variables were generally reduced from session 2 to session 3. The workload parts of the functions also changed. In session 3 there was a mixture of TLX and GWL ratings plus a second function contained GWL ratings only. In the session 3 the first function was similar, but included five out of six individual ratings plus three GWL ratings in one function, and a more concise combination of temporal demand and performance demand.

4.6   Generalisability of Results

The present study expanded on previous studies [24, 27] connecting elasticity-rigidity variables and subjective ratings of workload by including a wider range of elasticity constructs and group-level workload ratings. The previous tasks (vigilance and financial decisions making) were not comparable to the present one, nor were the experimental conditions, so the generalisability of results found here are limited to the following: (a) People with higher levels of emotional intelligence recognised greater mental demands. (b) Anxiety and emotional intelligence are more likely to be active variables to the extent that participants work with others rather than alone; in the present study team size was an important contributor to subjective workload. (c) Ratings of individual (or group) workload are affected by elasticity characteristics. The relative contributions of elasticity variables with TLX ratings were relatively equal when they occurred at all in the vigilance task. Vigilance tasks are known to be psychologically demanding because of their low workload most of the time. In the present task individual differences played a smaller role in predicting TLX ratings, a relatively equal role with GWL ratings, both of which reduced as the group became more mature. Field independence played an important role in TLX ratings in the financial decision task [27], in which participants worked alone in all experimental conditions. On the one hand, that variable was thought to have a specific role in financial decision making. On the other hand, it was thought to have a more general role with regard to the participant's utilisation of working memory capacity. Field independence only played a role as part of one emergent canonical function in the present study.

4.7 Limitations and Future Research Directions

The present study was an abstraction of emergency response functions, and not a real event in which life and death decisions are not merely a game and physical demands such as removing building rubble to excavate survivors or gunfire with perpetrators are involved. The present study does warrant closer attention to the personal characteristics of ER teams and tracking of their performance and reactions during their most demanding tasks to the extent possible. Laboratory research, however, does provide a safe and flexible environment for testing ideas in which the consequences of failure are "strictly academic."

The present study expanded the roster of elasticity variables compared to previous efforts, although the conscientiousness constructs were not included here. There was a limitation on the participants' available time, and it was necessary to confine the pre-testing to variables that warranted the most attention and save the remainder of time for learning the task. In this case the signature characteristics of conscientiousness – low impulsivity, high attention to rules and details – would not be relevant to the task which demanded strategy, adaptation, and random action to foil the opponents' efforts. Future research on elasticity and subjective workload should reinstate conscientiousness as a possible relevant variable insofar as it is relevant to the task.

Furthermore, no claim has been made here that the elasticity variables that have been identified are an exhaustive list; new variables should be considered and studied. Elasticity-rigidity variables are actually part of a cusp catastrophe model for workload and performance. The cusp model was not studied here, although it is on the agenda for continued research. Previous studies involved individual-level performance variables, but performance for the present task was group-level only. There are additional issues to be considered by which individual-level characteristics are organised into group-level metrics and then used to study group-level performance. Although they share a common function in the cusp model, adding the elasticity-rigidity variables together into one scale is not recommended. They are not all responsive to the same task conditions. Adding them together would only produce extraneous variance in the composite measure and thus reduce the correlation with other variables such as workload ratings and task conditions. Anxiety and conscientiousness (the latter not studied here) are already known to be factorially independent [59]. The coping strategies were developed by Cantwell and Moore [52] as independent factors also.

The time pressure manipulation was not as effective as we anticipated. Thus, it should be more demanding in future research. The effectiveness of time constraints would be relative to the task and other experimental conditions that are involved. Emergent leadership is a group dynamic that was not considered in the present study. The ER teams started as leaderless, but it is well-known that leaders emerge eventually as part of a self-organising social structure [68]. The effects of leadership styles (or other characteristics) on the distribution of workload is not known, however, either with regard to how workload is shared by team members or with regard to individual-level and group-level sources. The connection between leadership emergence dynamics and the simultaneous top-down vs. bottom-up processes in workload sources requires further investigation.

References

1. Simon, H.A.: Administrative Behavior, 2nd edn. Littlefield Adams, Totowa (1957)
2. Broadbent, D.E.: Perception and Communication. Pergamon Press, Elmsford (1958)
3. Kantowitz, B.H.: Channels and stages in human information processing: a limited analysis of theory and methodology. J. Math. Psychol. **29**, 135–174 (1985). doi:10.1016/0022-2496(85)90014-8
4. Hancock, A., Warm, J.S.: A dynamic model of stress and sustained attention. Hum. Factors **31**, 519–537 (1989). doi:10.7771/2327-2937.1024
5. Baddeley, A.: Working memory: looking back and looking forward. Nat. Rev. Neurosci. **4**, 829–839 (2003). doi:10.1038/nrnl201
6. Drag, L.L., Bieliauskas, L.A.: Contemporary review 2009: cognitive aging. J. Geriatr. Psychiatry **23**, 85–93 (2010). doi:10.1177/0891988709358590
7. Oberauer, K., Kliegl, R.: A formal model of capacity limits in working memory. J. Mem. Lang. **55**, 601–626 (2006). doi:10.1016/jml.2006.08.009
8. Reuter-Lorenz, P.A., Cappell, K.A.: Neurocognitive aging and compensation hypothesis. Curr. Dir. Psychol. Sci. **17**, 177–182 (2008). doi:10.1111/j.1467-8721.2008.00570.x
9. Schneider-Garces-, N.J., Gordon, B.A., Brumback-Pelz, C.R., Shin, E., Lee, Y., Sutton, B. P., Maclin, E.F., Gratton, G., Fabiani, M.: Span, CRUNCH, and beyond: working memory capacity and the aging brain. J. Cogn. Neurosci. **22**, 655–669 (2009)
10. Wickens, C.D.: Multiple resources and performance prediction. Theoret. Issues Ergon. Sci. **3**, 159–177 (2002). doi:10.1080/14639220210123806
11. Wickens, C.D.: Multiple resources and mental workload. Hum. Factors **50**, 449–455 (2008). doi:10.1518/001872008X288394
12. Ralph, J., Gray, W.D., Schoelles, M.J.: Squeezing the balloon: analyzing the unpredictable effects of cognitive workload. Proc. Hum. Factors Ergon. Soc. **54**, 299–303 (2010). doi:10.1177/154193121005400407
13. Hancock, P.A., Desmond, P.A. (eds.): Stress, Workload, and Fatigue. Lawrence Erlbaum Associates, Mahwah (2001)
14. Hancock, P.A., Szalma, J.L. (eds.): Performance Under Stress. Ashgate, Aldershot (2008)
15. Ackerman, P.L. (ed.): Cognitive Fatigue. American Psychological Association, Washington, DC (2011)
16. Matthews, G., Desmond, P.A., Neubauer, C., Hancock, P.A. (eds.): The Handbook of Operator Fatigue. Ashgate, Aldershot (2012)
17. Guastello, S.J., Boeh, H., Shumaker, C., Schimmels, M.: Catastrophe models for cognitive workload and fatigue. Theoret. Issues Ergon. Sci. **13**, 586–602 (2012). doi:10.1080/1463922X.2011.552131
18. Guastello, S.J., Boeh, H., Schimmels, M., Gorin, H., Huschen, S., Davis, E., Peters, N.E., Fabisch, M., Poston, K.: Cusp catastrophe models for cognitive workload and fatigue in a verbally-cued pictorial memory task. Hum. Factors **54**, 811–825 (2012). doi:10.1177/0018720812442537
19. Hart, S.G., Staveland, L.E.: Development of the NASA task load index (TLX): results of experimental and theoretical research. In: Hancock, P.A., Meshkati, N. (eds.) Human Workload, pp. 138–183. North-Holland, Amsterdam (1988). doi:10.1016/S0166-4115(08)62386-9
20. Dey, A., Mann, D.D.: Sensitivity and diagnosticity of NASA-TLX and simplified SWAT to assess the mental workload associated with operating an agricultural sprayer. Ergonomics **53**, 848–857 (2010). doi:10.1080/00140139.2010.489960

21. Hart, S.G.: NASA-task load index (NASA-TLX) 20 years later. Proc. Hum. Factors Ergon. Soc. **50**, 904–908 (2008). doi:10.1177/154193120605000909
22. Warm, J.S., Dember, W.N., Hancock, P.A.: Vigilance and workload in automated systems. In: Parasuraman, R., Mouloua, M. (eds.) Automation and Human Performance: Theory and Applications, pp. 183–200. Lawrence Erlbaum Associates, Mahwah (1996)
23. Wierwille, W.W., Eggemeier, T.F.: Recommendations for mental workload measurement in test and evaluation environment. Hum. Factors **35**, 263–281 (1993). doi:10.1177/001872089303500205
24. Guastello, S.J., Shircel, A., Malon, M., Timm, P.: Individual differences in the experience of cognitive workload. Theoret. Issues Ergon. Sci. **16**, 20–52 (2015). doi:10.1080/1463922X.2013.869371
25. Oron-Gilad, T., Szalma, J.L., Stafford, S.C., Hancock, P.A.: The workload and performance relationship in the real world: a study of police officers in a field shooting exercise. Int. J. Occup. Saf. Ergon. **14**, 119–131 (2008). doi:10.1080/10803548.2008.11076757
26. Guastello, S.J.: Catastrophe models for cognitive workload and fatigue: memory functions, multitasking, vigilance, financial decisions and risk. Proc. Hum. Factors Ergon. Soc. **58**, 908–912 (2014). doi:10.1177/1541931214581190
27. Guastello, S.J. (ed.): Cognitive Workload and Fatigue in Financial Decision Making. Springer, New York (2016). doi:10.1007/978-4-431-55312-0
28. Funke, G.J., Knott, B.A., Salas, E., Pavlas, D., Strang, A.J.: Conceptualization and measurement of team workload: a critical need. Hum. Factors **54**, 36–51 (2012). doi:10.1177/0018720811427901
29. Salas, E., Stevens, R., Gorman, J., Cooke, N.J., Guastello, S.J., von Davier, A.: What will quantitative measures of teamwork look like in 10 years? Proc. Hum. Factors Ergon. Soc. **59**, 235–239 (2015). doi:10.1177/1541931215591048
30. Helton, W.S., Funke, G.J., Knott, B.A.: Measuring workload in collaborative contexts: trait versus state perspectives. Hum. Factors **56**, 322–332 (2014). doi:10.1177/0018720813490727
31. Guastello, S.J.: Euler buckling in a wheelbarrow obstacle course: a catastrophe with complex lag. Behav. Sci. **30**, 204–212 (1985). doi:10.1002/bs.3830300405
32. Zeeman, E.C.: Catastrophe Theory: Selected Papers, 1972–1977. Addison-Wesley, Reading (1977)
33. Guastello, S.J.: Catastrophe theory and its applications to I/O psychology. In: Cortina, J.M., Landis, R. (eds.) Frontiers of Methodology in Organizational Research, pp. 29–61. Routledge, New York (2013)
34. Guastello, S.J.: Human Factors Engineering and Ergonomics: A Systems Approach, 2nd edn. CRC Press, Boca Raton (2014)
35. Guastello, S.J.: Nonlinear dynamical systems for theory and research in ergonomics. Ergonomics **60**, 167–193 (2017). doi:10.1080/00140139.2016.1162851
36. Guastello, S.J., Gregson, R.A.M. (eds.): Nonlinear Dynamical Systems Analysis for the Behavioral Sciences Using Real Data. CRC Press/Taylor Francis, Boca Raton (2011). doi:10.1080/00140139.2014.944325
37. Guastello, S.J., Reiter, K., Malon, M.: Cognitive workload and fatigue in a vigilance dual task: miss errors, false alarms, and the impact of wearing biometric sensors while working. Nonlinear Dyn. Psychol. Life Sci. **20**, 509–535 (2016)
38. Guastello, S.J., Boeh, H., Gorin, H., Huschen, S., Peters, N.E., Fabisch, M., Poston, K.: Cusp catastrophe models for cognitive workload and fatigue: a comparison of seven task types. Nonlinear Dyn. Psychol. Life Sci. **17**, 23–47 (2013)

39. Guastello, S.J., Malon, M., Timm, P., Weinberger, K., Gorin, H., Fabisch, M., Poston, K.: Catastrophe models for cognitive workload and fatigue in a vigilance dual-task. Hum. Factors **56**, 737–751 (2014). doi:10.1177/0018720813508777

40. Guastello, S.J., Reiter, K., Malon, M., Timm, P., Shircel, A., Shaline, J.: Catastrophe models for cognitive workload and fatigue in N-back tasks. Nonlinear Dyn. Psychol. Life Sci. **19**, 173–200 (2015)

41. Cox-Fuenzalida, L.-E., Swickert, R., Hittner, J.B.: Effects of neuroticism and workload history on performance. Pers. Individ. Differ. **36**, 447–456 (2004). doi:10.1016/S0191-8869(03)00108-9

42. Rose, C.L., Murphy, L.B., Byard, L., Nikzad, K.: The role of the big five personality factors in vigilance performance and workload. Eur. J. Pers. **16**, 185–200 (2002). doi:10.1002/per.451

43. Ein-Dor, T., Mikulincer, M., Doron, G., Shaver, P.R.: The attachment paradox: How can so many of us (the insecure ones) have no adaptive advantages. Perspect. on Psychol. Sci. **5**, 123–141 (2010). doi:10.1177/1745691610362349

44. Guastello, S.J., Lynn, M.: Catastrophe model of the accident process, safety climate, and anxiety. Nonlinear Dyn. Psychol. Life Sci. **18**, 177–198 (2014)

45. Taylor, J.A.: A personality scale of manifest anxiety. J. Abnorm. Soc. Psychol. **48**, 285–290 (1953). doi:10.1037/h0056264

46. Thompson, H.L.: The Stress Effect: Why Smart Leaders Make Dumb Decisions – and What to Do About It. Jossey-Bass, San Francisco (2010)

47. Schutte, N.S., Malouf, J.M., Hall, L.E., Haggerty, D.J., Cooper, J.T., Golden, C.J., Dornheim, L.: Development and validation of a measure of emotional intelligence. Pers. Individ. Differ. **25**, 167–177 (1998). doi:10.1016/S0191-8869(98)00001-4

48. Gerdes, K.E., Leitz, C.A., Segal, E.A.: Measuring empathy in the 21st century: development of an empathy index rooted in social cognitive neuroscience and social justice. Soc. Work Res. **35**, 83–93 (2011). doi:10.1093/swr/35.2.83

49. Lietz, C.A., Gerdes, K.E., Sun, F., Geiger, J.M., Wagaman, M.A., Segal, E.A.: The Empathy Assessment Index (EAI): a confirmatory factor analysis of a multidimensional model of empathy. J. Soc. Soc. Work Res. **2**, 104–124 (2011). doi:10.5243/jsswr.2011.6

50. Guastello, S.J.: Physiological synchronization in a vigilance dual task. Nonlinear Dyn. Psychol. Life Sci. **20**, 49–80 (2016)

51. Kato, T.: Development of the coping flexibility scale: evidence for the coping flexibility hypothesis. J. Couns. Psychol. **59**, 262–273 (2012). doi:10.1037/0022-3514.37.6.822

52. Cantwell, R.H., Moore, P.J.: The development of measures of individual differences in self-regulatory control and their relationship to academic performance. Contemp. Educ. Psychol. **21**, 500–517 (1996). doi:10.1006/ceps.1996.0034

53. Kane, M.J., Engle, R.W.: The role of prefrontal cortex in working-memory capacity, executive attention, and general fluid intelligence: an individual-differences perspective. Psychon. Bull. Rev. **9**, 617–671 (2002). doi:10.3758/BF03196323

54. Pascual-Leone, J.: A mathematical model for the transition rule in Piaget's developmental stages. Acta Psychologia **32**, 301–345 (1970). doi:10.1016/0001-6918(70)90108-3

55. Stamovlasis, D., Tsaparlis, G.: Applying catastrophe theory to an information-processing model of problem solving in science education. Sci. Educ. **96**, 392–410 (2012). doi:10.1002/sce.21002

56. Hakstian, A.R., Cattell, R.B.: Higher-stratum ability structures on a basis of twenty primary abilities. J. Educ. Psychol. **70**, 657–669 (1978). doi:10.1037/0022-0663.70.5.657

57. Rittle-Johnson, B., Star, J.R., Durkin, K.: The importance of prior knowledge when comparing examples: Influences on conceptual and procedural knowledge of equation solving. J. Educ. Psychol. **101**, 836–852 (2009). doi:10.1037/a0016026

58. MacLean, M.H., Arnell, K.M.: Personality predicts temporal attention costs in the attentional blink paradigm. Psychon. Bull. Rev. **17**, 556–562 (2010). doi:10.3758/PBR.17.4.556

59. Costa, P.T., McCrae, R.R.: Four ways five factors are basic. Pers. Individ. Differ. **13**, 653–665 (1992). doi:10.1016/0191-8869(92)90236-I

60. Cattell, H.E.P.: Development of the 16PF fifth edition. In: Conn, S.R., Rieke, M.L. (eds.) 16PF Fifth Edition: Technical Manual, pp. 1–20. Institute for Personality and Ability Testing, Champaign (1994)

61. Guastello, S.J., Marra, D.E.: External validity and factor structure of individual and group workload ratings: the potential influence of self-organizing processes (2016, manuscript under journal review)

62. Sellers, J., Helton, W.S., Näswall, K., Funke, G.J., Knott, B.A.: Development of the team workload questionnaire (TWLQ). Proc. Hum. Factors Ergon. Soc. **58**, 989–993 (2014). doi:10.1177/1541931214581207

63. Abich IV, J., Reinerman-Jones, L., Matthews, G.: Impact of three task demand factors on simulated unmanned system intelligence, surveillance, and reconnaissance operations. Ergonomics (2016, in press). 10.1080/00140139.2016.1216171

64. Sanjram, P.K., Gupta, M.: Task difficulty and time constraint in programmer multitasking: an analysis of prospective memory performance and cognitive workload. Int. J. Green Comput. **4**, 35–37 (2013). doi:10.4018/jgc.2013010103

65. Zander, A.: Making Groups Effective, 2nd edn. Jossey-Bass, San Francisco (1994)

66. Dennis, A.R., Valacich, J.S.: Computer brainstorms: More heads are better than one. J. Appl. Psychol. **78**, 531–537 (1993). doi:10.1037/0021-9010.78.4.531

67. Latané, B., Williams, K., Harkins, S.: Many hands make light the work: the cases and consequences of social loafing. J. Pers. Soc. Psychol. **37**, 822–832 (1979). doi:10.1037/0022-3514.37.6.822

68. Guastello, S.J.: Group dynamics: adaptability, coordination, and the emergence of leaders. In: Guastello, S.J., Koopmans, M., Pincus, D. (eds.) Chaos and Complexity in Psychology: Theory of Nonlinear Dynamical Systems, pp. 402–433. Cambridge University Press, New York (2009). doi:10.1177/0018720809359003

69. Bonito, J.A., Hollingshead, A.B.: Participation in small groups. In: Burleson, B.R. (ed.) Communications Yearbook, vol. 20, pp. 227–261. Sage, Thousand Oaks (1997). doi:10.1080/23808985.1997.11678943

70. Conrad, R.: Speed and load stress in a sensorimotor skill. Br. J. Ind. Med. **8**, 1–7 (1951)

71. Kantowitz, B., Sorkin, D.: Human Factors: Understanding People-System Relationships. Wiley, New York (1983). doi:10.1037/a0027770

72. Szalma, J.L., Teo, G.W.L.: Spatial and temporal task characteristics as stress: a test of the dynamic adaptability theory of stress, workload, and performance. Acta Physiol. **139**, 471–485 (2012). doi:10.1016/j.actpsy.2011.12.009

73. Prigogine, I., Stengers, I.: Order Out of Chaos: Man's New Dialog with Nature. Bantam, New York (1984). doi:10.1063/1.2813716

74. Goldstein, J.: Emergence in complex systems. In: Allen, P., Maguire, S., McKelvey, B. (eds.) The Sage Handbook of Complexity and Management, pp. 65–78. Sage, Thousand Oaks (2011)

75. Guastello, S.J., Liebovitch, L.S.: Introduction to nonlinear dynamics and complexity. In: Guastello, S.J., Koopmans, M., Pincus, D. (eds.) Chaos and Complexity in Psychology: Theory of Nonlinear Dynamical Systems, pp. 1–40. Cambridge University Press, New York (2009). doi:10.1017/CBO9781139058544.002

76. Sawyer, R.: Social Emergence: Societies as Complex Systems. Cambridge University Press, New York (2005). doi:10.1017/CBO9780511734892

77. Arrow, H., McGrath, J.E., Berdahl, J.L.: Small Groups as Complex Systems: Formation, Coordination, Development, and Adaptation. Sage, Thousand Oaks (2000)
78. Poole, M.S.: Decision development in small groups I: a comparison of two models. Commun. Monogr. **48**, 1–24 (1981). doi:10.1080/03637758109376044
79. Gersick, C.J.G.: Time and transition in work teams: toward a new model of group development. Acad. Manag. J. **31**, 9–41 (1988). doi:10.2307/256496
80. Claypoole, V.L., Szalma, J.L.: Social norms and cognitive performance: a look at the vigilance decrement in the presence of supervisors. Proc. Hum. Factors Ergon. Soc. **59**, 1012–1016 (2015). doi:10.1177/1541931215591288
81. Guastello, S.J., Marra, D.E., Perna, C., Castro, J., Gomez, M., Peressini, A.F.: Physiological synchronization in emergency response teams: subjective workload, drivers and empaths. Nonlinear Dyn. Psychol. Life Sci. **20**, 223–270 (2016)
82. Simulation Productions, Inc.: The Creature that Ate Sheboygan! Wreak Havoc with the Monster of Your Choice. Author, New York (1979)
83. Guastello, S.J., Bond Jr., R.W.: Coordination learning in Stag Hunt games with application to emergency management. Nonlinear Dyn. Psychol. Life Sci. **8**, 345–374 (2004)

Observations and Issues in the Application of Cognitive Workload Modelling for Decision Making in Complex Time-Critical Environments

K. Tara Smith[(⊠)]

Human Factors Engineering Solutions Ltd., Dunfermline, Scotland
Tara@hfesolutions.co.uk

Abstract. This paper presents some incidental findings and observations related to cognitive workload and situational awareness from a number of research projects investigating the impact of changes to systems used to support decision-making in complex time-critical situations. It is hoped that these observations will provide useful insights into the way cognitive workload affects decision-making as well as providing guidance to future research, in the form of specific aspects to investigate as well as considerations for the analysis process.

Keywords: Cognitive workload · Decision-making · Situational awareness · Predictive modelling

1 Introduction

This paper is based on the findings of a set of seven extensive research programmes undertaken for the UK Defence Science and Technology Laboratory (Dstl) over the past eleven years. These various projects were investigating the problem space from different angles or were concerned with specific sub areas: for this reason this paper is in effect multi-faceted rather than one continuous smooth narrative. The understanding of cognitive workload was developed in the context of predicting the benefits and/or disadvantages of the introduction of changes to the socio-technical system. The research was investigating the effect on decision making of making changes to the manned system; these changes could be to equipment, information presentation mechanisms, processes, procedures, manning levels, team structure, etc. or a combination of these: these changes (intended to be improvements) are referred to as "interventions" as they are an intervention to the current socio-technical system. All of these research projects were intended to recommend changes which would improve the decision-making process within a team working in a situation where these decisions:

- were based on a large amount of potentially complex and potentially uncertain information, usually from a variety of sources
- had to be made within a confined timeframe, and;
- where the results of these decisions could have critical consequences.

L. Longo and M.C. Leva (Eds.): H-WORKLOAD 2017, CCIS 726, pp. 77–89, 2017.
DOI: 10.1007/978-3-319-61061-0_5

The research conducted resulted in a number of findings related to how cognitive workload can affect the way people conduct their decision-making activities in this type of environment as well as mechanisms for visualising and analysing cognitive workload that support the research process. The projects from which the findings in this paper were drawn involved different environments and different decision-making contexts, therefore the individual studies differed in their scope, objectives, target user group and details. These projects were all carried out in a military context (in the Land and Maritime domains) and therefore the details cannot be reported here.

This paper presents a number of the incidental findings (i.e. those not directly related to the objectives of the research projects) that have potential value for other cognitive modelling projects. It is not intended to cover the mechanisms of collecting workload and related data, although it might touch on the problems of comparing the results of some of these mechanisms to the results of modelling approaches.

2 Context

The pressures of making operational decisions in safety-critical situations (which includes the military environment) is often exacerbated by tasks having to be performed within strict timescales. There are many human-related impactors on this decision-making process and also many decision support aids aimed at reducing the burden on the decision maker, however the relationships between the different impactors and between the impactors and the support tools are complex and inter-dependent, making it difficult to predict the effects of any changes to equipment, systems and/or operational processes and procedures. The nature of human factors is not just looking at equipments and environments; it is understanding the fundamental capabilities of the human in the system and relating those to the demands of their tasks in the context of the environment in which they have to work. Making critical decisions under pressure, whether that pressure is due to time constraints, environmental constraints, cognisance of the importance and consequences of that decision or a combination of pressures, puts considerable stress on the individual making those decisions. Another dimension to this problem is that the decision maker often does not have all the necessary information and evidence to hand: the interplay between the effort they are putting into gathering more information to make a better-informed decision and the requirement to make the decision quickly puts additional stress and pressure onto the individual.

There were several streams to the research projects that gathered the information presented in this paper:

- Investigation of two of the major impactors on decision making: cognitive workload and Situational Awareness (SA)
- Mapping of the gamut of human-related impactors on the decision-making process to identify causal relationships
- Investigation of why people do not always adopt or fully utilise tools and techniques that are introduced with the intention of aiding the decision-making process.

The projects that resulted in the observations presented in this paper varied in both the types of system under consideration and the military domain (Land and Sea) however, they all adopted a similar general approach, which can be summarised as model-experiment-model-experiment. A coherent modelling and analysis approach was used for these multiple research projects investigating decision making: this allowed results to be more easily read across from one domain or one individual study to other domains or studies in this space. This approach involves:

- modelling a set of representative example scenarios (this could be an extensive set) to predict the "hotspots" or points with the most likely potential for improvement: these hotspots are generally caused by the combination of cognitive demands upon the individual
- undertaking a representative human-in-the-loop/team-in-the-loop experiment (user trial) using one or more of the representative scenarios to validate the predicted results from the modelling
- modelling those interventions believed most likely to be beneficial
- undertaking a final team-in-the-loop experiment to verify the predicted benefits.

The modelling was conducted using a proprietary predictive model, which is known as Blizzard. This model makes an assessment across team structure, individual capability, training, workload and SA to provide a realistic prediction of the effect of the introduction of an intervention on human performance (workload, SA, etc.), facilitating early down-selection of concepts and ideas. More information on the development of this model can be found in previously published papers [1, 2].

The workload measures for the team-in-the-loop experiments were collected using a variation on NASA-TLX [3]: either the standard NASA-TLX questions, a subset of these or an extended version. SA measures were collected through subjective questionnaire, usually based upon the Mission Awareness Rating Scale (MARS) [4], the Crew Awareness Rating Scale (CARS) [5] or a combination of these. The questionnaires used to collect the workload and SA measures were individually tailored for the different studies to ensure that the questions were relevant to the participants in those studies and the scenarios being used for the experiments. They were administered at suitable points throughout the experiments; in some cases subsets of questions were used to minimise the impact of collecting the data, with the full question set only being used at the conclusion of the experiment. It is important to note that there are two aspects that were not considered in any of these projects:

1. The predictive model is not related to any physical indicators of cognitive workload, such as heart rate, brain activity or gaze information.
2. Although individual variations (such as fatigue, training, etc.) can have a substantial impact on an individual's capability to complete a cognitive task in the time required, the interventions considered during these research projects were not intended to affect these aspects: they were focussed on making the task of making a decision easier and/or more quickly.

One final point must be remembered when considering the observations made in this paper: human beings are infinitely varied and infinitely adaptable. They are capable of stretching their capabilities to perform when situations demand, even if these excessively high levels of workload can only be maintained for short periods of time or in extreme circumstances. This dynamic variability coupled with the complexity of human cognitive processes makes any generalised statement regarding predicted cognitive workload problematic and subject to both assumptions and points of view. The point of view taken in these research projects was to provide a mechanism to measure and rank improvements to the socio-technical system under investigation.

2.1   Definition of Cognitive Aspects

There is no one agreed definition of cognitive workload or SA and consequently not one agreed method of assessing or modelling it, therefore this subsection describes the paradigms adopted within these research projects. Both cognitive workload and SA are to some degree compartmentalisms of an individual's cognitive activity: i.e. they are conceptual entities constructed by psychologists and human factors practitioners to allow them to analyse cognitive processes. Like other similar cognitive conceptual entities such as memory, emotions or language processing they are interdependent components of what takes place in an individual's brain during the decision-making process. The Blizzard model builds on a number of established and emerging theories, including Hopkins' Integrated Skills Theory (unpublished: in effect based upon [6, 7]) and Tuckman's Group Development Model [8]. It utilises data capture and presentation methods, such as GOTA (Goals, Objectives, Tasks and Activities) [9] and ETLX (Extended Task Load Index – developed from NASA-TLX [3]). A number of accepted and validated models have been combined within this workload model: the key models within this model are Wickens' Multiple Resource Theory [10, 11], McCracken & Aldrich [12, 13] and Dstl's STORM model [14, 15] which allows the consideration of team and cultural dynamics.

Individual people develop their own mental model of the world around them, which includes cognitive representations of the past, the present and the future, based on how these affect them. These models are fuzzy, but people use their model as a basis for their decisions. Although there is no coherent representation of these models within human science, it is possible to have a coherent representation of the cognitive workload involved in using these models. A component of these mental models can be described as situational awareness (SA). The research projects adopted Endsley's definition of SA, "the perception of elements in the environment within a volume of time and space, the comprehension of their meaning, and the projection of their status in the near future" [16, 17].

Figure 1 below provides an overview of the conceptual framework that integrates all of these elements and was used as the context for the human factors work conducted during these research projects. In essence, this framework uses the stages of Wickens' Multiple Resource Theory (perception, processing/analysis and decision/action) to modify the rate (ability) of an individual to absorb and comprehend SA in terms of Endsley's levels of SA (perception, comprehension and projection). It also takes into consideration external impactors and cross-cutting factors relevant for the individual (or team) and the scenario. The three measures that cross over between experimental measures and modelling (predicted) measures are:

- Time to decision point
- Level of SA at decision point
- Workload to achieve decision point.

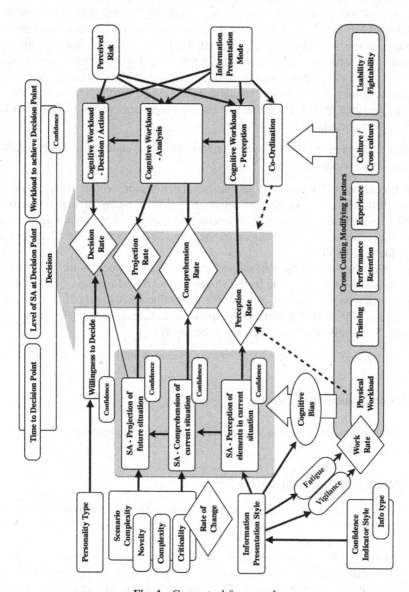

Fig. 1. Conceptual framework

The research resulted in some concepts related to cognitive workload, SA, decision-making and the relationships between them:

- Critical SA threshold: there is a clear indication that an individual aims to gain an acceptable level of SA prior to making a command decision, which is referred to as the critical SA threshold. The amount of SA needed to reach this critical SA threshold is dependent on the style and experience of the individual.
- SA trigger: the cycle of actively gaining additional SA was always initiated by a trigger event, such as a single report that posed a significant risk of significant change to the individual's SA picture at SA Level 2 (comprehension) and/or 3 (prediction), which is referred to as the SA trigger. If this SA trigger is late or wrong then it has a direct consequence to an individual's ability to reach an effective decision point (EDP). There is an additional threshold for the SA trigger in that if the information provided is inadequate the SA trigger does not initiate the proactive SA gathering cycle by the individual.

Other findings of the research which provide additional context for the observations reported in this paper include:

- the importance of having SA is not constant: i.e. it is more critical to the outcome to have better SA for non-standard situations, such as points of high information traffic, extraneous activity and unforeseeable events. These points/stressors are likely to cause additional workload on the individuals and therefore affect their SA and the time to EDP.
- the critical measure of operational performance in this context is the time to EDP, which is also affected by the level of cognitive workload required to maintain the individual's background SA and achieve their critical SA threshold.
- there is a strong indication that an individual will trade workload, and to some extent SA, to allow a faster decision to be made.

These findings and their consequences are discussed in the following sections.

3   Observations and Issues

This section discusses a number of the potentially useful incidental findings from the research projects.

3.1   Paradox of Workload and SA

It could be argued that all decisions fall somewhere in the continuum between a completely time-sensitive decision (making a decision as quickly as possible) and a completely quality-sensitive decision (waiting until you have enough information to make the best possible decision: i.e. a high level of SA). The research projects have found that in these military contexts, decisions tend to fall into two bunches: a mostly quality-sensitive decision or a mostly time-sensitive decision. An individual will decide to make either a more time-sensitive (faster) or a more quality-sensitive (more accurate) decision, depending on the requirements of the specific circumstance and their individual decision-making style, although it is often the case that secondary considerations in the scenario drive individuals to make time-sensitive decisions.

When analysing the effects of interventions in terms of cognitive workload, the relationships with SA and time can have a masking effect: i.e. workload is reduced but the effect shows in SA or time, the benefit is taken in improved SA or reduced time rather than reduced workload. Put simply, in the context of decision-making, workload benefit can be taken in three possible ways:

1. As a reduction in cognitive workload
2. As an improvement in the level of SA
3. As a reduction in the time to effective decision point.

In effect, these three potential benefits form the axes of the 3-D space in which benefits can be obtained. It should be noted that in reality, an individual is unlikely to take 100% of the benefits provided by the intervention in one of these aspects, but trade off the dimensions to best suit the circumstances. This relationship has a major impact when comparing predicted cognitive workload to measured cognitive workload. When modelling, all three axes cannot be left as variables: some assumptions must be made to provide fixed points on which to base the modelling. Typically when investigating the effect of the introduction of an intervention, the workload is calculated to achieve an equivalent level of SA; this might result in a lower workload and/or a different time to reach the decision point. However in an experiment, the individuals will select their own trade-off point between these three possible improvements. This effect was noted across five different human-in-the-loop experiments carried out in different domains, over four years. During analysis, it was clearly seen that because of the context of some of the experiments, all of the participants took the time-related advantage. In one experiment they preferred to gain better SA and in another there were clear distinctions between different individuals, some preferring to benefit in terms of SA and some in terms of time.

Working hypothesis: an individual can dynamically take the benefit provided by an intervention in different ways, dependent on the specific demands of the situation and their own personal decision-making style. This paradox needs further research, both to investigate its applicability in different domains and also to further investigate its causes, effects and drivers.

3.2 Impact of Coping Strategies

For all of the task demand stressors it can be generalised that there will be a threshold above which an individual cannot complete his tasks in the time required, however it is highly likely that an experienced decision-maker will adopt coping strategies to address each of these stressors. A simple example is to group objects into higher level units and then only consider the behaviour and actions of the higher level unit. Another coping strategy might be to hand off some tasks or some aspects of the decision to a colleague or subordinate. These coping strategies are either dynamic or pre-emptive. Dynamic coping strategies usually involve delaying lower priority tasks in preference to higher priority tasks, and then trying to catch up with those tasks if there is a lull. This can result in a "delay bow wave" where the delayed tasks build up to a level that affects subsequent tasks and ultimately can cause the individual to just stop coping completely, for the task not to be completed in the required time or for the individual to have to make the decision without sufficient information (low level of SA). This is in line with the Cynefin framework [18] (originally developed for IBM), which supports decision-making by making sense of human behaviours; it identifies domains or contexts of decision-making moving from complex to chaotic. Pre-emptive strategies are harder to identify: one strategy could be prior to any events the individual goes through classes of what they believe is going to happen and define their default response.

Working hypothesis: even for well formulated activities undertaken by well-trained and practised individuals, the fundamental coping strategies are inherent in their execution of the tasks, when the task tempo puts pressure on the individuals in the system.

3.3 Workload Sensitivity

Many of the initial team-in-the-loop experiments showed variations in the levels of workload across the different participants and the different runs of the experiment. Although this could be put down to imprecise or non-identical interpretations within the assessment process, it is more likely that it to some extent represents the variation between different individual's capabilities. It has long been argued in the anthropometric world that an "average" person does not exist (or is extremely rare) and it seems likely that this is also the case for cognitive capabilities, especially when differences due to training, experience, fatigue, concentration, etc. are also taken into account. To address this, the approach taken was that rather than investigating and modelling human capabilities, the research in effect turned this on its head, by modelling the level of human capability required to conduct the tasks within the scenario: i.e. the level of cognitive demand of the socio-technical system. Then, in order to determine the level of capability required for the tasks in the scenario, an arbitrary threshold was introduced in the model that triggered workload coping strategies (such as delaying a task or handing it over to a teammate). This threshold was incrementally decreased until the model predicted that the individual could no longer cope. Comparison of the differences between these incremental runs of the model allowed the determination of points of sensitivity: i.e. the "hotspots" where the introduction of an intervention that would (in some way) reduce workload would be beneficial. Reflection of this degraded performance caused by high workload into the consequences for acquiring SA also identified points where the SA was catastrophically reduced, which would then lead to insufficient SA to support the decision-making process. This gives both a workload and an SA sensitivity for the socio-technical system, indexed against the time-steps of the tasks in the scenario.

The team-in-the-loop validation exercise could then examine and identify an equivalent level of workload coping strategies for an equivalent scenario, to allow the band within that degradation set to be understood. This calibration of the model allows the investigation of the sensitivity of the socio-technical system to variations in its human component. The same calibration can also be applied to different scenarios in the modelling environment to reduce the necessity for additional or extensive team-in-the-loop trials. This approach proved to be useful in identifying where in the scenario workload problems would occur and understanding the data around any delay bow waves that were then observed in an experiment.

Working hypothesis: from the perspective of improving a socio-technical system, the surrogate measure of workload and SA sensitivity is sufficient to identify and measure performance improvements.

3.4 Tipping Points

As well as the (in effect) negative tipping points of high workload causing a situation where an individual cannot cope (cannot complete task in time, cannot complete task at all), one of the research projects identified a positive tipping point effect, where the combination of three elements reduced workload to such an extent that an individual operator could perform tasks at speed and to an accuracy that they had been unable to achieve with the predecessor (existing) system.

In essence, three independent interventions were derived that all showed individual improvement, but when all were implemented at the same time for the same task, the improvement was more than the sum of the individual improvements. It is the opinion of the author that this effect was due to the fact that they were truly independent interventions, in that not only did they address separate aspects of the design of the system but they also addressed different cognitive areas:

- The first intervention was concerned with decreasing the workload for perceiving the data that was being presented
- The second was concerned with decreasing the workload for navigation around the functions of the system
- The third was concerned with decreasing the workload related to psychomotive control of the system.

However as the aim of the research was not to understand this effect but to design a more effective system, there was no opportunity during this project to investigate the cause of this multiplying effect.

Working hypothesis: where the interventions address separate cognitive channel paths, their combinational effect on the overall performance can be greater than the sum of the effects of the individual interventions.

3.5 Robust Decisions

In this context, a robust decision is a decision that takes account of the uncertainty of multiple courses of action and is most likely to leave more degrees of freedom for future actions. In situations where a decision has to be made before the critical SA threshold has been reached, an experienced and well-trained individual will tend to make robust decisions. In effect this is changing the nature of the decision rather than affecting the time to EDP. This is in line with Gary Klein's Recognition-Primed Decision (RPD) model [19], in which the decision-maker generates a course of action, compares it to the constraints imposed by the situation and selects the first course of action that is not rejected. It is a model specifically representing the way in which people make quick, effective decisions in complex situations. The second stage of this model (the more important one) is that the individual imagines a range of likely consequences of actions arising from implementing the decision made in the first stage and then checks if they in themselves make sense in terms of the uncertainty they have about the first assessment. This theory is independent of the amount of SA that the individual has. Therefore, when a well-trained, experienced individual is faced with having to make a decision when they have significantly less than optimum SA, they construct a decision which they think is likely to lead to a positive outcome, understanding the information that they do not have, i.e. they are constructing the decision in the certainty that they do not have that information: this is a robust decision.

When measuring workload in a decision-making context, the lack of SA may force the individual to construct this robust decision, therefore the cognitive workload is biased towards the processing and action levels of Wickens' Multiple Resource Model [10, 11], whereas when an individual has gained as much SA as they think they need, the gaining of this SA is in the perception and processing level and the making of the decision becomes more obvious (requires less workload).

Working hypothesis: the differing nature of a decision and the process for arriving at that decision caused by different amounts of SA results in a bias in the type of cognitive workload required to make that decision.

4   Consequences for Interpreting Results

The first predicted results are not the end of the story. Two critical questions must be considered:

- What are the consequences for measuring and validating a predictive model, given some of the effects described in the previous sections?
- What are the consequences for interpreting and deriving meaning from the results of an experiment or a predictive model?

4.1   Measuring and Validating

Within the context of these research projects, it was important to consider and capture three separate elements:

1. The cognitive workload
2. The relevant SA and SA level
3. The decision points and the time taken to reach the decision points.

In all experiments, it is important to compare apples with apples: i.e. if by introducing an element intended to reduce the cognitive workload, the strategy adopted by the user to satisfy their overall intent of making a critical decision is affected, then the other elements that are varied must also be measured. This is equally important in the modelling, as well as in any measuring or validation experiments. This necessity for comparing like to like is further aggravated by the fact that a model can provide predictions second by second, whereas experimental data, particularly when concerned with what is going on in an individual's head, is usually collected at periodic intervals in order to minimise interference with the task being conducted.

There are a large number of techniques for collecting experimental data, but the issue is not how to collect it, but what needs to be collected to be able to compare between different experiments and between experimental and modelled data. This is further discussed in a chapter in the 2nd Edition of the Handbook of Standards and Guidelines in Ergonomics and Human Factors [20], which is specifically concerned with the interplay between cognitive measures taken and the measurement techniques used to collect these measures. Each of the working hypotheses presented in the previous sections must be taken in turn and the data examined in relation to these hypotheses in order to establish whether in order to compare like to like, adjustments must be made to the assumptions or the model in order to compensate for any differences between the expected behaviours and/or goals and those observed in an experiment. Given that there are a myriad of subtle impactors that affect the decision process, and that the individual trade-off between these impactors is rooted in the domain of the decision and the user population, it is highly unlikely (in the opinion of the author) that a universally applicable model of this trade-off process can be developed: it is likely that the best that can be achieved will be a framework and a process for considering a specific population and domain's trade-offs.

4.2   Interpreting and Deriving Meaning

Collapsing workload into a single figure can lose critical information. For example, during a user trial it was found that although visual workload was often very high, it was always the case that at the critical points it was the additional demands in linguistic/cognitive reasoning that pushed an individual over the workload threshold. This was true in that specific domain, but this combinational effect is highly likely to be apparent yet different in different domains. Similarly when analysing the data from experiments looking at the consequences of the introduction of new technology that is intended to improve SA, two cases must be recognised and considered separately:

1. Where increasing the effectiveness of the SA component has resulted in an individual making an earlier decision than baseline but with an equivalent level of SA;
2. Where increasing the effectiveness of the SA component has resulted in an individual making a decision at approximately the same time as for baseline, but with a higher level of SA.

Both of these cases can be considered as an improvement, but combining them in the analysis is likely to mask the extent of these two separate improvements: i.e. the average improvement in either speed of decision or level of SA across both groups is not likely to represent the full extent of the benefit. It must be noted that this is a generalisation and there are examples from previous studies where the data falls outside these assumed bunch points: for example, there was one experiment where a class of participants made a faster decision with a lower level of SA than baseline, as the new technology provided them with the SA they needed for the decision but with less extraneous SA resulting in a lower level of overall SA. These are two specific examples that illustrate the general case that the devil is in the detail. This implies the requirement for a set of understood and related views that allow the movement between levels of the data and perspectives on the data. These views should accommodate the difference between an individual task and a composite activity within a time window, as well as the different levels of view from detailed measures such as spatial reasoning, but also allow the metaviews related to issues such as task and activity sensitivity to workload requirements.

5   Conclusions

This paper is not intended to provide universally applicable conclusions or recommendations for methods and mechanisms for predicting and analysing cognitive workload. It is intended to present and describe a number of disparate observations, suggestions and hypotheses derived from a number of research projects in the hope that these will provide thought-provoking and useful inspiration to other researchers and further the understanding of how cognitive workload affects the decision-making process, especially in complex, time-critical situations. The working hypotheses presented are intended to illustrate some of the ways in which the author's understanding of workload has developed over the course of these projects and act as signposts to guide future research.

References

1. Smith, K.T., Mistry, B.: Predictive Operational Performance (PrOPer) model. In: Ergonomics Society 60th Anniversary Conference (2009)
2. Smith, K.T.: Building a human capability decision engine. In: Ergonomics Society Conference (2013)
3. Hart, S.G., Staveland, L.E.: Development of NASA-TLX (Task Load Index): results of empirical and theoretical research. In: Hancock, P.A., Meshkati, N. (eds.) Human Mental Workload, pp. 139–183. North-Holland, Amsterdam (1988)
4. Matthews, M.D., Beal, S.A.: Assessing situation awareness in field training exercises. U.S. Army Research Institute for the Behavioural and Social Sciences. Research Report 1795 (2002)
5. McGuinness, B., Foy, L.: A subjective measure of SA: the Crew Awareness Rating Scale (CARS). In: Presented at the Human Performance, Situational Awareness and Automation Conference, Savannah, Georgia (2000)
6. Morehouse, L.E., Gross, L.: Maximum Performance. Pocket Books, New York (1977). Cited in Bailey, R.W.: Human Performance Engineering: A Guide for System Designers. Bell Telephone Laboratories, Inc. (1982)
7. Gallwey, W.T.: The Inner Game of Tennis. Random House, New York (1974). Cited in Bailey, R.W., Human Performance Engineering: A Guide for System Designers. Bell Telephone Laboratories, Inc. (1982)
8. Tuckman, B.: Developmental sequence in small groups. Psychol. Bull. **63**, 384 (1965)
9. Smith, K.T.: A framework for modelling goals and objectives. In: Ergonomics Society Conference (1999)

10. Wickens, C.D.: Processing resources in attention. In: Parasuraman, R., Davies, D.R. (eds.) Varieties of Attention, pp. 63–102. Academic Press, New York (1984)
11. Wickens, C.D.: Processing resources and attention. In: Damos, D.L. (ed.) Multiple-task Performance. Taylor & Francis, London (1991)
12. Aldrich, T.B., McCracken, J.H.: A computer analysis to predict crew workload during LHX scout-attack missions. US Army Research Institute Field Unit, Fort Rucker, Alabama (1984)
13. McCracken, J.H., Aldrich, T.B.: Analysis of selected LHX mission functions: implications for operator workload and system automation goals (Technical Note ASI479-024-84). Army Research Institute Aviation Research and Development Activity, Fort Ruckers, AL (1984)
14. Mathieson, G., Holt, J., Mistry, B., Verrall, N.: Building Effective Representations of Social Networks and Culture in Models of HQ. DSTL/CR11545 V1.0 (2004)
15. Mistry, B.J., Waters, M.: Social Networks & Culture in HQ Modelling. Calibration and Integration of STORM with extant C2 model DARNOS (2007)
16. Endsley, M.R.: Toward a theory of situation awareness in dynamic systems. Hum. Factors 37(1), 32–64 (1995)
17. Endsley, M.R., Farley, T.C., Jones, W.M., Midkiff, A.H., Hansman, R.J.: Situation Awareness Information Requirements for Commercial Airline Pilots (1998)
18. Kurtz, C.F., Snowden, D.J.: The new dynamics of strategy: sense-making in a complex and complicated world. IBM Syst. J. 42(3), 462–483 (2003)
19. Klein, G.A.: Sources of Power: How People Make Decisions, pp. 1–30. MIT Press, Cambridge (1998)
20. Smith, K.T.: Measurement of situational awareness, cognitive workload and time to respond in decision-making: consideration of the interplay between these measures and the measurement techniques used. In: Handbook of Standards and Guidelines in Ergonomics and Human Factors, 2nd edn. CRC Press Taylor & Francis Group – Awaiting Publication

The Impact of Workload and Fatigue on Performance

Jialin Fan[⊠] and Andrew P. Smith

School of Psychology, Centre for Occupational and Health Psychology,
Cardiff University, 63 Park Place, Cardiff CF24 0DB, UK
{FanJ12, SmithAP}@cardiff.ac.uk

Abstract. Both workload and fatigue impair performance, and a high workload can lead to an increase in fatigue. This paper reports on two studies regarding workload and fatigue, and their impact on performance. Study 1 examined the risk factors for fatigue and the outcomes of it in relation to the rail industry. The results showed that workload is one of several predictors of fatigue. In Study 2 an online test integrating a single-item subjective measure and objective cognitive tests was used to examine the association between workload, fatigue and performance. Workload was found to be a factor that increased fatigue, which then resulted in a change in performance.

Keywords: Workload · Occupational fatigue · Performance · Online measures

1 Introduction

Fatigue refers to the effects or after-effects of diverse activities, such as spending a busy day at work, driving on a long journey, or even concentrating for a short duration of time on highly demanding physical exercises. In the domain of occupational fatigue, the terms 'workload' and 'job demands' may be interchangeable. A high workload may contribute to the development of fatigue, illness, and other issues which can lead to a reduction in performance. In previous studies, high job demands were considered to be a predictor of fatigue [1, 2] with a higher workload leading to greater subjective fatigue [3, 4]. Greth et al. [4] also suggested that the relationship between workload and fatigue could be dynamic, and the optimal level of workload could change over time. Both a high workload and fatigue result in performance impairments in daily work. A high workload (referred to as "mental workload") is related to the fit or gap between task demands and people's capacities. A study of driving examiners [5] provides an example of an easy definition of high workload. It showed that a high workload could be characterised by a person examining nine tests a day, while a low workload would be examining seven tests. A useful concept of workload was proposed by Jahns [6]. In this concept, Jahns suggested that workload involves three related components: input load, operator effort, and performance (or result). The input load consists of the external factors, such as work duration and workload, while the operator effort reflects the subjects' internal reaction to the input load, such as internal goals, motivation and task criteria adopted. The intensity of effort is probably one of the most important parts in determining workload [7]. The performance is the output of the above two components.

© Springer International Publishing AG 2017
L. Longo and M.C. Leva (Eds.): H-WORKLOAD 2017, CCIS 726, pp. 90–105, 2017.
DOI: 10.1007/978-3-319-61061-0_6

It is maintained by the person and influences their tolerated error level [8], which involves the probability of error, time to respond, response consistency, response range, and response accuracy, etc.

Based on Jahns' concept, two key features of workload can be measured, namely the subjective workload and performance changes. The first feature, subjective workload, reflects the personal feeling of the input load and the human effort (described above). Cain [9] reviewed mental workload measurements and suggests that an overall subjective workload measure is sufficient if task demands and the resulting workload can be characterised by one parameter. Subjective workload scores are usually related to the task load. They often increase in proportion to the increase in task complexity scores [10]. The second feature, performance changes, involves reduced functional capacity during the work. The effect of workload could also be measured with the before/after work technique. Broadbent [11] reviewed a series of fatigue tests, most of which studies task load using the after-effect method which involves measuring performance before and after work. The difference in performance between before work and after work reflects the workload effect. In particular, the difference in the before-after performance is greater with a high workload [5]. The after-effect symptoms were usually slower reaction times and less accurate responses. This was supported by Parkes' workload study [5]. This classic study found that the response speed and accuracy of visual search tasks and logical reasoning tasks showed a significant effect on workload. Fatigue has also been found to be associated with performance change. Although accurate fatigue data is difficult to obtain directly, fatigue can be assessed through cognitive performance tests because it impairs people's ability to perform efficiently. A review from Krueger [12] states that fatigue appears to result in increased reaction time, decreased vigilance, and perceptual and cognitive distortions.

Several cognitive tasks have been used in fatigue studies to investigate fatigue-related performance change [13], including reaction time testing, logical reasoning tasks, visual search tasks, the Stroop task, and so on. Some studies have assessed fatigue using subjective measures instead of cognitive tests. In earlier research, Bartley and Chute [14] and Cameron [15] argued that subjective fatigue has no predictive power. However, self-report of fatigue was found to be strongly associated with poor performance in later studies [16, 17]. This, again, shows the strong association between fatigue and performance change.

Two studies are described in this paper. The first involved a large-scale survey investigating whether workload (high job demands) was associated with fatigue. The second study (Study 2) then examined the effects of workload and fatigue on performance using online performance measures. It also examined whether workload increases fatigue, which then leads to changes in performance, or whether the effects of workload and fatigue are independent.

2   Study 1

2.1   Background

Fatigue in railway workers is defined as a state of 'perceived weariness that can result from prolonged working, heavy workload, insufficient rest and inadequate sleep' [18].

This definition points out that heavy workload is a factor contributing to fatigue. Since automation technology has been introduced into the workplace, work in the railway industry imposes more cognitive demands while physical demands have diminished [19]. Jobs in the modern railway industry requiring sustained vigilance may result in a heavy mental workload and increased fatigue. However, there has been very limited research investigating the risk factors and prevalence of rail fatigue, and this area has historically been less researched than aviation and road transport fatigue [20]. Fatigue is a daily stressor amongst workers. In the rail industry, fatigue can lead to issues such as reduced performance [21, 22], which then increase the risk of train accidents and incidents [23, 24] and ill health [25, 26]. This demonstrates that fatigue and its impact on safety-critical performance is a key issue in the rail industry.

In general, the causes of prolonged work fatigue are varied. Firstly, fatigue is considered to be a result of high job demands [1, 2] and low job control [27]. Job demands refer to workload, while job control refers to the personal ability to control work activities. Secondly, individual differences also play a role in fatigue, including personality [28], coping types [29], and health-related behaviours [30]. Thirdly, fatigue is closely related to shift work which disrupts the sleep-wake cycle [31] and deprives workers of sleep, therefore reducing levels of performance [32]. Also, in the railway industry, the working environment and tasks often require sustained vigilance which may increase fatigue [18]. Lal and Craig [33] state that the known environmental factors affecting vigilance are noise, vibration, environmental pollutants, and a variety of stimulations.

A Fatigue Model. Cameron [15] suggested that the term fatigue is synonymous with a generalised stress response over time. This provides the rationale for applying stress models, such as the Demands, Resources, and Individual Effects (DRIVE) model to assess fatigue. The DRIVE model includes the following three factors: job demands, job resources (support and control), and individual differences [34]. According to this model, people working in jobs with high demands and low control experience high levels of stress and poor well-being. Also, individual differences (such as coping style) play an important role in influencing health outcomes.

Rationale. To further manage and monitor rail fatigue, it is necessary to establish a profile of fatigue among train staff working in the rail industry. The present study first considered associations between occupational risk factors and perceived fatigue. It aimed to examine the prevalence of fatigue and identify potential risk factors in UK railway staff. The purpose was also to build a detailed picture of the relationship regarding workplace stressors, individual differences, fatigue, and well-being outcomes using the DRIVE model. The DRIVE model was applied as the theoretical framework to investigate fatigue. This study assessed fatigue and potential risk factors included in the DRIVE model, such as workload, job control and support, work environment, personality and lifestyle. It also aimed to investigate the associations between fatigue, work-related outcomes, and well-being during the last six months.

2.2 Methods

Participants. Participants were recruited from a train company in the UK, 1067 of whom completed the questionnaires (N = 1067, mean (±SD) age = 44.25 ± 10.763 yr.) with a response rate of around 50%. The main job types of participants were conductors, drivers, station workers, engineers, administrators, managers, at-seat catering stewards, and controllers.

Materials. This survey ran from 27th April to 18th May 2015. The questionnaire consisted of twenty-six single-item questions, some of which were chosen from Wellbeing Process Questionnaire (WPQ) [35]. It took approximately 15 min to complete. Most of the questions were on a 10-point scale, the remaining were Yes/No answers. The single-item measures were chosen because they have been noted to be valid and reliable [36]. This methodology allowed for the identification of the overall risks while saving time compared to administering multi-item measures. Fatigue was the main variable that this survey focused on. Participants rated their physical and mental fatigue from 1 (not at all) to 10 (very tired). The survey also measured the variables which might predict fatigue. It included questions regarding workload, job control and support, which were predictors in the DRIVE model and derived from WPQ. Questions regarding the working environment (levels of noise and vibration) and whether or not participants worked shifts or worked at night were also asked. In addition to fatigue and its potential risk factors, single item measures were also used to measure efficiency at work, work-life balance, and well-being (all measured from 1 [not at all] to 10 [very much so]).

Procedure. Participants were given a letter detailing the information of the study and an informed consent form. After the participants had signed and returned the forms, they were asked to answer a paper questionnaire that consisted of 26 questions. Volunteers were given the right to withdraw from the survey at any point. They were also informed that they had the right to refuse to answer any questions that made them feel uncomfortable. This study was reviewed and approved by the School of Psychology Research Ethics Committee at Cardiff University.

Analysis. Data analysis were carried out using SPSS 23. The independent variables tested were: workload, job control and support, shift work, exposure to noise and vibration, exposure to fumes, health-related behaviours (or health lifestyle) and personality. The dependent variables tested were fatigue and well-being outcomes. An analysis of the data assessed the associations between fatigue and risk factors, and between fatigue and efficiency at work.

2.3 Results

Descriptive. The most common job types were conductors (25.9%), drivers (22.6%) and station workers (21.3%), followed by managers, engineers, administrators and at-seat stewards. There were 57 participants with missing data about their profession. 58.3% of participants rated their fatigue as high (threshold = 6). Issues of fatigue were apparent in all the job roles mentioned. It was reported by the majority of the drivers (74.7%), engineers (71.1%) and controllers (82.4%), and by less than half of the administrators and station workers. In the following analysis, jobs that reported a high percentage of issues associated with fatigue were categorised as high fatigue job types, while the other jobs were categorised as low fatigue job types.

Analysing Predictors of Fatigue. Logistic regressions were run to investigate the predictors of low/high fatigue. These were used to assess the predictive ability of IVs while controlling for social demographic and individual difference factors. The variables used in this analysis were categorised into high/low through the use of thresholds. For example, fatigue scores above the thresholds were categorised as high fatigue, while the others were categorised as low fatigue. A median split was used to re-code both personality (M = 8, range = 1 to 10) and lifestyle (M = 7, range = 1 to 10) into positive/negative groups. The dependent variable used here was categorical fatigue (High/Low), and the independent variables were either categorical or continuous. The variables included in the model were social demographic variables (age and gender), personal risk factors (personality and lifestyle) and work-related risk factors (workload, job control and support, shift-work, being exposed to noise and vibration at work, being exposed to fumes at work, and fatigued job type), in which age was continuous, and all others were categorical. The OR effect size for each of the IVs is shown in Table 1 below.

Table 1. Odds ratio of each IV on fatigue.

Variables	Odds ratio	95% C.I for odds ratio
Social demographics		
Age	1.000	[0.986, 1.014]
Gender	0.893	[0.618, 1.288]
Personal characteristics		
Personality (negative)	1.590*	[1.174, 2.154]
Lifestyle (unhealthy)	1.477*	[1.089, 2.003]
Work characteristics		
Workload (high)	3.447**	[2.549, 4.659]
Job support and control (low)	1.692*	[1.030, 2.780]
Noise and vibration (high)	2.211**	[1.558, 3.140]
Fumes (high)	0.787	[0.546, 1.135]
Shift-work (yes)	1.745*	[1.207, 2.522]
Job type (high fatigued)	2.143**	[1.506, 3.049]

*p < 0.05, **p < 0.001

Workload and Fatigue. Workload was the strongest predictor of reported high fatigue in this model, recording an odds ratio of 3.45. This indicated that participants who reported a high workload were over three times more likely to report a fatigue problem than those reporting a low workload, controlling for all other factors in this model.

Other Job Characteristics and Fatigue. Other than workload, exposure to noise and vibration, highly fatigued job types, low job control and support and doing shift-work also predicted fatigue. The second strongest predictor was exposure to noise and vibration (OR = 2.21, p < 0.01). This was followed by shift-work with an odds ratio of 1.74, and low job control and support with an odds ratio of 1.69. Highly fatigued job types (OR = 2.1, p < 0.01) were 2.1 times more likely to report a fatigue problem than low fatigue job types. There was no unique statistically significant contribution from the factor "exposed to fumes" in this model.

Personal Characteristics and Fatigue. Both personality and lifestyle predicted fatigue. The odds ratio was 1.59 for personality, indicating that participants who had a negative personality were 1.59 times more likely to report high fatigue than those with a positive personality, controlling for other factors in the model. Similarly, the odds ratios of 1.47 for lifestyle indicated that participants who had a negative personality were 1.47 times more likely to report high fatigue.

Association Between Fatigue and Outcomes. The association between fatigue and outcomes was investigated using a Pearson correlation (shown in Table 2). The variables used were continuous. Fatigue showed a significant correlation with perceived stress at work (r(1064) = .52, p < .01) and negative work-life balance (r(1061) = .48. p < .01), with high levels of fatigue being associated with high levels of work stress and poor work-life balance. Fatigue was also significantly correlated with most of the negative well-being outcomes both in life and at work, including life satisfaction, job satisfaction, life stress, job stress, life happiness, work happiness, life depression and anxiety, job depression and anxiety, MSDs, and work-related ill health (r's ranged from .25 to .47, p < .01). Fatigue also showed a significant correlation with low-performance efficiency, high presenteeism (both p < .001), and the greater number of days absent (p < 0.05). The correlation between fatigue and the number of accidents at work was also close to being statistically significant in a positive direction (p = .059).

2.4   Summary

Fatigue is currently a general problem in the railway staff population. Investigating fatigue in railway staff requires the understanding and exploration of many potential risk factors. The present study indicated that high workload, poor job control and support, shift-work, exposure to noise and vibration, unhealthy lifestyle and negative personality would result in fatigue. As one of the several predictors of subjective

Table 2. Correlations between fatigue and main outcomes.

Variables	(1)	(2)	(3)	(4)	(5)	(6)	(7)
Fatigue (1)	1						
Perceived stress at work (2)	.516**	1					
Presenteeism (3)	.247**	.249**	1				
Performance efficiency (4)	−.136**	−.239**	−.093**	1			
Work-life balance (5)	.477**	.328**	.222**	−.172**	1		
Absenteeism (6)	.065*	.023	.041	−.106**	.050	1	
Accidents at work (7)	.059	.077*	−.015	−.153**	.039	.139**	1

*p < 0.05, **p < 0.001

fatigue, high workload results in higher levels of subjective fatigue. Meanwhile, both a high workload and high levels of subjective fatigue were found to correlate with poor subjective reports of performance efficiency. Therefore, a further study was warranted to provide an examination of the relationships between the workload, fatigue and objective performance outcomes.

3   Study 2

3.1   Links Between Study 1 and 2

Study 1 was a large-scale survey using a sample of rail staff, but with only subjective reports of the predictors and outcomes. Study 2 looked at the effects of subjective reports of workload and fatigue on objective performance using a student sample. The eventual aim is to use the objective performance measures with rail crew, but before that it is necessary to confirm that each part works. Hence, there were two studies. In Study 2, an online measure of fatigue was developed which integrated self-assessment, psychomotor vigilance task (PVT), visual search and logical reasoning. The purpose of the study was to use these online measures to examine whether workload increased fatigue, which then led to performance changes, or whether the effects of subjective fatigue and workload were independent.

3.2   Background

Online-based cognitive tests have been developed over the past two decades. A recent review of these tests confirmed the main advantages of computerised cognitive evaluation [37], which include the ability to provide realistic simulations of cognitive tasks in everyday life. Recently, there has been a growing interest in online experimentation due to the development of HTML5 and JavaScript. Although Garaizar [38] raised the problem an inherent timing issue in these technologies, the authors of QEREngine [39] resolved this by using internal chronometry, which involves using time stamps of the browser in milliseconds about the Unix epoch time, to check presentation and response timing. The precision of timing with the QRTEngine was validated using a photodiode time measurement, which was external chronometry.

Compared with offline tests or laboratory experiments, online tests are more convenient to apply in the occupational setting. Before using them, however, one needs to examine whether the online objective performance tests are sensitive enough to detect the effects of workload and subjective fatigue. Based on previous literature, it could be predicted that both workload and subjective fatigue would be associated with a change in performance. Parkes' workload study [5] has shown that response speed, and accuracy of cognitive performance of visual search and logical reasoning tasks show a significant effect on workload. Meanwhile, Krueger [12] states that fatigue appeared to result in a slower reaction time and decreased vigilance in several cognitive tasks. However, as Study 1 has shown, a high workload was one of several predictors of fatigue. This raises the question of whether workload and fatigue have independent effects on performance change, or whether workload increases fatigue first, which then leads to performance change. To test these conflicting views, this study aimed to examine the associations between workload, subjective fatigue, and objective performance change by using online cognitive tests.

This study involved a pre-study session (8–11 am) and a post-study session (3–6 pm). Four measurements were used in both sessions: the single-item self-assessment of fatigue, the psychomotor vigilance task (PVT), visual search and logical reasoning tasks. Use of the single item methodology for subjective fatigue and the online PVT were the central fatigue and workload measures. In addition to these measures of fatigue, online visual search tasks and logical reasoning tests were also selected as they have been found to be sensitive to the effects of the workload in previous studies [5, 40].

3.3   Methods

Participants. Before recruiting participants, G*Power [41] was used to calculate an appropriate sample size, setting the alpha level to 0.05 and power to 0.8. In this case, a sample of twenty-one participants per group were required to detect a large effect size of d = 0.8 using a one-tailed test. The one-tailed test was adopted because previous literature has reported performance change to be affected by time of day and workload. Forty-eight undergraduate students were recruited from Cardiff University. They were assigned to either a high or low workload group after the experiment, based on their self-rating of workload. This experiment was reviewed and approved by the School of Psychology Research Ethics Committee at Cardiff University. All of the participants were full-time undergraduate students.

Materials. Each session included a single-item self-assessment, a 10-min PVT, a visual search and a logical reasoning task which was used to measure workload, fatigue and performance. The fatigue self-assessment was used to measure subjective fatigue in both pre-work and post-work sessions, and subjective workload was also measured in the post-work session. The other three cognitive tests were used to assess objective performance. Also, the Visual Analogue Mood Rating Scale (VAS mood rating) was used to validate the single-item fatigue measure. All the tasks and data collection were performed on the Qualtrics online survey platform.

Single-Item Measures of Fatigue and Workload. Participants rated their fatigue level (measured from 0 [no fatigue] to 10 [maximally possible fatigue]) at the beginning of each session. This subjective fatigue rating was used to measure any change before and after work [42]. In the post-work session, participants also rated their workload level over the day (measured from 0 [no workload] to 10 [extremely high workload]). Participants were allocated to either high or low workload conditions. The allocation of high or low workload condition was based on the participants' self-rating of their workload.

PVT. The PVT was 10 min in duration and with 2 to 10 s random inter-stimulus intervals (ISIs) in each trial, as proposed by Dinges and Powell [43]. When the PVT started, it was followed by a blank screen. Then, a big empty box appeared on the screen. After the random ISIs, a small square appeared in the middle of the box and timing started until the participant responded by pressing the 'Space' key on the keyboard. The RT, type of response, the number of trials in each minute and total were measured. There were four different types of response which could be recorded; 1. the response was too fast (response before stimulus appears), 2. normal response, 3. lapse (RT $>$ = 0.6 s), and 4. sleep (RT $>$ = the 30 s). Only the type-2 response (normal response) was marked as correct. If the number of type-1 responses was greater than the sum number of type-2 and type-3 responses, the participant was excluded in the following analysis. Additionally, meta information of the device, date and time of task taken were also recorded. At the end of this test, the participants were presented with a hyperlink which linked them to the next test, a visual search task.

Visual Search Test. The visual search task consisted of 12 trials which randomly appeared from a total of 30 trials. On each trial, participants were shown a random 60-letter set and one target letter. They were required to find a set of target letters as quickly and accurately as possible. The response time and accuracy for each trial was recorded.

Logical Reasoning Task. This test was based on Baddeley's [44] grammatical reasoning test, and it consisted of 24 trials. It required the subjects to make a decision from two options as quickly and accurately as possible. The outcome features were response time and percentage of correct responses.

Visual Analogue Mood Rating Scale (VAS). This was a subjective assessment of mood using the VAS rating system [45]. It consisted of 18 items which ranged in value from 0 (negative end) to 100 (positive end), it also measured subjective mood. The outcomes consisted of four factors: alertness (which reflected fatigue, eight items), anxiety (6 items), depression (1 item itself) and hedonic tone (3 items). This paper only focuses on alertness which was used to validate single-item fatigue measure. The maximum value of alertness was 800.

Procedure. The study involved two sessions on each day: pre-work in the morning (8 to 11 am) and post-work at the end of the working day (3 to 6 pm). Before the day on which testing took place, a brief introduction to each cognitive test was emailed to participants. The introduction included an example of each cognitive test and a familiarisation session to ensure participants were able to complete the tasks correctly before starting the study. On the testing day(s), participants were asked to complete a series of tasks via a computer under a time frame. They were given two hyperlinks to access the tasks via email (one for each session). The study took approximately 45–60 min in total (20–25 min for each part). At the end of the experiment, the participants were debriefed.

Analysis. Data analysis was carried out using SPSS 23. Data was analysed using mixed ANOVAs. The independent variables tested were subjective fatigue and workload. The dependent variables were performance outcomes from each test, including mean reaction time and accuracy. The analysis assessed the associations between:

1. Subjective fatigue and workload ratings
2. Workload, subjective fatigue and performance outcomes
3. Subjective fatigue and alertness (to validate single-item fatigue measure).

3.4 Results

Forty-eight participants completed the tests, while two records were excluded in the data analysis due to missing data or unacceptable low accuracy (more than 50% incorrect response) in at least one task. Such low levels of accuracy were unusual and unacceptable since a familiarisation session had already been provided to participants to ensure they knew how to complete the tasks correctly before starting the experiment. The excluded data records were neither reliable in PVT, or in the logical reasoning test. Participants (N = 46) were in either the high or low workload condition. The allocation of a high or low workload condition was based on the participants' self-rating of workload.

Association Between Workload and Fatigue. The association between workload and fatigue was investigated using the Pearson correlation (shown in Table 3). The workload rating was significantly correlated with fatigue ratings at the end of the workday ($r(46) = .382$, $p < 0.01$), with higher workload ratings being associated with higher levels of fatigue after work. A higher workload was also significantly correlated with a greater post-pre change in fatigue rating ($r(46) = .382$, $p < 0.01$) which was calculated by subtracting the pre-work fatigue from the post-work score.

Table 3. Correlation between workload and fatigue.

Variables	(1)	(2)	(3)
Workload (1)	1		
Post-work fatigue (2)	.382**	1	
Post-pre change in fatigue (3)	.382**	.738**	1

*p < 0.05, **p < 0.001

Descriptive Statistics. Subjective workload scores were categorised into a high/low workload using a median split. The mean changes in performance are summarised in Table 4 below.

Table 4. Mean change of performance scores by workload and fatigue.

Mean (S.D)	High workload		Low workload	
Fatigue	Increased	Decreased	Increased	Decreased
PVT - RT (ms)	7.10 (28.39)	30.84 (20.56)	16.06 (22.49)	−8.03 (27.57)
- Accuracy (%)	−4.54 (7.86)	−3.20 (6.67)	−7.80 (8.28)	2.62 (6.96)
- Lapse	3.25 (5.40)	3.56 (3.32)	4.63 (7.19)	−0.88 (4.84)
- Total responses	0.42 (4.76)	−2.00 (4.53)	−0.50 (3.89)	0.35 (3.12)
Visual search - RT (s)	0.49 (3.98)	0.92 (4.18)	−0.08 (1.98)	1.18 (5.96)
- Accuracy (%)	−2.83 (9.65)	2.56 (11.11)	−3.37 (19.58)	10.24 (21.87)
Logical reasoning-RT(s)	1.27 (1.87)	−2.16 (3.84)	0.50 (2.63)	−0.15 (2.01)
- Accuracy (%)	−0.42 (13.61)	2.22 (23.95)	−11.13 (21.39)	−5.12 (18.12)
Alertness (% change)	23.33 (78.83)	31.69 (39.65)	−10.51 (27.55)	46.35 (41.60)

Effect of Workload and Fatigue on Performance. MANOVAs were used to analyse the effect of workload and the effect of a change in fatigue. The variables used in this analysis were categorised into two groups by using a median split. Workload was divided into high/low. The post-pre change of fatigue was split into increased/decreased fatigue.

Effect of Workload and the Interaction with Fatigue. A two-way MANOVA was conducted to explore the interaction between workload and change in fatigue. There was no main effect of workload nor interaction between workload and fatigue.

Effect of Fatigue on Performance. There was a statistically significant difference found between increased fatigue and decreased fatigue on the combined dependent variables, $F(8, 37) = 3.699$, $p < 0.01$, partial eta squared = 0.44. When the results for the dependent variables were considered separately, the differences that reached statistical significance were accuracy of PVT, accuracy of visual search and the reaction time for logical reasoning (shown in Table 5). In the PVT, response accuracy was significantly affected by fatigue ($F(1, 44) = 8.149$, $p < 0.01$, partial eta squared = 0.15). Increased fatigue not only reduced accuracy but also resulted in an increase in lapse responses ($F(1, 44) = 3.873$, $p = 0.055$, partial eta squared = 0.08) at the end of the workday. Also, an effect of fatigue was found to be significant for the performance of both the visual search and logical reasoning tasks. The accuracy of visual search declined more in the fatigue-increased condition than in the fatigue-reduced condition ($F(1, 44) = 4.423$, $p < 0.05$, partial eta squared = 0.91), while the reaction time for logical reasoning was slower ($F(1, 44) = 5.528$, $p < 0.05$, partial eta squared = 0.11). This, again, confirmed the association between subjective fatigue and the post-pre changes in performance.

Table 5. Significant univariate fatigue effect on performance.

	df	df error	F	Fatigue	Mean (SD)
PVT – accuracy (%)	1	44	8.149	Increased	−5.85 (7.98)
				Decreased	0.60 (7.29)
- Lapse	1	44	3.873	Increased	3.80 (6.03)
				Decreased	0.65 (4.81)
Visual search – accuracy (%)	1	44	4.423	Increased	−3.05 (13.97)
				Decreased	7.58 (18.96)
Logical reasoning - RT(s)	1	44	5.518	Increased	0.96 (2.17)
				Decreased	−0.84 (2.87)

Fatigue and Alertness in VAS. The results showed that increased fatigue significantly affected the change in alertness ($F(1, 44) = 106.425$, $p < 0.001$). It is not surprising that alertness and fatigue were associated since they represent the same thing. This result also showed that the single-item fatigue measure was validated by an established method of measuring alertness.

3.5 Summary

Overall, subjective fatigue was found to predict objective performance. Fatigue not only led to reduced accuracy and an increased number of lapses in the PVT, but it also reduced accuracy in the visual search task and was associated with slower RT in the logistic reasoning task. In PVT, performance reduced significantly further if subjective fatigue increased, and significantly improved if fatigue decreased. Similarly, in the other two cognitive tests, increased fatigue resulted in a greater reduction of performance. If fatigue increased, the response speed of logical reasoning was increased, and the accuracy in the visual search was further decreased.

The hypothesis predicted that either objective performance or subjective fatigue would be reduced at the end of the workday because of workload, and the reduction would be greater with a higher workload. The result showed that the effect of the workload was significantly associated with a greater change in fatigue, but no main effect of workload nor interaction between workload and fatigue was found.

The alertness dimension of VAS mood scale was used to validate the single-item fatigue measure. The result showed that the change in alertness and the change in fatigue strongly correlated with each other, and that increased fatigue resulted to reduced alertness.

4 Discussion

The field of railway fatigue has historically been less-researched in comparison to aviation and road transport fatigue. Study 1 sought to determine the risk factors and outcomes of fatigue in the rail industry. The results confirmed that workload is one of several predictors of fatigue, with a high workload resulting in higher levels of fatigue. Many of the results of this study are in line with work of the previous researchers using other professional group samples, such as truck drivers [22], seafarers [46] and nurses [36], and it also supports the use of the DRIVE model in the context of railway fatigue research. As expected, workload, job control and support, job characteristics, and personality characteristics predicted fatigue. These results support the main paths of the DRIVE model [34] and have initiated an investigation of risk factors for, and prevalence of, rail fatigue.

Fatigue was found to be significantly related to subjective reports of poor performance efficiency and presenteeism, which could increase the risk of accidents. Also, fatigue was associated with negative work-life balance and negative well-being outcomes in both daily lives and work life, including life satisfaction, job satisfaction, life stress, job stress, life happiness, work happiness, life depression and anxiety, job depression and anxiety. Both workload and fatigue were found to result in performance impairments in the previous literature, while workload was one of the strongest predictors of fatigue in Study 1. This raised the question of whether workload increases fatigue which then leads to a reduction of performance, or whether there are independent effects. Study 2 was designed to seek the answer to this by using single-item measures of workload and fatigue and online cognitive tests. The results showed that a change in subjective fatigue predicted impaired performance, while workload affected fatigue which then resulted in a change in performance.

The findings provide evidence for the effects of fatigue, but there was no independent effect of perceived workload found on performance change. The change in subjective fatigue significantly affected performance impairments in all three of the cognitive tests. Therefore, it is largely subjective fatigue that predicted the changes in objective performance. This probably reflects other factors affecting fatigue, and it may be these factors which then result in performance change.

The results showed that the online fatigue test (single-item measure and cognitive tests) did provide indicators of fatigue. The alertness dimension of VAS mood scales was used to validate the single-item fatigue measure. The result of alertness was consistent with the fatigue outcome which supported the validation of the single-item fatigue measure. Meanwhile, the change in PVT performance outcomes was affected by subjective fatigue and workload, indicating that the PVT was sensitive to these changes in state. Also, the outcomes of the three performance tests showed similar trends due to changes in fatigue. Therefore, these online measures were sensitive enough to study fatigue further, and were potentially applicable to the occupational setting.

In future research, such online measures will be applied for measuring perceived workload, perceived fatigue, and objective performance with railway staff. Mental workload has become a more important topic in the workplace as the work in modern railway industry requires more cognitive demands rather than physical demands [19]. Detecting work-related fatigue and poor time performance will allow organisations to provide adequate support to the staff and to take action to reduce the risks of incident or accident, especially in safety critical work.

5 Conclusion

Both workload and fatigue were associated with performance impairments. The results showed that workload is one of several predictors of occupational fatigue. High workload is one of the factors which increases fatigue and then leads to a reduction of performance. It is fatigue that mainly leads to performance impairments, and increased fatigue performance declines. The two-part online fatigue measure which integrates a single-item fatigue measure and cognitive tests acted as an indicator of the effects of subjective fatigue and workload.

References

1. Moos, R.H..: Psychosocial factors in the workplace. In: Handbook of Life Stress, Cognition and Health, pp. 193–209 (1988)
2. Hockey, G.R.J., Wiethoff, M.: Assessing patterns of adjustment to the demands of work. In: The Psychobiology of Stress, pp. 231–240 (1990). doi:10.1007/978-94-009-1990-7_21

3. Dorrian, J., Baulk, S.D., Dawson, D.: Work hours, workload, sleep and fatigue in Australian Rail Industry employees. Appl. Ergon. 42(2), 202–209 (2011). doi:10.1016/j.apergo.2010. 06.009

4. Grech, M.R., Neal, A., Yeo, G., Humphreys, M., Smith, S.: An examination of the relationship between workload and fatigue within and across consecutive days of work: is the relationship static or dynamic? J. Occup. Health Psychol. 14(3), 231 (2009). doi:10.1037/ a0014952

5. Parkes, K.R.: The effects of objective workload on cognitive performance in a field setting: a two-period cross-over trial. Appl. Cogn. Psychol. 9(7), 153–171 (1995). doi:10.1002/acp. 2350090710

6. Jahns, D.W.: A concept of operator workload in manual vehicle operations (1973)

7. Van Roy, K.S.: The Perceived Workload of ICU Physicians and Physician Extenders and Its Relationship to Burnout, Patient Safety, and Quality of Care. ProQuest, Ann Arbor (2008)

8. Johannsen, G.: Workload and workload measurement. In: Moray, N. (ed.) Mental Workload, pp. 3–11. Springer US, New York City (1979)

9. Cain, B.: A review of the mental workload literature. In: Defence Research and Development Canada Toronto, Human System Integration Section, Part II, vol. 4, pp. 1–34 (2007)

10. Park, J., Jung, W.: A study on the validity of a task complexity measure for emergency operating procedures of nuclear power plants - comparing with a subjective workload. IEEE Trans. Nucl. Sci. 53(5), 2962–2970 (2006). doi:10.1109/TNS.2006.882149

11. Broadbent, D.E.: The ergonomics society - the society's lecture 1979: is a fatigue test now possible? Ergonomics 22(12), 1277–1290 (1979). doi:10.1080/00140137908924702

12. Krueger, G.P.: Sustained work, fatigue, sleep loss and performance: a review of the issues. Work Stress 3(2), 129–141 (1989). doi:10.1080/02678378908256939

13. Craig, A., Cooper, R.E.: Symptoms of acute and chronic fatigue. In: Handbook of Human Performance, vol. 3, pp. 289–339 (1992)

14. Bartley, S.H., Chute, E.: Fatigue and Impairment in Man. McGraw-Hill Book Company, New York (1947). doi:10.1037/11772-000

15. Cameron, C.: A theory of fatigue. Ergonomics 16(5), 633–648 (1973). doi:10.1080/ 00140137308924554

16. Chalder, T., Berelowitz, G., Pawlikowska, T., Watts, L., Wessely, S., Wright, D., Wallace, E.P.: Development of a fatigue scale. J. Psychosom. Res. 37(2), 147–153 (1993). doi:10. 1016/0022-3999(93)90081-P

17. Kim, E., Jesus Lovera, M.D., Schaben, M., Bourdette, D., Whitham, R.: Novel method for measurement of fatigue in multiple sclerosis: Real-Time Digital Fatigue Score. J. Rehabil. Res. Dev. 47(5), 477 (2010). doi:10.1682/JRRD.2009.09.0151

18. British Office of Rail Regulation.: Managing Rail Staff Fatigue. http://orr.gov.uk/__data/ assets/pdf_file/0005/2867/managing_rail_fatigue.pdf (2012)

19. Young, M.S., Brookhuis, K.A., Wickens, C.D., Hancock, P.A.: State of science: mental workload in ergonomics. Ergonomics 58(1), 1–17 (2015). doi:10.1080/00140139.2014. 956151

20. Milner, C. J., Dick, G. L., Hammer, R. M.: Driver-somnolence and Eye-movements Studied in a Night-driving Simulation. (No. Monograph) (1984)

21. Beurskens, A.J., Bültmann, U., Kant, I., Vercoulen, J.H., Bleijenberg, G., Swaen, G.M.: Fatigue among working people: validity of a questionnaire measure. Occup. Environ. Med. 57(5), 353–357 (2000). doi:10.1136/oem.57.5.353

22. Charlton, S.G., Baas, P.H.: Fatigue, work-rest cycles, and psychomotor performance of New Zealand truck drivers. N. Z. J. Psychol. 30(1), 32–39 (2006)

23. British Rail Accident Investigation Branch.: Derailment of two locomotives at East Somerset Junction (2008). http://www.raib.gov.uk/publications/investigation_reports/reports_2009/report282009.cfm
24. Bowler, N., Gibbon, W.H.: British Rail Accident Investigation Branch.: Fatigue and its contribution to railway incidents (2015). http://www.rssb.co.uk/Library/risk-analysis-and-safety-reporting/2015-02-str-fatigue-contribution-to-railway-incidents.pdf
25. Mohren, D.C.L., Swaen, G.M.H., Kant, I.J., Borm, P.J.A., Galama, J.M.D.: Associations between infections and fatigue in a Dutch working population: results of the Maastricht Cohort Study on Fatigue at Work. Eur. J. Epidemiol. 17(12), 1081–1087 (2001). doi:10.1023/A:1021270924291
26. Leone, S.S., Huibers, M.J., Kant, I., Van Schayck, C.P., Bleijenberg, G., Knottnerus, J.A.: Long-term predictors of outcome in fatigued employees on sick leave: a 4-year follow-up study. Psychol. Med. 36(09), 1293–1300 (2006). doi:10.1016/j.jpsychores.2004.03.015
27. Karasek Jr., R.A.: Job demands, job decision latitude, and mental strain: implications for job redesign. Adm. Sci. Q. 24, 285–308 (1979)
28. Parkes, K.R.: Personality and coping as moderators of work stress processes: models, methods and measures. Work Stress 8(2), 110–129 (1994). doi:10.1080/02678379408259984
29. Cox, T., Ferguson, E.: Individual differences, stress and coping. Wiley (1991)
30. Laaksonen, M., Piha, K., Martikainen, P., Rahkonen, O., Lahelma, E.: Health-related behaviours and sickness absence from work. Occup. Environ. Med. 66(12), 840–847 (2009). doi:10.1136/oem.2008.039248
31. Ferguson, S.A., Lamond, N., Kandelaars, K., Jay, S.M., Dawson, D.: The impact of short, irregular sleep opportunities at sea on the alertness of marine pilots working extended hours. Chronobiol. Int. 25(2–3), 399–411 (2008). doi:10.1080/07420520802106819
32. Kjellberg, A.: Sleep deprivation and some aspects of performance. Waking Sleep 1(2), 139–143 (1977)
33. Lal, S.K., Craig, A.: A critical review of the psychophysiology of driver fatigue. Biol. Psychol. 55(3), 173–194 (2001). doi:10.1016/S0301-0511(00)00085-5
34. Mark, G.M., Smith, A.P.: Stress models: a review and suggested new direction. Occup. Health Psychol. 3, 111–144 (2008)
35. Williams, G.: Researching and developing mental health and well-being assessment tools for supporting employers and employees in wales. Ph.D. thesis, Cardiff University, Cardiff (2014)
36. Williams, J., Smith, A.P.: Stress, job satisfaction and mental health of NHS nurses. In: Contemporary Ergonomics and Human Factors 2013: Proceedings of the International Conference on Ergonomics and Human Factors 2013, Cambridge, UK, 15–18 April 2013, p. 95. Taylor & Francis (2013)
37. Crook, T.H., Kay, G.G., Larrabee, G.J.: Computer-based cognitive testing. in: Neuropsychological Assessment of Neuropsychiatric and Neuromedical Disorders, pp. 84–100 (2009)
38. Garaizar, P., Vadillo, M.A., Lopez-de-Ipina, D., Matute, H.: Measuring software timing errors in the presentation of visual stimuli in cognitive neuroscience experiments. PLoS ONE 9(1), e85108 (2014). doi:10.1371/journal.pone.0085108
39. Barnhoorn, J.S., Haasnoot, E., Bocanegra, B.R., van Steenbergen, H.: QRTEngine: an easy solution for running online reaction time experiments using Qualtrics. Behav. Res. Methods 47(4), 918–929 (2015). doi:10.3758/s13428-014-0530-7
40. Hughes, D.G., Folkard, S.: Adaptation to an 8-h shift in living routine by members of a socially isolated community. Nature (1976). doi:10.1038/264432a0
41. Buchner, A., Erdfelder, E., Faul, F.: How to use G*Power (1997). http://www.psycho.uni-duesseldorf.de/aap/projects/gpower/how_to_use_gpower.html

42. Volker, I., Kirchner, C., Bock, O.L.: On the relationship between subjective and objective measures of fatigue. Ergonomics, 1–5 (2015). doi:10.1080/00140139.2015.1110622

43. Dinges, D.F., Powell, J.W.: Microcomputer analyses of performance on a portable, simple visual RT task during sustained operations. Behav. Res. Methods Instrum. Comput. **17**(6), 652–655 (1985). doi:10.3758/BF03200977

44. Baddeley, A.D.: A 3 min reasoning test based on grammatical transformation. Psychon. Sci. **10**(10), 341–342 (1968). doi:10.3758/BF03331551

45. Bond, A., Lader, M.: The use of analogue scales in rating subjective feelings. Br. J. Med. Psychol. **47**(3), 211–218 (1974). doi:10.1111/j.2044-8341.1974.tb02285.x

46. Smith, A.P., Allen, P.H., Wadsworth, E.J.K.: Seafarer fatigue: the Cardiff research programme. Centre for Occupational and Health Psychology, Cardiff, UK (2006)

Estimation of Train Driver Workload: Extracting Taskload Measures from On-Train-Data-Recorders

Nora Balfe[1(✉)], Katie Crowley[1], Brendan Smith[2], and Luca Longo[3]

[1] Trinity College Dublin, Dublin, Ireland
balfen@tcd.ie
[2] Iarnród Éireann, Dublin, Ireland
[3] Dublin Institute of Technology, Dublin, Ireland
luca.longo@dit.ie

Abstract. This paper presents a method to extract train driver taskload from downloads of on-train-data-recorders (OTDR). OTDR are in widespread use for the purposes of condition monitoring of trains, but they may also have applications in operations monitoring and management. Evaluation of train driver workload is one such application. The paper describes the type of data held in OTDR recordings and how they can be transformed into driver actions throughout a journey. Example data from 16 commuter journeys are presented, which highlights the increased taskload during arrival at stations. Finally, the possibilities and limitations of the data are discussed.

Keywords: OTDR · Train driver taskload · Rail human factors

1 Introduction

In contrast to rail signalling, where several specific workload tools have been developed (e.g. [1]), train driver workload is under-researched. The train driver task has however been extensively discussed in the human factors literature, with numerous models, frameworks and task analyses produced to describe the task and influencers, and several studies investigating train driver visual behaviour (e.g. [2, 3]). This paper presents a new approach to investigating train driver workload using data from on-train-data recorders (OTDR) to capture train driver activity and calculate driver taskload. This section describes the work to date on measurement of workload in train driving, and Sect. 2 proposes a new method for calculating train driver taskload from OTDR. Section 3 presents a preliminary application of the methodology in a case study of 16 commuter train journeys. Finally, the limitations, possible applications and further research required are discussed in Sect. 4. Human factors research into the train driving task dates back to Branton [4], who, in 1979, published a paper discussing the nature of train driving and the need for drivers to anticipate future actions, develop internal representations of the railway (route knowledge), and test these representations against reality. Authors who have written about the train-driving task typically agree that the key tasks involve processing information collected from inside and outside the

L. Longo and M.C. Leva (Eds.): H-WORKLOAD 2017, CCIS 726, pp. 106–119, 2017.
DOI: 10.1007/978-3-319-61061-0_7

cab and applying route knowledge to correctly control the speed and braking of the train [5–7]. Additional tasks include:

- Maintaining an efficient speed profile [5]
- Making scheduled stops [5]
- Managing the train for fuel efficiency [6]
- Departing stations [8]
- Arriving at stations [8]

Gillis [9] notes that the train-driving task is primarily a visual-spatial task involving constant perception and processing of information, and the majority of a train driver's physical actions are driven by information received (e.g. moving the traction handle in response to a change in the speedometer). Hamilton and Clarke [10] include a high level cognitive task analysis (CTA) goal structure, which was used as the basis of a quantitative tool for the assessment of route drivability (Table 1).

Table 1. CTA of the train driver task [10]

Execute a train service	Prepare for service	Prepare driver for driving duty
		Assemble train (shunting)
		Prepare train for service
	Drive service	Start from scheduled stop
		Drive towards scheduled service stop in accordance with movement authority
		Stop for scheduled service stop
		Perform service operations at stop
		Perform operations for failed train
	Close out train after service	Relinquish possession of train
		Perform formalities after service

However, despite the apparent simplicity of the task, Naweed [11] describes the train-driving task as complex, dynamic, and opaque. Although the basic tasks may be described reasonably simply, the actual practice is complicated by changing conditions, event densities, and performance pressures that drive adjustments in motor skills and problem solving strategies. The complexity is often further increased by conflicting goals of time-accuracy, comfort and speed regulation, and the trade-offs of such required to optimise the overall journey. The dynamism comes from the constant need to regulate speed, while the opacity is due to the gaps in information when working with lineside signalling. Drivers must use their route knowledge to infer future requirements. Thus, driver performance is not simply a matter of perceiving and responding to stimuli as suggested by the use of simple information processing models, but is driven by continuous, proactive prediction and planning [12]. The consensus in the literature is that, despite the apparent simplicity, train driving is a complex task requiring processing and integration of vestibular, kinaesthetic, acoustic, and peripheral visual information [13].

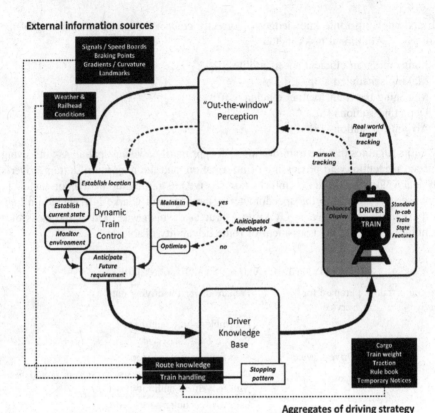

Fig. 1. Model of the train driver task [11]

Naweed [11] describes a closed loop system of train driver performance based on the perception of location from lineside features, and use of this information in conjunction with the drivers' knowledge base (i.e. route knowledge and train handling knowledge) to establish location and apply appropriate controls (Fig. 1). Driving strategies are informed by specific sources, including the rulebook and temporary notices. Hamilton and Clarke [10] describe how train-driving goals are selected by a plan (or rules) determined by operating conditions. For example, on passing a cautionary aspect, a driver should decelerate, but when and by how much will depend on situational factors including the specific aspect shown, railhead conditions, train performance characteristics, etc.

These models adequately describe moment-to-moment train control, but are less capable of representing the entirety of the train-driving task, particularly its contextual and situated nature [14]. McLeod et al. [14] suggest instead a situational model of driver performance which applies the concept of situation awareness to link driver knowledge and experience with their actions and strategies (Fig. 2).

In addition to this more complex model, McLeod et al. [14] discuss additional concepts that may be relevant to explore the complexity associated with the task:

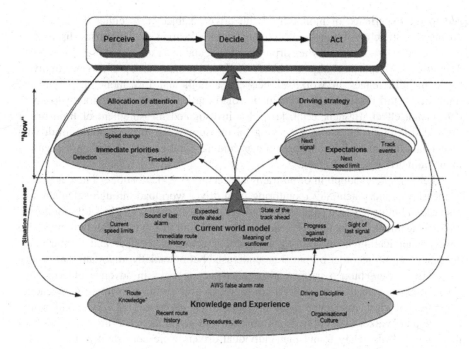

Fig. 2. Situational model of the train driver performance [14]

- Strategic behaviour – how do train drivers develop and apply strategies for managing workload, attention, and other influences?
- Situation awareness – how do drivers develop an understanding of the current situation and apply this to predict future state?
- Situated behaviour and distributed cognition – how do the context, situation, tools and surroundings inform and support or hinder driver actions?
- Distributed cognition – how do the artefacts and surrounding environment support or hinder driver performance?

1.1 Train Driver Workload Measurement

Despite the number of models of train driving, measurement of train driver workload has been specifically investigated in only a small number of papers. Dunn and Williamson [15] examined the effect of underload on train driver performance in a simulated train-driving environment. They suggest that the train-driving task can involve periods of relatively high workload, but also involves "periods of repetitive low workload activity, such as driving along a straight track at a steady speed and only responding to signals from the in-cab 'vigilance' control device." (pp. 998). As train drivers do not control lateral positioning of the train (although they must be vigilant approaching junctions that they do not take the 'wrong route'), their driving tasks are limited to controlling the throttle and brake. Dunn and Williamson [15] also state that the train-driving environment itself may add to the experience of monotony "with drivers subjected to either the repetitive, unchanging stretches of train tracks moving beneath the train and off into the distance, or the reduced external stimuli when driving underground in a tunnel or at night" (pp. 998). They used self-report techniques (NASA-TLX) and primary task performance to investigate the differences in workload between a high and low monotony simulated train-driving task and found the combination of low task demands and monotony to have a detrimental effect. Basacik et al. [16] also investigated measurement of train driver underload through the use of physiological measurements during a non-train driving related task, and produced some preliminary findings for the use of physiological sensors in the train driving environment.

The widespread adoption of on-train-data-recorders (OTDR) offers a new approach to measuring and potentially monitoring train driver workload through calculation of the taskload imposed on the driver. OTDR are primarily used for train fault monitoring and management, but as they log each and every input in the train cab they may also have an application in monitoring train driver activities. Walker and Strathie [17] suggest that train recorder output is an underused but potentially important data source for understanding human performance and detecting risks in advance of accidents. Their research used data from 107 train journeys over six days to investigate leading indicators of risks associated with in-cab warning devices [18]. A second study, Strathie and Walker [19] applied link analysis and graph theory to the movements of the train controls. They found that individual drivers were consistent in their movements, and there were differences between drivers in the pairs of movements. Broekhoven [20] used real-time data from operational signalling control systems to calculate an External Cognitive Task Load (XTL) for rail signallers. The approach uses four measures over five minute periods: the number of automatically executed plan rules (monitoring load), the number of manually adjusted plan rules (planning load), the number of non-executed plan rules (manual intervention load), and the percentage of seconds spoken through the telephone (communications load). The four measures were weighted to align with the Integrated Workload Scale for Signallers [1] and then summed. This result was then multiplied by a switching cost calculated from the number of trains delayed, the number of telephone calls made, and the number of incidents. The XTL formula was found to discriminate between high and low perceived workload in both the communication and manual actions.

The purpose of this paper is to describe a method of extracting train driver actions from the OTDR, and present the results of a case study describing train driver taskload as measured by the OTDR.

2 Method

2.1 Experiment Description

Data was collected from eight return journeys (16 journeys in total) over two routes. Five drivers participated in the study. Table 1 describes the driver and route for each journey included in the study. A researcher travelled with the driver on each journey and noted any unusual events or deviations from standard practices. The researcher also collected subjective and physiological data; this data will not be presented in this paper. The journeys were all scheduled passenger services, and the research did not cause any interference with the timetabled journey.

2.2 Dataset Preparation

Following the journey, the OTDR data was downloaded from the Teloc (Hasler, V3.11) via the Nexala remote condition monitoring system (Nexala, v2.8.01). The resulting Teloc files were parsed and cropped to the relevant time frame. Relevant signals were then selected, and exported to Excel using Eva 2 software (Hasler, v2.4 Pro). The following signals were regarded as relevant as they are directly attributable to driver actions:

- Brake demand – provided in three bitcodes
- Acknowledgement of Continuous Automatic Warning System (CAWS)
- Aspect logged in the CAWS system (Green, Yellow, Double Yellow, Red)
- Gear (forward/reverse)
- Emergency brake application
- Headlight (dipped beam and full beam)
- Horn switch
- Left door opening
- Power demand – provided in three bitcodes
- Right door opening
- Vigilance alarm acknowledgement

All these signals were logged as bitcodes (0/1); in addition, analogue signals of time, speed, and GPS coordinates were downloaded and exported for each journey.

The data was then pre-processed via the following steps:

1. Power and brake levels applied were determined from the relevant bitcodes for each line of data;
2. The aspect (signal colour) was determined for each line of data;
3. Journey phases were added according to the framework described by Balfe and Smith [21];

This dataset provided the basis for the analysis of train driver actions or taskload.

2.3 Driver Taskload Computation

The dataset was used to calculate driver taskload by identifying the times of driver actions. The actions identifiable from the dataset are:

(a) Initiate braking – Drivers must use their route knowledge and timetable knowledge to identify when they should start applying the brakes for the next station stop, red signal stop, or to reduce or control speed;
(b) Change braking – Drivers adjust the level of braking according to the train and braking performance;

(c) Stop braking – Drivers remove brakes when they no longer wish to reduce train speed, or the train is stopped;

(d) Change gear – Drivers may put the train into reverse – this is unusual during a normal passenger journey and would usually be performed in shunting or permissive working (e.g. separating previously joined trains) movements;

(e) Acknowledge CAWS warning – Drivers receive a buzzer warning when they approach a more restrictive aspect, and they must acknowledge this warning by pressing a button within 7 s, or the train emergency brake will be automatically applied;

(f) Headlights – Drivers change headlight settings as they move through the network;

(g) Horn switch – Drivers operate the train horn at required locations on the network, and often as they enter or leave a station;

(h) Door opening – Drivers operate the door switches to open and close the train doors at stations. There are several unlogged tasks associated with closing train doors – specifically checking for passengers trapped in doors and checking that the door interlock light has illuminated before leaving the station;

(i) Initiate power – Drivers apply power as they start from a stop, or to increase train speed due to a change in signal aspect, line speed, or to maintain a speed profile;

(j) Change power – drivers change the power according to the train performance;

(k) Acknowledge vigilance alarm – drivers receive a buzzer warning at periodic intervals, which they must acknowledge by toggling a foot pedal (vigilance device; also known as dead man's pedal). If they do not respond within 7 s, the train emergency brake will be automatically applied.

The data therefore provides information on all routine actions performed by the driver to control the train, and driver taskload can be calculated from this data by summing the number of actions taken within a set time period (e.g. the number of actions per minute). However, there are a number of driver tasks that are not logged in the data, particularly those of communication and passenger interaction (e.g. operating the passenger information system, responding to passenger queries, etc.) as well as perception and interpretation of the visual environment. The OTDR also gives limited insight into the cognitive processing associated with these actions. It may still be useful for monitoring and comparing different journeys and different journey phases.

3 Case Study Results

Figure 3 shows an example histogram describing the number of actions in each minute of one of the train journeys analysed. The graph clearly shows variation in activity levels over the course of the journey, with a maximum of 19 and a minimum of 1 actions in each minute.

The actions can be analysed in terms of journey phase, i.e. station duties, departing from stations, arriving at stations, and travelling between stations. The journey stages were demarcated according to the model described by Balfe and Smith [21]. Figure 4 shows a typical journey speed profile and describes the four main stages repeated throughout the journey.

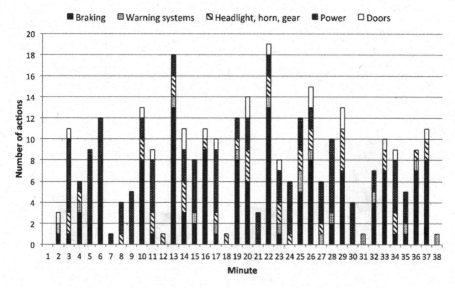

Fig. 3. Train driver actions over a typical journey

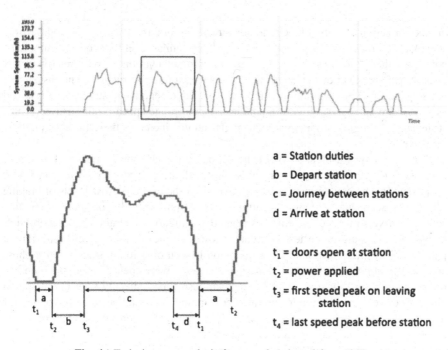

a = Station duties

b = Depart station

c = Journey between stations

d = Arrive at station

t_1 = doors open at station

t_2 = power applied

t_3 = first speed peak on leaving station

t_4 = last speed peak before station

Fig. 4. Train journey analysis framework (adapted from [21])

Figure 5 shows the mean number of actions per minute, along with the maximum and minimum number of actions, for each of the four journey stages across all 16 analysed journeys. The graph shows that the "arrive at station" stage has the highest

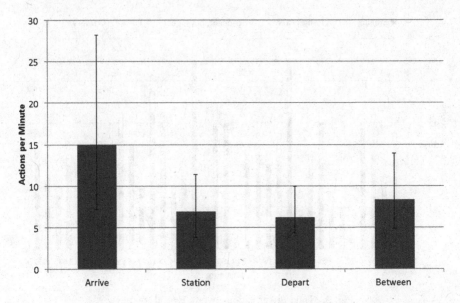

Fig. 5. Average, maximum and minimum actions per minute for each of the four journey stages

number of actions per minute, due to adjustments in braking levels while approaching stations. "Station duties" and "depart station" have similar levels of actions. It should be noted that the 16 journeys analysed were all commuter journeys, with relatively few instances of the "journey between stations" stage and three journeys had no instance of this stage at all. "Between stations" may be expected to generate relatively little taskload as drivers are simply required to maintain the appropriate speed profile. However this stage can also involve stopping at red signals and this increases the actions required by the driver.

Figure 6 shows a breakdown of the actions for each journey phase, shown as a percentage of the total actions in each phase. Braking, applying power, and door operations are the predominant activities. As would be expected, low levels of braking actions are seen during station departures (comprising only 3% of station departure actions). Drivers may apply the brakes when departing to test a train's braking abilities, known as a running brake test. Similarly, power applications are rare during arrival phases (2% of arrival actions). Door operation is seen only in the station duties phase and the arrival phase, as on some occasions the doors were opened before the train had registered coming to a stop. Gear changes are also predominantly seen in the station phase, as drivers put the train in neutral after stopping in the station and replace the gear to forward when preparing to depart. Warning acknowledgements, headlight operations and horn operations were spread across all four phases.

3.1   Weighted Method

Since all actions are not equal in terms of the underlying cognitive processing, a more nuanced measurement of taskload could be constructed by weighting the different

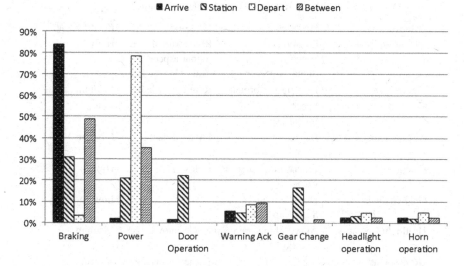

Fig. 6. Proportion of actions across each of the four journey stages

actions. A possible framework is described below as an illustration, although it should be noted that this framework is based only on preliminary task analyses, and has not been validated with train driving experts.

Table 2 shows the perception and memory activities associated with each of the physical actions logged in the OTDR. Actions with more cognitive activities associated with them can be assumed to place a higher load on the train driver. For example, initiating braking requires the driver to be aware of the location and speed of the train, drawing on route knowledge to determine the point at which to apply the brakes. The reason for the brake application may be to maintain line speed, to respond to a change of signal aspect, or to stop at a station. A more detailed framework could calculate individual factors for each of these events.

In this example initiating braking, applying the emergency brake, initiating power and closing train doors are all tasks with relatively higher load than the others. This is because they draw more deeply on the drivers' memory and/or require more perception and analysis of the environment. Concluding braking, gear changes, opening doors, and responding to the vigilance device are listed as low in relation to other tasks, as they are all simple responses to a stimulus. Weighted coefficients can then be applied to the high, medium and low rated actions for better estimation of cognitive task load based on actions undertaken. For purposes of illustration, high rated actions in this dataset were given a weight five times that of those rated low, and medium rated actions were given a weight three times that of those rated low. Further research would be required to determine the correct coefficients. Figure 7 shows the average, maximum and minimum weighted actions per minute for the four journey stages. Braking is still the dominant activity in this weighted method, and the braking associated with arriving at stations is further highlighted in the weighted method.

Table 2. Relative load for different actions

Action	Perception	Memory	Relative load
Initiate braking	Location Speed Signal aspect	Route knowledge Signal aspect Train characteristics	High
Change braking	Braking performance	Route knowledge	Medium
Conclude braking	Speed Signal aspect		Low
Acknowledge CAWS	Buzzer Signal aspect	Signal aspect	Medium
Emergency brake	Emergency situation Error	Rules	High
Gear change	Doors closed Signal upgrade		Low
Headlight operation	Approaching train Location	Route knowledge Rules	Medium
Horn operation	Sign Location	Route knowledge	Medium
Initiate power	Station checks Signal upgrade	Rules Signal aspect	High
Change power	Train performance Speed	Route knowledge	Medium
Remove power	Speed	Route knowledge	Medium
Doors open	Train speed Location		Low
Doors close	Station checks	Rules	High
Vigilance device	Buzzer		Low

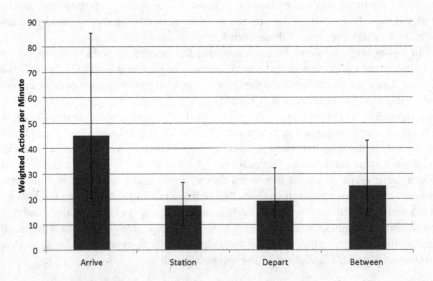

Fig. 7. Weighted average, maximum and minimum actions per minute

4 Discussion and Conclusions

This paper has presented a method for calculating train driver taskload from OTDR data, using transitions between states to infer driver actions. The results of this analysis of 16 journeys illustrate the increase in taskload during arrival at stations, primarily due to continuous adjustment of train braking. Of course, the taskload does not constitute the entirety of train driver workload, but it provides one piece of information that may be useful for monitoring driving performance, particularly in terms of underload. The method is completely unobtrusive, as it uses already existing data to construct the taskload model, and as such it may be a useful method of data collection in future studies involving train drivers. The advantage of the method outlined here is in providing a completely unobtrusive method to evaluate train driver taskload, and hence an aspect of their workload. This method could also be used to gather data in a variety of operational situations; for example, comparing the taskload of novice train drivers to that of more experienced drivers, in order to understand the strategies used by those experienced train drivers to manage underload. Another possible application is in comparing train driver taskload before and after infrastructure changes, in order to understand how the changes have affected the train driver task, whether positively or negatively. A further application could be the evaluation of overload through busy urban areas. As the data is already being collected on trains equipped with OTDR, there is no additional cost to collecting the data, only to the analysis.

In relation to the literature, the data presented here dovetails with the cognitive task analysis undertaken by Hamilton and Clarke [10], although only the 'Drive Service' elements were presented in this paper. However, in contrast to the models more focused on human information processing, the OTDR data only provides detailed insight into 'actions' performed by the driver. Where signal aspect data is available from the OTDR, some small insight may be gained into perception – particularly through analysis of reaction times to warnings of aspect changes. However this data is very limited, and the wide range of other information used by drivers (e.g. landmarks, signals from platform staff, etc.) throughout journeys is not captured by the OTDR. Referring to the model of Naweed [11] (Fig. 1), little of the contextual information and visual environment that drivers must perceive, analyse and respond to is directly covered by this method. Similarly, it is difficult to make any inferences on information analysis and driver decision-making from the data. The model of McLeod et al. [14] describes the more contextual and cognitive processes that comprise train driving and highlights the limitations of taskload calculation alone for estimating driver workload. However, further analysis of large datasets from OTDR may provide some insight into the range of strategies used by different drivers in different situations.

Future research could apply the methodology to more journey types (particularly longer, intercity or high speed journeys) to compare key metrics with the shorter, commuter-type journeys analysed here. As OTDR are in widespread international use, future research could also examine national differences. The example weighted method presented in this paper could also be further developed and the coefficients determined through structured manual observations of drivers and a comprehensive cognitive task analysis. They should also be validated with subject matter experts to ensure they accurately provide a more sensitive analysis of workload, as in Rizzo et al. and Rubio et al. [22, 23]. The data may also be analysed using frameworks [e.g. 24] to better aggregate heterogeneous records towards improved assessment of mental workload. The data collected in conjunction with the OTDR data described in this paper will also be analysed to determine whether there are any correlations between the OTDR taskload model and subjective or physiological measures of workload, providing some validation of the methodology.

References

1. Pickup, L., Wilson, J.R., Sharples, S., Norris, B., Clarke, T., Young, M.S.: Fundamental examination of mental workload in the rail industry. Theor. Issues Ergon. Sci. **6**(6), 463–482 (2005)
2. Naghiyev, A., Sharples, S., Ryan, B., Coplestone, A., Carey, M.: Real workload verbal protocol data analysis of European Rail Traffic Management System train driving and conventional train driving. In: 2016 IEEE International Conference on Intelligent Rail Transportation (ICIRT), pp. 191–196. IEEE (2016)
3. Luke, T., Brook-Carter, N., Parkes, A.M., Grimes, E., Mills, A.: An investigation of train driver visual strategies. Cogn. Technol. Work **8**(1), 15–29 (2006)
4. Branton, P.: Investigations into the skills of train-driving. Ergonomics **22**(2), 155–164 (1979)
5. Doncaster, N.: "By the seat of their pants" cues and feedback used by train crew. In: Wilson, J.R., Mills, A., Clarke, T., Rajan, J., Dadashi, N. (eds.) Rail Human Factors around the World: Impacts on and of People for Successful Rail Operations, pp. 484–494. CRC Press, Leiden (2012)
6. Hamilton, W.I., Clarke, T.: Driver performance modelling and its practical application to railway safety. Appl. Ergon. **36**, 661–670 (2005)
7. Buksh, A., Sharples, S., Wilson, J.R., Coplestone, A., Morrisroe, G.: A comparative cognitive task analysis of the different forms of driving in the UK rail system. In: Dadashi, N., Scott, A., Wilson, J.R., Mills, A. (eds.) Rail Human Factors: Supporting Reliability, Safety, and Cost Reduction, pp. 173–182. Taylor & Francis, London (2013)
8. Zoer, I., Sluiter, J.K., Frings-Dresen, H.W.: Psychological work characteristics, psychological workload and associated psychological and cognitive requirements of train driver. Ergonomics **57**(10), 1473–1487 (2014)
9. Gillis, I.: Cognitive workload of train drivers. In: Wilson, J.R., Norris, B., Clarke, T., Mills, A. (eds.) People and Rail Systems: Human Factors at the Heart of the Railway, pp. 91–101. Ashgate, Aldershot (2007)
10. Hamilton, W.I., Clarke, T.: Driver performance modelling and its practical application to railway safety. In: Wilson, J.R., Norris, B., Clarke, T., Mills, A. (eds.) Rail Human Factors: Supporting the Integrated Railway. Ashgate, Aldershot (2005)
11. Naweed, A.: Investigations into the skills of modern and traditional train driving. Appl. Ergon. **45**, 462–470 (2014)
12. Elliot, A.C., Garner, S.D., Grimes, E.: The cognitive tasks of the driver: the approach and passage through diverging junctions. In: Wilson, J.R., Norris, B., Clarke, T., Mills, A. (eds.) People and Rail Systems: Human Factors at the Heart of the Railway, pp. 115–123. Ashgate, Aldershot (2007)
13. Naweed, A., O'Keeffe, V., Tuckey, M.R.: The art of train driving: flexing the boundaries to manage risk within an inflexible system. Eat Sleep Work **1** (2015)

14. McLeod, R.W., Walker, G.H., Moray, N., Mills, A.: Analysing and modelling train driver performance. In: Wilson, J.R., Norris, B., Clarke, T., Mills, A. (eds.) Rail Human Factors: Supporting the Integrated Railway. Ashgate, Aldershot (2005)

15. Dunn, N., Williamson, A.: Driving monotonous routes in a train simulator: the effect of task demand on driving performance and subjective experience. Ergonomics 55(9), 997–1008 (2012)

16. Basacik, D., Waters, S., Reed, N.: Detecting cognitive underload in train driving: a physiological approach. In: Proceedings of the 5th International Rail Human Factors Conference, 14–17 September, London (2015)

17. Walker, G., Strathie, A.: Combining human factors methods with transport data recordings. In: Stanton, N., Landry, S., Di Bucchianic, G., Vallicelli, A. (eds.) Advances in Human Aspects of Transportation: Part 2 (2014)

18. Walker, G., Strathie, A.: Leading indicators of operational risk on the railway: a novel use for underutilised data recordings. Saf. Sci. 74, 93–101 (2015)

19. Strathie, A., Walker, G.: Can link analysis be applied to identify behavioural patterns in train recorder data? Hum. Factors 58(2), 205–217 (2015)

20. Broekhoven, R.F.G.: Comparison of Real-Time Relative Workload Measurements in Rail Signallers. University of Twente, Twente (2016)

21. Balfe, N., Smith, B.: A framework for human factors analysis of railway on-train data. Paper presented at HFES-Europe Chapter Conference, Prague, October 2016 (2016)

22. Rizzo, L., Dondio, P., Delany, S.J., Longo, L.: Modeling mental workload via rule-based expert system: a comparison with NASA-TLX and workload profile. In: Iliadis, L., Maglogiannis, I. (eds.) AIAI 2016. IAICT, vol. 475, pp. 215–229. Springer, Cham (2016). doi:10.1007/978-3-319-44944-9_19

23. Rubio, S., Díaz, E., Martín, J., Puente, J.M.: Evaluation of subjective mental workload: a comparison of SWAT, NASA-TLX, and workload profile methods. Appl. Psychol. 53(1), 61–86 (2004)

24. Longo, L.: A defeasible reasoning framework for human mental workload representation and assessment. Behav. Inf. Technol. 34(8), 758–786 (2015)

The Relationship Between Workload and Performance in Air Traffic Control: Exploring the Influence of Levels of Automation and Variation in Task Demand

Tamsyn Edwards[1](✉), Lynne Martin[2], Nancy Bienert[1],
and Joey Mercer[2]

[1] San Jose State University at NASA Ames Research Center,
Moffett Field, CA, USA
{tamsyn.e.edwards,nancy.bienert}@nasa.gov
[2] NASA Ames Research Center, Moffett Field, CA, USA
{lynne.martin,joey.mercer}@nasa.gov

Abstract. In an air traffic environment, task demand is dynamic. However, previous research has largely considered the association of task demand and controller performance using conditions of stable task demand. Further, there is a comparatively restricted understanding of the influence of task demand transitions on workload and performance in association with different types and levels of automation that are available to controllers. This study used an air traffic control simulation to investigate the influence of task demand transitions, and two conditions of automation, on workload and efficiency-related performance. Findings showed that both the direction of the task demand variation and the amount of automation influenced the relationship between workload and performance. Findings are discussed in relation to capacity and arousal theories. Further research is needed to enhance understanding of how demand transition and workload history affects operator experience and performance, in both air traffic control and other safety-critical domains.

Keywords: Air traffic control · Workload transitions · Workload history · Time-based metering · Automation

1 Introduction

Within the safety critical domain of air traffic control (ATC), workload "is still considered one of the most important single factors influencing operators' performance" [1, p. 639]. Workload has been defined within the ATC domain as the "activities, both mental and physical, which result from handling air traffic" [2, p. 3]. Air Traffic Controllers' (ATCOs') primary task is to ensure the safety of aircraft in their airspace [3]. They have to ensure at least standard separation between the aircraft in the airspace (sector) for which they are responsible, which includes changing the course of one or more aircraft if they predict that the paths of these aircraft will, in the future, come too close together (conflict). Secondly, controllers strive to efficiently manage their traffic,

© Springer International Publishing AG 2017
L. Longo and M.C. Leva (Eds.): H-WORKLOAD 2017, CCIS 726, pp. 120–139, 2017.
DOI: 10.1007/978-3-319-61061-0_8

which, in airspace where aircraft are descending to arrive at an airport, includes creating strings of evenly spaced aircraft to assist in maximizing landings. ATCO tasks can be thought of as a series of speed-time-distance trigonometry problems. Thus, their workload stems mainly from cognitive demands, and is "mental" in nature, although a sector that has many aircraft entering and exiting can have a high physical load, in terms of the communication required with pilots.

Although there are many factors that can increase the complexity of an event for a controller (e.g. sector structure, weather), amount of controller workload is closely related to traffic density[1]. While there are procedures in place to limit traffic density becoming too great in any one sector, controllers also manage task demand by employing a range of strategies [4]. This behavior can be described by resource theory [5], which assumes that the human operator has a limited capacity of cognitive resources available to be allocated to a task. More tasks are understood to demand more processing resources. At some point, the number of tasks lead to demands greater than the resources available, and performance suffers, unless the operator (in this case the ATCO) can change the task demand on cognitive resources. In ATC, safety performance is paramount, and so ATCOs develop a range of strategies to manage the demands of the task and therefore, the available cognitive resources, as observed by [6, 7].

In ATC, as with many other safety critical environments, task demand and workload are dynamic. ATCOs frequently experience changes in traffic load and the complexity of the traffic situation. These changes in task demand can potentially result in changes to the cognitive complexity of managing the traffic and subsequently, ATCOs' subjective experience of transitions between high and low workload. These transitions can be expected by the controller, such as when traffic load changes based on the time of day or known activities in surrounding sectors, or unexpected, for example, through increased complexity resulting from an emergency situation. Transitions may also be gradual or sudden [8]. Controllers, therefore, have to remain vigilant at all times when they are 'on position' to make sure they are aware of events as they build, even if the transition is sudden.

Research on task demand transitions, and the effect on both performance-influencing covariate factors (such as workload) and task performance is limited, with studies frequently utilizing a constant task demand [9] or changing demand only between experimental conditions. Of the research available on demand transitions, there appears to be conflicting findings. Some (e.g. [10]) have reported that overall performance efficiency on a vigilance task was not affected by task demand transitions, regardless of whether the transition was expected or unexpected. However, others (e.g. [10]) have found that performance on vigilance tasks was influenced by a low-to-high demand transition or high-to-low demand transition (e.g. [8]). Task demand and workload transition research specific to an ATC environment is particularly underrepresented. Consequently, there is limited understanding of the influence of demand transitions on workload and performance in air traffic environments. To contribute to understanding in this domain, [12] reported on a study that investigated task demand transitions on workload, fatigue and an efficiency performance measure, metering accuracy. Findings

---

[1] Traffic density refers to the number of aircraft an ATCO is managing in their sector.

showed that a change in task demand appeared to affect both workload and fatigue ratings, although not necessarily performance. In addition, participants' workload and fatigue ratings in equivalent task demand periods appeared to change depending on the demand period preceding the time of the current ratings. However, the findings reported specifically focused on a scenario in which the controller had full manual control. In both the current and future planned (i.e. NextGen) air traffic systems, automation is increasingly present to both assist (for example, the ground based separation assurance tools offered to air traffic controllers in studies reported by [13]), and in some cases, take over controller tasks (such as in automated handoffs). In order to increase National Airspace (NAS) capacity, it is therefore important to investigate the association of taskload variations, and taskload after-effects, with both current-day manual tasks and tasks with functions that will potentially be automated in the future.

As discussed in [14], there can be a tradeoff for the operator between the situation awareness (SA) that is generated by completing tasks and the accompanying workload and time pressure. Automation adds another layer to these tradeoff considerations; if implemented with the human/automation system in mind, automation can offer situation awareness-enhancing qualities, such as predictability and integrated information [14], which together help the human to build and maintain situation awareness.

It is important to understand for which tasks air traffic controllers can continue to be an effective part of the separation assurance system and which tasks are now more suitable for automation. The tradeoff between the levels of automated aid with human involvement in air traffic management performance was explored in a series of three studies, the third of which is mentioned in detail below. The addition of automation (that redefines a human system as a human/automation system) is intended to aid human performance and increase system capacity.

The data reported in this paper was generated from a larger study reported in [9]. The authors extend the findings reported in [12] by investigating the association of differing levels of automation on workload and efficiency-related performance in an ATC simulation. The aim of the study reported here was to investigate the influence of expected and gradual task demand transitions (high-low-high and low-high-low) on workload and performance under two different levels of automation, within a high fidelity ATC simulation environment. Due to the quantity of measures and data generated from this study, only a subset of the measures and findings that are most relevant to this research aim are presented. Initial findings are reported in [12] which are extended in the current paper.

2 Method

2.1 Design Overview

A within measures, en-route ATC human in the loop (HITL) simulation was utilized to investigate task demand variation on workload and performance. Participants operated a combined low and high altitude sector in Albuquerque Center (ZAB) and were assigned to meter aircraft into Phoenix (PHX) and manage overflights. Metering is a specific controller task of scheduling arrival traffic to meet a pre-planned schedule or time. Task demand was manipulated to create two scenarios. Efficiency-related performance was inferred from delay to metered aircraft (in seconds) at three nautical miles before a meter fix). Participants were eight retired-ATCOs who had previously worked in enroute airspace in Oakland Air Route Traffic Control Center (ARTCC). Pseudo pilots were paired with controllers, and completed standard pilot tasks such as controlling the aircraft in accordance with controller instructions and communicating with controllers. Each simulation session lasted for 90 min.

2.2   Airspace and Task Demand Scenarios

Participants operated a simulated, combined low and high altitude sector (segment of airspace, Fig. 1), in Albuquerque Center (ZAB) that handles aircraft beginning their arrival descent into the Phoenix Sky Harbor International Airport (PHX). This airspace was selected for the complexity it offered through a mix of arrivals and overflights. Scenarios were designed to have the mix of traffic present in this sector – overflights passing through at level altitudes and transitioning aircraft either climbing out from PHX and other airports in the area, or on a metered descent into PHX. The scenarios included winds for the area, which were constant-at-altitude with a nominal forecast error.

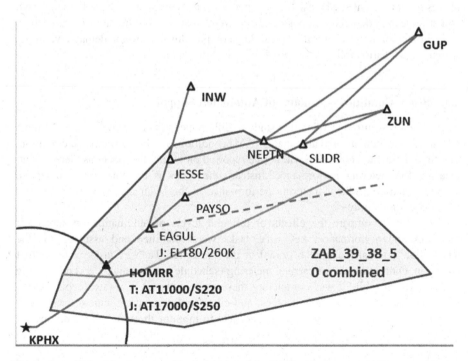

Fig. 1. Low-high altitude sector (shaded in grey) in ZAB with the routes that comprise the "EAGUL6 STAR" marked

Arrival traffic in both scenarios was metered through the HOMRR fix on the EAGUL6[2] arrival (Fig. 1). Aircraft were initiated in the scenario with up to two-minute delays (M = 76 s) as they entered the sector (on the right of Fig. 1). In addition, nine conflicts were created in each scenario where an overflight would lose separation with another overflight or an arrival if not adjusted. In the Start High scenario, four conflicts were built to occur in the first thirty minutes, two in the second thirty minutes, and three in the final thirty minutes. In the Start Low scenario, three conflicts were built to occur in each of the three thirty-minute segments.

The direction of the task demand transition was manipulated to create the two scenarios. Scenario 1 followed a high-low-high task demand pattern and scenario two followed a low-high-low task demand pattern. The creation of three task demand periods was implemented in order to better reflect the multiple task demand transitions that can be experienced within an operational environment. In addition, this permitted an extension of previous studies that had focused on the comparison of workload and performance for one transition period (e.g. [8]).

Each simulation session lasted for 90 min and consisted of three, 20 min [15] periods of stable task demand which alternated between high and low traffic levels, interspersed with a total of three, 10 min transition phases. Task demand was created by the number of aircraft under control [16] as well as the ratio of arrival aircraft and overflights. Arrival aircraft create complexity in the task, which also influences task demand. Task demand phases for equivalent stable task demand periods (i.e., high demand regardless of which scenario the high demand was positioned in) were created using the same aircraft counts and number of arrival aircraft, permitting comparability between demand variation scenarios. Scenarios followed a counterbalanced presentation.

2.3   Study Condition – Amount of Automated Support

Automation was introduced into the study to different extents to create three conditions: a manual condition, an arrival manager (AM) condition, and fully automated condition. The fully automated condition will not be reported on during this paper as there was no measure for metering performance. Instead, the focus is on comparing subjective workload and controllers' metering performance in the Manual and Arrival manager (AM) conditions only.

In order to compare the effects of different levels of automation on subjective measures and performance, key ATC tasks were identified and assigned to "the automation" (actually a suite of tools) or the controller. The key tasks were conflict detection, conflict resolution, arrival metering (schedule conformance), and monitoring the automation while it was completing these tasks. Other ATC housekeeping tasks, including handoffs, frequency changes, and climb and descent clearances, were automated for all conditions and the controller had to monitor these for all conditions.

---

[2] Lining aircraft up for a runway begins many miles out from an airport as aircraft begin their descent. Aircraft begin to fly on more formalized waypoint-to-waypoint routes that "channel" them to a runway. Each set of routes is given a name, in this case "EAGUL".

The four key tasks were combined in the study conditions. The first "mostly manual" condition was close to current day operations where the participants worked all four key tasks (including monitoring the automated housekeeping tasks). In the second, mid-level decision support condition (Arrival manager or "AM"), participants were responsible for "metering" and monitoring the automation. Metering refers to the controller task of contributing to arrival traffic schedule conformance. In this case, controllers in this low-altitude en route sector are required to deliver the PHX arrival traffic to meet a schedule. The scheduler is spacing aircraft to assure well-spaced runway arrivals. The controller does not have to keep the aircraft exactly on time but has to deliver them within a plus or minus ($\pm$)30 s window across a waypoint (HOMRR) that is at the lower left of the sector. The automation was allocated the tasks of conflict detection and resolution (CD&R) and housekeeping. The algorithms that alerted and resolved strategic conflicts (looking from 3 to 12 min ahead) were based on the Automated Airspace Concept [17, 18] and the tactical CD&R automation (looking 0–3 min ahead) was based on TSAFE [19].

During the study, each participant worked with each of the automation conditions for four runs. For half of the runs they worked the Start High traffic scenario and for the other half they worked the Start Low traffic scenario. Combined, this was a 3×2 design (level of automation by traffic density), which was repeated to give a data set of twelve 90-minute runs. It was predicted that the increased amount of automation would be reflected in lower workload ratings from the participants and increased efficiency performance, measured by greater schedule conformance (more arrival aircraft crossing the meter-fix in the $\pm$30 s window).

2.4   Participants

A total of eight male retired-controllers took part in the simulation. Age ranged from 50–64 years. Participants responded to grouped age ranges and so an average age could not be calculated. Participants had worked as en-route controllers in the Oakland, California, ARTCC. Participants' years of experience as active ATCOs (excluding training) ranged from 22–31 years (M = 26.56, SD = 3.90).

2.5   Procedure

Participants were asked to work the traffic, as they would normally do, ensuring separation and metering the arriving aircraft to deliver them within a $\pm$30 s delay window across the HOMRR fix. It was emphasized that the participants could work any of the traffic at any time in any condition if they wanted. That is, for the conditions with greater amounts of automation, the controller could intervene if they did not think the automation was going to achieve the separation criteria. In addition to the primary tasks, the participants completed two other sets of tasks. Firstly, they were prompted to rate their workload and then answer a situation awareness question every three minutes for the duration of each run. Secondly, they were asked to verbalize whenever they saw a "glitch" in the software, e.g., an aircraft not behaving as directed or overcorrecting.

The study was run over five consecutive days. The first day and a half was devoted to training the participants on the study environment and procedures. After an initial briefing, six training scenarios were run with increasing levels of traffic and complexity (two 45 min training runs and four 90 min training runs). Beginning in the afternoon of the second day, participants worked 13 data collection runs (12 planned runs and one repeat). They completed workload and awareness scales during each run and questionnaires at the end of each run, as well as a post-simulation questionnaire. The last session on the fifth day was a debrief that provided an additional opportunity for participants to offer feedback. As four of the twelve runs were under the "fully automated" condition, which incorporated metering in a different fashion to the other two conditions, these four runs were removed from the data for the analysis presented below.

Data from workstation logs and controller responses were analyzed from eight runs for each participant. The results section below compares data across the levels of automation to describe the relationships between automation and performance for efficiency. The discussion explores relationships between the performance factors.

3   Results

3.1   Task Demand Variation Manipulation Check

A review of the descriptive statistics suggests that task demand did vary in the intended direction (Fig. 2). Figure 2 confirms that the number of aircraft in the controller's sector were similar between equivalent task demand periods regardless of scenario (high-low-high demand or low-high-low demand). The number of arriving aircraft was also similar.

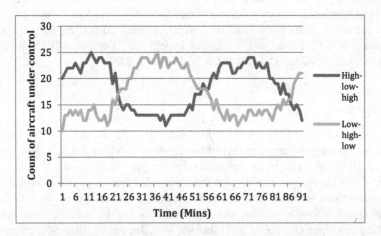

Fig. 2. Count of aircraft under control by minute for scenario 1 (high-low-high demand) and scenario 2 (low-high-low demand).

3.2   The Relationship Between Taskload and Workload

Two sets of data were chosen for comparison – participants' perceived workload, recorded through a real-time rating that indicated how controllers thought they were managing the scenario demands, and a task performance metric of schedule conformance that indicated how well the human-automation system was maintaining the delay goals for the sector.

Participants rated their workload in real time using an ISA-type rating scale and prompt. Every three minutes during a run, when the scale illuminated on the workstation banner, they rated their level of workload between 1 (very low) and 6 (very high). Figures 3 and 4 show the mean perceived workload ratings at each time point during the runs split by the type of scenario and then plotted by the two task-sets that

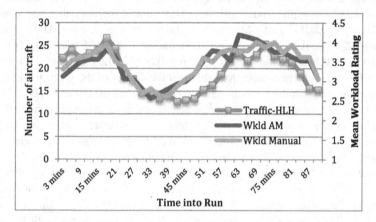

Fig. 3. Mean real time workload rating of the AM and manual conditions during the High-Low-High traffic scenario

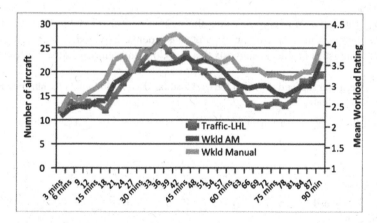

Fig. 4. Mean real time workload rating of the AM and manual conditions during the Low-High-Low traffic scenario

the controllers were given (Manual and Arrival manager). Overall, participants rated themselves as having low to moderate workload during the H-L-H scenario, with the lowest mean rating being 2.5, and the highest 4.1, out of a possible 6 (Fig. 3). Mean ratings for the Arrival manager task set were very similar to those given for the Manual task set. During the L-H-L scenario (Fig. 4), participants also rated their workload, on average, as moderate to low, with the lowest mean rating being 2.0, and the highest 3.6. Mean ratings for the two task sets were not so similar for this traffic scenario. The mean workload reported under the AM task set was consistently slightly lower than that given for the Manual task set.

As the level of traffic in the scenario was assumed to be one of the main influences on workload, the number of aircraft in each scenario (traffic count) is also plotted in Figs. 3 and 4. The correspondence between workload ratings and traffic count is very high (please note the two y-axes in the figures). Significant, positive relationships were found between the traffic count and workload ratings for both the AM condition ($r = 0.71$, $p < 0.001$) and Manual condition ($r = 0.79$, $p < 0.001$) in the High-Low-High demand scenario and workload and the AM condition ($r = 0.85$, $p < 0.001$) and Manual condition ($r = 0.81$, $p < 0.001$) in the Low-High-Low demand scenario. One point of interest is that, although the curves of the mean workload and traffic lines are very similar for both traffic scenarios when the traffic is increasing to a "High" phase, the mean workload reported begins to rise slightly before the traffic (see 39–63 min on Fig. 3 and 15–33 min on Fig. 4). Conversely, when the traffic is decreasing to a "Low" phase, the mean workload reported begins to decline slightly after the traffic (see 72–90 min on Fig. 3 and 42–69 min on Fig. 4). To further investigate any differences between the task demand and automation conditions on reported workload, a one-way repeated measures analysis of variance (ANOVA) was conducted for each scenario. The first reported findings [12] for the manual condition are repeated below, but did not extend the analysis to comparison with the arrival manager (AM) condition. Therefore the following analysis extends previous findings.

3.2.1 The Relationship Between Taskload and Workload in the AM Condition

Workload ratings were averaged across the 20 min periods of stable task demand to facilitate comparison between the separate task demand periods. A review of the descriptive statistics (Table 1) suggests that workload in both demand scenarios varied

Table 1. Mean and standard deviation for workload (as rated by ISA) in both transition phases for the AM condition.

Workload (ISA)	Task demand period 1 (0–20 min)		Task demand period 2 (31–50 min)		Task demand period 3 (61–80 min)	
	M	SD	M	SD	M	SD
Scenario 1 workload (High-low-high)	3.48	0.82	2.85	0.77	3.98	0.76
Scenario 2 workload (Low-high-low)	2.59	0.62	3.60	0.69	3.01	0.78

as expected with task demand. In the high-low-high demand scenario (scenario 1) workload appears to be rated slightly higher in the third task demand period (high demand) compared to the first task demand period (high demand). In the low-high-low demand scenario (scenario 2), workload was rated highest in the high demand phase. However, on average, participants perceived workload to increase in the second low demand period compared to the first. Comparing across low demand periods between conditions, workload is rated similarly in the first period of scenario 2 and the middle period of scenario 1. However, the low demand period in the third period of scenario 2 is rated as higher workload than either of the other low demand periods.

To further examine the changes in perceived workload, a one-way repeated measures analysis of variance (ANOVA) was conducted for each scenario [5]. In the high-low-high demand AM condition, Mauchly's test indicated that the assumption of sphericity had been violated ($X^2(2) = 7.08$, $p < 0.05$); therefore degrees of freedom were corrected using Greenhouse-Geisser estimates of sphericity ($E = 0.59$). The results show that there was a significant main effect of task demand period on self-reported workload $F(1.18,8.27) = 28.79$, $p < 0.001$. Pairwise comparisons revealed that workload was significantly lower in task demand period 2 (low demand) than high task demand period one ($p < 0.005$) and three ($p < 0.001$). Workload was not rated as being significantly different between high demand period 1 and high demand period 3($p = 0.2$). In scenario 2 (low-high-low demand) a significant main effect of task demand period was found on self-reported workload ($F(2,14) = 11.18$, $p < 0.005$). Pairwise comparisons revealed that workload was rated significantly higher in the high demand period than the first low demand period ($p < 0.05$) and was not significantly higher than the final low demand period ($p = 0.13$). Workload ratings in the second low demand period were not significantly higher than the first low demand period ($p = 0.061$).

3.2.2 The Relationship Between Taskload and Workload in the Manual Condition

Workload ratings were again averaged across the 20 min periods of stable task demand (Table 2). A similar pattern of workload between demand scenarios was seen in the manual condition and the metering condition. A review of the descriptive statistics (Table 2) suggests that workload in both scenarios varied as expected with task demand. In scenario 1 (high-low-high demand) workload appears to be rated slightly higher in the third task demand period (high demand) compared to the first task demand period (high demand). In scenario 2 (low-high-low demand), workload was rated highest in the high demand, here the second task demand phase. However, on average, participants rated perceived workload to increase in the third task demand period (low demand) compared to the first low demand period. Comparing between scenario 1 and 2, the high demand period is perceived to generate the most workload for participants in the low-high-low demand scenario, although the high demand periods were objectively equivalent between scenarios. Comparing across low demand periods between conditions, workload is rated similarly in the first period of scenario 2 and the middle period of scenario 1. However, the low demand period in the third period of scenario 2 is rated as higher workload than either of the other low demand periods.

Table 2. Mean and standard deviation for workload (as rated by ISA) in both demand transition scenarios for the manual condition.

Workload (ISA)	Task demand period 1 (0–20 min)		Task demand period 2 (31–50 min)		Task demand period 3 (61–80 min)	
	M	SD	M	SD	M	SD
Scenario 1 workload (High-low-high)	3.67	0.77	2.87	0.61	3.85	0.62
Scenario 2 workload (Low-high-low)	2.78	0.64	4.06	0.71	3.33	0.61

A repeated measures ANOVA was applied to each scenario, to explore differences within-scenarios. In relation to scenario 1 (high-low-high demand) a significant effect of task demand period was found on self-reported workload $(F(2,14) = 44.23, p < 0.001)$. Pairwise comparisons revealed that workload was significantly lower in task demand period 2 (low demand) than high task demand period one $(p < 0.005)$ and three $(p < 0.001)$. Workload was not rated as being significantly different between high demand period 1 and high demand period 3 $(p = 0.68)$. In scenario 2 (low-high-low demand) a significant main effect of task demand period was found on self-reported workload $(F(2,14) = 32.72, p < 0.001)$. Pairwise comparisons revealed that workload was rated significantly higher in the high demand period than the first low demand period $(p < 0.001)$ and second low demand period $(p < 0.005)$. It was also identified that the workload ratings in the second low demand period were significantly higher than the first low demand period $(p < 0.05)$.

3.2.3   Workload Across Demand Scenarios and Automation Conditions

Figure 5 presents a comparison of the mean workloads for the task demand periods for the task demand transition direction variable (low-high-low and high-low-high) and the

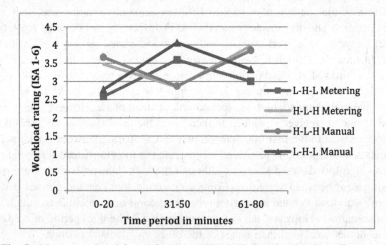

Fig. 5. Mean metering delay under two taskloads during the H-L-H traffic scenario

automation variable (AM or manual). It is interesting to note that based on the descriptive statistics, workload ratings in the low-high-low demand scenario overall are lower for the AM condition than the manual condition. The same pattern is not seen for the high-low-high scenario. In addition, the high workload period in the low-high-low manual condition is rated higher than either of the high workload periods in the metering and manual conditions for the high-low-high scenario.

3.3 The Relationship Between Taskload and Task Performance

The metering task involved reducing the scheduled delay on the arrival aircraft to meet the delay goal of being within ±30 s of the scheduled time at the HOMRR waypoint. The controller was required to do the metering with only the help of a trial planning function – a tool that marked on the sector display predicted route of the aircraft. The meter-fix accuracy metric describes an aircraft's successful delivery at HOMRR. Aircraft crossing the meter-fix were counted as successful if the aircraft arrived within ±30 s and crossed within the 3 nmi gate around HOMRR.

Overall, 90.4% of the aircraft were successfully delivered across the HOMRR meter-point. Approximately the same percentage of flights was successfully delivered under the two task-sets (91.0% and 90.4%). On average (when the mean was calculated with absolute values), aircraft in the Manual condition were delivered with 11.9 s of delay and they had 10.7 s of delay in the Arrival manager condition. The mean delay over time per task-set was calculated and is charted in Figs. 6 and 7. The pattern of delay for both task sets during the H-L-H scenario (Fig. 6) is similar, with larger mean delays occurring when the traffic is High, and lower mean delays during the Low traffic in the middle of the runs. While there is a good amount of variation in the delay over the meter fix, the goal for the arrivals was to be within ±30 s, and at most of the time-points the average delay across the aircraft within that time bin is less than 30 s. It should be noted that individual aircraft within that time bin may not have been delivered successfully (under 30 s) but that the group average is successful. For the AM task set, there was only

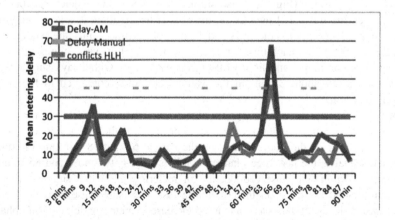

Fig. 6. Mean metering performance under two taskloads during the H-L-H traffic scenario

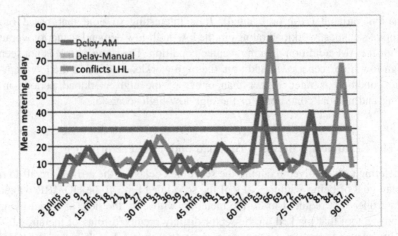

Fig. 7. Mean metering performance under two taskloads during the L-H-L traffic scenario

one time point when mean delay was above 30 s; this occurred at 66 min into the run when the traffic load was High. For the Manual task set, there were two time points when mean delay was above 30 s, again traffic load was High – at 12 min and 66 min into the run. Since both sets of data show a marked increase in metering delay at the beginning of phase 3 (66 min) and in the middle of phase 1 (12 min), it is possible that the controllers were more focused on other tasks at those times and this caused their metering efficiency to reduce. In the H-L-H scenario, there were two planned conflicts between 10 and 14 min into the scenario, and the seventh planned conflict was at 62 min. It is suggested that, even when CD&R was allocated to the automation in the AM condition, the participants traded-off fine-tuning aircraft in their metering task to ensure these conflicts did not occur. However, an important difference between the Manual and AM delay is that the standard deviation of delay for phase 3 (61 to 90 min) under the Manual task set is much larger (at 21.44 s) than for the other three High phases represented in Fig. 7 (which are 13.11, 13.53 and 13.73 s respectively). The pattern of delay for both task sets during the L-H-L traffic (Fig. 7) is also similar, with larger mean delays occurring in phase 3, when the traffic is Low. As for the H-L-H traffic, there is a good amount of variation in the delay over the meter fix and, at most of the time-points, the average delay across the aircraft within each time bin is less than 30 s. However, although the delay patterns are similar, they seem slightly offset from each other, with delay rising or falling slightly sooner (by about 3 min) in the Manual condition compared to the Arrival manager condition.

For both task sets, there are only two time points when mean delay is above 30 s; for the AM task set they are at 66 and 87 min into the run when the traffic load is Low or increasing; and, for the Manual task set, they are at 63 and 78 min into the run. In this L-H-L scenario, the last three planned conflicts were between 60 and 85 min into the scenario. Again, the observed decline in metering efficiency suggests that the participants traded accuracy on their metering task to ensure these conflicts did not occur. Since both sets of data show a marked increase in metering delay during phase 3 (61–90 min), the standard deviation of delay for this phase were compared. Under the

Manual task set, the standard deviation of the delay in phase 3 is much larger (at 16.43 s) than for the other three Low phases represented in Fig. 7 (which are 10.15, 9.55 and 9.43 s respectively).

3.4   The Relationship Between Task Performance and Workload

The main inquiry of this analysis was to explore the relationship between taskload, performance efficiency, and how these are related to perceived workload. The data that is shown in Figs. 3, 4, 5, 6 and 7 above was combined to compare workload with task performance (represented by metering delay) under each traffic scenario and automation set. Table 3 compares the mean metering delay and mean workload during the H-L-H traffic. For both the AM and Manual conditions, the delay was correlated with workload across the whole scenario and then by the three phases of traffic load. There is a significant correlation of the Arrival manager task set workload with delay ($p < .01$), which is above 0.5 overall and across each phase of traffic – broadly, as workload ratings rise and fall metering delay also rises and falls. The correlation between workload and delay in the Manual task set is lower, only 0.39 overall, but still significant ($p < .05$). While the correlations for phase 1 and 2 are close to the overall correlation, there is a noticeable reduction in the correlation during phase 3, down to 0.12 between workload and delay (Table 3).

Table 3. Correlation of workload with delay under H-L-H traffic load (**$p < .01$; *$p < .05$)

	Overall correlation	Phase 1 (High traffic)	Phase 2 (Low traffic)	Phase 3 (High traffic)
Metering task set	0.58**	0.53	0.51	0.58
Manual task set	0.39*	0.49	0.35	0.12

This process of correlation was completed for each task set under L-H-L traffic load (Table 4). The unexpected finding is that the correlations between workload with delay for both task sets are very low, the overall correlations are slightly negative for both task sets. Despite the correlations being so low, a slight trend similar to that in the H-L-H traffic load can be seen – the relationship between delay and workload reduces over the phases of the scenario. For both task sets, phase 3 shows the least correlation between workload and delay, which for the L-H-L traffic is negative.

Table 4. Correlation of workload with delay under L-H-L traffic load

	Overall correlation	Phase 1 (High traffic)	Phase 2 (Low traffic)	Phase 3 (High traffic)
Metering task set	−0.10	0.09	0.10	−0.13
Manual task set	−0.09	0.15	−0.26	−0.26

4 Discussion

A within-measures design was used to investigate task demand variation and automation levels on subjective workload and efficiency performance, measured by delay accuracy of arrival aircraft. The direction of the task demand transition was manipulated to create two scenarios: H-L-H and L-H-L. Results showed that task demand varied as intended. Descriptive statistics confirmed that equivalent demand periods, regardless of scenario or position, were composed very similarly in terms of controlled aircraft count and arrival aircraft count. This suggests that changes in the covariates or dependent variable are unlikely to be attributed to demand differences between the created scenarios.

4.1 The Relationship Between Taskload and Workload

In general, task demand and workload had high covariance for both H-L-H and L-H-L scenarios, across automation conditions. However, a key finding of interest is that perception of workload appears to differ depending on the demand period preceding the current ratings, in line with previous findings [5], and the level of automation in the control task. In the H-L-H condition, workload in the manual condition was reported on average a little higher than the Arrival manager condition, although this trend is reversed in the second high taskload period. This is an interesting data trend. As discussed in [14], more manual tasks can increase situation awareness (SA) for the operator. It may be possible that during the ramp up transition, the increased automation resulted in controllers requiring more cognitive effort to build the picture with the increasing traffic, creating a perception of higher workload.

In the L-H-L scenario there is still a high correlation between taskload and workload overall, but some differences can be observed compared to the H-L-H scenario. In the manual L-H-L condition, as expected, workload starts low with an average rating of around 2.5. This is similar to the workload ratings for the low taskload period in the H-L-H manual condition. However, when transitioning into the high workload period, the workload ratings appear to ramp up faster than in the comparable period of the H-L-H scenario. In addition, workload is rated higher than in either of the two high taskload periods in the H-L-H scenario, suggesting that there is a difference in perceived workload in the ramp up phases of the L-H-L scenario compared to the ramp up phase of the H-L-H scenario. As the traffic counts were the same in all high taskload periods for all scenarios, this is likely not due to objective differences in the traffic scenario. Workload is also perceived to be significantly greater in the second low demand period than the first, potentially suggesting that workload is perceived to be greater after the high demand period. This increased workload would not be the result of working to resolve delays from the previous period, as any remaining delays were absorbed in the 10-minute transition period between the stable demand periods. These findings indicate that the workload appears to be perceived differently depending on what precedes the time of rating. More specifically, results suggest that in this ATC task, a demand transition pattern of low-high-low demand may result in operators perceiving subsequent high and low demand periods after the initial low demand period as generating a greater workload than equivalent demand periods in a high-low-high demand transition pattern.

As expected, when comparing the workload ratings in the manual and Arrival manager conditions, reported workload appears to be lower in the AM condition than the manual condition in the L-H-L scenario. Interestingly and unexpectedly, this finding was not replicated in the H-L-H scenario, where manual and AM conditions appear to have similar workload ratings. In addition, the workload ratings in the high taskload period of the L-H-L AM condition were lower than the high taskload periods of the H-L-H scenario. This suggests that in the L-H-L condition, the application of automation, and the associated removal of specific controller tasks, provided support to the controller, and possibly increased available resources [5]. This results in lower workload ratings. As the same effect of the metering task was not observed in the H-L-H scenario, it may be that the L-H-L scenario created higher demand on the controller overall, and as such the removal of tasks in the AM condition had a noticeable effect on reported workload. If controllers did not feel that same demand in the H-L-H scenario, then the AM condition may not have had a notable influence on subjective workload.

4.2   Taskload and Task Performance

Task performance was assessed by the accuracy attained in metering arriving aircraft. Overall performance was good, with most aircraft arriving within the task criterion (30 s of the metered time). As expected, accuracy seems to co-vary with taskload, with higher delay seen in High workload times, in the H-L-H condition. This relationship is less obvious in the L-H-L condition however, with accuracy unexpectedly decreasing in the last low taskload period, possibly due to fatigue or time spent on task effects. Another interesting finding is that, in general, the AM and manual conditions do not appear to be too different in terms of metering, although there appears to be more variation between the conditions in the L-H-L scenario. This may suggest that the influence of the Arrival manager condition on workload that was found in the L-H-L scenario did not extend to improve performance. Finally, the standard deviations of delay in phase 3 are larger than the equivalent phase 1 period, for both conditions and scenarios. Performance variability therefore appears to have increased across task demand period. Increases in performance variability over time have been documented previously, although for vigilance-based performance [10]. The increase in performance variability may suggest that controllers have to work harder to maintain efficiency performance, with this becoming harder to maintain.

4.3   Workload, Automation Level and Performance

Analysis of the correlations between workload and arrival aircraft metering provides further detail about the relationship between workload and performance under different automation levels and taskload variation scenarios. In the H-L-H condition, a significant correlation was found between workload and metering; as workload ratings rise and fall metering delay also rises and falls. The correlation between workload and delay in the Manual task set was lower, although still significant. There is a noticeable reduction in this correlation during phase 3. The lower correlation is not unexpected, as in the Manual condition, participants had to work on conflict detection and resolution tasks in addition to the metering task. Controllers are not passive in their environment. With a higher experienced workload, controllers may have applied strategies to ensure maintenance of performance even under a high workload [7]. This is not seen in the Arrival manager conditions, however. The added automation may have resulted in less strategic options for maintaining performance. The differential application of strategy and how the controller elected to control and manage the traffic could contribute to the reduced covariance.

An unexpected finding was the low correlation between performance and workload for both manual and AM conditions in the L-H-L scenario. In fact, there appears to be hardly any relationship at all. The small covariance that is observed is often negative, with delay increasing with low workload and decreasing in association with high reported workload. There is therefore a clear effect of workload transition direction on the association between workload and performance. In the H-L-H scenario, the relationship between workload and performance is more predictable, although less so in the manual condition. This is potentially due to application of individual control strategies, or perhaps more choice in the control approach. In the L-H-L scenario, the transitions appear to influence the workload-performance relationship.

Although there is a lack of common agreement regarding the mechanisms by which task demand transitions may impact covariate factors [20], this collection of workload findings may be interpreted in the context of Limited Resource theory [5] and arousal theories. Potentially, in H-L-H scenario, the low demand period may have enabled controllers to use this time to recover resources and prepare for the next high task demand period. As has been previously documented in [6] this is an active control strategy that controllers use during low demand periods, when it is considered safe to do so. Arousal theories may provide some insight into why this effect may not be seen in the L-H-L demand transition pattern. Arousal theories suggest that low workload (or underload) may lead to lower arousal, which may limit attentional resources and create boredom and lack of motivation. If a human operator started a task from this point, it may be that the following demand periods are perceived to be more demanding. By the final low demand period, the operator may find it difficult to pay attention. Attentional resources theories suggest, however, that if preceded by a higher demand, lower demand periods can be utilized to replenish attentional resources, not necessarily reducing arousal to a level that would create negative effects. The application of these theories therefore potentially account for the disparate findings between the different task demand transition patterns. If this effect occurred in the L-H-L scenario but not the H-L-H scenario, this also may explain why the AM condition had noticeably lower workload rating in the L-H-L scenario but not the H-L-H scenario.

The result of improved metering may also be the result of controllers applying strategies to support performance across the demand periods.[7]. Although controller strategies were not a direct focus of this research, this finding highlights an important issue for future research considerations. Although this measure of performance (arrival metering) indicates that performance was maintained in the L-H-L scenario, controllers also reported greater perception of workload. It is therefore possible that controllers may have experienced having to work harder to maintain performance, even though this was not observable in the performance measure itself. This result emphasizes that in order to detect, and prevent, performance declines, further research should focus on measures that are sensitive to the operators' experience, and that can be monitored and utilized to detect potential performance decline prior to a performance related incident.

It is acknowledged that these results are provisional, and need to be interpreted within context. For example, in an air traffic environment, it is easier for the controller to build a picture of the traffic by gradually increasing demand levels alongside the increasing traffic, rather than beginning a session in the middle of a high demand period [6]. However, findings do have important implications for the prediction of controller performance in an operational environment. Findings suggest that high and low demand periods can affect controller perception of covariate factors such as workload differentially depending on what has happened prior to the current situation. Thus, supervisors may need to pay close attention to the number and direction of transitions that a controller experiences per session to most effectively support controller performance.

Future research should further explore the relationship between previous task demands and the relationship on present controller experience, including the exploration of sudden, and unexpected, transitions. Better predictions are needed to identify and prevent potential performance declines and associated performance-related incidents. Such predictions may be particularly relevant for adaptive automation technologies that support operator performance.

5   Conclusion

The effect of task demand transitions on workload, and one efficiency related performance measure, was investigated within the context of an air traffic control task. Initial findings suggest that task demand variations affected participants' perceptions of workload, although the effect appeared to be influenced by the direction of the previous demand periods. This was also influenced by the level of automation available to the controller, with the controller experiencing less workload when controlling with automation in an Arrival manager condition in the L-H-L scenario. Performance appeared to vary to some extent with taskload, in the direction expected, although findings were again disparate between scenarios. The most interesting findings suggest that the relationship between workload and performance was affected both by level of automation available to the controller, and direction of taskload. This finding has potential implications for the assessment of new automation and applying increased levels of automation in the control room. Previous research has infrequently considered transitions of task demand in an applied environment. Findings are consistent with the description of workload history effects [8], and suggest that equivalent task demand periods can elicit different experiences for a human operator depending on what precedes the time of rating. Attentional resource and arousal theories appear to support interpretation of the results. Further research is required to enhance understanding of demand transition and history effects. Practical applications include guidance for operations room supervisors, and implications for predictions of performance in high and low demand periods, with important implications for identifying and preventing potential performance declines and associated performance-related incidents.

References

1. Di Nocera, F., Fabrozo, R., Terenzi, M., Ferlazzo, F.: Procedural errors in air traffic control: effects of traffic density, expertise, and automation. Aviat. Space Envir. Md. **77**, 639–643 (2006)
2. Mogford, R., Guttman, J., Morrow, S., Kopardekar, P.: The Complexity Construct in Air Traffic Control: A Review and Synthesis of the Literature, DOT/FAA/CT-TN95/22. FAA, Washington (1995)
3. Loft, S., Sanderson, P., Neal, A., Mooij, M.: Predicting mental workload in en route air traffic control: critical review and broader implications. Hum. Factors **49**(3), 376–399 (2007)
4. Djokic, J., Lorenz, B., Fricke, H.: Air traffic control complexity as workload driver. Transp. Res. C-Emerg. **18**, 930–936 (2010)
5. Wickens, C.D.: Engineering Psychology and Human Performance. Harper Collins, New York (1992)
6. Edwards, T., Sharples, S., Kirwan, B., Wilson, J.R.: Identifying markers of performance decline in air traffic controllers. In: Di Bucchianico, G., Vallicelli, A., Stanton, N.A., Landry, S.J. (eds.) Human Factors in Transportation: Social and Technological Evolution Across Maritime, Road, Rail, and Aviation Domains (in press)
7. Sperandio, J.C.: Variation of operator's strategies and regulating effects on workload. Ergonomics **14**, 571–577 (1971)
8. Cox-Fuenzalida, L.E.: Effect of workload history on task performance. Hum. Factors **49**, 277–291 (2007)
9. Hancock, P.A., Williams, G., Manning, C.M.: Influence of task demand characteristics on workload and performance. Int. J. Aviat. Psychol. **5**, 63–86 (1995)
10. Helton, W.S., Shaw, T., Warm, J.S., Matthews, G., Hancock, P.: Effects of warned and unwarned demand transitions on vigilance performance and stress. Anxiety Stress Coping **21**, 173–184 (2008)
11. Moroney, B.W., Warm, J.S., Dember, W.N.: Effects of demand transitions on vigilance performance and perceived workload. In: Proceedings of the Human Factors and Ergonomics Society Annual Meeting, vol. 39, pp. 1375–1379. SAGE Publications (1995, October)
12. Edwards, T., Gabets, C., Mercer, J., Bienert, N.: Task demand variation in air traffic control: implications for workload, fatigue, and performance. In: Stanton, N., Landry, S., Di Bucchianico, G., Vallicelli, A. (eds.) Advances in Human Aspects of Transportation. Advances in Intelligent Systems and Computing, vol. 484. Springer, Cham (2017)
13. Homola, J., Morey, S., Cabrall, C., Martin, L., Mercer, J., Prevot, T.: Analysis of interactive conflict resolution tool usage in a mixed-equipage environment. In: AIAA Guidance, Navigation and Communications Conference, Boston, MA (2013)
14. Zeghal, K., Hoffman, E.: Delegation of separation assurance to aircraft: towards a framework for analysing the different concepts and underlying principles. In: ICAS 23rd Congress, Harrogate, UK (2000)
15. Galster, S.M., Duley, J.A., Masalonis, A.J., Parasuraman, R.: Air traffic controller performance and workload under mature free flight: conflict detection and resolution of aircraft self-separation. Int. J. Aviat. Psychol. **11**, 71–93 (2001)

16. Tenney, Y.J., Spector, S.L.: Comparisons of HBR models with human-in-the-loop performance in a simplified air traffic control simulation with and without HLA protocols: task simulation, human data and results. In: Proceedings of the 10th Conference on Computer Generated Forces and Behaviour Representation, Norfolk, VA (2001)
17. Erzberger, H.: The automated airspace concept. In: 4th USA/Europe Air Traffic Management R&D Seminar, Santa Fe, NM, December 3–7 (2001)
18. Farley, T., Erzberger, H.: Fast-time simulation evaluation of a conflict resolution algorithm under high air traffic demand. In: 7th USA/Europe Air Traffic Management R&D Seminar, Barcelona, Spain, 2–5, July (2007)
19. Paielli, R., Erzberger, H.: Tactical conflict alerting aid for air traffic controllers. AIAA J. Guidance Control Dyn. **32**(1), 184–193 (2009)
20. Wickens, C.D., Mabor, A.S., McGee, J.P.: Flight to the Future: Human Factors in Air Traffic Control. National Academy Press, Washington (1997)

Applications

The WASCAL-Tool: Prediction of Staffing for Train Dispatching as Part of the Design Process of Track Yards

Melcher Zeilstra[✉], Alfred van Wincoop, and Jouke Rypkema

INTERGO Human Factors and Ergonomics,
Pausdam 2, 3512 Utrecht, HN, The Netherlands
zeilstra@intergo.nl

Abstract. The Dutch infrastructure manager builds new track yards or enlarges existing track yards to facilitate service and maintenance of new rolling stock to be commissioned next few years. One of the design issues is the choice for a certain level of automation. A high level of automation requires higher investment in technology, but will result in lower mental workload of a train dispatcher and therefore require lower staffing and lower operational costs for the train dispatching process; a low level of automation result in higher mental workload of train dispatchers and has higher operational costs for train dispatching due to higher staffing. Or this design issue the WASCAL-tool was developed. The tool calculates staffing for train dispatching for all levels of automation, currently in operation in the Netherlands. The tool is validated based on observations of train service on several track yards. The output of the tool in terms of staffing is reliable enough for the choices to be made during the design process of a new track yard.

Keywords: Staffing · Workload · Train dispatching · Prediction · Design · Track yards · Level of automation

1 Introduction

In the period 2017 to 2022 the Dutch Railways (NederlandseSpoorwegen, NS) commission new rolling stock in train service. This new rolling stock is meant for extra or new train services on current and new trajectories in the Netherlands. The new rolling stock has to be serviced, cleaned and maintained on track yards. The currently available track yards do not have the capacity to facilitate these processes. Therefore ProRail, the Dutch infrastructure manager, must build new track yards or enlarge existing track yards. One of the design issues for building or enlarging a track yard is the choice of a certain level of automation. A high level of automation with signals and train detection enables computerized route setting, which lowers mental workload of train dispatchers. A lower mental workload will result in a lower level of staffing for train dispatchers. A low level of train automation (no signals, no train detection) requires procedural train dispatching with communication between dispatcher and train driver for use of routes along the yard. This will raise mental workload and therefore a higher level of staffing for train dispatchers is required. So a high level of automation requires higher

© Springer International Publishing AG 2017
L. Longo and M.C. Leva (Eds.): H-WORKLOAD 2017, CCIS 726, pp. 143–160, 2017.
DOI: 10.1007/978-3-319-61061-0_9

investment in technology, but has lower operational costs for the train dispatching process, a low level of automation is cheaper from the point of view of investments in technology, but has higher operational costs for train dispatching. For the design issue mentioned, the WASCAL-tool (Workload And Staffing Calculation tool) was developed. This tool calculates staffing for train dispatching, based on the levels of automation, and is currently in operation in the Netherlands.

2 Processes and Characteristics of a Track Yard in the Netherlands

In general, staff involved in the processes of logistics (normal line) and planning (dashed line) on a track yard can be represented as shown in Fig. 1.

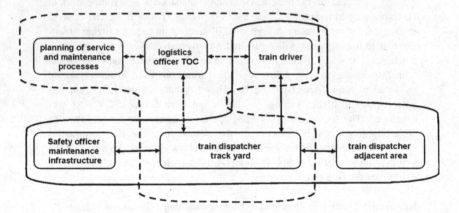

Fig. 1. Staff involved in processes for logistics and planning on a track yard in the Netherlands

Several service and maintenance processes can take place on a track yard. Currently these processes are:

- Servicing of rolling stock
- Maintenance of rolling stock (limited)
- Cleaning of the interior of rolling stock
- Cleaning of the exterior of rolling stock
- Combining or dividing carriages
- Parking of carriages

Planning of routes and setting of routes is highly dependent on the level of train automation, characteristics of the infrastructure, and computerized assistance of the train dispatcher. The several combinations of these elements, currently in operation in the Netherlands, are shown in Table 1. As shown in Table 1, train dispatchers are involved in different ways in the processes within a track yard. The higher the level of automation for route setting and planning, the fewer activities the train dispatcher performs. In order to incorporate activities of the train dispatcher in the desired tool for calculation of staffing for train dispatching, a task analysis is performed. Workload is calculated based on task performance, and staffing is calculated based on workload calculations.

Table 1. Characteristics of track yards in the Netherlands.

Level of automation	Infrastructure	Route setting/logistics	Planning
High level	Signals, train detection, automated control of switches	Computer-assisted route setting	Computer assisted planning of all routes
Medium level	Train detection, computerized control of switches by train dispatcher	Verbal route setting, computer assistance for judgment of safety of routes based on train detection	Computer assisted planning of routes into and out of the yard, manual planning of routes on the yard
Low level	Manual control of switches by train driver	Verbal route setting, computer assistance for judgment of safety of routes based on input of train dispatcher	Computerized planning of routes into and out of the yard, manual planning of routes on the yard

3   Staffing and Mental Workload

Staffing is, in a way, related to mental workload. When demands imposed by a task increase and level of automation and working organization cannot be changed, more staffing is needed to assure the required task performance with an acceptable workload for the operator. The character of the job of train-dispatching for a track yard is such that for determining acceptable workload, attention should be paid to longer-lasting workload and to peak load. When discussing workload, there are many terms and dimensions that can reflect workload. So, the first choice to be made is which dimension of workload should be assessed when calculating or predicting staffing.

Model of Mental Workload
In literature there are several terms and concepts regarding mental workload. Words like working pressure, workload, task load, mental strain, stress etc. are used [10] and there seems to be no clear definitions. Also, in international standards there are differences in terms regarding workload. To avoid the unintelligibility mentioned above, a model of the concept of workload based on ISO 10075 [4] is being used [19]. Figure 2 and Table 2 illustrate this model. The model shown is a heuristic model, suitable to explain the concept of workload to lay persons, but it is also connected to scientific views on the multidimensional construct of mental workload and determined by characteristics of the tasks (e.g. demands, performance), the operator (e.g. skill, attention) and, to a degree, the environmental context in which the performance occurs [10, 14].

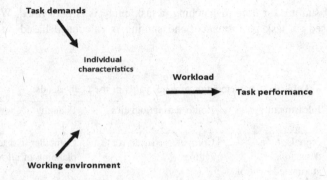

Fig. 2. Heuristic model of workload (based on ISO 10075 [4] and [19]).

Table 2. Elements of workload (based on ISO 10075, [4]).

Task demands	Individual characteristics (subjective/individual)	Working environment (objective)
Examples	*Examples*	*Examples*
- Amount of work	- Competencies	- Possibilities for regulation of task fulfilment
- Variation in complexity	- Stress resistance	
- Quality	- Coping	- Management support
- Speed of task performance	- Commitment	- Social pressure
	- Private circumstances	- Procedures/intelligibility
- ..	- Individual differences	- Management style
- ..	- ..	- Salary
- ..	- ..Etc.	- Support tools like MMI/GUI
- ..Etc.		- Working environment/workplace
		-..Etc.

The required tool should be part of the design process for a track yard, especially regarding the choice for a certain level of automation. The level of automation is part of the working environment within the model of mental workload, as presented in Table 2. Because of task allocation, (i.e. which tasks are performed by automation and which tasks are performed by humans) the choice of a certain level of automation directly impacts the task demands within a job (e.g. number of activities, complexity, time-occupancy etc.). The levels of automation to be chosen are all currently in operation in The Netherlands and all train dispatchers are skilled to perform the train dispatching process using the related systems. For the purpose of the tool individual characteristics, as representation of the characteristics of the operator, remain constant. Therefore, it was chosen to choose task demands as the basis for the tool to be developed. This choice also meets insights about objective task demands as input parameters for determination of acceptable workload [10].

The Task Weighing [TM] Tool for Calculation of Task Demands

For the calculation of task demands related to train dispatching in the Netherlands, the tool Task Weighing™ [1, 19]) was developed earlier. Development of this tool took place in close cooperation with train dispatchers. Task Weighing™ itself is a calculating formula, based on elements and descriptors of the job of train dispatching [19]. Task Weighing™ knows 5 base task components, which are described in base elements and descriptors:

1. Monitoring of trains;
2. Control by preparation of routes;
3. Communication by short messages;
4. Communication by consultation;
5. Adjustment of the plan.

An example of the base task component 'Communication by short messages' is a short telephone call with simple communication. For instance, a telephone call with a more complex request consisting of several information elements is an example of the base component 'Communication by consultation'. In Task Weighing™ judgement of information (puzzling and checking) is a separate base element, with distinction to judgment of timing of a required route and safety related judgements. Also, there are several base elements regarding control of the current computerized train dispatching systems with its current MMI characteristics. The mental workload related to the base elements and descriptors of Task Weighing™ are weighed by comparison of executing an activity that comes together with that certain element or descriptor [1, 19].

Standard for Staffing Based on Threshold Values for Task Demands

A calculated number of workload points has no meaning if there is not a threshold for acceptable workload. During the development process of Task Weighing™ these thresholds are formulated together with train dispatchers in a participative way. Table 3 outlines the Task Weighing™ thresholds for acceptable workload due to task demands. They represent the resources of 1 train dispatcher, comparable to the relationship between mental workload, demand for resources imposed by a task and the ability to supply the resources by the operator, as stated by Wickens [15, p. 161]. So, for example, regarding lasting workload with a duration of 4 h, in terms of Task Weighing™ a workload due to task demands of maximum 400 points per hour represents the resources of 1 train dispatcher.

In Table 3, the notice on each threshold in terms of workloads points due to task demands is related to workload. These notices are formulated with an 'average' train dispatcher performing his or her job in an 'average' working environment in mind. Of course, the actual occurring workload and performance delivered by a certain train dispatcher will depend on his or her own individual characteristics and environmental factors of the moment of task execution. It is difficult to formulate valid quantified thresholds for mental workload, which is also stated in [14], but the thresholds shown in Table 4 showed their purpose in workload assessment of train dispatchers, aimed for optimization of workload since the development of Task Weighing™.

Table 3. Task Weighing™ thresholds for acceptable workload due to task demands

Threshold in workload points due to task demands	Notice in terms of workload
Less than 150	Low workload, possible boredom
Around 250	Good workload for a shift of 8 h (average load per hour)
Between 250 and 400	Acceptable lasting workload during several hours (about 4 h). Overload possible if duration is longer than mentioned number of hours
Between 400 and 500	Acceptable peak workload during one (1) hour
Between 500 and 600	Acceptable peak workload during a maximum of one quarter of an hour (15 min)
Above 600	Overload, very high risk of human error

Table 4. Task demands of verbal authorization for a single route based on Task Weighing™

Activity	Workload points due to task demands
Interaction with the train driver	3
• Hearing telephone call (ringing)	
• Communication with train driver (request for route)	
Judgement and registration in computer system	3
• Selection of tracks	
• Judgment availability of route	
• Decision making: timing of route execution	
• Decision making (double check): safety	
Communication with train driver (authorization)	2

4   Task Analysis and Task Demand of Train Dispatching

Task analysis of train dispatching for a track yard is performed based on train dispatching regulation and manuals [3, 6–9, 13, 17, 18], as well as interviews and observations of train dispatching for several track yards.

Train Dispatching for a Track Yard in General

The first step in task analysis is performing a hierarchical task analysis (HTA, [12]) of train dispatching for a track yard. In general, the job of train dispatching consists of two elements: the setting of routes and the planning of routes. The planning of routes is more complex and more comprehensive than the setting of routes. Planning requires monitoring of the train service, updating the plan when a delay occurs, changing the plan when the original plan cannot be executed anymore, and (in the Netherlands) registering the causes of delays. Figure 3 shows results of the HTA for train dispatching for a track yard in general.

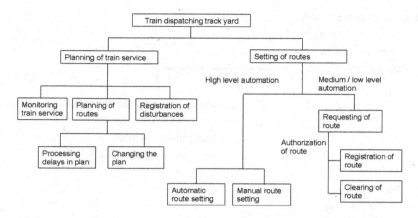

Fig. 3. Results of the HTA for train dispatching for a track yard in general.

Settings of Routes for a Track Yard

For a yard with a high level of automation, the setting of a route is relatively simple: either a route is set by an automatic route setting application, or a route is set by manual control of the computerized route setting system. When using automatic route setting, there is no mental workload accompanying the route setting itself. When using manual control of the computerized route setting system, mental workload is very limited, because the computerized route setting system performs all judgements regarding safe availability of the route on the required time.

In the Netherlands, the setting of routes for a track yard using medium or low level of automation requires at least 2 moments of communication by phone between the train dispatcher and the train driver. A train driver calls the train dispatcher and requests a certain route. The train dispatcher judges the safe availability of that route by using a computerized system (the train dispatcher puts the required route in into the computer system, the computer system shows the required route on the monitor together with other earlier requested routes which are being used at the moment, and the train dispatcher judges possible conflicts between routes) and authorizes the train driver for execution of the requested route or not. When not authorized, the train driver has to call again later to request the same route again. After having executed the authorized route completely, the train driver calls the train dispatcher to inform him about the clearance of the route.

The results of the HTA are linked to mental workload by performing a cognitive task analysis (CTA, [2]). Results of the CTA of setting routes for a track yard with medium and low level of automation are shown in Fig. 4.

Next step was 'weighing' all steps in the communication and decision making process of setting a route. For this weighing, the weighing scores of the base elements of Task Weighing[TM] were used. Table 4 shows the results of weighing task demands of all elements in the CTA for verbal authorization of a single required route.

Because the communication between the train dispatcher and the train driver regarding routes and the execution of routes takes a certain amount of time, e.g. the aspect of time-occupancy as part of task demand, the duration of the process of requiring and authorization of routes and the execution of routes was assessed. For the

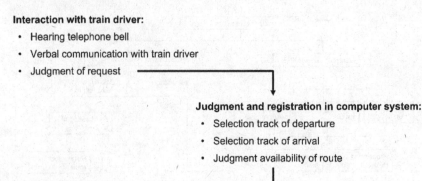

Interaction with train driver:
- Hearing telephone bell
- Verbal communication with train driver
- Judgment of request

Judgment and registration in computer system:
- Selection track of departure
- Selection track of arrival
- Judgment availability of route

- Decision making
- Double check (safety)
- Verbal authorization

Fig. 4. Results of the CTA of setting of routes, track yard medium and low level of automation.

communication process between the train dispatcher and the train driver, result was that it takes about 1.5 min per request and authorization of a route [13]. This means that a train dispatcher can handle a maximum of 3 requests for a route per 5 min. For the execution of routes, e.g. driving the train along the route, it is needless to say that the distance of a route is an important factor in process time. However, there are also differences in process time between a high and medium level of automation of the track yard, and a low level of automation. In high and medium level of automation, a computerized system controls the switches timely for the approaching train. For the low level of automation of the track yard the train driver has to control the switches manually, and this itself also takes time.

Planning of Train Service for a Track Yard

In the Netherlands the track yards with a medium and low level of automation do not have a plan for routes on the track yard, only a plan for routes into and out of the track yard. The track yards with a high level of automation also have a plan for routes on the track yard. Changes in the plan can be carried out in two different ways. One is with the aid of a computerized planning system. With the use of this system, the logistic officer of the train operating company requests a change of plan by filling in the time and track usage (route) related to the desired change for a specific train. The train dispatcher judges the desired change of plan and authorizes it when possible. After authorization,

Table 5. Task demands for judging a request for change of plan based on Task Weighing™

Activity	Workload points due to task demands
Perception of signal 'request for change of plan' and accepting request for judgment	1
Reading of request, judgment of request	4
Input result of judgement into planning system	1
Input of request for route in the execution plan	6

the train dispatcher processes the desired change of plan for execution. The other way is for the logistics officer to send a request to the train dispatcher by telephone. Table 5 shows results of the weighing of all steps in the process for a change of plan by the computerized planning system.

5   The WASCAL-Tool

5.1   Input for the Tool

The WASCAL-tool requires as input these characteristics of the track yard to be examined:

- Capacity of the track yard (number of trains, average carriages per train)
- Level of automation of the track yard
- Type of processes for service and maintenance on the track yard
- Number of routes necessary to move a train from one service or maintenance process to the other.

After inputting the characteristics, the tool makes it possible to calculate a prediction of staffing based on a concrete plan for routes during the day, or based on a frequency model for routes during the day. When applying the frequency model, a percentage of daily amount of trains per hour has to be chosen and filled into the tool. For each specific hour the tool randomly times the routes to be set and executed.

5.2   Output of the Tool

The WASCAL-tool delivers calculations for workload due to task demands over several certain periods of time. These periods are based on the thresholds mentioned in Sect. 3 Because the thresholds of Sect. 3 are related to resources of 1 train dispatcher, the results of calculation of workload due to task demands and comparison of the calculation results with the defined thresholds, an indication for staffing can be made. Figures 5 and 6 show the output of calculation of workload during a maximum duration of 4 h, as well as for a low level of automation and a high level of automation of train dispatching. The calculation of total workload during 4 h shown in Figs. 5 and 6 is the moving sum of calculated workload per 5 min over a period of 4 h prior to the moment of calculation. Both figures are based on a real life train service (track yard city of Groningen, Dec 12th, 2016, 18.00–24.00 p.m.), where the low level of automation of train dispatching represents the current situation for this specific track yard, and the high level of automation is fictional.

Figure 5 shows that in a low level of automation of train dispatching a single train dispatcher can handle the calculated workload due to task demands easily: the graph shows no exceeding of the upper straight line, representing acceptable workload during a maximum of 4 h. Figure 5 also shows that there is a reasonable chance of underload: the graph is below the lower dotted line during most of the time period, representing underload. In a high level of automation of train dispatching workload is very low with a certainty of underload (Fig. 6) and would be too low to be acceptable in real train dispatching.

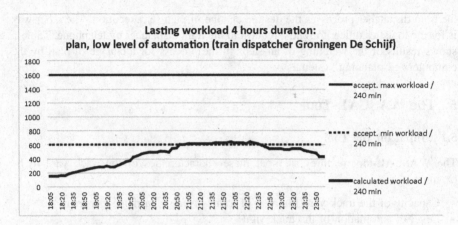

Fig. 5. Output of the WASCAL-tool: calculated lasting workload, duration of 4 h, low level of automation (track yard Groningen, Dec 12th, 2016, 18.00–24.00).

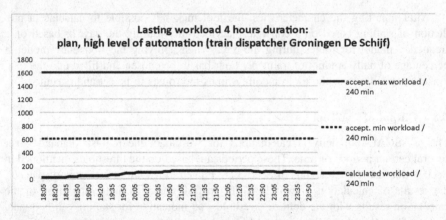

Fig. 6. Output of the WASCAL-tool: calculated lasting workload, duration of 4 h, high level of automation (track yard Groningen, Dec 12th, 2016, 18.00–24.00).

Figures 7 and 8 show for the same real life train service the output of calculation of peak load due task demands during a maximum of 15 min, again both in a low level of automation and in a high level of automation of train dispatching. The calculation of peak load due to task demands during 15 min shown in Figs. 7 and 8 is the moving sum of calculated workload per 5 min over a period of 15 min prior to the moment of calculation. Again the low level of automation of train dispatching (Fig. 7) represents the current situation for this track yard, and the high level of automation of train dispatching (Fig. 8) is fictional. Figure 7 shows that in a low level of automation of train dispatching a single train dispatcher can also handle peaks (short, maximum duration of 15 min) that occur: the graph is under the straight line the whole period. For a track yard with a high level of automation, Fig. 8, there are hardly any peaks in the workload.

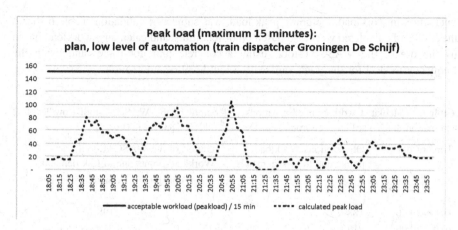

Fig. 7. Output of the WASCAL-tool: calculated peak workload, duration of 15 min, low level of automation (track yard Groningen, Dec 12th, 2016, 18.00–24.00).

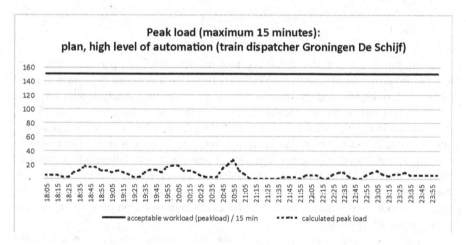

Fig. 8. Output of the WASCAL-tool: calculated peak workload, duration of 15 min, high level of automation (fictional, track yard Groningen, Dec 12th, 2016, 18.00–24.00).

5.3 Validation

The tool is validated by comparing calculation of mental workload based on observations of train dispatching in real train services with calculations applying the tool. Observations were enriched with loggings of the computer systems of the traffic control room to ensure that certain activities that were not observed, but took place, were part of the validation. Results of observations were discussed with train dispatchers during and after observation.

Validation took place for 2 track yards, during 6 h each: a track yard with a low level of automation (city of Groningen) and a track yard with a high level of automation (city of Amersfoort). Both mental workload over a period of one hour as fluctuation in workload, including peak load, was subject of validation. Table 6 shows the results of calculated workload based on observations and calculated workload based on the use of the WASCAL-tool (using a concrete plan for routes and using the frequency model) for the track yard with a low level of automation.

Table 6. Calculated workload: observations and output of the WASCAL-tool (low level of automation, track yard city of Groningen, Dec 12th, 2016, 18.00–24.00 p.m.).

Time of day	Observations Workload points due to task demands	Output of the WASCAL-tool Workload points due to task demands	
Dec 12th, 2016		Input: concrete plan	Input: frequency model
18.00–19.00	188	184	198
19.00–20.00	212	222	223
20.00–21.00	168	199	174
21.00–22.00	31	39	40
22.00–23.00	71	85	89
23.00–24.00	85	108	104

As shown in Table 6, the WASCAL-tool predicts workload per hour very well. Both the frequency model and the calculation based on a concrete plan show a good resemblance to the observations, in which the latter scores best. Analysis also delivered that the longer the period of calculation of workload and staffing (e.g. from 15 min peak load to lasting workload during a shift length of 8 h) the smaller differences between using a concrete plan and using the frequency model as input. For example, we analyzed the calculated number of workload points due to task demands per hour as output of the WASCAL-tool, and calculated workload points per hour based on observations. The output of WASCAL using a concrete plan as well as using the frequency model was strongly related to the calculation based on observations (Pearson's r, $r = 0.99$, $p < 0.01$).

Despite the good resemblance there are also differences between calculated workload based on observations and calculated workload applying the WASCAL-tool. This has several reasons:

- The monitoring of the train service is one of the task components within the job of train dispatching. The monitoring of the train service is difficult to recognize and related workload is difficult to assess when observing the train dispatcher doing his job. Therefore the monitoring of the train service is not part of the calculation of workload points based on observations, shown by the lower average number of points in Table 6. Bases for the way of monitoring of the train service are discussed with train dispatchers during observations. The WASCAL-tool uses a calculating formula for the monitoring of the train service based on results of observations and this formula incorporates the number of trains at the moment and the characteristics of routes along the track yard. For the monitoring of the train service during the observed hours of train dispatching, the WASCAL-tool calculates 5 to 20 workload points per hour more than the number of workload points calculated based on observations.

- Because of the short distances of routes in the specific track yard of the city of Groningen, there is less than 5 min between the telephone call of the train driver requesting for a route and the telephone call to confirm that the route is completely being used. For the track yard of the City of Groningen (low level of automation) the WASCAL-tool takes 10 min between both telephone calls as a basis. This means that calculated workload during observations is slightly differently distributed over the hours of observation than applying the WASCAL-tool. For the hours of validation the difference is about 10 points per hour.
- During observations there sometimes were activities with low workload, like short telephone calls or contact with a colleague train dispatcher, not related to route setting or planning of routes. These activities, weighing 5 to 10 points per hour, are not incorporated in the WASCAL-tool.

Also, the calculated number of workload points due to task demands per 5 min was analysed by comparing the output of the WASCAL-tool and the calculated workload based on observations (Pearson's r). The output of WASCAL using a concrete plan was strongly related to the calculation based on observations ($r = 0.78$, $p < 0.01$). The output of WASCAL using the frequency model was not strongly related to the calculation based on observations ($r = 0.19$, $p = 0.11$). This difference can be clarified by assessing the fluctuation in calculated workload points per 5 min.

Figure 9 shows the result of the calculation of fluctuation in workload per 5 min based on observations. For the same hour, Fig. 10 shows output of the WASCAL-tool using a concrete plan for routes. Figure 11 shows output of the WASCAL-tool using the frequency model. Fluctuation in calculated workload using a concrete plan as input for the tool (Fig. 10) most resembles fluctuation in workload during observations (Fig. 9). This good resemblance occurred for all hours which were subject of validation.

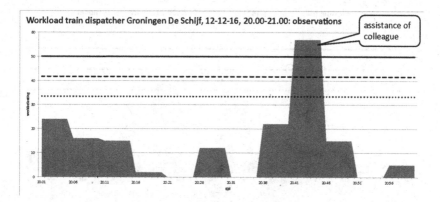

Fig. 9. Fluctuation in calculated mental workload based on observations (low level of automation, track yard Groningen, Dec 12th, 2016, 20.00–21.00).

Differences between calculated workload based on observations and calculated workload using the tool were present for several reasons. For the hour of train dispatching as shown in Figs. 9, 10 and 11 there was this following clarification: during observations, workload exceeds the straight upper line of overload (peak load) between 20.40 and 20.45. In this short period there were 3 telephone calls from a train driver related to requested routes and during observation, a colleague train dispatcher assisted the train dispatcher of track yard Groningen. The tool using a concrete plan (Fig. 10) doesn't count on assistance of a colleague, but has a different strategy for this kind of situations: when there are 3 or more telephone call in 5 min, all fourth and more request will not be authorized, and these routes will be requested later again. This explains the second peak of workload around 20.50 h shown in Fig. 10. The tool using the frequency model as input (Fig. 11) distributes requests for routes randomly on a hourly basis, so fluctuation in calculated workload will differ from observations by definition, but can be more like workload during the observations by simulating several times.

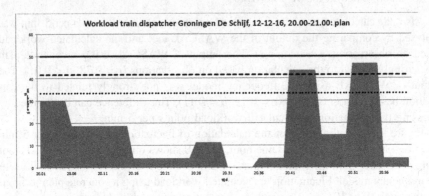

Fig. 10. Output of the WASCAL-tool with input of a plan for routes: fluctuation in workload (low level of automation, track yard Groningen, Dec 12th, 2016, 20.00–21.00).

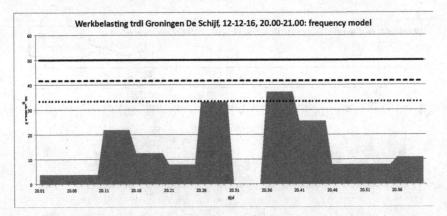

Fig. 11. Output of the WASCAL-tool with use of the frequency model for routes: fluctuation in workload (low level of automation, track yard Groningen, Dec 12th, 2016, 20.00–21.00).

The validation of the WASCAL-tool was concentrated on the calculation of workload due to task demands, because the calculation of staffing is based on application of the thresholds for workload points due to task demands per train dispatcher (see Sect. 3). But task demands are not the only relevant issue for the decision about staffing. Cooperation between train dispatchers, as seen during observations of train dispatching for the track yard of the city of Groningen, can be a solution to handle peak load, without increasing the total staffing. Also, the choice for a higher level of automation can be a way to handle peak load for the same situation, see Figs. 7 and 8 as an illustration of the possible influence of level of automation on peak load. Another way to handle peak loads is to change the planning of routes in order to avoid too many requests for a route within a limited time frame. The WASCAL-tool doesn't incorporate these issues at the moment.

6 Discussion

The study showed that the WASCAL-tool predicts workload due to task demands per hour very well. Both the calculation using the frequency model as the calculation based on a concrete plan show a good resemblance with the observations, in which the latter scores best. Differences in results of calculated workload per hour between the tool and real life observations are limited and can be clarified.

Predictions of the fluctuation in workload are less accurate. However, the calculations of the tool using a concrete plan are still fairly good, including peak load. The longer the period of calculation of workload and staffing, e.g. from 15 min peak load to lasting workload during a shift length of 8 h, the smaller the differences between output of the tool using a concrete plan as input and output of the tool using the frequency model as input. For track yards with medium and low level of automation perhaps the frequency model could predict peaks in workload in a more accurate way if time between the telephone call for request for a route and the call for clearance of a route can be configured in a dynamic way instead of a solid starting point only depending on the level of automation. Application of the WASCAL-tool using a concrete plan requires much more detail and higher accuracy in required input information than using the frequency model as input for the tool. Application of the tool using a concrete plan as input is more appropriate in the final design stage in designing a track yard when a final decision has to be made about the level of automation for the track yard and therefore about the way of train dispatching and related staffing. A reliable assessment of peak load requires the application of the WASCAL-tool using a concrete plan as input.

Because of the lower required accuracy, the use of the frequency model is more convenient early in the design process of a track yard. When using the frequency model as input for the tool, the output of 1 simulation run of the tool must not be regarded as the only result. Because of the nature of the frequency model, with execution of routes randomly distributed over an hour, several simulation runs are necessary to gain a more reliable image of workload, especially peaks in workload, and related staffing necessary for train dispatching for the track yard to be designed.

In its origin, the weighing of activities in terms of workload points and the thresholds for acceptable workload, used for calculation of staffing, date to the early nineties of the last century when a high level of automation was introduced for the process of train dispatching in the Netherlands [5]. In the middle of the first decade of this century, the weighing of activities and thresholds for acceptable workload were assessed again based on experience with the high level of automation with automatic route setting [19]. In these assessments the train dispatching process for a track yard was not taken into account. When it is considered that a higher accuracy of calculations of workload due to task demands and related staffing for the low level of automation of train dispatching is necessary, it is desirable to assess possible differences in the weighing of activities in a highly automated train dispatching process and in a train dispatching using a low level of automation. This could be done in the same partici- pative way as was performed when developing Task Weighing^{TM} for a high level of automation for train dispatching. Also, the validity of the thresholds for acceptable workload for train dispatching with high level of automation should be assessed for train dispatching with a low or medium level of automation. This could be done by parallel assessment of workload in observations using the WASCAL-tool and assess- ment of experienced workload using a validated tool for assessment of experienced workload of train dispatchers, for example a tool like the Integrated Workload Scale (IWS) [11]. In [16] it was shown that several train dispatching activities, like time spent on monitoring, communication by phone, communication with colleagues, reading and writing correlated significantly with IWS-workload scores and these activities are also distinguished in the cognitive task analysis, performed for the development of the WASCAL-tool.

The WASCAL-tool is developed as input for the decision making process regarding the level of automation for a track yard under design in conjunction with workload and staffing. But there are more choices to be made when it comes to making a final decision about staffing for train dispatching of a track yard, especially when the outcome of the tool indicates the necessity to pay special attention to underload or peak load. Choices to be made are related to:

- Cooperation between train dispatchers for the track yard and train dispatcher for the adjacent area (in the case of an unacceptable peak load).
- Expansion of the train dispatching area or combining the train dispatching process for the track yard under design with the train dispatching process for another area.
- A more robust plan for train service with a decreased chance of 'simultaneous' requests for routes within a limited time frame.
- Performance criteria for execution of train service in terms of delay or deviation from the original planned train service.
- Explication of the business case in terms of monetized consideration of investment in technology and operational costs for train dispatching.

Currently the WASCAL-tool doesn't incorporate the issues above, but can provide a basis for development of a complete decision support tool.

Acknowledgments. We thank the train dispatchers of the traffic management control room of the city of Groningen and the city of Amersfoort for their support and cooperation during the validation of the tool. We also thank all the other train dispatchers for other track yards in The Netherlands who were involved in the development of the tool.

References

1. Bruijn, D.W., de, Zeilstra, M.P.: Development of Task Weighing™, report 2937-b, version 1.0, February 2007 (Intergo, Utrecht, confidential). In Dutch: Bruijn, D.W., de, Zeilstra, M. P.: OntwikkelingTaakWeging™, rapport 2937-b, versie 1.0, februari 2007 (Intergo, Utrecht, vertrouwelijk) (2007)
2. Chipman, S.F., Schraagen, J.M., Shalin, V.L.: Introduction to cognitive task analysis. In: Schraagen, J.M., Chipman, S.F., Shalin, V.L. (eds.) Cognitive Task Analysis, pp. 3–23. Lawrence Erlbaum Associates, Mahwah (2000)
3. Handbook train dispatcher, version May 2016, ProRail Traffic Management Department, reference EDMS#3884910; in Dutch: Handboektreindienstleider (2016)
4. ISO 10075: 1991 (E), Ergonomic principles related to mental workload - General terms and definitions (1991)
5. Lenior, T.M.J., Gobel, M.P.: Predicting mental workload for train traffic control tasks. In: Seppala, P., Luopajarvi, T., Nygard, C.H., Mattila, M. (eds.) Proceedings of the 13th Triennial Congress of the International Ergonomics Association From Experience to Innovation - IEA 1997, pp. 358–360. Finnish Institut, London (1997)
6. Manual LOA-online (all levels of automation), ProRail Traffic Management Department, in Dutch: Handleiding LOA-online, beknopte handleiding voor het aanvragen/beoordelen van lokale orderaanvragen; Handleiding LOA Online versie4 | 20 juli 2016 | definitief (2016)
7. Manual EBI/LWA (medium level of automation), ProRailAssetmanagement, versie 1.0, June 1st, 2014, GVS60232-21, in Dutch: Gebruiksvoorschrift EBIScreen 300 Treindienstleider (2016)
8. Manual TRON-web based application (low level of automation), ProRail Traffic Management Department, version 4.3a, March 1st, 2016, in Dutch: TRON-webapplicatie - Functionaliteiten TREINDIENSTLEIDER - Versie 4.3A (2016)
9. Manual control of switches and signals with assistance of the system Process Control Routes, ProRail ICT Services, version 1.0, December 1st, 2015, GVS00102, in Dutch: Gebruiksvoorschriftvoor de bediening van wissel- en seininrichtingen met behulp van ProcesleidingRijwegen (2015)
10. Pickup, L., Wilson, J.R., Sharples, S., Norris, B., Clarke, T., Young, M.S.: Fundamental examination of mental workload in the rail industry. Theoret. Issues Ergon. Sci. 6(6), 463–482 (2005). doi:10.1080/14639220500078021
11. Pickup, L., Wilson, J.R., Nichols, S., Smith, S.: A conceptual framework of mental workload and the development of a self- reporting integrated workload scale for railway signallers. In: Wilson, J.R., Norris, B., Clarke, T., Mills, A. (eds.) Rail Human Factors: Supporting the Integrated Railway, pp. 319–329. Ashgate, Aldershot (2005)
12. Stanton, N.A.: Hierarchical task analysis: developments, applications, and extensions. Appl. Ergon. 37, 55–79 (2006)
13. Time occupancy study, train dispatching NCBG (low level of automation), Accent OrganisatieAdvies B.V., commissioned by ProRail Traffic Management and NedTrain, December 16th, 2009, confidentaial, in Dutch: NCBG Onderzoektijdstudie in opdracht van ProRail en NedTrain (vertrouwelijk) (2009)
14. Young, M.S., Brookhuis, K.A., Wickens, C.D., Hancock, P.A.: State of science: mental workload in ergonomics. Ergonomics 58(1), 1–17 (2017). doi:10.1080/00140139.2014. 956151
15. Wickens, C.D.: Multiple resources and performance prediction. Theret. Issues Ergon. Sci. 3, 159–177 (2002)

16. Wilms, M.S., Zeilstra, M.P., Subjective mental workload of Dutch train dispatchers: validation of IWS in a practical setting. In: Proceedings of the Fourth International Conference on Rail Human Factors, London, pp. 633–640, London (2013)
17. Working methods train dispatching (high level of automation) version May 2016, ProRail Traffic Management Department, in Dutch: WerkwijzeTreindienstleider (2016)
18. Working methods train dispatching NCBG (medium and low level of automation), version May 2016, ProRail Traffic Management Department, in Dutch: WerkwijzeTreindienstleider NCBG (2016)
19. Zeilstra, M.P, Bruijn, D.W., de Weide, R., van der, Development and implementation of a predictive tool for optimizing workload of train dispatchers. In: Proceedings of the European Conference on Rail Human Factors, Lille (2009)

Adaptive Automation and the Third Pilot: Managing Teamwork and Workload in an Airline Cockpit

Joan Cahill[1(✉)], Tiziana C. Callari[1], Florian Fortmann[2], Stefan Suck[2],
Denis Javaux[3], Andreas Hasselberg[4], Sybert H. Stoeve[5],
and Bas A. van Doorn[5]

[1] Centre for Innovative Human Systems, School of Psychology,
Trinity College Dublin, College Green, Dublin 2, Ireland
cahilljo@tcd.ie
[2] R&D Division Transportation, OFFIS – Institute for Information Technology,
Escherweg 2, 26121 Oldenburg, Germany
[3] Symbio Concepts & Products S.P.R.L, Sur les Coteaux,
264690 Bassenge, Belgium
[4] Institut für Flugführung, Deutsches Zentrum für Luft- und Raumfahrt e.V.
(DLR), Lilienthalplatz 7, 38108 Brunswick, Germany
[5] Aerospace Operations Safety Institute, Netherlands Aerospace Centre NLR,
Amsterdam, The Netherlands

Abstract. The objective of this paper is to present a new adaptive automation concept which offers an innovative 'team' centred approach to solving human factors/workload management problems. The A-PiMod concept/approach is defined by the concept of partnership – specifically, the "Third Pilot" and the crew and automation are in charge together. We are proposing partnership as opposed to dynamic changes in control function where changes can be controlled autonomously by the system. In support of this, a new multimodal concept is proposed which supports improved assessment of crew state/workload (i.e. information inputs re crew activity/interactions provides a means to communicate with the crew in relation to crew state and decision support, and allows for flexible crew/cockpit interaction).

Keywords: Adaptive automation · Workload · Crew state monitoring · Pilot decision making · Stakeholder evaluation · Multimodal interaction and cockpit displays

1 Introduction

Given automation advances over the last decade, pilots share responsibility for different flight tasks with cockpit systems. Adaptable systems are systems which require human delegation of task and 'function authority' to automation during real-time operational performance (i.e. the task distribution is controlled by the user) [1]. Adaptive automation (AA) is defined as a 'form of automation that allows for dynamic changes in control function allocations between a machine and human operator based on states

© Springer International Publishing AG 2017
L. Longo and M.C. Leva (Eds.): H-WORKLOAD 2017, CCIS 726, pp. 161–173, 2017.
DOI: 10.1007/978-3-319-61061-0_10

of the collective human–machine system' [2, 3]. As such, task distribution changes can be controlled autonomously by the system.

Today's automation is indifferent to the emotional and cognitive state of the crew. Automation only supports the crew based on explicit and static task assignments, with no adaptive capabilities, even though it is capable of higher or lower levels of support if needed or when the capabilities of the crew are challenged.

The air accident and flight safety literature reports on the many still-open issues in relation to automation design. For example, Flight Air France 447 (2009) [4], Flight Spanair 5022 (2008) [5], Flight Helios Airways HCY 522 (2005) [6], Flight China Airlines 140 (1994) [7], and Flight Air Inter 148 (1992) [8]. Critically, several human factors problems have been documented. This includes: automation surprises, degraded situation awareness, unintentional blindness, workload concerns and issues pertaining to over-reliance on automation.

Human operators and automated systems have to act together, cooperatively, in a highly adaptive way. They have to adapt to each other and to the context in order to guarantee fluent and cooperative task achievement maintaining safety at all times. With increasing flight hours, fatigue and increased traffic growth, all crews can benefit from an "experience aid". Ideally, the user and the "experience aid" (or assistance system) constitute a cooperative system - they share tasks and perform them as a team.

1.1   Introduction to the a-PiMod Project

The Applying Pilots' Model for Safer Aircraft (A-PiMod) project aims to address problems relating to crew/automation teamwork and workload management. The objective of the A-PiMod project is to demonstrate a new approach/concept (and associated technologies) for an adaptive automation and multimodal cockpit which will reduce human error. Specifically, the objective is to support adaptive distribution of tasks between the crew and automation, based on real-time analysis of the crew's cognitive state and behavior and on the risk associated with the mission. In relation to cognitive state, the focus is on situation awareness and workload and not emotional state. This research was funded by the European Commission and has been undertaken between September 2013 and September 2016.

2   Research Design

2.1   Overview

The high level Human Machine Interaction (HMI) design/evaluation methodology combines formal HMI design/evaluation activities (i.e. interviews and simulator evaluation), informal HMI design/evaluation approaches (i.e. participatory design activities), along with an integrated stakeholder approach to evaluation [9–11]. The A-PiMod safety case addresses the cockpit team concept (i.e. third pilot concept) and Human Multimodal Interaction (HMMI). Overall, the A-PiMod safety case has supported (1) the definition of user requirements and associated user interface design activities, and (2) the assessment of potential impact/benefits. This has involved twenty seven COP sessions and two phases of simulator evaluation. For more information about specific methodologies, please see [9–11]. The assessment of potential impact/benefits has been undertaken in relation to actual end user/operational scenarios. Scenarios have been developed as part of (1) formal evaluation activities (VC1 and VC2), and ongoing research with the A-PiMod COP.

2.2 Quantification of Safety Impact

The safety impact of the A-PiMod adaptive automation and multimodal cockpit concept was quantified by a systematic approach using the Total Aviation Risk model and structured feedback on change factors for base events in this risk model. The assessment of safety impact was undertaken for the A-PiMod concept, rather than for its particular implementation as achieved in the A-PiMod project (i.e. software/technology). For more information, please see [12].

2.3 Community of Practice and Stakeholder Participation

The concept of a Community of Practice (COP) proposed by Wenger underpins the stakeholder evaluation approach [13]. Stakeholder participation involves consultative interaction along with engagement in technical research tasks [14]. Overall, twenty seven COP sessions and two phases of simulator evaluation have been undertaken. The first phase of simulator evaluation involved eight participants, while the second phase involved twelve participants. The COP panel comprised fifteen participants (see Fig. 1 below). The Radar Diagram below (see Fig. 1) shows the two overlaying levels of expertise both from the internal and external stakeholders. The composition of the internal stakeholders is represented in blue, while the composition of the external stakeholder is represented in amaranth. The red dotted line corresponds to the 2-level expertise.

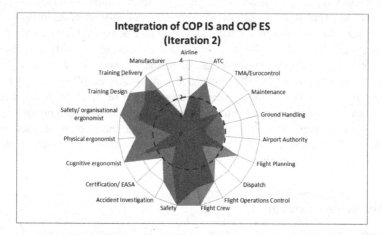

Fig. 1. Current state of stakeholder competency knowledge in A-PiMod (Color figure online)

3   Adaptive Automation and Multimodal Concept

3.1   Objectives and Overall Concept

The goal is to support crew in situations when they may need help irrespective of experience and/or in situations when the crew has less experience, and/or in situations where the crew is experiencing high workload, under pressure and potentially fatigued. Automation is conceptualized as a third crew member, providing support to crew in both high and low workload situations, to optimize flight safety and ensure the mission level goal is achieved.

The A-PiMod concept/approach is defined by the concept of partnership – specifically, the "Third Pilot" and the crew and automation are in charge together. The team comprises the pilot flying (PF), the pilot monitoring (PM) and automation. Automation is a virtual team-member. The team co-operates in relation to mission level decisions. Critically, this partnership concept is underscored by a core notion of Pilot authority. The system continuously monitors the operational situation and the allied crew/automation/aircraft state, to determine the tasks the team has to perform together, and how to best distribute them between the crew and automation. A-PiMod flags potential risks - providing operational guidance in relation to managing those risks. The crew forms their own judgement/ideas as to risk status of situation and the appropriate course of action. The crew is not mandated to follow the decision support provided by A-PiMod (this is an aid, not a requirement). Overall, the crew can over-ride system proposals/decisions, except in certain critical situations (i.e. incapacitation). As such, the crew have final control (i.e. make the final decisions), but are responsible and accountable for their decisions/actions.

A-PiMod adopts a team-centred approach as opposed to a crew centred approach. We are focusing on the outcome; considering what is best for the safe and efficient completion of the mission/flight, and not particularly trying to adapt to human needs. If the Pilot Flying/Pilot Monitoring is overloaded and this threatens the completion of the mission, the task distribution is adapted at the agent level. Automation is adapted to the crew states and capabilities, so that at all times the cockpit-level tasks that have to be performed for safe and efficient mission completion are achieved. The emerging Third Pilot concept can be conceptualized on several levels - (a) automated task distribution, (b), crew workload monitor, (c) crew task performance monitor, (d) scanning cycles monitoring, and (4) a risk assessment/decision support aid, enabling briefing and situation awareness. The Third Pilot concept is underpinned by the A-PiMod multimodal cockpit – which (1) enables monitoring of crew interactions with cockpit systems (i.e. provides inputs to crew state inference module), (2) facilitates crew interaction with automation (MCM Display) and (3), allows for flexible and natural interactions (i.e. touch and voice) with cockpit displays.

3.2   Architecture Concept

The adaptive automation system integrates three key components: (1) model-based evaluation of flight crew state, (2) real-time automated risk assessment, and

(3) adaptation of the Human Machine Interface. These components are currently missing in cockpit systems and are essential for safe crew-automation interaction. The A-PiMod architecture allows adapting the organization of the cockpit (task distribution between the crew and automation) and the circulation of information between the crew and the cockpit systems (including automation) to the current - and forthcoming - situation(s).

As detailed in Fig. 1, the whole A-PiMod architecture is based on a 3-layers hierarchy of tasks. The highest level is the mission level. The middle one is the cockpit level. The lowest level is the agent level, where tasks are executed by the agents in the cockpit: the crew and automation.

Tasks at a given level are translated - or instantiated - into the tasks of the level below based on the context of their execution. For the mission level for example, the context of execution is the context in which the A/C is flying (e.g., weather, ATC, traffic) and the A/C state. At the cockpit level, the cockpit context is mostly defined by the state of the cockpit agents (crew & automation) and of the cockpit equipment (e.g., displays). This contextual adaptation of tasks into the tasks of the level below is one of the main mechanisms by which adaptiveness is provided by the A-PiMod architecture each level providing additional degrees of freedom to perfectly tune the execution of the mission to current circumstances (at each level).

We are proposing partnership as opposed to dynamic changes in control function (where changes can be controlled autonomously by the system). A main aspect of the concept is the A-PiMod architecture, which describes at a high level the means for the adaptive distribution of tasks between the crew and automation, such as the real-time analyses of the crew's state (situation awareness and workload), and the mission risks. The new, improved automation system will permanently assess what the crew is - or is not - doing, as well as what they should be doing at the current time (i.e. recover from a stall, avoid ground obstacles etc.). How automation is adapted is through task distribution. Task distribution is the end result of the situation management process where the crew and other automated processes cooperate to assess the situation, its risks, what has to be done (cockpit level tasks), their risks, and produce an appropriate task distribution.

The cockpit is viewed as a 'cooperative system of human and machine agents that adapts its task distribution at all time in order to perform a mission, safely and efficiently'. Automation is adapted to the crew states and capabilities, so that at all times the cockpit-level tasks that have to be performed for safe and efficient mission completion are achieved (Fig. 2) .

3.3 Pilot Interaction in the Cockpit and User Interface Design

Pilot interaction in the cockpit can be characterized in relation to the following points:

- User friendly and flexible information/decision support
- The crew interact using voice/touch and traditional controls
- This interaction is tracked by the system (i.e. what tasks performing, level of fatigue, involvement in activity): this is referred to as 'crew state monitoring'

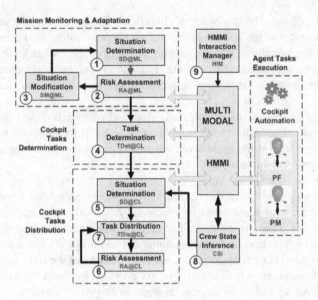

Fig. 2. Architecture concept

- The crew obtain feedback via a new cockpit user interface (Mission and Cockpit Level Management Display - MCMD) as to:
- The risk status of the operational situation (this includes an assessment of the status of joint crew/automation system)
- What to do – including the provision of best options/alternatives based on different 'technical' contributing factors (i.e. fuel remaining, status of alternates etc.)
- The proposed MCMD features two related sub-displays – the mission and cockpit level displays
- The crew can over-ride system proposals/decisions – except in certain critical situations (i.e. incapacitation)

The A-PiMod MC-M Display (i.e. the Mission & Cockpit Management Display) is the A-PiMod interface between the user and the proposed A-PiMod adaptive automation technologies. The MC-M Display supports all crew activities related to Mission management, as well as to Cockpit management. The Cockpit is seen as a team made of the crew itself and a series of dedicated A-PiMod modules that provides adaptive automation (Fig. 3).

The MC-M Display has been implemented on a tablet/Microsoft Surface. The tablet/Microsoft Surface is a touch display, and it can be operated via touch by the crew. High level features of the MC-M Display include:

- The device was shared for use by both the PF and PM
- The screen had a portrait orientation to include both the ML (Mission Level, top half) and CL (Cockpit Level, bottom half) interfaces.

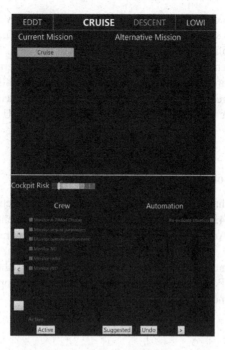

Fig. 3. MCMM display (Prototype)

3.4   Systems to Monitor Observed Behavior

Several systems (i.e. eye tracking, gesture recognition and head pose) are linked to the A-PiMod components (i.e. crew state estimation/task determination), to infer possible errors, missed events and missed piece of information. Specifically, visual analysis of pilots' behavior is recorded to infer human operator's (pilot's) mental state, stress level, and general workload. For more information, please see Appendix 1.

3.5   Benefits & Impact

This research indicates that the 'Third Crew Member' will provide many operational and safety benefits. This includes:

- Improving teamwork between crew and automation
- Providing task support in safety critical situations (i.e. operational risk assessment/decision support)
- Providing task support in high workload situations (i.e. operational risk assessment/decision support)
- Supporting workload management
- Improving team situation awareness
- Augmenting Pilot monitoring performance (i.e. avoid monitoring errors, link to error chain)
- Providing support in relation to error detection and management

Overall, this new concept/approach will significantly improve the safety of flight, especially in abnormal situations and during situations of crisis management. Critically, A-PiMod will not eliminate human error. Rather, it will reduce it. That is, it will reduce the accident rate, given improvements in error detection and error management. As validated in field research, the A-PiMod concept/approach will allow for an improved partnership between crew and automation (the "team players" idea), which will reduce human error and make substantial progress in relation to the EU aim of reducing the accident rate by 80%.

3.6 Quantification of Safety Impact

Overall it is assessed that the A-PiMod concept facilitates a reduction in the probability of fatal accidents by 43% from 4.0E−7 to 2.2E−7 fatal accidents per flight. This is about half of the FP7 Area 7.1.3 objective to reduce the accident rate by 80%. For more information, please see [12]. A cockpit that is designed with the A-PiMod approach in mind will extend automation capabilities in an adaptive way, to the extent necessary to support a safer flight. Potentially, such an adaptive automation approach might prevent many accidents. For more information, please see [11, 12].

4 Discussion

4.1 Innovation

The Third Pilot/A-PiMod system (1) reflects a mix of the logic associated with adaptable systems and adaptive automation, and (2) provides something new (i.e. multimodal cockpit concept). In relation to (1), we are

- Going beyond notions of assistance (adaptable systems), where the crew are fully in charge (i.e. in all situations/all of the time)
- Adopting certain aspects of adaptive automation – that is, supporting the pilots based on an understanding of crew state (situation awareness and workload)
- Proposing partnership as opposed to dynamic changes in control function where changes can be controlled autonomously by the system

  In our concept, the crew is in charge together with automation (team concept)

- In principle, the pilot remains in charge/in command
- However, there are certain special situations when automation can take charge (i.e. fully adaptive)

In relation to (2), we have developed new multimodal concepts which supports improved assessment of crew state/workload (i.e. information inputs re crew activity/interactions), provides a means to communicate with the crew re crew state and decision support (i.e. MCM Display – enabling assistance), and allows for flexible crew/cockpit interaction.

The third pilot has different modes of operation. This includes (1) passive monitoring, (2) active monitoring and (3) over-ride. In relation to A-PiMod, we expect that

(1) and (2) will be the standard/typical modes - operating as an adaptive automation supporting the pilots, based on understanding of crew state/workload. In extreme cases (3) will occur. Here A-PiMod/third pilot will take charge of the aircraft control (i.e. fully adaptive). We are calling (1) + (2) + (3) a third pilot or partnership concept. If automation would progress, aspect (3) might become more normal and (1) and (2) less typical. Of course major development and certification would need to be taken, especially for (3).

The A-PiMod architecture has been developed to support the transition towards more automation while staying in the same framework (something that is impossible in the assistive paradigm). This is possible because each component in the architecture is a small cooperative system made of the crew + a module. When there is no crew (full automation), there is just the module. When there is no automation (manual flight), there is just the crew (or a single pilot). A single pilot during manual flight superposes all the components.

4.2   Cockpit Centred vs. Task Centred Approach

A-PiMod adopts a team centred approach as opposed to a crew centred approach. We are focusing on the outcome; considering what is best for the safe and efficient completion of the mission/flight, and not particularly trying to adapt to human needs. As indicated in the architecture concept [15, 16], if the pilot flying/pilot monitoring is overloaded and this threatens the completion of the mission, the task distribution is adapted at the agent level.

Underpinning the A-PiMod concept is the idea that automation operates with a better understanding of the Pilots/crew state. In this way, automation is a 'true' member of the team. That said, we are trying to see what is best for the safe and efficient completion of the flight, and not particularly trying to adapt to human needs (that's a means more than an end). As such, automation delivers on mission/cockpit requirements (i.e. what is best for the safe and efficient completion of the flight). If we see that the human is overloaded and this threatens the completion of the mission at the mission level we will adapt the task distribution, at the agent level. This is not necessarily at odds with human centred automation insofar as it considers the Pilot position (i.e. situation awareness and workload status) and the Pilot provides feedback as to whether he/she accepts the suggestions of the automation system (i.e. decision support and task functions undertaken by automation).

4.3   Partnership Concept

A-PiMod is intended as an 'experience aid', a 'Smart Pilot Assistance'. This does not mean that A-PiMod will supplant Pilot experience; rather, it is intended to complement existing experience, and compensate for when someone might not be at his or her best. As such, A-PiMod needs to be seen as, and behave as a team-player. Anything that could be interpreted as undermining the authority or command held by the Captain will undermine A-PiMod's effectiveness in strengthening the team. A-PiMod should be a support, and not thought of as behaving like a tell-tale child constantly running to the teacher. Thus, it is important that changes are implemented at the 'right' pace, to enable to address safety issues properly.

4.4   Crew State Monitoring

The real gain in A-PiMod relates to crew state monitoring – that is focusing the pilot's attention on their state (i.e. crew state) along with that of their crew member - and on the current and future state of the aircraft. If over-loaded and/or under pressure, pilots may forget or not consider all the safe options. However the 3rd crew member (automation) will not, so a quick check will refresh the possible options, to allow a safe decision to be made. In this context, a key challenge is how to get the two human crew members to share their 'current state' with the 3rd crew member such that it is mean-influx, informative but not self-incriminating in any post hoc analysis. Normal human interactions can easily accommodate this in simple pre-flight social interactions. Formalizing it such that the 3rd crew member can make useful sense of it may be more problematic.

The assessment of crew state is not just about workload, it's about the crew experience, flight hours, familiarity with route, when last flown there and training background. If the Pilots are not familiar with the route, then the crew state might be assessed as less optimal. From a pilot's perspective, the starting point for crew state monitoring is the crew briefing/flight planning. This might occur a week before the flight. Or at least, at the time of the preflight, flight planning and briefing task. For crew state monitoring to work, we need to establish a picture/sense of the crew state from the very beginning of the flight. The A-PiMod system needs to know what the join crew status is and any threats associated with this. Potentially, we will need the crew to provide feedback about their state in advance of the flight. Further, it takes into account real-time crew behavior. This involves monitoring the crew state via the assessment of (1) crew activity (gesture), and (2) crew interaction with cockpit systems including new multi-modal input (i.e. touch, voice and gesture) and traditional controls.

4.5   Airline SOP

The introduction of the A-PiMod concept might drastically change airline SOP. Existing SOPs are premised on enabling different crew members with different levels of experience, knowledge or skill find 'common ground' to conduct consistent and safe operations. One significant factor to be considered in that respect would be how to handle introducing the A-PiMod concept on a mixed fleet basis, given that it would inevitably be introduced over a considerable period of time and pilots would have to operate on mixed aircraft (with and without the system). Given the nature of the system, this could prove quite challenging. Furthermore, final authority to override the A-PiMod systems' actions should reside with the operating crew. As a specific exception to that principle, the occasions on which A-PiMod could take action that could not be overridden by the crew would need very careful and very detailed SOP specification.

5   Conclusions

The A-PiMod concept/approach is defined by the concept of partnership – specifically, the "Third Pilot" and the crew and automation are in charge together. A-PiMod adopts a team centred approach as opposed to a crew centred approach. We are proposing partnership as opposed to dynamic changes in control function where changes can be controlled autonomously by the system. A main aspect of the concept is the A-PiMod architecture, which describes at a high level the means for the adaptive distribution of tasks between the crew and automation, such as the real-time analyses of the crew's mental state and the mission risks. Automation is a virtual team-member (third pilot) and the team co-operates in relation to mission level decisions. Task distribution is the end result of the situation management process where the crew and other automated processes cooperate to assess the situation, its risks, what has to be done (cockpit level tasks), their risks, and produce an appropriate task distribution.

An advanced A-PiMod system cannot supplant experience. However, it is ready to provide extra information in relation to risks/hazards and potential courses of action – if required by crew. In this way, an advanced A-PiMod system features different "levels" of response, similar to the way a Captain would have with different co-pilots of varying experience. Ideally, the A-PiMod system would provide an airline with the most experienced and capable crew possible in any situation, where skill level is constant, across all weather/routes/airports/time zones. A-Pimod helps avoid dramas – everything is routine (i.e. the crew is briefed about all possibilities). The third pilot/cockpit team concept and HMMI has been demonstration at two levels – namely (1) at a conceptual level and (2) at a level of software demonstration. The assessment of safety impact mostly relates to what has been advanced at a conceptual level (i.e. A-PiMod concept), rather than for its particular implementation as achieved in the A-PiMod project.

In the course of the A-PiMod project a particular implementation of the concept was achieved by development of a set of tools, and these tools were used in validation experiments in a flight simulator context (i.e. validation sessions 1 and 2). This set of tools can be viewed as a first technical instantiation of the A-PiMod system, and the sophistication, scope and integration of the tools can be improved in future research and development.

Acknowledgments. The research leading to these results/preliminary outcomes has received funding from the European Commission's Seventh Framework Programme (FP7/2007-2013) under grant agreement N. 605141 - Applying Pilot Models for Safety Aircraft (A-PiMod) Project. We would like to thank member of the A-PiMod Project Team and our COP members – particularly, Paul Cullen, William Butler, Martin Duffy and Stephen Duffy.

Appendices

Systems to Monitor Observed Behavior

Eye Tracking. In both sets of simulator evaluation sessions, SMI Eye Tracking Glasses 2 were used to measure the gaze positions. Please note that his was demonstrated – but not implemented in real time. SMI Eye Tracking Glasses is a binocular tracking device which operates with 60 Hz. It is connected with a Laptop via USB on which videos of the eyes and the scene camera are recorded and the gaze position is calculated. The system is combined with an A.R.T Optical Head Tracking system. Retro reflective targets are attached to the glasses which are recorded by infrared cameras installed in the simulator. This system allows us to calculate the head position and orientation. With both systems combined, it is possible to calculate a 3D gaze vector for each eye.

Gesture Recognition. The Gesture recognition is meant to recognize the upper body parts of a human operator – aeronautic pilot – in order to detect "implicit gestures". Implicit gestures refer to movements of the upper body parts, which are normal actions taken by the crew (e.g. controlling different parts of the cockpit, or interaction among the crew).

Head Pose Recognition. The head pose estimation functionality serves to provide information about where the pilot is looking within the cockpit (which instruments, screens, control elements, etc.). The technology is designed to be completely passive and non-intrusive in the sense that the pilot does not wear (or otherwise consciously interact with) any additional pieces of equipment, such as eye-tracking glasses. Also, the head pose estimation device does not emit any infrared light, which would be the case for contemporary remote eye trackers or depth cameras (based on structured light projection or infrared time-of-flight sensors). In A-PiMod, the first application of the said technology in the cockpit is detecting "missed events" – when the pilot is provided with a piece of information by the cockpit, but she misses it by not looking at the appropriate display for a time period. The cockpit display (MC-M Display) provides a notification of the missed event. Depending on the Pilots response, the saliency of such message is increased. The second application is contribution to the estimation of the pilot's state of mind and workload level from the patterns of the head motion.

References

1. Kaber, D.B., Prinzel, L.J.: Adaptive and Adaptable Automation Design: A Critical Review of the Literature and Recommendations for Future Research. NASA/TM-2006-214504 (2006)
2. Hilburn, B.J., Byrne, E., Parasuraman, R.: The effect of adaptive air traffic control (ATC) decision aiding on controller mental workload. In: Mouloua, M., Koonce, J.M. (eds.) Human–Automation Interaction: Research and Practice, pp. 84–91. Lawrence Erlbaum Associates Inc, Mahwah, NJ (1997)
3. Kaber, D.B., Riley, J.M.: Adaptive automation of a dynamic control task based on secondary task workload measurement. Int. J. Cogn. Ergon. **3**, 169–187 (2006)
4. Flight AF 447 Final Report on the accident on 1st June 2009 to the Airbus A330-203 registered F-GZCP operated by Air France flight AF 447 Rio de Janeiro (Published July 2012). Retrieved from Bureau d'Enquêtes et d'Analyses pour la sécurité de l'aviation civile (BEA), 1 June 2009. http://www.bea.aero/docspa/2009/f-cp090601.en/pdf/f-cp090601.en.pdf

5. Flight Spainair 5022. Final Report on the accident on 20th August 2008 involving a McDonnell Douglas DC-9-82 (MD-82) registration EC-HFP operated by Spainair at Madrid-Barajas Airport (Published 8 October 2008). Retrieved from Comisión Investigatión de Accidentes e Incidentes de Aviación Civil (CIAIAC), 20 August 2008. http://www.fomento.es/NR/rdonlyres/EC47A855-B098-409E-B4C8-9A6DD0D0969F/107087/2008_032_A_ENG.pdf
6. Flight Helios Airways HCY522. Final Report on the accident on 14th August 2005 involving a Boeing 737-31S registration 5B-DBY operated by Helios Airways at Grammatiko, Hellas (Published November 2006). Retrieved from Air Accident Investigation & Aviation Safety Board (AAIASB). 14 August 2005. http://www.moi.gov.cy/moi/pio/pio.nsf/All/F15FBD7320037284C2257204002B6243/$file/FINAL%20REPORT%205B-DBY.pdf
7. Flight China Airlines 140. Final Report on the accident on 26th April 1994 involving an Airbus Industrie A300B4-662R registration B1816 operated by China Airlines at Nagoya Airport (Published 19 July 1996). Retrieved from Aircraft Accident Investigation Commission. 26 April 1994. http://www.skybrary.aero/bookshelf/books/808.pdf
8. Flight Air Inter 148. Final Report on the accident on 20th January 1992 involving an Airbus A320 registration F-GGED operated by Air Inter Airlines in Vosges Mountains (near Mont Sainte-Odile). Retrieved from Bureau d'Enquêtes et d'Analyses pour la sécurité de l'aviation civile (BEA), 20 January 1992. http://www.bea.aero/docspa/1992/f-ed920120/htm/f-ed920120.html
9. Cahill, J., Callari, T.C.: A novel human machine interaction (HMI) design/evaluation approach supporting the advancement of improved automation concepts to enhance flight safety. In: de Waard, D., Sauer, J., Röttger, S., Kluge, A., Manzey, D., Weikert, C., Toffetti, A., Wiczorek, R., Brookhuis, K., Hoonhout, H. (Eds.). In: Proceeding of the Ergonomics Society Europe Chapter 2014 Annual Conference "Human Factors in high reliability industries", Lisbon, Portugal. (2015a). http://www.hfes-europe.org/human-factors-high-reliability-industries-2/
10. Cahill, J., Callari, T.: Stakeholder involvement in evaluation: lessons learned in the A-PiMod Project. Presentation at the Annual Meeting of the Irish Ergonomics Society. Dublin, Ireland, May 2015 (2015b)
11. Cahill, J, Callari, T. Javaux, D., Fortmann, F., Hasselberg, A. A-PiMod: a new approach to solving human factors problems with automation Paper presented at the HCI 2016 International Conference, Toronto Canada, July 2016
12. Stroeve, S., Van Doorn, B.A., Cahill, J. A Safety impact quantification approach for early stage innovative aviation concepts: Application to a third pilot adaptive automation concept. Paper presented at SESAR Innovation Days, Delft, November 2016
13. Wenger, E., McDermott, R.A., Snyder, W.: Cultivating Communities of Practice: A Guide to Managing Knowledge. Harvard Business Press, Boston (2002)
14. Cousins, J.B., Whitmore, E., Shulha, L.: Arguments for a common set of principles for collaborative inquiry in evaluation. Am. J. Eval. 34(1), 7–22 (2013)
15. Javaux, D., Fortmann, F., Möhlenbrink, C.: Adaptive human-automation cooperation: a general architecture for the cockpit and its application in the A-PiMod project. In: Proceedings of the 7th International Conference on Advanced Cognitive Technologies and Applications (COGNITIVE 2015). International Academy, Research, and Industry Association (IARIA) (2015). ISBN: 978-1-61208-390-2.
16. Fortmann, F., Cahill, J, Callari, T. Javaux, D., Hasselberg, A. (2016). Developing a feedback system to augment pilots monitoring performance. Paper presented at 2016 IEEE International Multi-Disciplinary Conference on Cognitive Methods in Situation Awareness and Decision Support (CogSIMA), San Diego, US, 1–25 March 2016

Quantification of Rail Signaller Demand Through Simulation

Lise Delamare[1,2], David Golightly[2]([⊠]), Graham Goswell[1],
and Peter Treble[1]

[1] Hitachi Information Control System Europe Ltd (Hitachi ICSE),
Manvers House, Kingston Road, Bradford-on-Avon BA151AB, UK
lise.delamare@hitachi-infocon.com
[2] Human Factors Research Group (HFRG), University of Nottingham,
Nottingham NG72RD, UK
David.Golightly@nottingham.ac.uk

Abstract. Demand factors are understood to play a substantial role in the experience of workload in rail signalling operations. Quantifying these demand parameters in signalling operations can inform both decisions about operational practice as well as technology design. To date, however, tools to estimate demand have either relied on assessor judgement of static or aggregated parameters, can be time-consuming to produce, and challenging when a workstation is changing or being developed. In order to anticipate the evolution of railway signalling, the Dynamic Modelling of Operator Demand (D-MOD) tool uses signalling simulation to derive accurate demand parameter measurements. This paper presents the architecture and design of the D-MOD platform, as well as the types of parameters that have been identified and quantified. Different categories of parameter, including static, dynamic and performance parameters have been captured and validated. Future directions for the tool are discussed.

Keywords: Rail signalling · Demand · Workload · Simulation · Quantification

1 Introduction

There has been a steady transition from distributed, physical control of railways in signal boxes located close to their area of control, to centralised control centres, sometimes located at several miles from their controlled area. Recently, the appearance of automation has further reduced even more the physical actions required by signallers, putting them in a more intense monitoring role [1]. These modifications have generated major changes in terms of signalling tasks, shifting from physical to cognitive tasks, and requiring the consideration of an increasing level of information from expanding areas of control. Great Britain, like many other countries, is experiencing further, rapid transition with the launch of new Traffic Management Systems (TMS), which brings greater unification of the traditional signalling/dispatch type function with higher order traffic replanning functions into a single role. This will have several consequences on organisation of work, workstation boundaries, and number of staff. All of this is taking place at a time of unprecedented demand on the railway system that must seek new ways of generating capacity within the existing infrastructure wherever possible [2].

L. Longo and M.C. Leva (Eds.): H-WORKLOAD 2017, CCIS 726, pp. 174–186, 2017.
DOI: 10.1007/978-3-319-61061-0_11

The rail sector is cognizant of the need to design both technology and processes (including timetables, and planning of track maintenance) with a view to their implications for workload for those who regulate trains [3]. A key component of workload is the demand associated with running a particular service pattern over a given area of infrastructure. [3] conceptualise the relationship as overt task characteristics, leading to specific signaling goals and an imposed load. Combined with internal load, perceived load and individual characteristics, an input load generates demands that lead to effort, effects on performance and wellbeing and, ultimately, the work result. The challenge to date has been to capture and articulate the nature of the task characteristics. These task characteristics underpin demand, and therefore drive both objective and experienced workload, but are highly sensitive to the very specific nature of not only the workstation, but the physical reality of the geography and traffic that are controlled through the workstation [4].

While tools such as ODEC [5] and Presto [6] are available, and have a successful pedigree within rail workload, there are limitations

(1) Tools such as Operational Demand Evaluation Checklist (ODEC) involve quantifying key parameters that represent demand, and therefore shape workload. Some of these are static infrastructure parameters (e.g. numbers of points in the area of control) but the relevance of some of this infrastructure (e.g. how often a point is actually used or not) is rarely accommodated in the estimate.

(2) Additionally, tools such as ODEC aim to capture more dynamic operational factors such as number of services per hour or day. The limitation is that these numbers are averages based on the timetable and may fail to capture the experience of running the service. For example, are the trains regularly spaced or do they come in clusters and/or involve combinations of fast and slower or freight trains? This is crucial given that workload is generated as much by a small but concurrent tasks, including regulation decisions, as it is by significant singular events [7].

(3) For both of the above points, this data are captured through inspection of the workstation and timetable and discussion with the staff controlling them. This requires experience, and time, and is open to variability and interpretation with less experienced assessors.

(4) While tools such as Presto more accurately capture time occupancy for particular infrastructure, the challenge is to have accurate timetable information and models of the infrastructure. This may be particularly problematic when the infrastructure is at a design (or re-design) phase.

The solution to these problems is to have a tool that can accurately and objectively capture the demand-shaping characteristics of a work-station. Furthermore, it should do so in a manner that captures not just static or averaged demand estimates, but can reflect moment to moment changes in demand resulting from the interaction between trains and the infrastructure. Finally, it would be highly desirable that planned changes and design options could be reviewed (for either infrastructure or timetable) as well as being able to evaluate current operations.

The Dynamic Modelling of Operational Demand (D-MOD) project [8, 9] is a collaboration between Hitachi Information Control Systems Europe and the University of Nottingham Human Factors Research Group. Funded as a 2 year Knowledge Transfer Partnership, the project aimed to apply Hitachi ICSE's (HICSE) capability in providing signalling simulation software and tools to the problem of workstation demand measurement. The remainder of this paper describes existing measures of demand and workload in the rail signalling domain. It then discusses the architecture of the D-MOD platform, before presenting the types of measures that are possible. The paper then presents indicative test results, concluding with ideas for how the tool could be used in future.

2 Existing Measures

Many demand simulating tools exist and have been applied to many domains such as aircraft, defence, nuclear, automobile. [10] used Dynamic Density (DD) metrics to measure and predict air sector complexity. This model based on mathematical variables includes several complexity factors which are defined as the reason that contributes to the difficulty. Their algorithms were tested with a panel in order to compare DD predictions with subjective workload ratings through regression analysis. The results obtained through regression analysis showed coherent results between subjective rating and DD predictions.

Aldrich et al. [11] introduced a workload computer model in 1989 called the VACP model (Visual, Auditory, Cognitive and Psycho-motoric) applied in defence. This model is based on task analysis and task demands, in which each task demand is detailed in micro entities which are then linked with a resources, time to perform an action/mental process, and complexity or estimated workload ratings provided by experts. This method provides good prediction of workload profile but requires a lot of time dedicated for the task analysis, and provides a granularity for the results which are sometimes not required. Balfe [9] also confirmed this point of view after applying a similar method called Multiple Resource Questionnaire in a signalling study.

In railway several tools have been developed: such as ODEC (Operator Demand Evaluation Checklist) [5], PRESTO [6] (Prediction of Operator Time Occupancy), AAT (Activity Analysis Tool) [5], IWS (Integrated Workload Scale) [5] and ASWAT (Adaptative Subjective Workload Tool) [5]. ODEC is a tool which provides an indication of the workload associated with a workstation by the study of its operational rules, infrastructure features and events that can occur. Key factors listed in the checklist (number of trains, number of phone calls), are mostly objective and provided by control centres through data analysis. This method is applied in the railway and known to be efficient, easy to set up, however the output it can provide is sometimes viewed as "limited": results obtained cannot help in the definition of solutions to be adopted in context of high and medium workload. Furthermore, the level of detail of the analysis sometimes omit important information about the traffic pattern and its operation (i.e. parameter "number of regulating locations" is probably not sufficient to describe regulating tasks).

AAT is another objective method which aims to record signallers activities during a day, provides indications on when, how long, and why these activities were performed (i.e. 5 min phone call at 10am: due to point failure). This technique is very useful in order to provide an indication of the distribution of signallers activities in terms of time and amount of tasks performed in parallel. This method is sometimes considered as limited in some human factors studies to the extent that even if activities are objectively tracked, and workload is not necessarily proportional with the amount of activities performed by the signaller.

PRESTO is another objective method which allows the definition and replay of a signalling scenario in a subarea of the workstation. This method is presented as a software in which the human factors professional is invited to enter information from the workstation (level crossings, routes, reaction time, phone calls duration...), a simulation is then made which consist in running the trains according to the timetable in the workstation. Outputs provided are detailed as much as in the AAT analysis, and also include a prediction of the level of occupation of the signaller. This tool h is efficient and provides a good overview of the traffic pattern and operation. However, the overheads in terms of time and effort for the analyst can be high.

IWS and ASWAT aim to capture the signaller's perceptions of workload using different rating scales. IWS rating scale focus on the rating of the perception of the demands and way to cope with them. ASWAT focus more on the rating of indicators such as time pressure, mental effort and pressure (same principle as NASA TLX [12] method). These methods are applied worldwide and succeeded to capture relevant data, which confirms their relevance and consistency. However, Human Factors professional often feel the need to complete these subjective methods with more objective data as the focus on subjective methods only provide subjective inputs and thus different point on views depending on individuals.

Other researchers [6, 13], have further methods using complexity/weighing ratings to quantify signalling effort during regulating context. These methods consisted in describing regulating tasks into different demand factors which can be measured (number of regulating locations, number and types of train movements, number of movements in parallel etc.) and can be factorised according with complexity rules defined.

In the context of our project, the requirements linked with the existing simulator called TREsim were clear from the beginning: the new module D-MOD must include parameters related with the infrastructure, timetable and technology – as these are data with which the simulator is actually working. Data shall be as much as possible objective to provide indicators totally external from human point of view (this is reinforced by the fact that subjective tools already exist and efficient). Manual inputs can be provided to add external data to the analysis but has to be limited and controlled. Keeping in mind these requirements, the D-MOD project started with a wide explo-ration of existing human factors tools (described above) in the railway and other domains, capable to evaluate workload related with task demands. In parallel, an internal study on demand parameters was performed with signalling experts from HICSE. From these studies, we extracted a preliminary list of demand parameters which were analysed in collaboration with a Subject Matter Expert. After this analysis, the project had to take a first direction to build its first proof of concept software in order to evaluate the capacity of the simulator to deliver awaited data. The analysis of the simulating tools pointed towards ODEC as a starting set of parameters, as it provides an indication of task demand with an acceptable level of granularity for our proof of concept: "ODEC is related to the view that workload is a function of the work that loads, and thereby a demand independent of the individual, and assesses the key factors of the system within which a rail signaller works which might impact on their workload" [3].

3 Architecture

TREsim is a simulator platform, primarily used for the training of new signallers, familiarisation of existing simulators with design or process changes, or new locations, and with the ability to replay events both derived from the simulator or capture through operational data. As well as giving feedback on performance, TREsim allows the introduction of faults or events into a signalling scenario. TREsim is integrated with a larger portfolio of tools allowing the testing of new signalling scheme designs, or integration with automatic route setting. Critically, the TREsim platform is very high fidelity, with accurate models of trains, timetable and infrastructure that can faithfully recreate actual or envisioned operational scenarios.

TREsim is divided into two entities, see Fig. 1: one signaller (trainee) workstation, and one observer (trainer) workstation. Underpinning the TREsim platform are a number of elements that, as well as enabling the simulator, also enable demand estimation.

- Infrastructure model – each simulated workstation has a model of the track, including points and signals, it comprises. Therefore it is possible to scan this model to quantify any modelled infrastructure elements to capture potential demand shaping parameters (e.g. number of points, number of platforms).

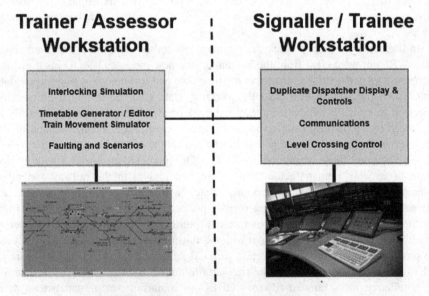

Fig. 1. Overview of TREsim simulation suite.

- Timetable model – this is a model of the planned trains for a workstation. As well as generating trains to run on the simulation, this model can also be scanned to calculate number of trains (and types of trains) expected for a given timetable (e.g. number of trains per day, per hour). There is also a timetable editor.
- Train movement simulator – this generates the movement of trains across the workstation given either a planned train according to the timetable, or as inserted by an assessor in real-time (e.g. to simulate the arrival of an unplanned freight train). The train movement simulator therefore presents an accurate simulation of *actual* (rather than aggregated) train movements.
- Interlocking simulation – this functional aspect of the simulator allows a realistic recreation of signal and route setting given input from either a signaller or an automated route setting module. As a result, permission cannot be granted to another route once a route is set or a train is in a signalling section, thereby preventing collisions between trains. Therefore, once routes have been set and trains are moving across a workstation, the impact of these events is linked realistically to the availability of other infrastructure, which can be a source of demand or impact performance.
- Faulting and scenarios – The assessor has control over events such as infrastructure faults, arrival of unplanned trains, or can mimic phone calls to the signaller using the simulator. In real-time use of the simulation, this can generate demand, with a subsequent implication for performance. Additionally, faulting can be used to restrict infrastructure and therefore change the more static parameters that can be scanned to calculate demand.
- Automatic route setting – Many workstations in Great Britain are now supported by some form of automatic route setting, and many of the simulated workstations available on TREsim are therefore supported by automation. This allows many simulation scenarios/timetables to be run with minimal intervention from a signaller.

When running in combination, all interactions from the signaller or automation, and impact on the interlocking, can be recorded. Additionally, all train movements, including delays and deviations from the timetable, down to positions in specific track sections, are also recordable. As a result, a high level of accuracy of both planned and actual train movements is possible. The D-MOD proof of concept has been developed to include different functionalities to enable end-users to perform their analysis in an accurate and optimised way.

Here are listed below some of the main functions of the software:

- A "navigation tree" providing information about the TT, start time, workstation simulated and displaying the list of areas created by end-users.
- A "period" tool enabling end-users to choose an hour/day slot for results granularity.
- A "colour filter" tool enabling end-users to have access to the most busy/used places in the infrastructure.
- A "selection area" tool enabling end-users to select any portion of the workstation that requires an evaluation.

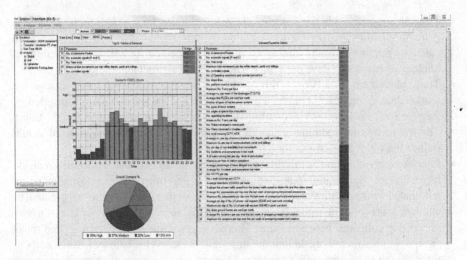

Fig. 2. D-MOD demand dashboard incorporating tabbed interface for different parameters. The current view shows ODEC scores on the right with a calculation of trains per hour on the left. Red, orange and green indicates high, medium and low ODEC scores. See [5] for further explanation. (Color figure online)

And different tabs displaying results:

- Data tabs: external parameters available in control centres can be entered manually and complexity levels (high/medium/low) are listed in these tabs (see Fig. 2).
- ODEC tab: ODEC results of each D-MOD parameters are displayed in these tabs, as well as a graph displaying the number of timetabled trains per hour.
- Flow tabs: train traffic is displayed. These tabs report both the expected number of timetabled trains and the number of trains in a simulation run. These indicators aim to reflect signallers work according to a timetable and the feasibility of a timetable.
- Route tabs: total of route sets manual/ARS is reported.

4 Parameters

From the architecture described above a number of classes of parameters are open to capture. These are:

(1) *Static infrastructure parameters* – These are parameters based around the unchanging aspects of the infrastructure for a given workstation design, such as the number of points. For the purposes of proof of concept, several of these parameters have been adopted from ODEC. The advantage of D-MOD is that they can be calculated swiftly and accurately.

(2) *Aggregated parameters* – These are parameters regarding train movements but, as per the original ODEC, rely on aggregated totals. However, with D-MOD they can be calculated swiftly and accurately, and include detail regarding the head-code of the services involved.

(3) *Dynamic parameters* – These are parameters arising from running trains and the inputs required to regulate them. This can be captured in great detail (specific train movements or specific route settings at a sub-second accuracy), that in practice can be averaged at an appropriate level of granularity.

(4) *Performance parameters* – As well as generating data regarding demand on the workstation, TREsim also generates metrics of performance. This can be in terms of delay accumulated, though signallers may also be able to improve the delay associated with trains that arrive on the workstation in a delayed state. Also, recording specific events such as trains approaching red signals can be used as a measure of safety, as approaching a red signal when this is not in accord with usual operations or timekeeping increases the risk of a signal passed at danger [15].

Table 1 presents a list of these categories with indicative parameters, along with the origin of that parameter – ODEC indicating a parameter taken from the ODEC tool, whereas D-MOD indicates a parameter that has been developed specifically within the context of the current project.

Table 1. List of parameters generated by D-MOD

Parameter name	Origin	Category
Number of platforms used to terminate trains	ODEC	Static
Number of point ends	ODEC	Static
Number of controlled signals	ODEC	Static
Number of automatic signals (R&E)	ODEC	Static
Number of locations for permissive working/No. permissive routes	ODEC	Static
Number of types of traction power systems	ODEC	Static
Maximum number of trains per hour	ODEC	Aggregated
Maximum number of trains per day	ODEC	Aggregated
Subtract the slowest traffic speed from the fastest traffic speed to obtain Min and Max class speed	ODEC	Aggregated
Number of trains per hour (Timetabled and simulated)	D-MOD	Dynamic
Number of trains per minute (Timetabled and simulated)	D-MOD	Dynamic
Flow per hour on track circuit block	D-MOD	Dynamic
Flow per day on track circuit block	D-MOD	Dynamic
Number of static routes in workstation	D-MOD	Static
Total number of route sets per hour (both ARS and manual)	D-MOD	Dynamic
Number of cumulating delay	D-MOD	Performance
Number of trains stopped at red signals	D-MOD	Performance
Duration of trains stops at red signals	D-MOD	Performance
Number of minutes gained/lost per train service	D-MOD	Performance
Initial and terminal delay per train service	D-MOD	Performance
Delay curves per train service	D-MOD	Performance

5 Validation

Following on from a phase of requirements, software development and piloting [6], the project has looked to validate a number of performance metrics. Prior evaluation activities in the project have demonstrated the general feasibility of quantitative demand measures, showing that static demand measures can be rapidly captured from a workstation simulation. Additionally, dynamic demand measures can be captured and show surface validity in comparison to other forms of demand and workload analysis such as AAT. However, to date these pilots had been conducted on only one type of workstation, and had not included performance measures. Therefore, the final phase of validation had two aims:

1. To demonstrate the feasibility of capturing performance measures - in this case cumulating delay and number of trains stopped at a red signal. NB Those signals where trains routinely stop at a red signal (e.g. at the end of a station platform can be and, in this case, were filtered out of the analysis).
2. To demonstrate that the metrics could be applied to a different workstation.

The validation was therefore conducted with a new workstation (Upminster) under three conditions – with normal operating conditions with or without automation and a third trial without automation and with an unplanned delay. This was a train running at a restricted speed resulting in a queue of trains building behind until the issue was resolved. In each scenario an experienced signaller operated the workstation therefore static, dynamic and performance data were generated. Each trial was conducted in real time covering approximately one hour of service (7.30am to 8.30am) at the morning peak. The delayed train was inserted at 7.29am. To provide more feedback on scenario complexity, the Integrated Workload Scale (IWS) tool was used to provide measures of the signaller's workload reported every 1 min. This subjective tool aimed to provide additional information about workload variation. Also AAT was used to check the signallers interactions with the workstation against the automated measures.

Scenario Results. Figure 3a, b and c show graphs of several key dynamic and performance parameters.

Actual and timetabled trains – The data shows a steady increase from the start of the scenario up to typically 19 or 20 trains concurrently on the workstation. In all three scenarios the operator (and in scenario 1, the combination of operator and automation) is able to able to keep pace though delay in both manual conditions is significant.

Number of manual route sets – Scenarios 2 and 3 indicate significant levels of input from the operator to maintain the service. In particular, there is a building spike in scenario 3 around 8.10 min where the signaller is working to clear the backlog of trains that has built up behind the slow running service. The number of routes set by the signaller is greatly reduced in the automated condition (1) but still involves a peak of input around 8.00am.

Cumulating delay – There is a large cumulating delay in scenario 3, demonstrating the viability of this metric. Notably, the cumulative delay drops to a similar level as other scenarios as the signaller is able to work clear the backlog.

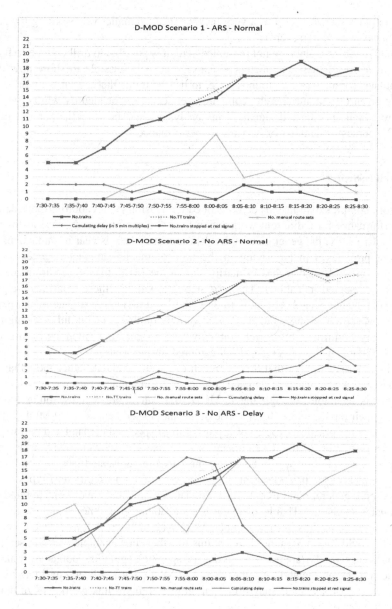

Fig. 3. a, b and c – Demand and performance measures for automated and non-automated normal condition, and non-automated with delay. X axis represents 5 min time blocks for period of evaluation. Y axis represents counts for number of trains, minutes of cumulating delay, number of timetabled trains, number of trains stopped at red signal and number of manual routes set.

Number of trains stopped at a red signal – There is a small increase in the number of trains held at a red signal in scenario 3 over the other two scenarios. This, again, indicates the ability to extract this metric from the simulation, though it may be more useful in other scenarios (e.g. if a very inexperienced signaller was working the panel, or the delay was more severe).

Finally, while the data are not presented here, it is possible to drill down into further detail on many of these parameters. For example, it is possible to show how delay accumulates for any specific train service, to list the trains that are on the workstation for any given instant and thereby compare over scenarios, or identify which trains are held by which specific red signals. This analysis could be essential for identifying specific sources of demand or impacts on performance.

6 Discussion

The work completed so far has demonstrated the feasibility of capturing both demand and performance for a different workstation from the one previously used as the basis of trials. Critically, the generation of the data presented here is near instantaneous, and therefore provides a major saving in the time of the human factors assessor. The emphasis on work to date has primarily shown the feasibility of capturing the kind measures presented in Table 1. The next step is to validate these measures are representative of actual events. The work to date [8, 9] and review by subject matter experts of trails data so far strongly indicates good validity on this data, but this validation can be formally confirmed by correlation between the data presented here, and other sources of data such as AAT and IWS captured during trials.

It is important to note that this approach does not invalidate other tools that have previously looked to capture demand. Rather, it is anticipated that the rich source of data that is available through the D-MOD tool can facilitate these other tools by allowing their rapid capture. Indeed, one of the anticipated benefits of D-MOD is that it can expedite the practical process of capturing most specified demand and performance measures in support of the development of new theory of demand and workload. For example, one aspiration would be to use the measures presented here in combination with eye-tracking or physiological data. The combination of different types of data raises a more general point that, to date, the data streams that have been captured have been treated as distinct. That is, there has been no attempt yet, other than through visual inspection of the results, to link one parameter with another. A future development of D-MOD would look to couple data streams together. For example, can the setting of specific routes or the approach of trains to specific regulation points be linked to specific sources of demand? Another use of D-MOD that has been considered is also how strategies of signallers may differ and how this might link to sources of demand and performance.

There are three limitations of D-MOD tool and process. First, as noted above, there needs to be more concrete comparison between existing measures such as ODEC and the data generated by the D-MOD tool. Second, is that the tool is currently only concerned with demand associated with the core tasks of managing the workstation. In practice, many other tasks can be a source of demand including the communications with other rail staff or public, completing or reading paperwork associated with protection arrangements, or dealing with level crossings [17]. It may be possible to 'overlay' non-signalling events into a scenario to indicate time occupancy. Related to this point is the third limitation, that D-MOD is focused on demand at this stage and rather than the implications for workload. At some point, the D-MOD tool could be use D-MOD to study the tighter coupling between either demand *or* performance (as knowing you are behind the timetable may be a considerable source of pressure), in order to establish the link with experienced workload.

7 Conclusion

The changing face of rail signalling demands new approaches to anticipating the workload implications for those operating the network. The D-MOD project has applied simulation capabilities to help in the quantification of one crucial aspect of workload, operational demand. It goes beyond existing tools (though can also accommodate and complement these existing tools) by providing a platform for the rapid capture of static workstation characteristics and detailed data on dynamic demand and performance factors. While the D-MOD tool is yet to cross the bridge between demand and experienced workload, the aspiration is that D-MOD can present a valuable tool in both the practical development of workload assessment tools for signalling, and serve as a research incubator for the development of theory.

Acknowledgement. Thank you to all Human Factors consultants, Network Rail, RSSB for their attendance to our Human Factors signalling working group. This project is co-founded by Innovate UK and EPSRC as part of the Knowledge Transfer Partnership programme.

References

1. Sharples, S., Millen, L., Golightly, D., Balfe, N.: The impact of automation on rail signalling operations. Proc. Inst. Mech. Eng. Part F: J. Rail Rapid Transit **244**, 1–13 (2010)
2. Wilson, J.R., Farrington-Darby, T., Cox, G., Bye, R., Hockey, G.R.J.: The railway as a socio-technical system: human factors at the heart of successful rail engineering. Proc. Inst. Mech. Eng. Part F: J. Rail Rapid Transit **221**(1), 101–115 (2007)
3. Pickup, L., Wilson, J.R., Sharpies, S., Norris, B., Clarke, T., Young, M.S.: Fundamental examination of mental workload in the rail industry. Theor. Issues Ergon. Sci. **6**(6), 463–482 (2005)
4. Pickup, L., Balfe, N., Lowe, E., Wilson, J.R.: 'He's not from around here: the significance of local knowledge. Rail Hum. Factors: Supporting Reliab. Saf. cost Reduction, **357** (2013)
5. Pickup, L., Wilson, J., Lowe, E.: The operational demand evaluation checklist (ODEC) of workload for railway signalling. Appl. Ergon. **41**(3), 393–402 (2010)
6. Wright, K., Crabb, R.: Making the invisible visible: an objective measure of cognitive workload for signallers. In: Proceedings of the Fifth International Conference on Rail Human Factor, London (2015)
7. Golightly, D., Wilson, J.R., Lowe, E., Sharples, S.: The role of situation awareness for understanding signalling and control in rail operations. Theor. Issues Ergon. Sci. **11**(12), 84–98 (2010)
8. Delamare, D., Golightly, D., Treble, P., Lumby, A.: D-MOD dynamic modelling of operator demand a new simulator module for the evaluation of signaller's demand. Presented at IEEE ICIRT 2016, Birmingham, UK (2016)

9. Delamare, D., Golightly, D., Goswell, G., Treble, P.: D-MOD The use of full-fidelity simulators for the quantification of signaller's demand. In: 7th International Conference on Railway Operations Modelling and Analysis (2017)
10. Kopardekar, P.H., Schwartz, A., Magyarits, S., Rhodes, J.: Airspace complexity measurement: An air traffic control simulation analysis. Int. J. Ind. Eng.: Theory Appl. Pract. **16**(1), 61–70 (2009)
11. Aldrich, T.B., Szabo, S.M., Bierbaum, C.R.: The development and application of models to predict operator workload during system design. In: McMillan, G.R., Beevis, D., Salas, E., Strub, M.H., Sutton, R., Van Breda, L. (eds.) Applications of Human Performance Models to System Design, pp. 65–80. Springer, Heidelberg (1989)
12. Hart, S.G., Staveland, L.E.: Development of NASA-TLX (Task Load Index): results of empirical and theoretical research. Adv. Psychol. **52**, 139–183 (1988)
13. Krehl, C., Balfe, N.: Cognitive workload analysis in rail signalling environments. Cogn. Technol. Work **16**(3), 359–371 (2014)
14. Weeda, C., Zeilstra, M.P.: Prediction of mental workload of monitoring tasks. In: Nadashi, N., Scott, A., Wilson, J.R., Mills, A. (eds.) Rail human factors supporting reliability, safety and cost reduction. Proceedings of the Fourth International Conference on Rail Human Factors, London pp. 633–640 (2013)
15. Gibson, W.H., Mills, A., Basacik, D., Harrison, C.: The incident factor classification system and signals passed at danger. Paper Presented at the 5th Conference of Rail Human Factors, London, UK (2015)
16. Shanahan, P., Gregory, D., Lowe, E.: Signaller workload exploration and assessment tool (SWEAT). In: Wilson, J.R., Mills, A., Clarke, T., Rajan, J., Dadashi, N. (eds.) Proceedings of 3rd Rail Human Factors Conference, pp. 434–443 (2012)

Mental Workload as an Outcome in Medical Education

Aidan Byrne[(⊠)] [iD]

Medical School, Swansea University, Swansea, UK
aidan.byrne27@swansea.ac.uk

Abstract. Educational theory derives from a number of disparate scientific disciplines, which provides an opportunity for rich dialogue. However, in a time of austerity and reduction in the budgets of many educational organisations, it has refocussed research into educational activities which provide real and measurable benefits to students. With a focus on medical education, this paper outlines the position that mental workload theory provides both a unifying theory and the methodology required to evaluate the learning of students.

Keywords: Mental workload · Educational theory · Medical education

1 Introduction

Education lacks a unifying theoretical perspective, but rather derives its principles from a range of associated scientific sources to provide both its philosophy and experimental methodology. This is important, as every education endeavour is inevitably situated within the confines of its chosen sources, which perhaps explains why education remains a subject around which argument frequently rages. This paper particularly references medical education, but the principles are generalizable to other educational domains. While Mental Workload has developed as a theoretical concept with validated measures and proved itself to provide unique insights into human performance [1], it has had little impact on the measurement of educational outcomes. Cognitive load theory has an established literature [2] and uses the principle that excessive mental workload impairs learning. It has been used to ensure that educational materials both present critical information in easily understood formats and to reduce the inclusion of extraneous information. A critical weakness in this approach is that the experimental evidence is based on classroom-based educational activities with outcomes measured by performance in written assessments. While such an approach may be valid within purely academic disciplines, it must be questioned whether such an approach is applicable to educational activities which aim to prepare students for real world activities. An example of the above is the difference between a study of tracheal intubation (a key clinical skill) in the laboratory, which suggested that it is possible to train a complete novice using three attempts in the laboratory using success as the criteria [3] compared to a real world study of experienced staff who required an average of 76 attempts to master the same skill. The role of complexity in educational design will be further explored below.

© Springer International Publishing AG 2017
L. Longo and M.C. Leva (Eds.): H-WORKLOAD 2017, CCIS 726, pp. 187–197, 2017.
DOI: 10.1007/978-3-319-61061-0_12

This paper is an attempt to outline a coherent philosophy which can guide its use in educational activities with practical real world outcomes. Unfortunately, the huge range of educational philosophies makes it impossible to include them all in a single paper and I have, therefore, chosen three philosophies to illustrate what such a philosophy would imply. In each case, the philosophy is described in terms of its theoretical source, its view of learning, the teaching/learning methods adopted, the assessment tools used and its chosen outcomes.

Firstly, the philosophy of Behaviourism [4] is based on laboratory studies of (often animal) behaviour in response to changes in their environment, with the work of Pavlov [5] on dog salivation as perhaps the best known. Learning is viewed as a 'conditioned response' to an environmental stimulus with the organism (learner) changing their behaviour in response to a reward or punishment. The educational process is therefore simple; repeatedly present the learner with a problem and if the answer is right, provide a positive stimulus and if the answer is wrong, a negative stimulus. In the past this may have been characterised as a ferocious teacher teaching mathematics using frequent application of the edge of a ruler on the knuckles and a rare sweet. However, the same principles apply to learning high level skills such as sports, where athletes usually repeat the same processes over and over, receiving feedback from their coach. Assessment is therefore a simple matter of providing the correct stimulus and measuring how often the learners pick the correct response. The lab rats press a lever in the cage and the human learners pick the correct answer in multiple choice tests. Success is a simple matter of measuring the % of correct responses and with a direct correlation between % correct and educational success, often published in the media as 'pass rates', 'A grades' or 'core indicators'. While such an approach is undoubtedly effective, it is frequently denigrated by higher level educators as mindless 'training' which can produce high levels of performance within a narrow domain, but which does not develop understanding, wider knowledge or the ability to transfer skills to other domains. The view of learners as little more than lab rats to be punished or rewarded sits uncomfortably with professional values.

Secondly, the philosophy of 'competence' [6] developed from workplace based analysis of tasks splits any complex task into a series of 'competences' which can be taught and then assessed in a structured and objective way. For example, during the induction of anaesthesia, the doctor needs to insert a cannula (tube) into a vein to give drugs, needs to communicate effectively with the patient and needs to administer an appropriate dose of drug. These tasks can be taught and tested separately, so for example, the insertion of cannula can be tested in the laboratory on a plastic arm, communication can be tested with an actor in an office and the dosage of drugs tested with a paper based exercise in an examination setting. The abilities of learners can therefore be easily tested in a series of structured assessments with each competency achieved 'ticked off' and when all the competencies have been achieved, then the learner is defined as fully competent and fit to practise. Unfortunately, for many practitioners, this logic is a flawed. For example, if you assume that if any musician can demonstrate that they can play each note of their instrument in turn, comment on some recorded music and also identify all the notation marks on a musical score, they are competent to play in an orchestra, you are likely to be disappointed. Complex tasks are far more than the sum of their components and need to be assessed as wholes.

Thirdly, the concept of Situated Learning [7], developed from ethnographic studies and views the learner starting as an outsider and then gradually becoming a full member of a community. The focus is therefore not so much on the acquisition of specific knowledge or skills, but rather on personal change and development. The primary learning activity is therefore working within the community alongside peers/mentors and with success attained when the individual is accepted by the community as one of their own. The medieval apprenticeship with the apprentice working alongside masters and being finally accepted once they produce their own 'masterpiece' perhaps illustrates this philosophy best. While such a philosophy has obvious attractions, its lack of objectivity and scope for excluding minority groups means that it is rarely used in professional settings as the sole means of assessment.

Although the above are described as distinct and mutually exclusive philosophies, in practice, they are often combined. While such combinations are understandable in response to external pressures such as cost, the need to provide a hard pass/fail boundary and the need to defend decisions against legal challenge, the results are predictably incoherent. For example, trainee anaesthetists, who are already qualified doctors with at least two years' work experience are required to join a training programme [8] (apprenticeship) and work alongside senior staff (masters) who provide mentorship and ultimately decide whether the learner has achieved the level of skill required to be accepted to the community of (master) anaesthetists. However, during this period, they are also required to learn vast amounts of abstract knowledge and pass multiple choice examinations, as well as being required to demonstrate specific competencies in real world and laboratory settings. The result is entirely predictable, with some trainees rated as excellent by senior staff who fail the exams and others who are regarded as incompetent who nevertheless pass the exams. The result is frustration, wasted resources and a failure to reliably discriminate between those who will perform to a high standard in the workplace and those who will not.

2 Mental Workload as Educational Theory

The question then, is how Mental Workload should be viewed as an educational philosophy?

Wicken's Multiple Resource Theory [9] is widely cited within the Mental Workload literature and provides a framework on which to base a wide range of assessment methodology. However, it also underpins a philosophy of perception and cognition which can be brought into the educational domain. These can be expressed as:

- The world is a highly complex and rapidly changing environment which cannot be fully comprehended by our limited perceptual resources.
- Our senses can be trained to convert the overwhelming complexity of reality into a manageable and coherent 'perception' of our world. However, by necessity that perception is fragmentary and may be inaccurate.
- Our decisions are largely driven by subconscious processes, with consciousness perhaps seen as a largely retrospective and rationalising process.

- Our responses to our environment are highly dependent on learned and complex patterns of response which coordinate a wide range of resources to achieve each task.

For example, this can easily be applied to the role of a pilot in combat. The environment is complex and there are a lot of things to do, such as fly, navigate and use weapons. Pilots gradually learn strategies to simplify their world, so that radar contacts are either 'friend' or 'foe' and firing weapons, at least initially, becomes a simple matter of eliminating a 'foe'. Pilots also learn that the majority of rapid responses cannot be thought through, but have to become automated responses to specific problems. In the same way, responses cannot be theoretical notions of how to respond, but rather as highly automated psychomotor patterns learned through long practice. However, the same principles can be applied to a doctor in General Practice seeing a patient, with for example, an older lady with back pain. While the symptoms are usually simple, a consultation provides a wealth of verbal and nonverbal cues as to the severity and nature of the pain, so that the way the patient opens the clinic door, their gait across the room, the way they sit down and their facial expression as they describe the pain may be far more informative than the symptoms as described. Further, doctors need years of practice to learn how to notice these clues, but also may miss or misinterpret clinical information. The subconscious nature of these processes is readily evident in the common descriptions of doctors who refer patients for further investigation because they 'knew something was wrong' (rather than what) and those who describe the identification of a diagnosis 'before the patient even sat down'. However, the two examples above provide a key distinction in the work of those investigating the use of Mental Workload as a method to improve performance and that difference is in how we view the complexity of our environment.

In high risk industries, such as aviation, complexity has been seen as a challenge to the limited capacity of the human mind, with the result that it has been systematically designed out of high risk processes [10]. The main application of studies involving mental workload has been to identify processes where cognitive demand are too high so that the workload can be reduced, for example, through simplification, workload sharing or better training. The most widely known example in the UK is perhaps the ban on the use of mobile phones while driving, partly at least based on simulation studies using a secondary task methodology [11]. In the above cases, the theoretical stance taken supports the use of laboratory or simulation based studies in that the task and operator actions can usually be reduced to a small number of defined correct and incorrect options and the environment can be reproduced to a high degree of fidelity. If the mental workload of subjects is measured within a simulator, then interventions which produce a reduction in their workload can be accepted as a successful intervention. For example, if redesigning a computer interface reduced the workload of operators, then we can predict that the performance of operators will increase and their error rates will decline [12].

In contrast, within domains such as medicine, the environment, actions and possible outcomes are in most cases very poorly defined and the mental workload associated with the task can be extremely high [13]. As noted above, a doctor in a clinic setting is required to monitor a wide range of verbal and nonverbal clues, to consider whether each clue is relevant to an existing diagnosis, to consider whether a new diagnosis is possible, to run through the usual questions, to develop new questions depending on previous answers and at the same time, to appear calm, sympathetic and to respond appropriately to whatever they are told. It is perhaps no wonder that patients complain that doctors 'don't listen' as they are engaged in so many different tasks [14]. Although the distinction between the 'complexity' of aviation and the 'complicatedness' of medicine can be seen as medical hubris, its reality is evidence by the failure of simulation to produce improved clinical performance in many studies [15–17]. The key suggestion here is that in complex systems it is still possible to design training and assessment systems which closely link to operator performance; for example, pilots can be tested on a simulator using outputs like approach speed and altitude, with a high certainty that those outputs will predict real world performance. In contrast, in complicated domains like medicine, where there are no high fidelity simulators and few agreed outputs, it is not possible to use the same educational strategies.

As an educational philosophy, therefore, learning is seen as the ability to deal with complexity without excessive mental workload. That is, someone who has learned effectively can make sense of complex information/situations and respond effectively without evidence of mental workload, with the maximum complexity that can be accommodated as a measure of performance. So for example, the performance of a doctor could be measured by the complexity of patients with which they can cope and the performance of a musician with the complexity of the musical score they can play. While the units with which complexity are measured are domain-specific, the principles are universal.

3   Practical Application to Education

What is suggested here is that our view of complexity is the key to the use of mental workload studies in the educational domain. If complexity is viewed as a problem, then it suggests that educational processes should be simplified with material introduced to learners within controlled environments and with the complexity of the material gradually increased once they have mastered the basic elements. In contrast, if we view complexity as the essential characteristic of the domain, then it suggests that exposing learners to that complexity at the earliest possible stage and maximising their exposure to it during their educational is essential. This approach is supported by studies which appear to characterise expertise as 'knowing where to look' rather than 'knowing what to look for' [18], and those which characterise expertise as highly context dependant [19]. This conclusion is controversial in that most educational processes have relied in the past on the principle that learners must 'understand the basic principles' before they engage in realistic practice. This has led to, for example, a medical student being ejected from an operating theatre because they hadn't studied enough anatomy on the basis that if they didn't know anatomy, they couldn't learn from the experience of observing surgery. It's difficult to determine whether some of this resistance is based on educational belief, on a feeling that anyone without appropriate professional knowledge is not worthy to be admitted to a professional environment or it is a case of 'I had to go through two years of lectures to get here, so you should too'.

An adherence to existing methods and assessment techniques also obscures the problem that the accepted measures of student performance in medical schools, such as the results of entrance interviews, multiple choice exams, essays and projects do not predict future performance as a doctor and do not even correlate well with each other [20]. What we do know is that 'knowing' and 'understanding' or even 'doing in a laboratory setting' are not adequate to define 'safe to practice'. The explanation suggested here is that they fail to predict future performance because they provide a challenge which avoids the complexity of the real world.

In other high risk domains such as aviation, this problem has been addressed through the development of simulation [21], so that learners can be developed through a programme of part task simulators which mimic small aspects of a single task in real-time, such as navigation computers, to full scale, high fidelity simulators which allow an entire day's work to be completed in real time. For many industries, including healthcare, simulators have limited utility, for three reasons [22]. Firstly, people do not come with a manual and individual people do not always behave the way you would expect. This means that people can suddenly behave in unexpected and unusual ways, but also, their physiology can also confound expectation. When learners have to deal with real people, they have to be prepared for the unexpected and it is hard to design simulators that do not behave predictably. Secondly, most industries where simulation has become embedded deal with information provided either verbally or in the form of instrumentation, both of which can be simulated relatively easily. In contrast, the simulation of skin colour, joint movement or nonverbal communication are extremely difficult and unlikely to be simulated effectively in the near future. Thirdly, pilots are few in number and the cost of flying an aircraft for training is very high, making simulation a financially viable option. Healthcare workers are numerous and training on the job is cheap, making simulation training financially impossible. While simulation provides obvious advantages, it can prove to be prohibitively expensive to implement in low income areas [17]. A shift to mental workload as an educational outcome can shift the focus from how a simulator works (anatomical fidelity) and works (functional fidelity) toward more simple devices which just target the effectiveness of training (psychological fidelity) [23, 24].

Mental workload provides us with a new way of looking at the problem of assessing the performance of individuals dealing with complex environments in that the ability of an individual to deal with a complex situation without becoming cognitively overloaded can be used to define expertise [1]. This is characterised by sensory systems which effectively reduce the complexity to comprehensible concepts, an ability to make sense of those concepts as a whole as well as the ability to rapidly produce a coordinated and effective response. The difference between the novice and expert is perhaps most graphically described by those involved in large scale conflicts, where those new to combat are described as becoming overwhelmed by the situation and becoming completely paralysed and unable to respond at all. In contrast, with even a few days experience, soldiers become able to deal with the experience and start to respond appropriately [25].

4 Links to Other Education Theories

This concept of expertise links closely to the concept of the four stages of competence [26], with novices moving from Unconscious incompetence, conscious incompetence, conscious competence and finally unconscious competence. However, while the label of 'unconscious competence' is correct in that the primary reason for the improved performance is the development of subconscious cognitive processes which allow the operator to complete the task without conscious effort (low mental workload), the suggestion here is that the process of developing expertise does not pass through four different developmental stages. Rather, the subconscious processes are the key elements of expertise and are developed from the beginning of the training process. The conscious monitoring of action and the decision to practice are obviously important to make sure an individual continues to train, but is not an essential part of the development of expertise. For example, those learning to play the piano usually go through a process of being told about musical notation, learning how to convert the notes to key strokes and eventually, at the highest level, being told to 'forget the notes and just play the music'. However, there are many people who have just sat down at a piano and learned to play music without any instruction or theory. That is, they develop unconscious competence without going through a stage of unconscious incompetence or conscious competence. In this context, the use of the term 'competence' is also problematic as noted above.

Often linked to the concept of unconscious incompetence is Miller's pyramid of competence [27], which describes an increase in performance from Knows, Knows How, Shows How and Does. That is a learner progressing from knowing theory, to being able to describe how something would be done in practice, to being able to demonstrate how and finally being able to complete the task in the real world. However, the problem with this description of learning is that it is a greater reflection of the teaching methods commonly used than the development of expertise. That is, learners are usually taught the theoretical principles first, the practicalities next and then taken through simple practical teaching before being allowed to move into the workplace. The example of the self-taught pianist readily demonstrates that it is not necessary to acquire theoretical knowledge before engaging in practice. However, an important distinction must be made here between what is necessary for effective learning and what is possible in the real world. For example, while it might be acceptable to allow a novice free rein on a piano to learn through experimentation, the same would not apply to those learning how to control a nuclear reactor. The suggestion is that Mental Workload can provide the basis for a new educational concept of expertise in that learning is a process by which we learn to respond to complexity without developing cognitive overload. The level of educational attainment achieved is therefore defined by the complexity/speed of the task which can be completed successfully. 'Command' appears an appropriate term to describe an individual who has achieved a level of expertise at which they have acquired the ability to cope with the cognitive demands of the most difficult predicted situation and yet still maintain a cognitive workload within their capacity so that they retain spare capacity to monitor their own performance. Such an individual would therefore be able to explain and justify their decisions after the event. While this concept is perhaps most easily applied to pure psychomotor tasks, such as typing, where expertise can be defined in terms of 'words per minute', it can also be applied to much more complex tasks. An objection to this definition could be that professional occupations perceive their own occupations as far more than the successful completion of tasks, but this does not negate the concept of mental workload as an educational outcome.

5 Practical Implementation

The follow will describe previous studies using mental workload within an educational setting to demonstrate these principles. As noted above, a medical consultation provides a complex cognitive challenge for even experienced healthcare workers due to the need to ask questions, monitor the answers, watch for nonverbal clues, make diagnoses, empathise etc. There are few studies of mental workload during consultations, but they appear to confirm that the consultation is a high workload task [28]. An interesting observation is that the observed levels of workload appear consistent with periods of overload that could be associated with significant levels of error or poor performance.

A recent study [unpublished] in medical students measured the effect of combining a listening task with the physical task of taking a blood sample. While the simple task of listening to a recording of clinical information appeared to be a low workload task, students taking a blood sample showed evidence of cognitive overload. The more interesting finding was that when the two tasks were combined, there was no increase in mental workload, which was unexpected. However, the performance of the students on the listening task deteriorated. The explanation appears to be that in response to the excessive cognitive workload, the students 'shed' the listening task in order to be able to complete the physical task of taking blood. If confirmed in future studies, the implication is that during a consultation, healthcare workers are routinely overloaded and are likely to ignore patients in order to complete tasks such as filling in forms or entering data into a computer. This would provide an explanation of the problem that patients frequently complain that healthcare workers don't listen to them and suggest that rather than staff being uncaring, they are simply overwhelmed with the number of tasks they have to perform.

Studies in medicine have largely used subjective reporting of workload using the NASA-TLX scale [29], and secondary task methods using mental arithmetic/visual change/vibrotactile stimulus as outcomes. Although the methodology varies, all studies have used deterioration in second task performance as evidence of cognitive overload. These studies confirm that the mental workload of staff correlates well with their perception of the difficulty of the tasks, with, for example, higher levels of mental workload during the induction of anaesthesia and emergence from anaesthesia (often compared to takeoff and landing for pilots) and lower during the maintenance (cruise) phase. Although the average levels of workload appear closely linked to the task, the workload of individuals appears to vary widely, which was an unexpected finding and one at odds with studies in other fields. The explanation may be that while admission to many high risk occupations depends on a selection process which includes a range of psychomotor and cognitive tasks, admission to medicine is almost exclusively based on written examinations and interviews. It is therefore possible for an individual with cognitive problems with psychomotor coordination (dyspraxia) or other limitations to qualify as a doctor who would never qualify, for example, as a pilot. This suggests that the inclusion of mental workload as an educational outcome could provide learners with valuable feedback on their aptitude for a variety of medical specialities at an early stage of their career and avoid them investing years in a speciality for which they are unsuited.

A study looking at the mental workload of anaesthetists during their seven year training programme confirmed that delivering anaesthesia appears to be a high work-load task and confirmed that training reduces mental workload, with a near linear decrease in workload in relation to the number of years training completed [30]. Interestingly, those tested in their final year of training, who should have completed all the compulsory aspects of their training and were engaged in training for sub-specialist tasks did not show evidence of cognitive overload, suggesting that a seven year programme successfully trains subjects to an appropriate level of expertise and that this expertise can be reliably determined by measuring mental workload. The interesting finding from this research was that the mental workload of qualified, permanent staff was also measured and was shown to be higher than that of final year trainees. This unexpected finding indicates that either the expertise of qualified staff had deteriorated once they had completed their training or could be associated with a decrease in cognitive capacity with age, as qualified staff were inevitably older than trainees. This suggests that healthcare workers in high cognitive load tasks could face significant and different challenges as they get older.

In addition to the challenges of healthcare working, we have observed that the assessment process can also be challenging for observers. For example, the most common assessment of clinical practice involves the observation of a learner by a trained observer, who then ticks off each aspect of the performance that has been completed. A study of observers during a practice exam suggested that the mental workload of the observers was indeed very high, which is explained by the need to observe for up to 28 different actions, to rate the completeness of each action and then to record the action on a chart [31]. Importantly, a follow-up study showed that a short training period had no effect on either the accuracy or mental workload of observers which supports the concept that the performance of complex tasks depends on sub-conscious processes developed through long periods of practice rather than simply understanding or knowing what to do [32].

6 Conclusion

In conclusion, this paper suggests that human performance should be viewed as three tightly-knit and largely subconscious processes: a highly sophisticated analysis of sensory input to derive comprehensible wholes, the synthesis of those wholes into situational awareness and the coordinated response to the situation. Expertise is defined as the ability to complete those three processes in response to a complex situation without cognitive overload and professional expertise requiring the ability to consciously justify the actions taken. This level of performance is characterised by not just the ability to perform at an expert level, but to also retain enough spare cognitive capacity to monitor the performance and adapt as necessary and therefore should be regarded as achieving 'Command'. Mental workload therefore provides a unifying theory of educational activity with well-developed links to appropriate assessment methodologies.

References

1. Wickens, C.: Multiple resources and mental workload. Hum. Factors **50**(3), 449–455 (2008)
2. de Jong, T.: Cognitive load theory, educational research, and instructional design: some food for thought. Inst. Sci **38**(2), 105–134 (2010)
3. Ayoub, C.M., Kanazi, G.E., Al Alami, A., Rameh, C., El-Khatib, M.F.: Tracheal intubation following training with the GlideScope® compared to direct laryngoscopy. Anaesthesia **65**(7), 674–678 (2010)
4. Skinner, B.: Reflections on Behaviourism and Society. Prentice-Hall, Eaglewood Cliffs (1904)
5. Pavlov, I.P.: Conditioned reflexes: an investigation of the physiological activity of the cerebral cortex. Ann. Neurosci. **17**(3), 136 (2010)
6. Talbot, M.: Monkey see, monkey do: a critique of the competency model in graduate medical education. Med. Educ. **38**(6), 587–592 (2004)
7. Lave, J., Wenger, E.: Situated Learning. Legitimate Peripheral Participation. Cambridge University Press, Cambridge (1991)
8. Anaesthetists RCo. CCT in Anesthetics, Edition 2, Version 1.6. London (2010)
9. Wickens, C.: Situation awareness and workload in aviation. Curr. Dir. Psychol. Sci. **11**, 128–133 (2002)
10. Cambell, R., Bagshaw, M.: Human Performance and Limitations in Aviation. Blackwell Publishing, Hoboken (2002)
11. Recarte, M.A., Nunes, L.M.: Mental workload while driving: effects on visual search, discrimination, and decision making. J. Exp. Psychol. Appl. **9**(2), 119–137 (2003)
12. Charabati, S., Bracco, D., Mathieu, P.A., Hemmerling, T.M.: Comparison of four different display designs of a novel anaesthetic monitoring system, the integrated monitor of anaesthesia (IMATM). Br. J. Anaesth. **103**(5), 670–677 (2009)
13. Byrne, A.: Measurement of mental workload in clinical medicine: a review study. Anesthesiol. Pain Med. **1**(2), 90–94 (2011)
14. Davis, D.H.J., Oliver, M., Byrne, A.J.: A novel method of measuring the mental workload of anaesthetists during simulated practice. Br. J. Anaesth. **103**(5), 665–669 (2009)
15. McGaghie, W.C., Issenberg, S.B., Petrusa, E.R., Scalese, R.J.: A critical review of simulation-based medical education research: 2003–2009. Med. Educ. **44**(1), 50–63 (2010)
16. Stefanidis, D., Scerbo, M., Sechrist, C., Mostafavi, A., Heniford, B.: Do novices display automaticity during simulator training. Am. J. Surg. **195**(2), 210–213 (2008)
17. Ersdal, H.L., Vossius, C., Bayo, E., Mduma, E., Perlman, J., Lippert, A., et al.: A one-day "Helping Babies Breathe" course improves simulated performance but not clinical management of neonates. Resuscitation **84**(10), 1422–1427 (2013)
18. Balslev, T., Jarodzka, H., Holmqvist, K., de Grave, W., Muijtjens, A.M.M., Eika, B., et al.: Visual expertise in paediatric neurology. Eur. J. Paediatr. Neurol. **16**(2), 161–166 (2012)
19. Godden, D., Baddeley, A.: Context-dependant memory in two natural environments: on land and underwater. Br. J. Psychol. **66**(3), 325–331 (1975)

20. Wilkinson, D., Zhang, J., Byrne, G.J., Luke, H., Ozolins, I.Z., Parker, M.H., et al.: Medical school selection criteria and the prediction of academic performance. Med. J. Aust. **189**(4), 235 (2008)
21. Lancaster, G., Dodd, S., Williamson, P.: Design and analysis of pilot studies: recommendations for good practice. J. Eval. Clin. Pract. **10**(2), 307–312 (2004)
22. Bradley, P.: The history of simulation in medical education and possible future directions. Med. Educ. **40**(3), 254–262 (2006)
23. Byrne, A.: What is simulation for? Anaesthesia **67**(3), 219–225 (2012)
24. Bannister, S., Hilliard, R., Regehr, G., Lingard, L.: Technical skills in paediatrics: a qualitative study of acquisition, attitudes and assumptions in the neonatal intensive care unit. Med. Educ. **37**(12), 1082–1090 (2003)
25. Beevor, A.: D-Day: The Battle for Normandy. Penguin, Westminster (2009)
26. Adams, L.: Learning a new skill is easier said than done. Gordon Training International, Solana Beach (2011)
27. Miller, G.: The assessment of clinical skills/competence/performance. Acad. Med. **65**(9), S63–S67 (1990)
28. Byrne, A.J., Oliver, M., Bodger, O., Barnett, W., Williams, D., Jones, H., et al.: Novel method of measuring the mental workload of anaesthetists during clinical practice. Br. J. Anaesth. **105**(6), 767–771 (2010)
29. Yurko, Y., Scerbo, M., Prabhu, A., Acker, C., Stefanidis, D.: Higher mental workload is associated with poorer laparoscopic performance as measured by the NASA-TLX tool. Simul. Healthcare. **5**(5), 267–271 (2010)
30. Byrne, A.J., Jones, J.G.: Responses to simulated anaesthetic emergencies by anaesthetists with different durations of clinical experience. Br. J. Anaesth. **78**(5), 553–556 (1997)
31. Byrne, A., Tweed, N., Halligan, C.: A pilot study of the mental workload of objective structured clinical examination examiners. Med. Educ. **48**(3), 262–267 (2014)
32. Byrne, A., Soskova, T., Dawkins, J., Coombes, L.: A pilot study of marking accuracy and mental workload as measures of OSCE examiner performance. BMC Med. Educ. **16**(1), 191 (2016)

Effect of Control-Display Compatibility on the Mental Workload of Submarine Helmsmen

Philippe Rauffet[1(✉)], Christine Chauvin[1], Chiara Nistico[1],
Samantha Judas[1], and Norbert Toumelin[2]

[1] Université Bretagne-Sud, Lab-STICC UMR CNRS 6285, Lorient, France
{philippe.rauffet, christine.chauvin,
chiara.nistico, samantha.judas}@univ-ubs.fr
[2] DCNS Group, Lorient, France
norbert.toumelin@dcnsgroup.com

Abstract. The purpose of the study is to analyse the directional compatibility of control-display design and its effects on the mental workload of helmsmen. An experiment is then carried out on a simulator designed by a world leader in military naval shipbuilding. This experiment follows a unique scenario including four usual submarine maneuvers. It is achieved by two groups, each carrying out a perceptual-motor task on a specific steering control-display configuration, proposed by the naval shipbuilder (one with a standard numeric display and one with a new visual-spatial representation, both tasks controlled by the same joystick). The findings of this study show that the control-display compatibility produces increased mental workload when a direction-of-motion stereotype is violated (upward-forward relationship).

Keywords: Direction-of-motion stereotype · Control-display compatibility · Mental workload

1 Introduction

Submarine steering is a specific case in the activities of complex system supervision. Controlling the three-dimensional movement of the submarine is carried out without direct visualisation, neither of the environment nor of the submersible actuators. Moreover, activities consist of a set of routine procedures and phases carried out by a helmsman, usually inexperienced, responding to compass heading and immersion instructions transmitted by the Chief of the Watch (COW). This relative inexperience is explained by the low level of decisions taken by these operators, who only execute the instructions. The position of the helmsman is one of the first appointments of young submariners. Helmsmen are generally recruited with an A-level diploma, and they are assigned to steering tasks after just a short formation lasting 8 weeks, with 20 h spent on a simulator. A few authors have investigated the working activities carried out in a submarine control room. For instance, McLane and Wolfe [15] focused on display concepts for submarine manual control, and more recently, Stanton and Bessell [22]

© Springer International Publishing AG 2017
L. Longo and M.C. Leva (Eds.): H-WORKLOAD 2017, CCIS 726, pp. 198–212, 2017.
DOI: 10.1007/978-3-319-61061-0_13

proposed a work analysis of the activities involved in returning the submarine to periscope depth. However, these analyses relative to submarine control were mostly descriptive or narrative, and were little concerned with performance and the effects experienced by the driver [25]. The lack of in-depth studies is explained by the difficulties of accessing the domain context because of the physical constraints and confidentiality issues. There is, however, a startling contrast with the research conducted in the aviation or automotive domains, where numerous studies provide fine-scale modelling of cognitive steering tasks [1, 16, 19], an analysis of perceptual-motor interactions with a human-machine steering interface [13, 23], and a regular or periodic, objective or subjective, assessment of the effects of steering on mental workload. This assessment is often carried out in simulation environments with strong ecological validity, and it is based on, inter alia, physiological and ocular measurements or questionnaires such as the NASA Task Load Index (NASA-TLX) to determine mental workload [7, 10, 17, 20].

The purpose of this article is thus to partially open this "black box" by analysing submarine steering and measuring the effects of perceptual-motor tasks on the helmsmen's mental workload. Submarine steering can be carried out according to different modes ranging from full automation to complete manual control. This paper deals with the manual mode only, because it is the most "costly" for helmsmen in terms of task load. To this end, through a simulator-based experiment, we present an analysis of helmsmen's cognitive and perceptual-motor tasks in an ecologically valid scenario.

2 Related Works

In this section, we first present a state-of-the-art review of models related to direction-of-motion stereotypes, and we then transpose the models to the case of submarine steering in order to analyse perceptual-motor requirements and the way pilots interact manually with steering controls and displays (Sect. 2.1). Finally, we present studies on the assessment of steering effects on mental workload (Sect. 2.2).

2.1 Models of Perceptual-Motor Tasks, and Analysis of Manual Steering in New Submarines

In the later generations of submarines, all the elements needed for helm supervision (control and display) are found in one unit: the steering station. The monitoring and the command of three-dimensional steering parameters (immersion gap, compass heading deviation, trim of the vessel), within tactical and operational phases, involve low-level perceptual-motor tasks with the steering control-display configuration [18, 25]. These perceptual-motor tasks are often dependent on the activation of a direction-of-motion stereotype, i.e. the expectations of the relevant user population in terms of directional control-display compatibility [27]. The following paragraphs explore these generic stereotype issues that are then used to compare the perceptual-motor tasks resulting from the interactions with two different control-display configurations for submarine steering.

Generic Models About Direction-of-Motion Stereotypes

Once the physical requirements for display readability and control motions have been met, the direction-of-motion stereotype or movement compatibility is a preponderant key factor for the successful design of controls and displays [16]. The design of systems that do not follow stereotypes reduces performance or safety, especially in emergency situations or under time pressure [30]. An important study evaluating possible types of directional stimulus-response compatibility for systems, in which a control must be moved to bring about the goal-oriented motion of an object, is that of Worringham and Beringer [29]; the issue is also dealt with in the work of Burgess-Limerick et al. [3] and Chan and Hoffmann [6]. In particular, these authors refer to two common stereotypes that may exist between control and display movements and should guide the design of compatible configurations:

- Control-display compatibility (CD): the directional relationships in which the control and resulting movement on the display moved in the same direction were the least likely to cause error.
- Visual Field compatibility (VF): The principle suggests that compatible control-response relationships are those in which the direction of movement of the response in the operator's visual field matches the direction of movement of the control in the operator's visual field if the operator is looking at the control. This principle has been demonstrated to predict task performance correctly.

Wickens et al. [26] also analyse these direction-of-motion stereotypes when visual spatial thinking requires transformations between the different reference frames of the control and the display. In particular, they investigate the case where the control is in the horizontal frame whereas the display is vertically oriented. Contrary to the rather symmetrical lateral axis, where left and right are easy to confuse, the vertical and the fore-aft axes share an asymmetry (due to the gravitational forces, up is different from down, and because of the vision and the locomotion systems, forward is different from backward). As a consequence, the authors notice a strong association between the two marked endpoints of these two asymmetrical axes, especially between "forward" and "upward" directions.

The Specific Case of Two Specific Submarine Steering "Control-Display" Configurations

As part of the development of a submarine, studies were conducted in close collaboration with a shipbuilder. Work focused on the design of a new steering configuration, i.e. a visualisation interface coupled with a joystick as a motion control. This new configuration (henceforth called configuration B) could be deployed in future boats, as an alternative to the standard interface currently in use in submarines (henceforth called configuration A). As shown in Table 2, the joystick must be pushed for diving and pulled for rising.

The interface of configuration B aims at replacing the numerical data related to steering parameters by a visual-spatial information synthesis. In particular, it uses certain proposals from Temme et al. [23] who used two metaphors to build an aircraft cockpit display for the US Naval Air Station. These metaphors were adapted to the submarine case:

- The "starfield" metaphor shows the system's behaviour and its localisation in the external world. It is a reference framework that showcases the vertical and horizontal translations as well as the transverse rotations of the submarine.
- The "aircraft" metaphor (in the present case, "submarine") is a 2D image that symbolizes the vessel. Its position is fixed on the screen; the relative position of the starfield metaphor shows the vessel's behaviour and trajectory. Breakdowns (e.g. jammed rudder blades) may also be shown on this metaphor, which accounts for the orientation and movement limits of the system.

Application of Stereotype Models to the Two Control-Display Configurations
Table 1 shows a comparative analysis of the two control-display configurations A and B, where only the interface changes (the joystick stays the same). The stereotype violation in configuration B was confirmed by the feedback of submariners of two French naval bases, to whom this new configuration was submitted. Several submariners pulled the joystick to increase the submarine immersion, which caused the opposite effect of the desired goal. It is worth remembering that when pushing the joystick, the star moves towards the lower end of the submarine and the latter dives, whereas when pulling the joystick, the star moves towards the high end of the diamond shape and the submarine rises (see Fig. 1).

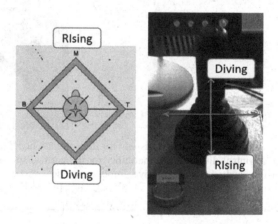

Fig. 1. The disturbing reverse motions in configuration B

This control system thus follows the usual pattern, particularly in the aviation domain: when pilots pull back the stick, the aircraft ascends, and when they push, it descends. The interface, more precisely the diamond-star set-up, may have misled some participants. They may have pulled back the joystick to try and bring the star towards the bottom of the diamond: "When you try to make the star go up, you pull the joystick and then you reverse the command". At the opposite, the movements of control and display are parallels for counter clockwise and clockwise turns.

Table 1. Comparison of the two control-display configurations in terms of direction-of-motion stereotype

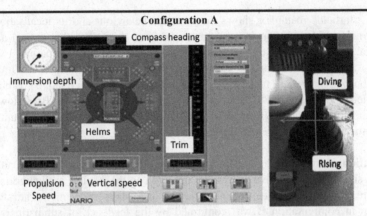

Configuration A

No direction-of-motion stereotype is involved between control and display. The interface is spatially static; only digits change over time for vertical speed and compass heading.

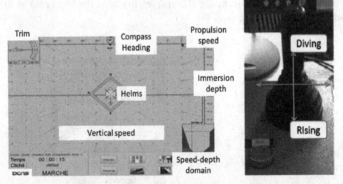

Configuration B

There is a compatibility of control and display for the compass heading monitoring, but there is also a control-display incompatibility for the vertical speed control. The joystick must be pushed forward to dive, implying vertical descending of the diamond-star inside the aircraft metaphor on the display. Hence, the upward/forward stereotype is violated (see [26]).

2.2   Analysis of Helmsmen's Mental Workload

The foregoing literature review enables us to make hypotheses related to these perceptual-motor aspects of submarine steering tasks. The perceptual-motor tasks require indeed compliance with the "upward/forward" direction-of-motion stereotype. To assess the effects of this aspect of steering tasks, helmsmen's mental workload need to be measured. According to the literature, different indicators can be identified.

Many studies propose subjective and objective measures to assess mental workload. Among the subjective techniques, there are two main multi-dimensional methods: SWAT [21] and NASA-TLX [11]. When the SWAT scale is compared to the NASA-TLX, the TLX scale is generally considered to be the better scale for measuring mental workload [12]. The NASA-TLX rating scale (TLX stands for task load index) is designed to assess the different factors causing mental workload in a questionnaire that enables a periodic, multidimensional, and subjective evaluation of the load experienced. This questionnaire examines six dimensions of workload assessment: cognitive demand, physical demand, temporal demand, effort, performance, and frustration. Hence, the different dimensions characterise the perception of the demand by the participants and their cognitive activity and effort. At the end of the main task, the participants score each dimension from 0 to 100. These six dimensions are then displayed in pairs and the participants select the dimension that contributed most to their load. Byers et al. [4] proposed an alternative to Hart and Staveland's [11] NASA-TLX, called NASA-rTLX (standing for raw task load index), whereby the weight gradings of the different dimensions are identical instead of being weighted by each subject. The authors showed a strong correlation between the two indicators. In addition to this subjective assessment, many studies have shown the contribution of objective, physiological measures for estimating mental workload, such as heart rate or skin conductance [24, 28]. In particular, several authors focused on another physiological indicator, the pupillary diameter, as remote eye tracking sensors are minimally intrusive and do not interfere with operators' activity. Hence, Beatty and Lucero-Wagoner [2] showed that an increase of the mean value of pupillary diameter results from the cognitive effort increase needed to face a more difficult task. Cegarra and Chevalier [5] argued that pupillary response can be considered a very sensitive indicator that can complement and be combined with the NASA-TLX technique. Dehais et al. [8], De Greef et al. [9], Marshall [14], and Recarte et al. [16] also identified this relationship in real or simulated activities, under various driving or steering tasks such as piloting an airplane, driving a car or operating a naval warship.

The next paragraphs present an experiment designed to verify the modelling of the specific case of manual submarine steering proposed in Sects. 2.1 and to determine precisely the effect of this perceptual-motor activity on the mental workload of helmsmen with the indicators presented in Sect. 2.2.

3 Material and Method

A first experiment designed to measure the effect of steering tasks upon mental workload and performance had already been conducted with 20-odd submariner helmsmen in two French naval bases. The sample, however, was highly heterogeneous, whether in terms of length of service in the Navy (ranging from 18 months to 10 years), campaigns at sea, or job profiles (certain participants had received helmsman training only while others had added COW or Officer of the Deck training). Moreover, configuration A (see Sect. 2.2) was familiar to all these submariners, which consequently skewed the configuration comparison. Additionally, a helmsman's job is to execute simple instructions; it can be entrusted to inexperienced submariners. Hence, we decided to reproduce the experiment with a novice homogeneous population having a solid scientific knowledge level. The population knew neither of the two steering interfaces (hence the bias of the first experiment was avoided) but was knowledgeable enough to comprehend and control the dynamic behaviour of the submarine; the group of participants thus closely resembled the average submarine helmsman profile. The experiment protocol is detailed in the following sections.

3.1 Participants

The participants were recruited from undergraduate and doctoral students in an engineering school in Brittany, France. Twenty students participated in the study (average age = 23.80; standard deviation = 3.105); they were randomly distributed into two equal groups corresponding to the two experimental conditions: one group carried out the simulation with configuration A, the other with configuration B (see Sect. 2.1). Furthermore, all subjects worked with the same experimental scenario (see Sect. 3.2). Group homogeneity was controlled through two variables: video game playing and visual correction. Both groups had the same number of participants who did not play video games (N = 3), the same number of participants who played video games at least once a week (N = 3), and the same number of participants wearing contact lenses or glasses (N = 4).

3.2 Simulation Set-up and Experimental Situation

The Simulator

The simulation set-up was designed to reproduce an ecological situation:

- at the operating level, the participants used a joystick; this device corresponds to what will replace the current supporting-bracket system in the future submarines;
- at the visualisation level, the interface of configuration A reproduced the current interface in submarines but on a smaller scale, and the interface of configuration B was an alternative tested by the shipbuilder for the future submarines;
- finally, at the behaviour level, the software part of the simulator reproduced a submarine's hydrodynamic model for both standard maneuvers and degraded situations (technical breakdown, damage, etc.). In accordance with the instructions issued through the commands, the simulation software computed the submarine behaviour in real time and displayed the information as it normally would appear on the submarine steering station.

The Scenario

For this study, an ecological scenario with four steering maneuvers was developed and validated in association with a submarine captain (see Fig. 2). The values of speed, immersion, and trim limits of the scenario were chosen with this expert; the French Navigation School of Submariners also validated this scenario. The four maneuvers result from the repetition of two sequences; each sequence included one submersion maneuver carried out at fast propulsion speed (16–20 knots) and one surfacing maneuver carried out at moderate speed (8–10 knots).

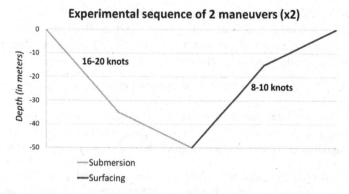

Fig. 2. Experimental scenario with 4 maneuvers (2 repeated sequences of one submersion and one submersing)

These maneuvers reflected the pilots' response to instructions regarding immersion depth changes (± 50 m on a relative basis); their difficulty depended upon the propulsion speed and the steering phase (i.e. steering time requirements and reactive approach or proactive stabilization (see Sect. 2.1)), manipulated by the experimenter. Participants had to reach the ordered immersion depth (within ± 7 m of receiving the instruction) and stabilise the submarine for 10 s so that the maneuver was evaluated as completed. There was no time limit but each participant was given a maximum of four attempts per maneuver to reach immersion depth. If all four attempts were used, the experimenter ended the maneuver. This threshold of four attempts was chosen for a practical reason; namely to prevent underperforming participants from being subjected to never-ending sessions. Moreover, in agreement with the submarine captain helping to design the scenario, it was considered a good indicator of the operators' (in)ability to achieve the requested task. To change immersion depth, pilots act on the trim of the vessel only, hence on the submarine's rate of climb.

3.3 Data Collection and Processing

Mental workload was evaluated using the NASA-rtlx and the analysis of pupil diameter.

Using the NASA-rtlx to Measure Mental Workload

After each maneuver, participants answered the French, pen-and-paper version of the NASA-rtlx questionnaire: it is an alternative to Hart and Staveland's [8] NASA-TLX, whereby the weight gradings of the different dimensions are identical, instead of being weighted by each subject. Byers et al. [3] showed a strong correlation between the two indicators. The questionnaire retained its six dimensions. For each of these, participants answered on a Likert-type scale ranging from weak to high levels. Each dimension was explained verbally.

Using Eye-Tracking Data to Estimate Mental Workload

For this study, we used a binocular eye-tracker with a 60 Hz recording frequency allowing precision readings of between 0.5° and 1.0°. The recorded data was then processed using Seeing Machines software:

- faceLAB™ 5 enables the continuous measure of pupil diameter, head posture, and gaze direction.
- EyeWorks™ provides the link between the ocular data and the experimental environment. It provides screenshot video capture and records gaze direction and data breakdown according to the phases of the scenario or areas of interest.

The eye-tracker was placed at the bottom of the screen and behind the control box (see Fig. 3). To avoid ocular behaviour variations (pupil diameter, blinks, etc.) resulting from changes in ambient light conditions, the luminosity of the test venue was kept constant.

Fig. 3. Experimental set-up (eye-tracking system, questionnaire, control box and interface)

The raw data were cleansed and processed with MATLAB software (see Table 2). Consistent with the literature [2, 10], physiological ocular data (pupil diameter) is considered an indicator of mental workload. Only pupil diameters between 2 and 8 mm were retained (which corresponds to the maximal dilation range of the human eye); similarly, fixation time was taken into account from 15 hundredths of a second (0.15 s) only. Pupil diameter was also subject to centring-reducing operations so as to eliminate inter-subject differences related to average diameter and dilation variations.

Synthesis of the Selected Indicators

Dividing the scenario in four maneuvers was performed by coding the starting times of each maneuver from the video captures. This division enabled the calculation of indicators for each maneuver; these were the dependent variables (DVs) under investigation in this study.

Statistical Processing

Analysis of the distribution of the dependent variables and of the control variables then helped determine the nature of the applicable statistical tests. The conditions of

Table 2. Synthesis of the dependent variables

Variable	Raw data	Filtered and standardized data	Calculation
NASA-rtlx (for each manoeuvre)	Likert-type scale for each dimension	Overall indicator calculated from the mean of all dimensions	$NASA - rtlx = \begin{bmatrix} \textit{experienced physical demand} \\ \textit{experienced mental demand} \\ \textit{experienced temporal demand} \\ \textit{experienced effort} \\ \textit{experienced performance} \\ \textit{experienced frustration} \\ \textit{overall indicator of experienced load} \end{bmatrix}$
PD (for each manoeuvre)	Raw pupil diameter	Cleaned and z-normalized pupil Diameter DPz (Diameter between 2 and 8 mm, then z-normalizing operations)	Mean pupil diameter for each phase $PD = \sum\limits_{DPz \in phase}^{1...n} \frac{PDz}{n}$

normality, homogeneity, and sphericity of variances were met by only the mean of z-normalized pupil diameter and certain dimensions of NASA-rtlx. Repeated measures univariate ANOVA and a t-test were then applied using STATISTICA software.

3.4 Experimental Protocol

The experiment was conducted in the LOUSTIC laboratory (Brest, France), a multi-disciplinary research platform for the uses of information and communication technology. Participants took the test individually. The test lasted about 2 h and was divided into six phases:

1. greeting participants: completing the profile questionnaire;
2. explaining the steering principles: a slide presentation was used to explain (verbally) the steering tasks and the interface;
3. practicing: participants carried out three maneuvers to familiarise themselves with the steering activities, the control box, and the interface;
4. eye-tracking parameter and calibration setting: Eye-Works Record software was launched to record the participants' eye movements after faceLAB software had calibrated the head, eyes, and test environment;
5. carrying-out the steering task: participants carried out the maneuvers and completed the NASA-rtlx questionnaire at the end of each maneuver;
6. debriefing and thanking: participants were questioned regarding the set of maneuvers, the interface, and the simulator in order to obtain their comments, and the test purpose was revealed. To ensure the inter-subject independence of the collected data, participants were asked not to reveal test contents to those around them.

3.5 Experimental Design

The protocols of only 16 out of 20 subjects were analysed because of a problem with pupil diameter data acquisition for certain maneuvers. In the end, the configuration A group included 8 subjects and the configuration B group included 8 individuals; the control-display configuration thus constituted an inter-subject variable. All of them were subject to the same scenario (presented in Fig. 1), with 2 repeated sequences of 2 different maneuvers (submersion and surfacing). Our experimental design was thus a mixed factorial design, written as in

Subject8 < ControlDisplayConfiguration2 > *Sequence2*Maneuver2.

The tables presented below show these independent variables (related to perceptual-motor requirements) and the dependent variables (related to mental workload) (Table 3).

Table 3. Independent and dependent variables

DV	Indicator of
NASA-rtlx : dimensions of experienced workload	Mental workload
PD : pupil diameter (z-normalized)	Mental workload

IV	Groups	Categories
Control-Display Configuration	2 Independent	Configuration A Configuration B
Sequence	2 Paired	Sequence 1, Sequence 2
Maneuvre	2 Paired	Submersion at rapid speed, Surfacing at moderate speed

3.6   Hypotheses

In terms of the distinction between perceptual-motor tasks and different control-display configurations (stereotype compliance or violation), presented in Sect. 2, we posit the following hypothesis:

H – The control-display configuration has an effect on the operators' mental workload. The mental workload experienced by operators for steering tasks should be higher for participants using configuration B due to the control-display incompatibility. Hypothesis H is broken down into two operational hypotheses:

H1 – The interface type has an effect on mental workload as measured by the NASA-TLX. We expect the NASA-TLX score to be higher for participants using configuration B.

H2 – The interface type has an effect on mental workload as measured from pupil dilation. The pupil diameter of participants using configuration B should be higher than that of participants using configuration Λ.

4   Results

4.1   Effect of Control-Display Compatibility upon NASA-rtlx

The dimensions investigated in the mental workload questionnaire were mental requirements, physical requirements, time requirement, effort, performance, and frustration (variance homogeneity was controlled and accepted for all dimensions of the questionnaire with the value $\alpha = .05$). For a macroscopic analysis, the dimension-based means of all maneuvers were examined (the means normality was controlled and accepted, and variance homogeneity was controlled and accepted for all means of all four maneuvers with the value $\alpha = .05$). Results show a significant effect of the interface on the mean of the Effort dimension (t (18) = 2.45; p < 0.05). Configuration B users (mean = 70.00; standard deviation = 9.57) report a perceived effort higher than that of configuration A users (mean = 58.75; standard deviation = 10.86). More detailed analyses were performed to check whether there were differences according to the different maneuvers. Distribution normality was checked, then parametric and nonparametric tests were carried out (normality was respected for all questionnaire dimensions except for the Effort dimension in maneuver 1).

The score statistical analysis showed a significant effect of the interface on the Effort dimension only in the first maneuver (Mann-Whitney U Test: U = 1.98; p < 0.05) and the second maneuver (t test: t (18) = −2.22; p < 0.05). The mean values of the Effort dimension of the first two maneuvers are significantly higher for configuration B users (maneuver 1 mean = 71.00; standard deviation = 11.25, maneuver 2 mean = 68.00; standard deviation = 16.02) than for configuration A users (maneuver 1 mean = 55.00; standard deviation = 18.86, maneuver 2 mean = 52.50; standard deviation = 15.14). In other words, configuration B brought about a higher perceived effort than configuration A.

4.2 Effect of Control-Display Compatibility upon Pupil Diameter

Table 4 shows the analysis of the "mean of z-normalized pupil diameter" variable in terms of the variables interface, sequence, and maneuver in the entire scenario.

Table 4. Effects of the independent variables on pupil diameter

Significant effects of pupil diameter upon	F	P	Power	Group means
Control-display type	F(1,14) = 10,13	0,007	0,84	Configuration A: −0,01 Configuration B: 0,27
Maneuver	F(1,14) = 8,79	0,010	0,79	Rapid: 0,16 Moderate: 0,01

The analysis highlighted two main observations:

- The pupil diameter mean is significantly higher with configuration B than with configuration A.
- The pupil diameter mean is significantly higher in submersion maneuvers carried out at fast propulsion speed than in surfacing maneuvers carried out at moderate propulsion speed.

5 Discussion

These findings confirm all the hypotheses posited regarding the effects of the perceptual-motor requirements (stereotype compliance or violation) on mental workload: those effects do exist and are significant. Consistent with hypotheses H1 and H2, there is a significant effect of the perceptual-motor requirements on mental workload. The participants using configuration B experienced higher mental workload concerning the Effort dimension measured by NASA-rtlx. Similarly, the participants' average pupil diameter was significantly higher than that of the other participants using configuration A, regardless of the maneuver or the phase being examined (approach or stabilization phase).

The statistical results regarding the performance and mental workload experienced with configuration B therefore confirm the comments and the observed behaviours of submariners (see Sect. 2.1). The subjective assessment of these professionals matches completely with the objective measures carried out in our experiment. The joystick moves, opposite to the diamond-star moves on the display of configuration B, increases errors and mental workload. The violation of the upward/forward stereotype defined by Wickens [20] is consequently demonstrated by these results.

6 Conclusion

This experiment has brought useful information on methodological and practical aspects. It also has limitations that should be emphasised. From a methodological perspective, it demonstrates the benefits of combining several measures to enable interface comparison and evaluation. The two measures of mental workload (NASA-rtlx and pupil diameter) provided convergent and complementary input for discussion. Following Cegarra and Chevalier [4], we observe that the pupil diameter measure is more fine-tuned than that of NASA-rtlx (as it is carried out online, it distinguishes the different phases of a maneuver) and that NASA-rtlx helps to account for the load participants perceived. In this case, the issue is that of effort, namely the effort that is necessary to go against what appears to be the right action. From a practical point of view, the experiment has also shown that it is necessary to rethink the control-display configuration B design, so as to comply with the direction-of-motion stereotypes (especially the upward-forward compatibility of joystick and interface), to simplify the perceptual-motor tasks and to avoid overload. However, this study presents some limitations that should be taken into account. It has been conducted in an experimental situation with participants who were not helmsmen. Although the situation and the scenario were designed in order to be as ecological as possible, the study must be considered as a first approach to the activity of submarine helmsmen. Ideally, this approach should be complemented and strengthened through an analysis of helmsmen's activity in a naturalistic setting.

Acknowledgment. This paper is an adapted and shortened version of: Rauffet, P., Chauvin, C., Nistico, C., Judas, S., and Toumelin, N. (2016). Analysis of submarine steering: effects of cognitive and perceptual–motor requirements on the mental workload and performance of helmsmen. Cognition, Technology and Work, 18(4), 657–672.

References

1. Anzai, Y.: Cognitive control of real-time event-driven systems. Cogn. Sci. **8**(3), 221–254 (1984)
2. Beatty, J., Lucero-Wagoner, B.: The pupillary system. Handb. Psychophysiol. **2**, 142–162 (2000)
3. Burgess-Limerick, R., Krupenia, V., Wallis, G., Pratim-Bannerjee, A., Steiner, L.: Directional control-response relationships for mining equipment. Ergonomics **53**(6), 748–757 (2010)
4. Byers, J.C., Bittner Jr., A.C., Hill, S.G.: Traditional and raw task load index (TLX) correlations: are paired comparisons necessary? In: Mital, A. (ed.) Advances in Industrial Ergonomics and Safety, pp. 481–485. Taylor & Francis, London (1989)
5. Cegarra, J., Chevalier, A.: The use of Tholos software for combining measures of mental workload: toward theoretical and methodological improvements. Behav. Res. Methods **40**(4), 988–1000 (2008)
6. Chan, A.H.S., Hoffmann, E.R.: Movement compatibility for configurations of displays located in three cardinal orientations and ipsilateral, contralateral and overhead controls. Appl. Ergon. **43**(1), 128–140 (2012)
7. Chen, S., Epps, J.: Using task-induced pupil diameter and blink rate to infer cognitive load. Hum.-Comput. Interact. **29**(4), 390–413 (2014)
8. Dehais, F., Causse, M., Pastor, J.: Embedded eye tracker in a real aircraft: new perspectives on pilot/aircraft interaction monitoring. In: Proceedings from the 3rd International Conference on Research in Air Transportation. Federal Aviation Administration Fairfax, March 2008
9. de Greef, T., Lafeber, H., van Oostendorp, H., Lindenberg, J.: Eye movement as indicators of mental workload to trigger adaptive automation. In: Schmorrow, D.D., Estabrooke, I.V., Grootjen, M. (eds.) FAC 2009. LNCS, vol. 5638, pp. 219–228. Springer, Heidelberg (2009). doi:10.1007/978-3-642-02812-0_26
10. Engstrom, J., Johansson, E., Ostlund, J.: Effects of visual and cognitive load in real and simulated motorway driving. Trans. Res. **8**, 97–120 (2005)
11. Hart, S., Staveland, L.: Development of NASA-TLX (Task Load Index): results of empirical and theoretical research. Adv. Psychol. **52**, 139–183 (1988). Elsevier
12. Hill, S.G., Iavecchia, H.P., Byers, J.C., Bittner Jr., A.C., Zaklade, A.L., Christ, R.E.: Comparison of four subjective workload rating scales. Hum. Factors **34**(4), 429–439 (1992)
13. Jamson, A.H., Merat, N.: Surrogate in-vehicle information systems and driver behaviour: effects of visual and cognitive load in simulated rural driving. Trans. Res. Part F: Traffic Psychol. Behav. **8**(2), 79–96 (2005)
14. Marshall, S.P.: Identifying cognitive state from eye metrics. Aviat. Space Environ. Med. **78**(5), B165–B175 (2007)
15. McLane, R.C., Wolf, J.D.: Symbolic and pictorial displays for submarine control. IEEE Trans. Hum. Factors Electron. **2**, 148–158 (1967)
16. McRuer, D.T., Allen, R.W., Weir, D.H., Klein, R.H.: New results in driver steering control models. Hum. Factors: J. Hum. Factors Ergon. Soc. **19**(4), 381–397 (1977)
17. Nilsson, R., Gärling, T., Lützhöft, M.: An experimental simulation study of advanced decision support system for ship navigation. Trans. Res. Part F: Traffic Psychol. Behav. **12**(3), 188–197 (2009)
18. Peters, B., Nilsson, L.: Modelling the driver in control. In: Cacciabue, C. (ed.) Modelling driver Behaviour in Automotive Environments, pp. 85–104. Springer, London (2007)

19. Ranchet, M.: Effet de la maladie de Parkinson sur la conduite automobile – Implication des fonctions executives. Thèse de doctorat, Université de Lyon 2 (2011)
20. Recarte, M.A., Perez, E., Conchillo, A., Nunes, L.M.: Mental workload and visual impairment: differences between pupil, blink and subjective rating. Span. J. Psychol. **11**, 374–385 (2008)
21. Reid, G.B., Nygren, T.E.: The subjective workload assessment technique: a scaling procedure for measuring mental workload. Adv. Psychol. **52**, 185–218 (1988)
22. Stanton, N.A., Bessell, K.: How a submarine returns to periscope depth: analysing complex socio-technical systems using Cognitive Work Analysis. Appl. Ergon. **45**(1), 110–125 (2014)
23. Temme, L.A., Still, D.L., Kolen, J.: OZ: a human-centered computing cockpit display. In: 45th Annual Conference of the IMTA, Pensacola, Florida (2003)
24. Veltman, J.A., Gaillard, A.W.K.: Physiological indices of workload in a simulated flight task. Biol. Psychol. **42**(3), 323–342 (1996)
25. Verney, J.: Pilotage intégré pour sous-marins. Navigation **43**(171), 372–387 (1995)
26. Wickens, C.D., Vincow, M., Yeh, M.: Design Applications of Visual Spatial Thinking: The Importance of Frame of Reference. Cambridge University Press, Cambridge (2005)
27. Williams, K.W.: A Summary of Unmanned Aircraft Accident/incident Data: Human Factors Implications (Technical report DOT/FAA/AM-04/24). U.S. Department of Transportation, Federal Aviation Administration, Office of Aerospace Me, Washington, DC (2004)
28. Wilson, G.F.: An analysis of mental workload in pilots during flight using multiple psychophysiological measures. Int. J. Aviat. Psychol. **12**(1), 3–18 (2002)
29. Worringham, C.J., Beringer, D.B.: Directional stimulus-response compatibility: a test of three alternative principles. Ergonomics **41**(6), 864–880 (1998)
30. Zupanc, C.M., Burgess-Limerick, R.J., Wallis, G.: Performance consequences of alternating directional control-response compatibility: evidence from a coal mine shuttle car simulator. Hum. Factors **49**(4), 629–636 (2007)

Neuroergonomics Method for Measuring the Influence of Mental Workload Modulation on Cognitive State of Manual Assembly Worker

Pavle Mijović[1(✉)], Miloš Milovanović[2], Vanja Ković[3],
Ivan Gligorijević[1], Bogdan Mijović[1], and Ivan Mačužić[4]

[1] mBrainTrain LCC, Belgrade, Serbia
{pavle.mijovic,ivan,bogdan}@mbraintrain.com
[2] IT Department, Faculty of Organizational Sciences,
University of Belgrade, Belgrade, Serbia
milos.milovanovic@mmklab.org
[3] Department for Psychology, Faculty of Philosophy,
University of Belgrade, Belgrade, Serbia
vanja.kovic@f.bg.ac.rs
[4] Department for Production Engineering, Faculty of Engineering,
University of Kragujevac, Kragujevac, Serbia
ivanm@kg.ac.rs

Abstract. In this study, we simulated a manual assembly operation, where participants were exposed to two distinct ways of information presentation, reflecting two task conditions (monotonous and more demanding task condition). We investigated how changes in mental workload (MWL) modulate the P300 component of event-related potentials (ERPs), recorded from wireless electroencephalography (EEG), reaction times (RTs) and quantity of task unrelated movements (retrieved from Kinect). We found a decrease in P300 amplitude and an increase in the quantity of the task unrelated movements, both indicating a decrease in attention level during a monotonous task (lower MWL). During the more demanding task, where a slightly higher MWL was imposed, these trends were not obvious. RTs did not show any dependency on the level of workload applied. These results suggest that a wireless EEG, but also Kinect, can be used to measure the influence of MWL variation on the cognitive state of the workers.

Keywords: Wireless EEG · Kinect · Reaction times · Mental workload · Attention

1 Introduction

Modern industry tends to automate industrial processes to a wide extent in order to optimise mental workload imposed on the operators. However, the industry still consists of many processes where automation does not apply. This is especially notable in assembly tasks and processes where costs related to the process automation are

© Springer International Publishing AG 2017
L. Longo and M.C. Leva (Eds.): H-WORKLOAD 2017, CCIS 726, pp. 213–224, 2017.
DOI: 10.1007/978-3-319-61061-0_14

generally not justifiable [1]. Manual assembly work is often repetitive and monotonous and as such, it carries low mental workload (MWL). Importantly, mental underload can be as dangerous as overload [2, 3] because the probability of error occurrence and MWL exposure are mutually related, according to the U-shaped curve [4], i.e. extremely high/low MWL increases the probability of error occurrence, while the optimal MWL leads to the smallest probability of error occurrence. Therefore, there is an increasing need to find the methodology for objective assessment of the influence of MWL on human operators for both the automated and manual processes. Human factors and ergonomics (HF/E) is the scientific discipline that investigates the interaction between system and human operators [5–7]. Classical ergonomics' approach to studying human cognitive state and the interaction between humans and operating systems mainly utilises qualitative and subjective methods, such as questionnaires and measurements of overt performance [8]. However, these methods are often unreliable and unable to investigate the covert cognitive processes of workers during their everyday routine in industrial environments [8]. For that reason, neuroergonomics emerged as a novel path in ergonomics research [8, 9]. Neuroergonomics merges knowledge from ergonomics and neuroscience, and it is defined as the science discipline that studies the human brain in relation to work [10].

One of the most powerful neuroimaging methods in neuroergonomics research is electroencephalography (EEG), since wireless EEG is capable of direct recording of electrical brain activity in real world [11]. A commonly employed EEG method for evaluating cognitive state is the extraction and investigation of event related potentials (ERPs). ERPs are defined as voltage fluctuations in continuous EEG signal that are associated in time with certain physical or mental occurrences [12]. ERP components are usually defined in terms of polarity, and latency with respect to a discrete stimulus, and have been found to reflect a number of distinct perceptual, cognitive and motor processes. In that sense, the so-called P300 component is represented by the positive deflection in terms of voltage, appearing around 300 ms after the stimulus presentation [13]. The P300 component is often used to identify the depth of cognitive information processing and is not influenced by the physical attributes of the stimuli [13]. For these reasons, the P300 ERP component is assumed to reflect the attention level of the person [14] and its amplitude is modulated by mental workload [15].

It is important to stress that the goal of neuroergonomics is not only to investigate the brain's functions, but also to put it in the context of human behavior in everyday environments [9]. As such, it is important to investigate the neural basis of physical performance, e.g. body movements and reaction times (RTs). Traditionally, RTs were used to estimate the cognitive state of the person. The main reason behind the wide use of RT measurements is that they are easy to measure and simple to interpret [16]. RT represents a time interval from the indicated start of a work process or operation (stimulation), until the moment of the action initiation. However, as it was pointed out in [17], reaction-time experiments usually consist of a stimulus followed by the response, without direct possibility to observe the mental processing that occurs in between.

Physical performance measurements are ubiquitous in ergonomics studies, mainly in the domain of physical ergonomics. These became even more prominent with rapid development of the motion capture (MoCap) sensors that are nowadays affordable and unobtrusive. The majority of research related to operators' motion is related to posture estimation or action recognition [18], while significantly less studies are oriented towards linking cognitive processes to motor actions. One study that investigated the relationship between gestures and the cognitive state of the person showed that during the task that carries less mental workload, the quantity of the task unrelated movement increases [19]. This study investigated behavioral activity offline and indirectly, since the participants were recorded with a video camera and manual analysis was subsequently performed with replaying the video [19]. Advances in computer vision technology (namely structured light technology) nowadays allows for automated analysis. This enabled us to develop and use a simple behavioral model, based on movement energy (ME; [20]). Ultimately, the combination of brain dynamics and behavioral modalities can open a deeper understanding of the influence of the mental workload on human mental states during complex work activities [21].

The aim of the present study is to investigate how changes in mental workload during a simulated industrial manual assembly task are influencing the P300 ERP component's amplitude, but also the behavioral modalities of RTs and ME. We investigated the influence of the task duration on these modalities, where the expectation was that the ME and RTs should show an increasing trend, while the P300 component's amplitude should decrease as the task progresses. Additionally, we investigated whether the changes in mental workload modulate the P300 component's amplitude.

2 Methods

2.1 Participants

Ten subjects, aged between 19 and 21 years old. volunteered as participants in the study. Participants were instructed not to drink any alcohol on the day before and the day of their participation in the study, as well as not to drink coffee at least three hours prior to their participation in the study. All participants had normal or corrected-to-normal vision. They had agreed to participation and had signed the informed consent, after reading the experiment summary. The study was approved by the Ethical Committee of the University of Kragujevac.

2.2 Replicated Workplace

Reliable EEG recording still relies on wet electrodes, thus the on-site industrial EEG recording still represents a big challenge, since it may cause discomfort to the workers on the industrial floor. For that reason, we replicated a workplace (Fig. 1) in the building of the Faculty of Engineering (University of Kragujevac) and we simulated the production process of the rubber hoses, used in the hydraulic brake systems in automotive industry. Once the replicated workplace was created, the participants in the study were equipped with the wearable EEG. Participants' movements were recorded using Kinect sensor, which was placed in front and above the participants. Foot switch was used with the aim of recording the RTs, as will be explained in Sect. 2.7. The sensor placement is presented in Fig. 1.

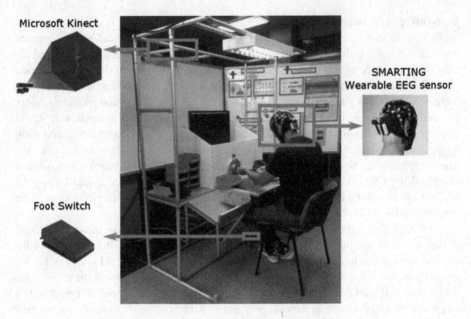

Fig. 1. Replicated workplace and the sensors placements

2.3   Sensors Used in the Study and Multimodal Synchronization

EEG data were recorded with the SMARTING (mBrainTrain, Serbia) wireless EEG system. The small and lightweight EEG amplifier (85 × 51 × 12 mm, 60 g) was tightly connected to a 24-channel electrode cap (Easycap, Germany). The communication between the SMARTING and the recording computer was established through a Bluetooth connection. The electrode cap contained sintered Ag/AgCl electrodes that were placed based on the international 10–20 System. The experimental procedure imposed that the electrode impedances must be set below 5 kΩ, which was confirmed by the device acquisition software.

To investigate the body movements, we used the Microsoft Kinect sensor. Kinect has a sampling frequency of 30 frames per second (fps) and it is capable of representing the human body with a stick figure, where the most prominent human body joints (e.g. shoulder, elbow) are represented with the key-points. For this study, we used a 10 key-point seated model, since in the experimental setup. the replicated machine occluded the lower part of the participants' body.

To synchronize the data coming from different, above-mentioned, sensors, we used the Lab Streaming Layer (LSL) framework (https://github.com/sccn/labstreaminglayer). As explained in [21], LSL is a real-time data collection and distribution system that allows multiple continuous data streams as well as discrete marker timestamps to be acquired simultaneously by Lab Recorder, in an eXtensible Data Format (XDF). This data collection method provides synchronous, precise recording of multi-channel, multi-stream data that are heterogeneous in both type and sampling rate [21], and all of the sensors mutually communicate over a local area network (LAN).

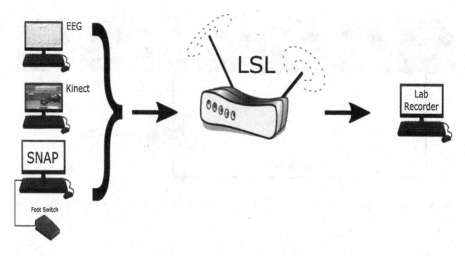

Fig. 2. Overall system architecture

For running the experimental tasks (explained in detail in Sect. 2.4) we used the SNAP environment. SNAP allows relatively simple, script-level development of complex, interactive experimental paradigms and it can retrieve the signals from various input devices. This feature was used to attach the foot switch through a USB port to the recording computer, with the aim of recording the RTs. with the aim of extraction of the behavioral modality of RTs.

The overall system architecture for synchronous recording of all described streams is graphically depicted in Fig. 2.

2.4   Experimental Task

Simulated Assembly Task

In the production process, an operator carries out the crimping operation in order to join a metal extension to a rubber hose. This single operation, carried out in a sitting position, consists of eight simple steps (actions). The simulated operation consists of eight major production steps that can be summarised as follows (Fig. 3): first, the information to initiate the simulated assembly operation is presented to the participant, in the form of visual stimulus (step 1), upon which he is instructed to instantly initiate the operation by taking the metal part (step 2) and the rubber hose (step 3). Following this, participants should place the metal part on the hose (step 4) and place both inside the crimping machine (step 5). The participants then proceed by promptly pressing the pedal, which initiates the improvised machine and replicates the real machines' crimping sound (step 6). Upon completion of the simulated crimping process, the participant removes the component and places it in the box with completed parts (step 7). Finally, the participant sits still and waits for subsequent stimulus (step 8).

Experimental Procedure

Experimental procedure was similar for all the experiments and it was described in detail in [11]. The participants were subjected to the modified sustained attention to

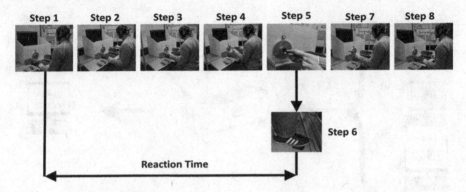

Fig. 3. Graphical presentation of the step-by-step simulated crimping operation (Color figure online)

response task (SART) and Arrows task, simultaneously with the simulated task. The tasks were balanced across the participants and duration of each task was around one and a half hours, upon which the participants had a 15 min break, before starting the second task. Both tasks were presented on a 24" screen from a distance of approximately 100 cm. Upon presentation of the stimuli on the screen, the participants were instructed to complete the previously explained assembly operation.

As explained in [11], the original SART paradigm consists of consecutively presenting digits from '1' to '9' and participants are required to give the speeded response on all stimuli, with the exception of digit '3'. The main difference between the original SART and in modified SART paradigm is that the digits in Numbers are randomized, with the condition that forbid the appearance of two consecutive digits '3' ('no-go' stimulus) and in between two 'no-go' conditions at least two 'go' conditions must appear. The participants in the study were instructed to initiate the assembly operation as soon as the digit appeared on the screen, with whichever hand they felt more comfortable (they could freely choose, previously explained step 2 and 3, presented in Fig. 3).

The Arrows task was presented and explained in [11]. The Arrow task is a choice reaction "go/no-go" task, where the arrows pointing to the left and right appear on the screen; the white arrows represent the 'go' (target) condition, whereas the red arrows represent the "no-go" stimulus. Similarly to the SART task, the stimuli sequence in Arrows was randomised with the condition that forbade two consecutive appearances of the "no-go" stimuli. Contrary to SART, the participants were required to initiate the action altering the hand according to the direction in which the white arrow on the screen was pointing, i.e. in the Arrows task the participants should initiate the action with the right hand (step 2) if the white arrow is pointing to the right, or with the left hand (step 3) if pointing left. Regardless of the task, all the stimuli were presented for 1000 ms on a black screen background. Each task consisted of 500 stimuli, where the probability of the appearance of the 'no-go' stimuli was set to 10% (50 in total), while the 'go' stimuli were presented 450 times.

2.5 EEG Processing

EEG signal processing was performed offline using EEGLAB [20] and MATLAB (Mathworks Inc., Natick, MA, USA). EEG data were first bandpass filtered in the 1–35 Hz range, followed by re-referencing to the average of the TP9 and TP10 channels. Further, an extended Infomax Independent Component Analysis (ICA) was used to semi-automatically attenuate contributions from eye blinks [21]. After the data pre-processing, ERP epochs were extracted from −200 to 800 ms with respect to times-tamp values of "go" and "no-go" stimuli. Baseline values were corrected by subtracting mean values for the period from −200 to 0 ms from the stimuli occurrence. The identified electrode sites of interest for the ERP analysis in this study were Fz, Cz, CPz and Pz, as the P300 component is most prominent over the central and parieto-central scalp locations [14]. The P300 amplitude was calculated for both the "go" and "no-go" conditions and for each experimental condition, using mean amplitude measure [12] in the time window from 350 to 450 ms, with regard to the timestamps of the stimuli.

2.6 Movement Energy (ME) Calculation

During the simulated assembly operation, the upper-body movement of participants was recorded with the Kinect. The Kinect was placed in a position above and in front of participants (as shown in the Fig. 1). The motion data are acquired in a form of a stick figure with the 10 key-points seated model that represent the joints of the upper body.

Automatic quantification of the task unrelated ME was based on the kinetic energy of the key-points. The motion data were extracted and analyzed in the period between the operators' completion of each operation and the consecutive stimuli that was pre-sented to the participants (Step 8, Fig. 3). In that period, the participants had no pre-scribed activity and the expectation was that they would spend that time relatively still. Further, the kinetic energy of movement was calculated for each simulated operation and for each of the key-points in all-three axes (as explained in [20]). Finally, the ME for each trial was calculated as the summation of kinetic energies in all three axes.

2.7 Reaction Times

The experimental design did not allow subjects to react to the button press on seeing the visual 'go' stimulus, thus the reaction time (RT) could not be measured in the traditional way (as the time elapsed between the stimulus presentation and the speeded response by the participants). For that reason, RTs in our study were defined as the time elapsed between the stimulus presentation (step 1) and the foot switch press (step 6 from Fig. 3). This allows the calculation of RTs, as the difference between timestamps from simu-lated operation initiation and the beginning of the machine simulated crimping process.

2.8 Statistical Analysis

Prior to statistical analysis, we averaged our data using a 15-point and one-step moving average window, as explained in [22]. The statistical analysis was performed using IBM SPSS software. We performed Spearman correlation in order to investigate the

Table 1. Spearman correlation results

Task/task order	ME	RTs	Fz P300	Cz P300	CPz P300	Pz P300
SART first	.512[**]	−.309[**]	−.501[**]	−.538[**]	−.567[**]	−.595[**]
SART second	.473[**]	−.277[**]	−.274[**]	−.375[**]	−.218[**]	−.217[**]
Arrows/first	.183[**]	−.322[**]	−.693[**]	−.621[**]	−.593[**]	−.531[**]
Arrows/second	−.265[**]	−.194[**]	.311[**]	.385[**]	.414[**]	.546[**]

changes in behavioral and neural features as the time of the task progressed, i.e. the general trend of P300 amplitude, RTs and ME.

Additionally, in order to investigate whether the mental workload modulates the P300 amplitude, we performed a paired t-test between P300 amplitude in SART and the Arrows task, on four electrode sites of interest (Fz, Cz, CPz, Pz). It is noteworthy that we compared the values of P300 amplitudes only in the "go" condition.

3   Results

The Spearman correlation results are presented in Table 1. These results revealed the general negative trend of RTs, regardless of the task and order of the task presentation. Regarding other modalities, the ME data showed a positive trend, whereas the P300 amplitude showed a negative trend in most of the task conditions, with an exception in the case of the arrows task presenting as the second task, i.e. when a more demanding task was following the monotonous task.

The general trends of P300 amplitude at the Pz electrode location and ME are graphically shown in Fig. 4. Regarding the P300 amplitude's analysis, we found that P300 component's amplitude in the "go" conditions elicited higher P300 amplitude in the Arrows task, compared to the SART task ($p < .05$). The t-test results for all four electrode sites are provided in Table 2.

4   Discussion

In this study, we investigated the influence of mental workload on the cognitive state of the workers during the manual assembly operations. We imposed two different levels of mental workload on the workers during the simulated manual assembly operations and observed its effect on the behavioral modalities of ME and RTs, as well as on the modulation of the P300 component's amplitude. P300 component's amplitude and ME showed comparable results. From Table 1 and Fig. 4, it can be seen that the P300 amplitude is decreasing during the task, reflecting that the attention of the participants is showing negative trend, the amount of the task unrelated movement (ME) is increasing in almost all experiment conditions (also shown in Fig. 4). These results are in line with our hypothesis that the amount of task unrelated movement should increase during the monotonous task [19], while the P300 amplitude is expected to decrease. The exception from the general trend is the experimental condition in which the task that carries higher

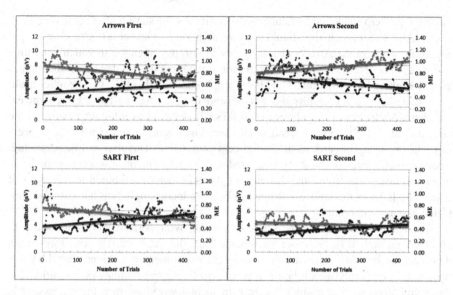

Fig. 4. graphical representation of general trends of P300 amplitude from Pz electrode site (red color) and ME (black color). (Color figure online)

Table 2. T-test results for P300 amplitude comparison between the task conditions (Arrows/SART task) and for all electrode sites under study.

Electrode site	Task	N	Mean	STD	STD error mean
Fz	Arrows	40	4.45	5.23	0.70
	SART	40	2.38	5.04	0.67
Cz	Arrows	40	4.81	4.70	0.63
	SART	40	2.57	4.85	0.65
Cpz	Arrows	40	5.35	4.32	0.58
	SART	40	2.76	3.99	0.53
Pz	Arrows	40	6.36	4.17	0.56
	SART	40	3.22	3.41	0.46

MWL (Arrows) is performed upon completion of the more monotonous (SART) task. The difference in MWL is the consequence of the choice action in the Arrows task that does not exist in the SART task. Our results suggest that if the more monotonous task is followed by the more demanding task, the amount of the task unrelated movements is decreasing, while at the same time, there is a positive influence on the participant's attention level, as the P300 amplitude shows an increasing trend as the task progresses. Additionally, the t-test revealed that the P300 amplitude elicited during the Arrows was of higher magnitude than during the SART task. This can be expected, since in the Arrows task the participants are exposed to slightly higher demands of the arriving stimuli evaluation, as they are unaware of the arrow stimuli direction. On the contrary, the digit stimuli from SART task carries significantly lower information, which can cause the participants to stop evaluating the content of the stimuli after some time [11], i.e. in SART task participants should just pay attention to whether it is a "go" or "nogo" condition, while in the Arrows task they should also pay attention to which hand they will initiate the operation. All these results confirm our hypothesis that the modulation of mental workload also modulates the P300 amplitude, but also ME. On the other hand, we found that the RT results did not depend on the level of the imposed mental workload. Although we hypothesised that RTs will decrease over the time course of the task, they showed a negative trend in all cases under study, i.e. the participants were faster in executing the task as the experiment progressed. This may not be surprising, since the participants in the study were students, without any prior working experience in similar tasks. Therefore, the decrease of the RTs can be attributed to the effect of rehearsing [23], as the students seemed to become increasingly familiar with the simulated assembly operation.

The results from this study suggest that the overt performance monitoring, as observed through RTs, may not be reliable enough, since we did not observe any difference in reaction times between different experiment conditions. Notably, this finding is in line with one of the main premises of neuroergonomics [8]. Additionally, this study suggests that a slight increase in mental workload in a manual assembly operation, compared to an entirely repetitive and monotonous task, has a positive influence on the cognitive state of the operators. Finally, findings from this study may be also implemented in the job rotation strategy in factories. Job rotations in assembly lines are often proposed as a method of reducing the monotony of the task, thus keeping the workers more focused [24]. We propose that job rotations on assembly tasks should be organised in such a way to avoid cases in which a more demanding task is followed by a task that is more monotonous in nature. However, this observation should be investigated thoughtfully in future studies.

5 Conclusion

This study demonstrated how neuroergonomics methods can be successfully applied in investigating the influence of changes in mental workload to the cognitive state of the workers. The monotonous task showed a decrease in P300 component's amplitude and an increase in ME, both indicating a decrease in the attention level of a worker, as the task progresses. It is noteworthy that in the more demanding task, this result was not consistent. Furthermore, we also showed that the P300 amplitude was more prominent in the task that carried a slightly higher cognitive demand, in comparison to a highly monotonous and repetitive task. All these results suggest that the wireless EEG, but also Kinect, can be successfully utilised in the measuring of the influence of mental workload modulation on the cognitive state of the workers.

Acknowledgments. This research is financed under EU—FP7 Marie Curie Actions Initial Training Net-works—FP7-PEOPLE-2011-ITN, project name "Innovation Through Human Factors in Risk Analysis and Management (InnHF)", project number: 289837.

References

1. Tang, A., Owen, C., Biocca, F., Mou, W.: Comparative effectiveness of augmented reality in object assembly. In: Proceedings of the SIGCHI Conference on Human Factors in Computing Systems, pp. 73–80. ACM (2003)
2. Larue, G.S., Rakotonirainy, A., Pettitt, A.N.: Driving performance impairments due to hypovigilance on monotonous roads. Acc. Anal. Prev. **43**(6), 2037–2046 (2011)
3. Young, M.S., Stanton, N.A.: Attention and automation: new perspectives on mental underload and performance. Theoret. Issues Ergon. Sci. **3**(2), 178–194 (2002)
4. Desmond, P.A., Hoyes, T.W.: Workload variation, intrinsic risk and utility in a simulated air traffic control task: evidence for compensatory effects. Saf. Sci. **22**(1), 87–101 (1996)
5. Karwowski, W.: The discipline of human factors and ergonomics. In: Salvendy, G. (ed.) Handbook of Human Factors and Ergonomics, pp. 3–37. Wiley, Hoboken (2012)
6. Parasuraman, R.: Neuroergonomics: research and practice. Theoret. Issues Ergon. Sci. **4**(1–2), 5–20 (2003)
7. Parasuraman, R., Rizzo, M.: Introduction to neuroergonomics. In: Parasuraman, R., Rizzo, M. (eds.) Neuroergonomics: The Brain at Work, pp. 3–14. Oxford University Press, Oxford (2008)
8. Mehta, R.K., Parasuraman, R.: Neuroergonomics: a review of applications to physical and cognitive work. Front. Hum. Neurosci. **7**(889), 1–10 (2013)
9. Mijović, P., Ković, V., De Vos, M., Mačužić, I., Jeremić, B., Gligorijević, I.: Benefits of instructed responding in manual assembly tasks: an ERP approach. Front. Hum. Neurosci. **10**(171), 1–13 (2016)
10. Picton, T.W., Bentin, S., Berg, P., Donchin, E., Hillyard, S.A., Johnson, R., Miller, G.A., Ritter, W., Ruchkin, D.S., Rugg, M.D., Taylor, M.J.: Guidelines for using human event-related potentials to study cognition: recording standards and publication criteria. Psychophysiology **37**(2), 127–152 (2000)
11. Polich, J., Kok, A.: Cognitive and biological determinants of P300: an integrative review. Biol. Psychol. **41**(2), 103–146 (1995)
12. Polich, J.: Updating P300: an integrative theory of P3a and P3b. Clin. Neurophys. **118**(10), 2128–2148 (2007)
13. Causse, M., Peysakhovich, V., Fabre, E.F.: High working memory load impairs language processing during a simulated piloting task: an ERP and pupillometry study. Front. Hum. Neurosci. **10**, 1–14 (2016)
14. Salthouse, T.A., Hedden, T.: Interpreting reaction time measures in between-group comparisons. J. Clin. Exp. Neuropsych. **24**(7), 858–872 (2002)
15. Luck, S.J., Woodman, G.F., Vogel, E.K.: Event-related potential studies of attention. Trends Cogn. Sci. **4**(11), 432–440 (2000)
16. Diego-Mas, J.A., Alcaide-Marzal, J.: Using Kinect™ sensor in observational methods for assessing postures at work. Appl. Ergon. **45**(4), 976–985 (2013)
17. >Rogé, J., Pebayle, T., Muzet, A.: Variations of the level of vigilance and of behavioural activities during simulated automobile driving. Acc. Anal. Prev. **33**(2), 181–186 (2001)
18. Mijović, P., Milovanović, M., Ković, V., Mijović, B., Gligorijević, I., Minović, M., Mačužić, I.: Communicating the user state: introducing cognition-aware computing in industrial settings. Saf. Sci. (2017, in revision)
19. Gramann, K., Ferris, D.P., Gwin, J., Makeig, S.: Imaging natural cognition in action. Int. J. Psychophys. **91**(1), 22–29 (2014)

20. Delorme, A., Makeig, S.: EEGLAB: an open source toolbox for analysis of single-trial EEG dynamics including independent component analysis. J. Neurosci. Methods **134**(1), 9–21 (2004)
21. De Vos, M., De Lathauwer, L., Van Huffel, S.: Spatially constrained ICA algorithm with an application in EEG processing. Sig. Proc. **91**(8), 1963–1972 (2011)
22. Mijović, P., Ković, V., De Vos, M., Mačužić, I., Todorović, P., Jeremić, B., Gligorijević, I.: Towards continuous and real-time attention monitoring at work: reaction time versus brain response. Ergonomics **60**, 1–14 (2016)
23. Awh, E., Jonides, J.: Overlapping mechanisms of attention and spatial working memory. Trends Cogn. Sci. **5**(3), 119–126 (2001)
24. Michalos, G., Makris, S., Rentzos, L., Chryssolouris, G.: Dynamic job rotation for workload balancing in human based assembly systems. CIRP J. Manuf. Sci. Technol. **2**(3), 153–160 (2010)

The Benefits of Task and Cognitive Workload Support for Operators in Ground Handling

M. Chiara Leva[1]([⊠]) and Yilmar Builes[2]

[1] School of Environmental Science, Dublin Institute of Technology,
Dublin, Ireland
chiara.leva@dit.ie
[2] Tosca Solutions Ltd., The Tower, Trinity Technology & Enterprise Centre,
Pearse Street, Dublin, Ireland

Abstract. The scope of the present work is to report an action research project applied to the relationship of task and cognitive workload support on one of the most important aspects of an airport: ground handling. At the beginning of the project workload management was not in the scope of work but as the project progressed and preliminary results and feedback were gained the researcher came to realize that some form of workload management support was also achieved as a by-product. The present paper is an attempt to account for what was achieved and how. Safe and efficient ground handling during departure and arrival of an aircraft requires coordinated responsibilities amongst qualified operators collaborating together simultaneously in a time constrained environment. The context is one of medium-high workload due to the number of activities covered in a short time, such as: passenger, baggage and cargo handling, aircraft loading, the provision and use of ground support equipment, etc. This paper presents the introduction of a tool aimed at performance monitoring and task support and discusses how the use of it can play a key role in the adequate management of workload by operators in Ground Handling. The core elements of the tool under analysis are electronic checklist and digitized shift handover, and it aims at highlighting how they have impacted performance, reducing operational and human related issues.

Keywords: Performance management · Safety management · Cognitive workload · Task support · Electronic checklist · Shift handover · Aviation

1 Introduction: Ground Operations and Human Workload

In aviation, ground operations is the aspect that deals with the airport handling procedures ensuring passengers and baggage are safely on board the aircraft prior to departure [1]. Safe and efficient ground handling during departure and arrival of an aircraft requires coordinated responsibilities amongst qualified persons at the same time, which generates heavy workload due to the high number of activities covered in a short time, such as: passenger, baggage and cargo handling, aircraft loading and handling, baggage preparation for loading and weight and balance sheet, use of ground support equipment, etc. [1].

The effects of task demands on human performance are increasingly under the spotlight, as the move towards automation has shifted the nature of human work from

© Springer International Publishing AG 2017
L. Longo and M.C. Leva (Eds.): H-WORKLOAD 2017, CCIS 726, pp. 225–238, 2017.
DOI: 10.1007/978-3-319-61061-0_15

working with the body to working more with the mind. Furthermore the increased responsibilities transferred to complex technological tools along with more complex procedures have imposed more demands on operators [2]. Instead of physical endurance and strength, sustained attention and problem solving skills have become more important [3]. This element is relevant for ground operations together with the observed effect of how physically demanding work that is performed simultaneously with a cognitive task can influence mental workload by weakening mental processing or decreasing performance [4]. In this context the aim of this paper is to explore the benefits of a web based application developed as a form of task support in ground handling tasks. Specifically the initiative introduced in a regional airport the use of an electronic checklist and shift handover as key element in fostering a safer and more efficient work environment. The digitization of daily electronic checklist and support systems for the shift handover which list the operations of the "turnaround" to be performed for each aircraft, and other maintenance activities required for equipment and/or infrastructure (e.g. runway inspections) was a platform able to provide the opportunity to collect real time performance and reporting on day to day anomalies and issues that was not available before. The tool has been used for two years and in this study we collected feedback from front line personnel and management on what were the perceived impacts the tool had on performance. At the beginning of the project workload management was in fact not in the scope of work but as the project progressed and preliminary results and feedback was gained the researcher came to realize that some form of workload management support was also achieved as a by-product. The present paper is an attempt to account for what was achieved and how.

1.1 Cognitive Workload and Task Support

A comprehensive definition of cognitive workload is "an amount of mental resources required to perform a specific task or sequence of tasks in a given environment" [5]. Excessive cognitive workload is generated when the satisfactory performance of a task demands from the operator more resources than are available at any given time [6]. A task can become complex after simple manipulations, for example, increasing the number of elements, changing the number of decisions required to complete an action, or the display duration as these changes can influence attention, effectiveness, and the time needed to complete a task [7]. The assignment of additional tasks to a worker has been one of the workload manipulations most commonly done even when the individual is already performing a complex task. The use of executive control processes becomes essential to guarantee the successful performance of multiple concurrent tasks [8]. The successful execution of several tasks simultaneously is more vulnerable as the workload increases. The workload is shouldered by the cognitive capability known as 'executive functions'. Executive functions are necessary for goal-directed behavior, as they include the ability to initiate and stop actions, to monitor and change behaviors, to plan future actions when faced with new situations [8]. A task support in this sense can be one able to sustain some of the executive functions such as working memory (that has to do with the capacity to hold and manipulate information "on-line" in real time) and sequencing (the ability to break down complex actions into manageable units and prioritize them).

To do so a necessary cornerstone is a clear task description. Task analysis in this sense is a necessary requirement to the design of task support. A proper acquisition of relevant information about a task in a safety-critical environment is the foundation of every sound human factor analysis. More and more studies have highlighted that this critical first step of the analysis cannot be neglected as it needs to provide the design stage with structured information about the tasks and contexts to be addressed, particularly when there are relevant time constraints during workload. This step of the study was carried out using a tool previously developed to support data collection and able to provide a structure for the interviews with the workers based on a simultaneous graphical representation of the task. It was used as a common means of communication between the technical personnel involved in the interviews & the human factors practitioners involved in the action research. This was aimed at supporting a common understanding of the tasks, their main objectives, challenges and criticalities whilst performing the actual task description [9]. The task analysis lead to the development of revised check lists for the key turnaround tasks and to the inclusion of shift handover provisions for the other activities not covered by checklists and not related to flight turnaround time. The checklists were used as a real time sign off for the tasks and delivered task support as they reminded key steps in detail and gave the possibility to report quickly any possible anomalies or issues in carrying out the tasks. Furthermore the shift handover page was designed to give the possibility to allocate tasks outside peak time, check status quickly and report once again issues as they arise. The information is managed by back office and feedback can be provided through the same dashboard where the shift handover occurs. We will discuss in the following paragraph the rationale for these very simple choices and their current outcomes.

2 Electronic Checklist and Shift Handover: Their Role for Task Support & Workload Management

The National Transportation Safety Board of United States recommends the use of checklist to carry out highly proceduralised work such as for instance the proper aircraft configuration for each phase of the flight. However, the improper use of these items can be a contributing factor to incidents and accidents [10]. The paper checklists that have been digitised were however already in use at the airport where the study occurred and they were exposed to a number of design weaknesses [11]. The most relevant issues included the inability to mark skipped items or the lack of a pointer for each item, and the lack of support for switching between several checklists. All these obstacles were mitigated with the use of an electronic checklist [11].

Electronic checklists offer several benefits to support a faster execution as they supply an external memory support for pending or completed steps of a procedure as well as serving as a reminder of omitted steps. At the same time, the electronic checklist can "detect" and show the current status for every single procedure. This can support status awareness for long tasks and help to ensure the completion and control of many simultaneous tasks. The incorporation of a touch-operated function into the electronic checklist also permit a faster information manipulation in switching from one procedure to another without losing track of partially completed checklists or getting lost through many tasks. The electronic checklist system was designed specially to reduce four types of common errors present in traditional paper checklists. Firstly, as a help to avoid forgetting the tasks at hand, and avoid skipping tasks. Secondly, it is inevitable to suffer from distractions or interruptions during a day's work, an electronic checklist can minimise the issue, supporting the resumption of work after any interruption/distraction. Thirdly, share the information in real time, asking support to someone if it is necessary and last but not least offer data analytics on daily perfor- mance KPI, key issues and need for solutions, it also offer insight into how a solution seems to work on the shop floor after implemented [11]. Just as the electronic checklists play an important role to guarantee the proper performance of the tasks connected with aircraft turnaround, in the same way electronic shift handovers are an important factor for non-recurrent tasks, safety critical activities such as runway inspections and coordination between operators at various level (passengers handling operators and ramp operators with airport duty manager).

The importance of proper shift handovers is often discovered in accident analysis where improper communications and assignment transfer occurred between shifts. In 2005 for instance Texas City submitted the final investigation report about the fatal Isomerization Unit Explosion in its city; the report explicitly mention poor shift han- dover as a key root cause of the accident [12]. Reliable communication is crucial for safety critical tasks and a proper shift handover is highly relevant in this context [13]. This is why the Health and Safety Executive in the UK [13] has contributed a guidance document HSG48 in which they provide information to improve shift handover. The most relevant advice consists in specifying the information more carefully before it is communicated, including aids such as semi structured log books that are a task support of sort for the activity of communicating the right information about the non-recurrent tasks handed over from one shift to the next. NASA demonstrated in a study how the design weaknesses of the traditional checklist and the improper human interactions associated with it can reduce the effectiveness of procedures, especially in complex socio technical systems where the role of the human is key. The same study also points out that merely improving the engineering design and the procedural sequence of the checklist will not eliminate the problem [11]. A recent report from the Aviation Safety Reporting System (ASRS) published in September 2015 highlights how the implementation of a new working methodology supported with a proper checklist has allowed the orderly execution and sequential collection of vital steps as well as facilitating the resolution of abnormal situations. Nevertheless, ASRS still receives incident reports associated with checklist errors, perhaps it's worth taking another look at some of the factors affecting proper checklist usage, including workers commitment and engagement [14].

3   The User Participation in Developing the Task Support Tool

The design of a workspace and associated task is one of the key drivers to allow people to carry out their role in an organization effectively and enjoy their work. Inspection methods can be applied in Human Computer Interface design to assess usability of interactive systems. However, they do not consider the state of the operator while executing a task, the surrounding environment and the task demands [15]. As a result, all too frequently, heavy troubleshooting is still necessary in the real-world during the ramp-up phase once the system has been build. Furthermore, the involvement and commitment of staff is crucial to ensure ownership of any task support tool. Participatory design is a process based upon involving front line staff in assessing the workplace including activities and tools at an early stage to ensure feedback is incorporated into user informed design choices. It provides a good platform to enhance frontline staff's awareness and involvement in activity management, by allowing them to take control of the necessary knowledge and an understanding even of the risk involved in their day to day activities [16].

The IT system developed as part of this study in the regional airport was delivered in 2014. Its aim was to support performance management and change in the airport considering the challenges faced in commercial aviation: the need to grow traffic, increase effectiveness of existing staff as there was no budget to upscale resources to match the required traffic increase. This situation can potentially lead to increased workload and time pressure for operators during turnaround. The operators suggested to adopt for their day to day a more organised approach to task assignment similar to the one used in the past for short-term periods of significant traffic growth due to special events (such as extra chartered flight during Mediterranean Olympic games in the region). This led to the development of a new integrated platform where operators at all levels could share all their required tasks, information and indicators in functional processes to create the transport service [17]. The case study involved University researchers and the staff of a small regional airport in Italy. The final result was an IT tool called "Daily Journal" configured as a databased to support, monitor and analyse day to day performance on the key activities in the airport. To start the process a mock-up was built to single out all the data that needed to be migrated form the paper format of the check lists used by Ramp and Operations for each flight into an electronic format.

Furthermore the data collected was extended to incorporate the managing of small deviations and anomalies. The previous paper forms were simple checklist that did not collect any info regarding who performed a task, if the task had any issues, or if there was the need to pass on any follow up or request for interventions from one shift to the next. The checklist was restructured around the subtask performed for Ramp and Handling operations identified during the process mapping exercise. Furthermore it is now possible to record who is in each turn and who are the shift leaders, and any possible anomaly that might occur during the operations and its associated criticality level and follow up. Critical anomalies can be escalated into accident reporting at any point.

Additionally, this tool also supports the management of the Safety Assessment of existing and planned operations. This feeds into the reporting against key performance indicators required by the Airport Council international for benchmarking purposes [19]. The Daily Journal provides an integrated platform for performance monitoring, reporting, task support, procedure documentation and proactive risk assessment. Proactive risk assessment is required by ICAO guidance document on Safety management systems [18]. To guarantee a proper shift handover design, a mock-up was built to single out all the data that needed to be migrated from the paper format of the checklists used by Ramp and Operations for each flight into an electronic format [17]. The checklist was structured around the subtask performed for Ramp and Handling operations identified during the process mapping exercise. The system has been built as a management system and it is configured as a Web Application. The application is connected to the existing company's databases and can show all required data using an interface protected by password [17].

4 Daily Journal in Operation: How It Supports Ground Handling Operators' Workload Concretely

Before the Daily Journal implementation it was found that the airport activities were perceived as constant firefighting, and the majority of the people interviewed pointed out that there was no clear assignments of roles and responsibilities for each turn. 70% of people interviewed proposed a use of shift planning around each flight which was the method used for short-term periods of significant traffic growth due to special events. Among the suggestions it was also proposed to allow automatic collection of data for ground handling task performance for every turnaround (already manually collected with the Trip File associated to each flight). Around 80% of people interviewed said that there wasn't a clear form of performance appraisal and they would have liked to have one.

One of the main change management activities carried out was to mitigate these issues providing an electronic checklist about what needs to be done by whom, so that the process of turnaround in ground handling can be integrally monitored. Figure 1 shows a checklist for a flight that arrives, where for each operation the sign off requires to select the name of the operator that executed it. There is the option to open a sub-task located to the right, where it can insert the anomalies that can happen during the execution of a step, and classify them by giving a kind of "severity" and insert them in

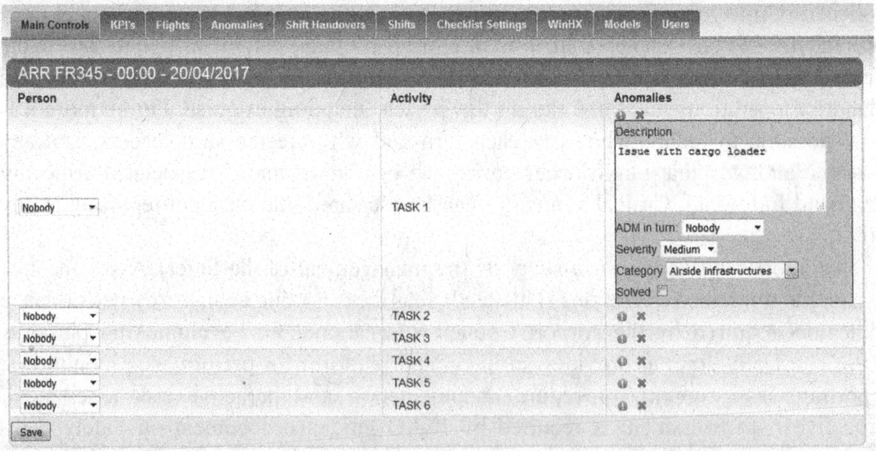

Fig. 1. Example of a checklist to monitor operations on incoming flights.

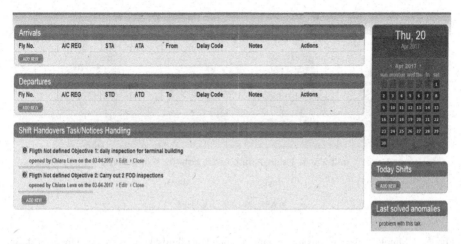

Fig. 2. Example of the main screen with the daily flights to manage and the activities derived from the handovers (shift handovers).

the context of the impact on safety, quality, security or environment, etc. The prototype can be used in at least three PC workstations, two in the Airport Duty Manager (ADM) office, situated in front of the aircraft parking apron and one in the ramp station, also located in front of the apron. The turnaround display is user friendly and easy to handle which allows users to enter information in a short time and share it instantly.

Figure 2 shows the main screen of the Daily Journal, where all flights arriving and departing daily should be loaded automatically. Several items have been grouped into a single box called "Actions" for each flight. The first item corresponds to "checklists" with all the operations and the operators involved in the flight. The second item allows users to add cases of passengers with reduced mobility or those need of assistance. The third element includes loading instructions and the last one is used to insert the "anomalies". The main screen also shows the activities derived from handovers (shift handovers). The reporting around those activities is completed by the airport-duty-managers. He/she may also report problems even when they have already been investigated and resolved. Any abnormality reported remains in the system, even if it has been resolved, and they are analyzed and discussed during scheduled during management review meetings.

One of the main advantages of this tool is to give a real picture of routine operations available in a shift versus their timeline. As this data can be used to show a precursor of workload based on the task performed by the resource available in each shift by cumulating the turnaround and routine tasks with the non-recurrent tasks performed during each shift. It was also used to identify latent risks and potential anomalies in the procedures, equipment, training and the human factor component, deviations which otherwise would have never been highlighted as well as providing a lever on the monitoring of key performance in the context of business management for long-term strategies. This leads to improved efficiency and avoids substantial costs that may arise from possible accident scenarios. It can also highlight if there are potential correlations

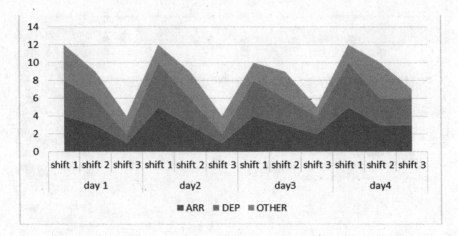

Fig. 3. Example of the analysis for amount of ground handling activities recorded for each shifts coming from different categories.

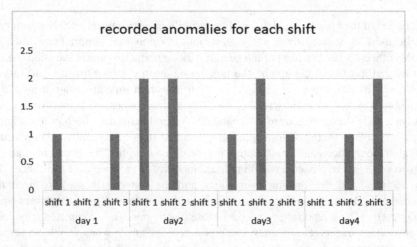

Fig. 4. Example of sample data for amount of anomalies recorded for each shift

between certain type of issues and different workload levels, Figures 3 and 4 shows a sample of the data analysis function for activities performed for each shifts, and the amount of anomalies recorded for each shift.

As a byproduct the daily journal also supports better communication as before its introduction some of the operational time was taken up coordinating and passing on information through VHF radio, the workload requirement due to this has greatly decreased. Below some comments received by employees/users of the Daily Journal: "The shift handover has become a mirror for operations activities, even in retrospective mode, with a greater control over the things that we do and that need to be done". Or "now we know better the potential consequences on the next shift if we perform certain operations in a superficial (routine) way". Or "It changed the way we think, we have a bigger awareness and responsibility on our operations". Or "while performing a task, whether the loading of cargo or push-back, now we think about the risks involved in the various steps".

For the managers and the operators on shift it is now possible to see over time what was done by whom in each shift and monitor not just the normal activities but also all the extra issues and anomalies that were handled and closed in each shift which added to the actual task requirements.

Regarding competences, the people interviewed were happy with the training provided by the organization and knowing that system would allow them to obtain certifications required and enabled most workers to be flexible and cover many positions. What they pointed out as missing firstly is the monitoring of actual tasks covered to make sure that there is a picture of the workload managed by each operator over time and the skills that need to be retained through experience. This feature of the tool effectively supports performance appraisal and feedback for the workers. The key success factor in this process of change is the human factor connected to technological development, without a proactive and constructive involvement by the majority of internal staff resistance to change of a work methodology rooted and consolidated over time would have probably compromised the tool uptake even if technically flawless. There is a development path both technological and human to be undertaken to achieve the improvement of performance and the desired innovation. Some details must be included during this path, such as training, ongoing communication and "no blame policy" towards staff involved in the reporting of errors or irregularities in the process. These are key factors for a successful tool uptake together with process transparency and the involvement of the entire staff.

5 Day to Day Task Support and the Long Lasting Implications on Error Reduction and Safety

The tool needs to support the full cycle for performance management.
The functionalities developed are:

1. Checklist to be used for task support on critical operations available in the on line repository of procedures directly derived from the Process mapping.
2. Digital signoff of the checklist and extra tasks connected to Shift handovers.
3. Review of procedures and processes performing participatory risk assessment (it takes the shape of structured hazard identification exercise focused on each operation of the airport operations manual). This will lead to the initial shaping of a risk registry for the main activities of the company to be further updated with risks identified through reporting and periodic reviews.
4. Management of recommendations coming from reporting and updating of risk registry through suggestions of the "Management Review and Safety Board"
5. Monitoring and data analytics capacity on workload managed for each shift over time and recurrent issues (see Figs. 3 and 4)

The first two aspects of the tool provide the advantage of making more readily available on the job the forms that can support the workload of the normal daily signed off procedures for all the operators on site. Only now the intention is to perform the sign off closer to real time and support the assignment of the extra tasks as part of the shift handovers notes that can be followed up to monitor task execution and workload precursors (number of activities over time) for shift and operators.

This has dramatically reduced the amount of miscommunication and lack of clarity in respect to who is supposed to do what during the turnaround. The tool contributed to reduce human errors as some of the issues reported were around steps of the tasks that were occasionally previously neglected.

The reduction of human error achieved is estimated to be in the range of 20% only accounting for the human error that are now reported and corrected on the job while they were previously not even noted (The 20% accounts for anomalies reported and closed almost immediately, and/or near misses currently recorded).

As an example it is relevant to mention the near misses and anomalies reported around the part of the pushback when the "NOSE GEAR LOCKPIN" is inserted. This pin acts on the valve that inhibits pressure to the nose gear. Then the steering height must be checked so as to avoid the tractor from impacting and damaging the landing gear doors. Possible errors around this part of the task can be forgetting to insert the Lock pin (often detected and corrected immediately before pushback, also thanks to the special notes used in the checklist and on the pushback vehicle, or that during the push, the towing tractor must be maneuvered so as to not exceed the maximum steer radius and speeds; should the safety pin break there would be a loss of directional control.

Furthermore the system has been able to dramatically address the issue of under reporting at the airport. *After the first year of using it the airport has been able to increase by a factor of 10 the amount of information reported to management about operational issues* [18]. The tool was introduced also to improve reporting levels and address some of the causal factors identified by previous studies for underreporting [19–21]:

1. a definition of operational anomalies and near misses relevant to the issues normally encountered on everyday tasks
2. a reporting framework that can avoid the extra paperwork
3. the provision of feedback on reported problems and operational issues.

The new reporting framework introduced in this change initiative linked the effect of an online task support to support the management of workload for highly proceduralised tasks in the form of a check list with an embedded reporting function (that is inherent to the signoff process already part of on-site operational requirements).

The advantage of using existing tools for near misses and in general event reporting is that the use of ad hoc reporting forms fail to provide a real-time picture of routine operations and possible peaks of task requirements due to anomalies and disturbances to be managed in the process [22].

6   Interim Results and Future Work

The new task support tool and reporting framework introduced in this change initiative has the advantage of being based on the forms that were already used as part of the normal daily operations for all the operators on site. This advantage effectively helped the goal of providing a real-time support and a picture of routine operations aimed at performance improvement and predictive risk management. As already stated the checklists were used as a real time sign off for the tasks and delivered workload management support as they reminded key steps in detail and gave the possibility to report quickly any possible anomaly or issue in carrying out the tasks. Furthermore the shift handover page was designed to give the possibility to allocate tasks outside peak time, check status quickly and report once again issues as they arise. Therefore the new tool presented the advantage of seamlessly integration in a pre-existing workflow.

The data collected through it have the potential to identify latent hazards in tasks, equipment, and procedures that may otherwise go unnoticed, and will also provide a better overview of everyday performance in the context of growing airport traffic demand. In the first months after its introduction was already able to change the rate of reporting from 40 accidents reports in 6 years to 209 anomalies collected with the trip file plus 201 activities reported through the shift handover in 1 month. Key success factors in this process have been:

1. Enthusiasm and proactive attitude of many ramp/operational agents; the desire for a change of work methodology and a new way of supporting their daily activities and the appraisal of their performance, different from the obsolete methods of evaluation.
2. Top management continuous support, proactive and positive attitude towards the initiative. That also led the management to use the tool to allocate tasks on shift handovers considering the workload already shouldered in each shift (related to the amount of turnarounds to be handled).
3. The possibility of keeping records of data collected over time; an overall evaluation of all processes of work and evidence of good performance and possible anomalies leading to integrated data monitoring.

The support of training sessions on "human factor issues" were organized in connection with the introduction of the new tool in the airport among which the exchange of information for the turnaround process between ramp operators and check in and gate operators. The feedback received was very positive and, it is perhaps interesting to report comments made by some of the Ramp operators: "by working on these check-lists and filling up the form with the tasks and the name of the agent who carried out the activities, we have become more conscious on our role and we have gone "back to the basics of our tasks", or "It is something everyone sees, something everyone deals with everyday but when you change your perspective and method of working (e.g. with the Daily Journal) or perform a risk assessment by working as a team with different departments, (as done during the Human Factor training sessions) something begins to change as if you were suddenly awakened" (Fig. 5) .

The interim successes are a very important part of the initiative. As Kotter (1995) noted "Real transformation takes time and a renewal effort risks losing momentum if there are no short-term goals to meet. Without short-terms wins, too many people give up or actively join the ranks of those people who have been resisting change" [23]. The tool can have the long lasting implications to support the achievement of improvement and leverage on the every-day performance within the context of the long term strategy of growth pursued by the airport, were the human factors and the capacity to deal effectively with required workload are key. However in the next stage of the project we

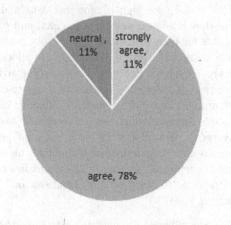

"The DJ provides benefits for task support on site"

■ strongly agree   ■ agree   ■ neutral   ■ disagree   ■ strongly disagree

Fig. 5. Example of feedback collected from the operators about task support provided

now need to actually assess workload levels for primary tasks measures and see how the tool can be used to monitor workload, human error and guide management in assigning extra tasks during less busy times to avoid peaks of workload requirements. For the subsequent stage of the project therefore formal methods to assess current perceived workload for different shift conditions and different roles will be deployed using the NASA TLX as a starting point [24] and moving progressively if needed towards more advanced models [25, 26] also able to discriminate between different types of activities (e.g. pushback or baggage handling are tasks associated with different cognitive workload demands). In choosing the appropriate methodology for the next stage the criteria of validity (i.e. to determine whether the Workload measurement instrument is actually what extent a method can explain objective performance measures, such as task execution time) and sensitivity (i.e. the capability of a method to discriminate significant variations in workload and changes in resource demand or task difficulty) [27]. The assessment will be focusing on primary task performance and it is important to remember that given the 'live' context we can not impact negatively on operators' functioning as the main goal is to achieve an even better level of support for human performance and an improved understanding of the key drivers behind it.

References

1. Irish Aviation Authority.: Ground Operations. (2017). https://www.iaa.ie/commercial-aviation/ground-operations. Accessed 13 Jan 2017
2. Stanton, N., Salmon, P., Walker, G., Baber, C., Jenkins, D.: Human Factors Methods: a Practical Guide for Engineering Design. Ashgate, Burlington, Farnham (2010)

3. Bommer, S.C., Fendely, M.: A theoretical framework for evaluating mental workload resources in human systems design for manufacturing operations. Int. J. Ind. Ergon. (2016)
4. DiDomenico, A., Nussbaum, M.: Effects of different physical workload parameters on mental workload and performance. Int. J. Ind. Ergon. **41**(3), 255–260 (2011)
5. Embrey, D., Blackett, C., Marsden, P., Peachey, J.: Development of a human cognitive workload assessment tool. Dalt. Hum. Reliab. Assoc. (2006)
6. Meyer, D., Kieras, D.: A computational theory of executive cognitive processes and multiple-task performance: part 1. Basic Mech. Psychol. Rev. **104**, 3–65 (1997)
7. Ackerman, P.L.: Determinants of individual differences during skill acquisition: cognitive abilities and information processing. J. Exp. Psychol. Gen. **117**, 288–318 (1988)
8. Borkowski, J.G., Burke, J.E.: Theories, models, and measurements of executive functioning: an information processing perspective. In: Lyon, G.R., Krasnegor, N.A. (eds.). Attention, Memory, and Executive Function, pp. 235–261 (1996)
9. Leva, M.C., Kay, A.M., Mattei, F., Kontogiannis, T., Ambroggi, M., Cromie, S.: A dynamic task representation method for a virtual reality application. In: Harris, D. (ed.) EPCE 2009. LNCS, vol. 5639, pp. 32–42. Springer, Heidelberg (2009). doi:10.1007/978-3-642-02728-4_4
10. National Transportation Safety Board.: Aircraft accident report, NTSB/AAR-88/05. Washington, DC (1988) https://www.ntsb.gov/investigations/AccidentReports/Pages/AAR8805.aspx. Accessed 2 Feb 2017
11. Degani, A., Wiener, E.L.: The Human Factors of Flight-Deck Checklists: The Normal Checklist (NASA contractor report 177549). NASA Ames Research Center, Mountain (1990). ViewMoffett Field, CA
12. British Petroleum.: Fatal Accident Investigation report – Isomerization Unit Explosion Final Report –Texas City, Texas, USA (2005)
13. The Health and Safety Executive.: Reducing Error and Influencing Behaviour. (2003). http://antarisconsulting.com/docs/guides/unit_a/A7_HSG48_Reducing_Error_and_Influencing_Behaviour.pdf. Accessed 19 Jan 2017
14. Aviation Safety Reporting System.: NASA. Callback, a checklist, issue 428. (2017). https://asrs.arc.nasa.gov/publications/callback.html. Accessed 17 Jan 2017
15. Longo, L.: Designing medical interactive systems via assessment of human mental workload. In: Proceedings of the 2015 IEEE 28th International Symposium on Computer Based Medical Systems, CBMS 2015, pp. 364–365. (2015) doi.10.1109/CBMS.2015.67
16. Leva, M.C., Naghdali F., Balfe, N., Gerbec, M., Demichela, M.: Remote risk assessment: a case study using SCOPE software. Chem. Eng. Trans. (43) (2015)
17. Leva, M.C., Sordo, D., Mattei, F.: Performance management in a small regional airport: the role of change in the day to day task support for an integrated SMS. J. Cogn. Technol. Work Arch. **17**(2), 237–248 (2015)
18. ICAO.: Safety Management Manual (SMM) Doc 9859 AN/474. (2017) http://www.icao.int/safety/SafetyManagement/Documents/Doc.9859.3rd%20Edition.alltext.en.pdf. Accessed 31 Jan 2017
19. Airport Council International Airport Benchmarking To Maximise Efficiency. Published By ACI World Headquarters Geneva – Switzerland (2006)
20. Pransky, G., Snyder, T., Dembe, A., Himmelstein, J.: Under-reporting of work-related disorders in the workplace: a case study and review of the literature. Ergonomics **42**, 171–182 (1999)
21. Clancy, P., Leva, M.C.: Hrymak, V., Sherlock, M.: Safety and or hazard near miss reporting in an international energy company. In: Proceedings of the Irish Ergonomics Society Annual Conference 2011 Edited by Leonard W. O'Sullivan and Chiara Leva (2011). ISSN: 1649-210 2011

22. Leva, M.C., Cahill, J., Kay, A., Losa, G.: Mc Donald, N.: The advancement of a new human factors report – 'the unique report' - facilitating flight crew auditing of performance/operations, as part of an airline's safety management system. Ergonomics **53** (2), 164–183 (2010)
23. Kotter, J.P.: Leading change: why transformation efforts fail. Harvard Bus. Rev. **73**(2), 59–67 (1995)
24. Hart, S.G., Staveland, L.E.: Development of NASA-TLX (task load index): results of empirical and theoretical research. In: Hancock, P.A., Najmedin, M. (eds.) Human Mental Workload (PDF), pp. 139–183. Advances in Psychology. North Holland, Amsterdam (1988). doi:10.1016/S0166-4115(08)62386-9
25. Longo, L.: A defeasible reasoning framework for human mental workload representation and assessment. Behav. Inf. Technol. **34**(8), 758–786 (2015)
26. Rizzo, L., Dondio, P., Delany, S.J., Longo, L.: Modeling mental workload via rule-based expert system: a comparison with NASA-TLX and workload profile. In: Iliadis, L., Maglogiannis, I. (eds.) AIAI 2016. IAICT, vol. 475, pp. 215–229. Springer, Cham (2016). doi:10.1007/978-3-319-44944-9_19

Workload Differences Between On-road and Off-road Manoeuvres for Motorcyclists

Simon Tong, Shaun Helman[(⊠)], Nora Balfe, Camila Fowler,
Emma Delmonte, and R. Hutchins

Transport Research Laboratory, Crowthorne, UK
shelman@trl.co.uk

Abstract. This paper describes the results of a study comparing motorcycle manoeuvres on-road (in live traffic) and off-road (in designated test centres). Workload was measured using NASA-RTLX with rider performance used as a secondary measure, and the results are discussed in terms of the different dimensions that were affected by the change in setting. The study found that both faults and workload increased in the on-road condition, with the frustration, performance and time pressure components of workload showing the largest increases. The results may have implications for conducting testing in protected environments, which might not fully reflect the workload associated with on-road manoeuvring.

Keywords: Motorcycle workload · NASA-TLX

1 Introduction

Motorcyclists are a particularly vulnerable group of road users with a higher risk of mortality on roads than other groups [1–3]. This greater incidence of fatalities among motorcycle riders has prompted previous research into the skills and workload associated with the task. Rutter and Quine [4] reported that age is the dominant factor in the high crash rate of motorcyclists; this coincides with the well-known statistic reported in the young and novice *driver* literature showing that young drivers are at particular risk [5]. (Inexperienced drivers of any age are also at a much greater risk of being in a collision than their more experienced counterparts [5]). Horswill and Helman [3] conclude that although behaviour plays a small role in the extra risk faced by motorcyclists, physical vulnerability plays a much greater part. Whatever the underlying factors, the importance of proper licensing for motorcyclists, including proper testing of their suitability for riding before being allowed access to the road system, is critical. Di Stasi et al. [6] describe the motorcycle riding task as "a dynamic and complex psychomotor activity demanding simultaneous processing of information on different cognitive levels as well as a variety of physical activities in a constantly varying setting" (pp. 362). Primary tasks involved in motorcycle riding include steering, adjusting throttle and brakes, controlling speed, monitoring the environment for hazards, negotiating lane changes, and navigating. All these tasks must be mastered and

© Springer International Publishing AG 2017
L. Longo and M.C. Leva (Eds.): H-WORKLOAD 2017, CCIS 726, pp. 239–250, 2017.
DOI: 10.1007/978-3-319-61061-0_16

tested before motorcyclists can be granted a licence. At present in Great Britain (GB), motorcycle tests of specific manoeuvres (captured in European Directive 2006/126/EC[1], and termed 'module 1' tests) are conducted in off-road test centres where manoeuvres are examined in a reduced risk environment. The reasoning behind this is that riders should not be tested on-road (the so-called 'module 2' or 'riding' test) until they have demonstrated basic manoeuvring skills in a relatively safe environment. There are some practical issues associated with this approach however; the main one is that some riders who are learning may live a great distance from their closest test centre. This presents both practical and safety challenges (as the inconvenience of having to get to a test centre, and the extra exposure to risk presented if this journey is undertaken on an L-plated motorcycle).

The study discussed in this paper sought to compare off-road manoeuvre testing of new motorcycle riders with proposed on-road manoeuvre testing, as part of a wider research project examining the feasibility of on-road module-1 motorcycle tests in GB (in order to overcome such practical issues as noted above). The work was undertaken as part of a project for the Department for Transport in GB, in 2013. Workload and performance were measured for a set of manoeuvres in both settings as part of the comparison. Workload was measured using the NASA Raw TaskLoad IndeX (RTLX) [7, 8] while performance was evaluated by experienced test assessors using the framework applied in official tests.

Workload can be defined as the human cost of completing a task [8] and mental workload as the amount of cognitive capacity required to perform a given task [9]. In this study, the NASA RTLX was used to provide workload scores [7]. This instrument uses six scales, each scored between 1 and 21, with higher numbers representing higher levels of workload. Overall workload is taken here as the average of individual ratings of the six subscales – mental demand, physical demand, temporal demand, performance, effort, and frustration. Brief descriptions of each subscale are provided in Table 1, adapted from [8]. NASA-TLX has previously been used to measure workload in driving research, for example Hancock et al. [10] have previously used NASA TLX to compare workload during left and right turns for car drivers, in a piece of research motivated by the high fatality rates among motorcycle riders. They found no significant relationship between driving manoeuvre and perceived workload, although other measures used in the same experiment found higher workload during turn sequences. In another example, specific to motorcyclists, Filtness et al. [11] undertook a study to compare novice and experienced motorcycle riders driving under the influence of three levels of alcohol intake (sober (0% blood alcohol level (BAC), 0.02% BAC, 0.05% BAC). They used a modified NASA-TLX to compare subjective workload between the groups and between alcohol levels. They found a significant difference between the 0% BAC group and both alcohol conditions for overall workload measuring using NASA-TLX. The difference between novice and experienced riders in this case approached significance. In terms of the individual dimensions, mental demand and effort scored highest in both groups, followed by performance. They also found a

---

[1] http://eur-lex.europa.eu/legal-content/EN/TXT/PDF/?uri=CELEX:32006L0126&from=EN.

Table 1. NASA-TLX subscales [8]

Subscale	Explanation
Mental demand	How much mental and perceptual activity was required (e.g. thinking, deciding, calculating, remembering, looking, searching, etc.)? Was the task easy or demanding, simple or complex, exacting or forgiving?
Physical demand	How much physical activity was required (e.g. pushing, pulling, turning, controlling, activating, etc.)? Was the drive easy or demanding, slow or brisk, slack or strenuous, restful or laborious?
Temporal demand	How much time pressure did you feel due to the rate or pace at which the mission occurred? Was the pace leisurely or rapid and frantic?
Performance	How successful do you think you were in accomplishing the goals of the task? How satisfied were you with your performance in accomplishing these goals?
Effort	How hard did you have to work (mentally and physically) to accomplish your level of performance?
Frustration	How discouraged, stressed, irritated, and annoyed versus gratified, relaxed, contented, and complacent did you feel during the task?

significant effect of sub-scale between urban and rural settings, and concluded that the workload sub-scales were measuring distinct aspects of the motorcycle riding task.

The aim of this study was to compare workload and performance between on- and off-road manoeuvres used in GB motorcycle licence tests.

2   Method

A repeated measures design was used to compare the two conditions (on- and off- road). 151 participants completed the trial, with 73 completing the off-road manoeuvres first and 78 completing the on-road manoeuvres first. All participants were learner riders who were judged by their instructors to be ready to take their motorcycle test. The trials were held at 11 different sites across GB, with a maximum of 67 riders and a minimum of 2 riders at each site (the median was 8). Learners were paid £55 for their involvement.

2.1   Materials

NASA Raw Task Load Index (RTLX) [7] was used to measure subjective workload. This is a multi-dimensional scale designed to obtain subjective estimates of workload from people immediately after they have performed a task. It has been used in a variety of domains, including the operation of automobiles [e.g. 12], since its original development in the aviation context and has been shown to be a reliable and valid measure of workload (for a review, see [8]).

2.2   Participants

In total, 151 learner riders took part in the trials. Participants had a mean age of 30 years and the majority (92%) were male. More than three-quarters (77%) were training on motorcycles with larger engines with no restrictions on power outputs. The remainder were using motorcycles with smaller engines and restricted power outputs of up to 35 kW. Learners had received a mean of 13 h of motorcycle training overall.

2.3   Procedure

Participants were recruited for the study from approved motorcycle training providers and were requested to be 'test ready'. On arrival at a trial site, each participant was given an opportunity to ask questions about the study and was invited to complete a consent form, in line with the ethical approval for the study. They were then invited to complete the on- and off-road manoeuvres. During the manoeuvres, experienced Driving Standards Agency (DSA)[2] examiners rated the performance of the participants, and in particular noted any faults in the performance of the manoeuvres (using the same faults form as used during formal tests). At the end of each set of manoeuvres, riders answered a series of questions to rate the workload associated with the activities they had just completed. After completing both sets of manoeuvres, riders answered a final set of more general questions before finally being thanked and paid for their participation. Table 2 describes the manoeuvres undertaken in the study. Four of the five manoeuvres were the same in both conditions. It was not possible to replicate the original 'on and off the stand' manoeuvre in the on-road condition, so this was replaced by a 'pushed U-turn' manoeuvre in the off-road condition. These tasks are not comparable, although they were part of the trial for reasons associated with the proposed changes in the motorcycle test. Descriptions of the manoeuvres tested off-road can be found online[3]. Brief descriptions of the manoeuvres tested on road as part of this study are as follows:

- Pushed U-turn – pushing the bike from one side of the road to the other, in a U-turn
- Ridden U-turn – riding the bike from one side of the road to another, in a U-turn
- Slalom – riding the bike in a slalom through five cones spaced in a straight line 4.5 m apart, 2.1 m from the kerb

Table 2. Manoeuvres included in the study.

Off-road	On-road
On and off the stand/manual handling	Pushed U-turn
Ridden U-turn	Ridden U-turn
Slalom	Slalom
Emergency stop after curve	Emergency stop after 85 m straight
Hazard avoidance after curve	Hazard avoidance after 85 m straight

---

[2] Since renamed to the Driver and Vehicle Standards Agency (DVSA) after merging with the previous Vehicle and Operator Services Agency (VOSA).

[3] https://www.gov.uk/government/uploads/system/uploads/attachment_data/file/316690/motorcycle-manoeuvring-area-multi-purpose-test-centre.pdf.

- Emergency stop after 85 m straight – riding for 85 m and achieving a speed of 28–30 mph before performing an emergency stop
- Hazard avoidance – riding for 85 m and achieving a speed of 28–30 mph before performing an avoidance manoeuvre in line with the dimensions shown in the link above.

3   Results

The results are presented relating to the performance (fault) data (Sect. 3.1) and the workload ratings (Sect. 3.2).

3.1   Fault Data

Figure 1 shows fault data broken down by fault type (minor, moderate, serious and dangerous) for both the on-road and off-road conditions. Dangerous faults involve immediate danger to the rider, the examiner, the public or property. Serious faults present a serious risk to safety that could develop into a dangerous situation. A single example of either of these two categories would result in a failed test at the time the trial was undertaken. Moderate faults are not potentially dangerous but could become serious if repeated (up to five of these were allowed per test, at the time during which the trial was undertaken). Minor faults were defined here as errors that would not merit a fault in a real test, but were captured here for more comprehensive data analysis based on the judgement of the examiner.

It is clear from Fig. 1 that there were more faults recorded during the on-road manoeuvres (227 in total) compared with the off-road condition (111 in total). In particular, the 'Serious Fault' category showed a steep increase for the on-road condition. A paired samples t-test showed that the mean number of faults on-road was

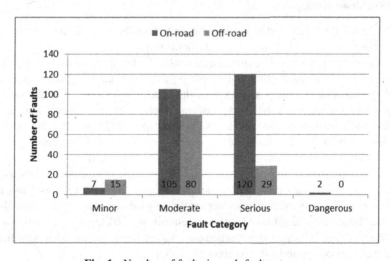

Fig. 1. Number of faults in each fault category

significantly greater ($p > .001$) than for the off-road condition. The number of faults per manoeuvre in both conditions are shown in Fig. 2. For all manoeuvres, there were more faults recorded during the on-road test than during the comparable manoeuvres off-road, with the exception of the on-road pushed U-turn. The mean number of faults for each manoeuvre was compared across the two conditions using paired samples t-tests. The results showed significant differences between the two conditions for the ridden U-turn and hazard avoidance. The result for the pushed U-turn may be explained by the difference in the on-road and off-road manoeuvres. The differences between the manoeuvres were further explored through the NASA-RTLX workload data.

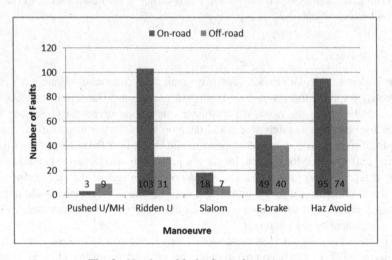

Fig. 2. Number of faults for each manoeuvre

3.2 Workload Ratings

Figure 3 shows the mean overall workload reported for the on-road manoeuvres. Note that the NASA-RTLX scale used was a 21-point scale.

Workload for the on-road manoeuvres tended to be approximately equal to, or higher than the workload for the comparable off-road manoeuvres. Analysis (using an ANOVA) of workload ratings showed that the condition (on- or off-road) had a significant effect on the workload scores overall ($p = .029$). The interaction between condition and manoeuvre type was also significant ($p = .047$) showing that workload differences existed only for some manoeuvres. The difference was subject to further analysis to identify which manoeuvres were responsible for this difference in workload. Statistical comparison of the mean workload within each manoeuvre across the two conditions was conducted using paired samples t-tests. The results showed that mean overall workload was significantly greater for the on-road versions of the ridden U-turn, emergency brake and hazard avoidance manoeuvres ($p = .013$, $p = .013$, and $p = .016$ respectively). This indicates that participants found these manoeuvres significantly more difficult to complete in the on-road condition.

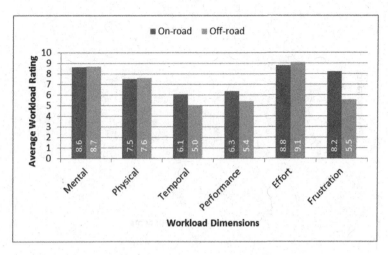

Fig. 3. Mean NASA-RTLX scores for each manoeuvre

The mean ratings for each of the six components of the NASA-RTLX were also compared. Figure 4 shows that the average workload rating for each dimension in both the on- and off- road conditions.

Effort was the highest rated dimension for both conditions, followed by mental demand and both these dimensions showed only small differences between the two conditions. Physical demand is also relatively high and shows little difference between the two conditions. However, frustration is lower for the off-road condition and shows a sharp rise in the on-road condition. Temporal demand and performance are the two lowest rated dimensions in both conditions, but both see a rise in the on-road condition. Figure 5 shows the mean ratings for each of the six components of the NASA-RTLX workload measure for the on- and off- road conditions for the ridden U-turn.

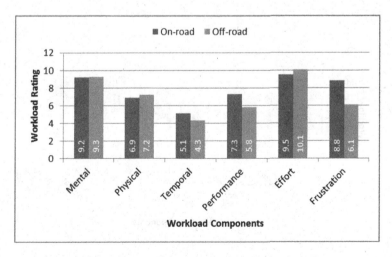

Fig. 4. Average workload scores for both conditions across all manoeuvres

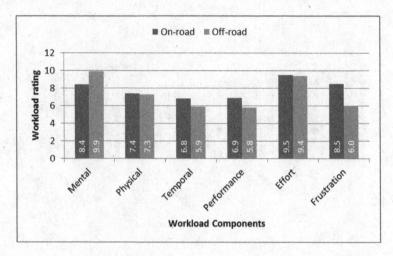

Fig. 5. Workload breakdown for ridden U-turn

Overall, participants rated the workload for this manoeuvre as significantly greater on-road, and the data here show this is driven by the temporal, performance and frustration components of workload, which were all significantly greater on-road ($p = .028$, $p = .003$, and $p < .001$ respectively). This means that participants:

- Experienced greater time pressure on-road, and felt more hurried and/or rushed
- May have had greater insight into performance on-road and may have been more aware of their errors
- Experienced greater frustration on-road, including feelings of stress and insecurity.

Figure 6 shows the mean ratings for the six components of workload for the on- and off- road versions of the emergency brake manoeuvre. Participants rated the overall

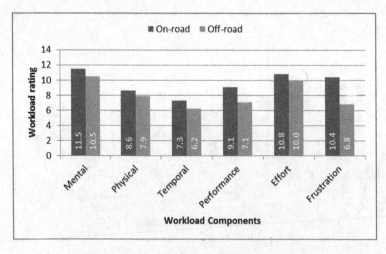

Fig. 6. Workload breakdown for emergency brake

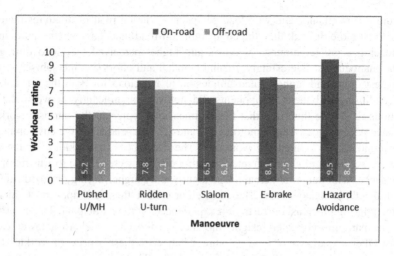

Fig. 7. Workload breakdown for hazard avoidance

workload for completing the emergency brake manoeuvre as significantly greater on-road; the data here shows that this is due to the performance and frustration components of workload being significantly greater for on-road riding ($p = .036$ and $p < .001$ respectively). This indicates that participants:

- May have had greater insight into their performance on-road and may have been more aware of their errors
- Experienced greater frustration on-road

Figure 7 shows the mean ratings for the seven components of workload for the on- and off- road conditions of the hazard avoidance manoeuvre. Participants rated the overall workload for the hazard avoidance as significantly greater on-road, and the data here shows that this is because the performance and frustration components of workload were both significantly greater on-road ($p = .008$ and $p < .001$ respectively). The means that participants:

- May have had greater insight into their performance on-road and may have been more aware of their errors
- Experienced greater frustration on-road

4   Discussion

The aim of this study was to compare performance and workload between on-road and off-road conditions for the manoeuvres used in GB motorcycle licence tests. With regard to performance, the main finding of the study was that learner riders were more likely to receive faults on the on-road versions of the ridden U-turn and hazard avoidance manoeuvres, when compared with the off-road versions. In terms of workload, the ratings from learners showed that all manoeuvres except the pushed U-turn and slalom had significantly higher workload ratings in the on-road than the off-road condition.

From a performance and workload perspective, the on-road manoeuvres therefore appear to be more difficult than the comparable off-road manoeuvres, with participants experiencing a greater number of errors and higher perceived workload during the on-road manoeuvres. Interestingly, mental demand and effort (i.e. the sub-scale) were the highest or second highest rated dimension of workload for both the on- and off-road conditions and these components did not vary significantly between the two conditions. It can be theorised that these dimensions represent the intrinsic workload associated with manoeuvring a motorcycle, and are independent of the environment or any external factors influencing workload. The differences in workload for the three manoeuvres with significantly greater overall workload were all due to frustration and performance, with temporal demand also significantly higher during on- road riding in one of the three manoeuvres. The road environment therefore appears to increase workload through increasing frustration experienced by the participant. This frustration gives the participant greater insight into their performance and, to a lesser extent, increases their experience of time pressure. Changes to these aspects of workload may partly explain the greater number of faults made. These dimensions may represent external influences on workload that will vary under different conditions and situations. Differentiation between intrinsic and extrinsic workload is not commonly found in the human factors workload literature, (see the Task Capability Interface Model [13] for more information on this), but intrinsic and extraneous load are differentiated in Cognitive Load Theory [14] in the education domain. Here, intrinsic load is defined as the load resulting from the nature of a learning task, while extraneous load is the load created by the instructional design [15]. The results of this study suggest that a similar differentiation may be relevant to broader workload measurement and is worthy of further investigation.

The data collected in this study found clear differences between the conditions in on- and off- road riding, highlighting the role of the environment in experienced workload and driving performance. The environment did not appear to significantly change the intrinsic workload (comprised primarily of mental demand and effort), but did increase perceived frustration, performance and sometimes time pressure. These are important elements of the real world task. The findings may be generalised to any workload study using a protected or simulated environment, where it is likely that some additional factors associated with workload are controlled and workload evaluations in these settings are therefore likely to be an underestimate. Further research investigating the differentiation between intrinsic and extrinsic workload may lead to the development of tools capable of partially overcoming this limitation.

When considering making changes to motorcycle testing, attention must of course be paid to the trade-off between how well the test prepares a candidate for riding, and what is practical and safe for candidates (and others) as they progress through the licence acquisition process. The barriers to having the Module 1 motorcycle test delivered on-road go beyond the measures reported here. In particular, the extra risks that may be present to examiners and other road users from on-road testing in live traffic need to be considered. This point notwithstanding, this research highlights the importance of on-road testing; even after competence in manoeuvres has been demonstrated in off-road settings, only through gaining experience on-road can motorcyclists be prepared for real road conditions.

Acknowledgments. This research was funded by the UK Department for Transport. The broader project from which the data in the current paper is sourced is published in the form of two TRL reports [16, 17], available from trl.co.uk.

References

1. Wulf, G., Hancock, P.A., Rahimi, M.: Motorcycle conspicuity: an evaluation and synthesis of influential factors. J. Saf. Res. **20**, 153–176 (1989). doi:10.1016/0022-4375(89)90025-X
2. Chesham, D.J., Rutter, D.R., Quine, L.: Mapping the social psychological determinants of safe and unsafe motorcycle riding. In: Grayson, G.B., Lester, J.F. (eds.) Behavioural Research in Road Safety. Transport and Road Research Laboratory, Crowthorne, UK (1991)
3. Horswill, M.S., Helman, S.: A behavioural comparison between motorcyclists and a matched group of non-motorcycling car drivers: factors influencing accident risk. Accid. Anal. Prev. **35**, 589–597 (2003). doi:10.1016/S0001-4575(02)00039-8
4. Rutter, D.R., Quine, L.: Age and experience in motorcycling safety. Accid. Anal. Prev. **28**(1), 15–21 (1996). doi:10.1016/0001-4575(95)00037-2
5. Maycock, G., Lockwood, C.R., Lester, J.: The accident liability of car drivers. TRRL Report RR315. Transport and Road Research Laboratory, Crowthorne (1991)
6. Di Stasi, L.L., Álvarez-Valbuena, V., Cañas, J.J., Maldonado, A., Catena, A., Antolí, A., Candido, A.: Risk behavior and mental workload: Multimodal assessment techniques applied to motorbike riding simulation. Transp. Res. Part F **12**, 361–370 (2009). doi:10.1016/j.trf.2009.02.004
7. Hart, S.G., Staveland, L.E.: Development of NASA-TLX (Task Load Index): results of empirical and theoretical research. In: Hancock, P.A., Meshkati, N. (eds.) Human Mental Workload. North Holland Press, Amsterdam (1988)
8. Hart, S.G.: NASA-Task Load Index (NASA-TLX); 20 years later. In: Proceedings of the Human Factors and Ergonomics Society 50th Annual Meeting, pp. 904–908. HFES, Santa Monica (2006)
9. O'Donnell, R.D., Eggemeier, F.T.: Workload assessment methodology. In: Boff, K.R., Kaufman, L., Thomas, J. (eds.) Handbook of Perception and Human Performance. Cognitive processes and performance, vol. 2, pp. 42–49. Wiley, New York (1986)
10. Hancock, P.A., Wulf, G., Thom, D., Fassnacht, P.: Driver workload during differing driving maneuvers. Accid. Anal. Prev. **22**(3), 281–290 (1990). doi:10.1016/0001-4575(90)90019-H
11. Filtness, A.J., Rudin-Brown, C.M.: Drinking and riding: is subjective workload related to performance? In: Australasian Road Safety Research, Policing and Education Conference, 4–6 October 2012, Wellington, New Zealand (2012)
12. Benedetto, S., Pedrotti, M., Minin, L., Baccino, T., Re, A., Montanari, R.: Driver workload and eye blink duration. Transp. Res. Part F **14**(3), 199–208 (2011). doi:10.1016/j.trf.2010.12.001
13. Fuller, R.: From theory to practice: implications of the task-capability interface model for driver training. In: Proceedings of the 10th Seminar on Behaviour Research in Road Safety Behavioural Research in Road Safety. DETR, London (2001)
14. Plass, J.L., Moreno, R., Brünken, : Cognitive Load Theory, p. 15. Cambridge University Press, Cambridge (2010)
15. Wiebe, E.N., Roberts, E., Behrend, T.S.: An examination of two mental workload measurement approaches to understanding multimedia learning. Comput. Hum. Behav. **26**, 474–481 (2010). doi:10.1016/j.chb.2009.12.006

16. Tong, S., Helman, S., Fowler, C., Delmonte, E., Hutchins, R.: Motorcycle manoeuvres review: the feasibility and safety implications of carrying out modified module 1 test manoeuvres on-road. Phase 1 - off-road trials with learner riders. Published Project Report (PPR667). Transport Research Laboratory, Crowthorne (2013)
17. Tong, S., Helman, S., Fowler, C., Delmonte, E., Hutchins, R.: Motorcycle manoeuvres review: phase 2 and phase 3 report. Published Project Report (PPR659). Transport Research Laboratory, Crowthorne (2013)

Workload, Fatigue and Performance in the Rail Industry

Andrew P. Smith$^{(\boxtimes)}$ ⓘ and Hugo N. Smith

Centre for Occupational and Health Psychology, School of Psychology,
Cardiff University, 63 Park Place, Cardiff CF24 0DB, UK
SmithAP@Cardiff.ac.uk

Abstract. Recent research has addressed the topic of workload in the rail industry. Much of this has been concerned with developing measures for use by signallers and there has been less research about the workload of passenger rail staff. The present studies addressed this issue using single item measures of workload, effort, fatigue and performance. Results from two diary studies with conductors/guards and maintenance engineers showed that high workload was associated with increased fatigue. Fatigue was associated with increased risk of incidents and slower reaction time. In the third study, results from a large scale survey showed both that high demands increased fatigue and demands were associated with perceptions of reduced performance. Overall, these results confirm the importance of workload for operational efficiency and show that the use of single item measures makes further study in real-life settings acceptable.

Keywords: Workload · Job demands · Fatigue · Performance · Rail industry

1 Introduction

The aim of the research described in this paper was to investigate workload, fatigue and performance/safety in a passenger train company in the UK. This was done using subjective reports of workload and fatigue and relating these to subjective reports of job characteristics and work outcomes. In addition, objective indicators of performance and safety were also used in some of the studies. This research was intended as a preliminary approach that will eventually be supported by studies involving objective measurement of workload and more objective outcomes (e.g. physiological measures). Although the studies were conducted using rail crew, the approach is transferable to other contexts and industries. Three studies are presented to address the initial aims. These studies are described separately as they involve different samples and differences in methodology. Brief discussions are given after each study, followed by an overall discussion of the programme of research. The next section reviews several approaches to workload that have been adopted in the UK rail industry.

There has been an increase in the importance of human factors in the rail industry [1]. In the case of workload this has led to the development of many measuring instruments and the design of standard operating procedures that will aid assessment of workload [2]. An initial aim has been to develop a function complexity index linking number of inputs to perception of workload [3]. This issue has been widely studied in

L. Longo and M.C. Leva (Eds.): H-WORKLOAD 2017, CCIS 726, pp. 251–263, 2017.
DOI: 10.1007/978-3-319-61061-0_17

other contexts and requires an examination of the relationship between the demand for resources imposed by the task and the ability of the individual to supply those resources [4, 5]. The aim was to develop a set of quantitative criteria and a model to define systems that provided appropriate workloads.

Workload is a multi-dimensional concept with consideration for time, mental tasks, physical tasks and stressors [6]. It could be used to plan crew sizes, allocate functions and assess effects of working practices on operator efficiency and health. Workload can be measured independently (what is imposed by the system) or by rating the workload of the individual. The term workload is used in different ways in the rail industry which has led to it being considered in a functional context (see [7] for a review). An initial starting point for earlier research was to review dimensions of workload and classify them in terms of effort (e.g. resource capacity), demand (e.g. task difficulty) or effect (e.g. performance). Workload tools used in previous studies with rail signallers were also reviewed (e.g. [8, 9]). Many of these, developed in laboratories or designed for military samples, were not suitable for real-time use or civilian populations. Interviews were also carried out with rail staff; the consensus being that the level of mental effort required to complete the work formed the major workload component. This confirms that perception of load is central to an understanding of mental workload and that the effort expended by the person to accommodate work demands is a critical dimension of mental workload [10]. Kahneman [11] specified three questions which can be applied to evaluation of demands, namely:

1. What makes an activity more or less demanding?
2. What factors control the level of capacity available?
3. What are the rules regarding allocation of resources?

Much of the literature assesses the effects of workload in terms of performance. Strategies may be adopted which are effort-conserving and standards of performance may be lowered to conserve effort. Effects of workload on wellbeing are often referred to as stress or fatigue, and it may be these states that mediate the effects of workload on performance. Tools have been developed to assess these dimensions of workload in rail signalling (see [12]). These include an Integrated Workload Scale (IWS) and an Operational Demand Checklist (ODEC). Other methods have been developed to assess the workload of train drivers (e.g. Train Driver DRAWS - Defence Research Agency Workload Scales; Acceptable Workload Evaluation; Train Driver Workload Probe; Time Line Analysis – [13]).

One of the major problems with the UK rail industry's approach to workload is that it does not address human mental workload (see [14–16]). In addition, although a number of measuring instruments have been developed for use in the rail industry, there is little evidence that they are currently being used by UK train operating companies. There are two main reasons for this; the first is that workload does not fit into any clear occupational health and safety category. It might, for example, be put under the heading of fatigue, but in this case it is often considered as secondary to factors like working hours. Indeed, job demands are included in the calculation of the HSE Fatigue and Risk Indices but they are usually set at a constant level for all staff. Workload could be put in the 'stress at work' category, however this is usually considered a HR issue rather than one of occupational health and safety, meaning that relationships with safety outcomes may not be examined. The other problem is that of having a very simple measure that can be easily used in real-life settings. Recent research has shown that single questions can often be as useful as longer scales [17–19]. This allows one to measure a number of concepts which can lead to the testing of more sophisticated models (e.g. the Demands-Resources-Individual Effects (DRIVE model – [20]). Both the single item approach and the DRIVE model have largely been applied to stress and wellbeing but can now be applied to workload and fatigue also. Indeed, the research described in this article is one of the first studies to do this. Multi-methodologies have been used to assess workload (or demands) in rail staff. The first study described here was a diary study where conductors rated their workload and fatigue each day for a week. The second study involved similar ratings from engineers at the start and end of the first and last day of their working week. Objective measures of performance were also taken at these times. Finally, the last study involved a survey of demands, fatigue and reported performance efficiency across different sectors of a rail company. All the studies described here were carried out with the approval of the ethics committee of the School of Psychology, Cardiff University, and with the informed consent of the volunteers. They were paid a small honorarium for participating.

2   A Diary Study of Workload and Fatigue of Conductors and Guards

2.1   Methods

2.1.1   Participants
The sample consisted of 33 conductors and guards, 23 male (69.7%) and 8 female participants (24.2%) (2 participants (6.1%) did not disclose their gender). The mean age of the group was 44.9 years and the range was 27-66 years. The participants worked as conductors and guards for a passenger rail company and were on day shifts with varying start times.

2.1.2   The Diary
The diary consisted of 10 questions, five questions that were to be answered before work and five questions to be addressed after work. These questions are shown in Appendix 1. The diary was completed every day for a working week (4 days). The questions answered before work covered sleep duration and quality, time taken to travel to work, alertness before starting work and general health status. Those completed after work recorded workload, effort, fatigue, stress and breaks during the day.

2.1.3   HSE Fatigue and Risk Index Scores
In addition to the diary data, information was available on the HSE fatigue index and risk index scores [21] for 22 of the participants. These 22 participants were representative of the whole sample in that their diary data did not differ from those with no Fatigue and Risk Index scores. The Fatigue and the Risk Index are the major outcomes from the HSE fatigue and risk calculator tool. Both are calculated from three separate components of the person's working hours and the nature of their job, namely:

- *A cumulative component.* This relates to the way in which individual duty periods or shifts are 'put together to form a complete schedule. The cumulative component associated with a particular shift depends on the pattern of work immediately preceding that shift.
- *A component associated with duty timing*, i.e. the effect of start time, shift length and the time of day throughout the shift.
- *A job type/breaks component.* This relates to the content of the shift, in terms of the activity being undertaken and the provision of breaks during the shift.

These measures were included in the study to determine whether subjective reports of workload and fatigue were associated with the scores from these mathematical models of fatigue (the fatigue index) and risk of an incident (the risk index).

2.2   Results

Initial analyses examined whether ratings of workload changed over the working week and whether workload on successive days was correlated. Workload increased over the week (Day 1 workload mean = 5.97 s.d. = 2.79; Day 4 workload mean = 7.34 s. d. = 7.34 t = -2.59 df = 32 p < 0.05). The correlations between ratings of workload, effort and fatigue for individual days were significant (all p's < 0.05) and the average ratings were used for subsequent analyses. The correlations are shown in Table 1.

Table 1. Correlations between average ratings of workload, effort, fatigue, sleep duration and HSE fatigue and risk index scores

	Workload	Effort	Fatigue	Sleep duration	Fatigue index	Risk index
Workload	1					
Effort	0.66**	1				
Fatigue	0.58**	0.38*	1			
Sleep Duration	−0.01	−0.07	0.12	1		
Fatigue Index	0.08	0.32	0.00	−0.60**	1	
Risk Index	0.27	0.33	0.60**	0.18	−0.03	1

$**p < 0.01, *p < 0.05$

Workload ratings were significantly correlated with effort and fatigue ratings. Fatigue ratings were significantly correlated with the risk index whereas workload was not significantly correlated with it. The fatigue index was significantly correlated with sleep duration but not the ratings of workload, effort or fatigue.

2.3   Discussion

These results show that single item measures of workload, effort and fatigue show the usual pattern of correlations. Workload increased over the working week and the rating of workload was associated with fatigue which in turn was associated with higher risk of an incident as indicated by the HSE risk index. In contrast, the HSE fatigue index was predicted by sleep duration rather than workload or by the subjective report of fatigue.

These results suggest that a very short audit of workload, effort and fatigue can demonstrate the expected relationships between these variables. Furthermore, the rating of fatigue was correlated with the risk of having an incident (as calculated by the HSE Risk Indicator) which indicates the potential of using these short subjective reports in combination with mathematical models of risk. It is now important to determine whether these measures are of use for other jobs in the rail company. The next study aimed to replicate these findings with volunteers doing a different job (maintenance engineers) and working both night and day shifts. The HSE fatigue and risk calculations were not available for this group and an objective measure of performance (a variable fore-period simple reaction time task, often known as a psychomotor vigilance task [PVT]) was submitted along with the recording of the subjective reports of workload, effort and fatigue.

3 Study 2: Before and After Work Assessment of Rail Engineers

This study used a technique (the After-Effect method) that has been used for examining fatigue [22, 23] and workload [24]. It is very similar to the diary method from the previous study but it only involved the first and last day of the working week.

3.1 Methods

Testing occurred immediately before starting work and immediately after finishing work on each of those days. The diary questions were the same as those of the conductor study. A simple reaction time task was also given at these times.

3.1.1 Participants

Thirty six volunteers (all maintenance engineers) took part in the study (all male; mean age = 44.9 years, range 21–64 years).

3.1.2 Simple Reaction Time Task

In this task a box was displayed in the centre of the screen and at varying intervals (from 1-8 s) a target square appeared in the box. As soon as they detected the square participants were required to press a response key using the forefinger of their dominant hand only. Reaction times were measured to the nearest millisecond. This task lasted for 3 min. The measure of interest here was the mean reaction time (test-re-test reliability: r = 0.65). The mean reaction time from the before work session was subtracted from the after work mean reaction time to obtain an indication of the effects of the working day.

3.2 Results

Results from the first and last day of the working week were averaged. Table 2 shows the correlations between variables. The results were almost identical to the conductors study. Workload, effort and fatigue were correlated. Fatigue was significantly correlated with the before-after difference in reaction time but workload and effort were not.

Table 2. Correlations between workload, effort, fatigue and RT difference

	Workload	Effort	Fatigue	RT difference
Workload	1			
Effort	0.66**	1		
Fatigue	0.65**	0.46*	1	
RT differences	0.11	0.24	0.55**	1

$^{**}p < 0.01,\ ^{*}p < 0.05$

3.3 Discussion

This study with rail maintenance engineers working a range of shifts has confirmed that the single item measures of workload and effort are correlated with a single item measure of fatigue. Fatigue is then correlated with performance impairment due to working, as measured using the simple reaction time task before and after work.

These first two studies have been small scale and focused on specific time periods. It is now important to determine whether similar results are obtained in a wider range of different jobs and locations, and whether these effects occur generally. The next study aimed to extend these findings using a survey methodology and a much larger sample covering a wide variety of jobs in a rail company. The goal was to see which outcomes are associated with job demands, and to try to replicate the results obtained in the diary studies. A different measure of performance was used in this study, namely a single question regarding performance efficiency.

4 Study 3: A Survey of Demands, Fatigue and Performance in Rail Staff

A detailed account of this survey is given in another paper [25]. The main features of the study are briefly summarised here. This, plus details of the actual questionnaire, should provide enough methodological detail. The questionnaire used was based on the Smith Wellbeing Questionnaire (SWELL, [19]). It was designed to provide a detailed profile of the wellbeing of the organisation. It also allows consideration of specific issues and the one of interest here was the association between job demands, fatigue and performance.

4.1 Methods

4.1.1 Sample

1067 employees of a train company completed the questionnaire (Mean age: 44.25 years). This represented a response rate of approximately 50%. The main job types were train drivers, conductors, engineers, station staff, administrators, managers and catering stewards. Participants were entered into a prize draw.

4.1.2 Questionnaire

This is given in Appendix 2.

4.2   Results

Job demands, the current measure of workload, were significantly correlated with fatigue ($r = 0.43$ $p < 0.001$). Demands were also associated with reduced efficiency at work ($r = -0.11$ $p < 0.01$). Fatigue was also associated with reduced performance ($r = -0.14$ $p < 0.01$).

Demands were not the only predictors of fatigue; it was also predicted by lifestyle, control/support at work, noise and shift work. A multiple regression put all of these predictors of fatigue, along with fatigue itself, into an analysis to predict performance. The results of this are shown in Table 3.

High job demands, an unhealthy lifestyle, shift work, and low control/support ($p <$ were all predictors of poor performance. Fatigue was no longer a significant predictor of performance when these variables were included.

Table 3. Regression predicting performance efficiency

Variable	Unstandardised coefficients beta	Unstandardised coefficients std error	Standardised coefficients beta	t	sig
Lifestyle	0.111	0.020	0.156	5.41	0.001
Noise	0.022	0.013	0.050	1.63	0.103
Shiftwork	0.289	0.091	0.096	3.20	0.001
Control/Support	0.227	0.019	0.346	11.79	0.000
Demands	−0.047	0.020	−0.075	−2.38	0.017
Fatigue	−0.019	0.020	−0.031	−0.95	0.344

4.3   Discussion

The present results confirm that high workload is associated with greater fatigue. At a univariate level, both workload and fatigue were associated with perceptions of reduced performance efficiency. However, the survey showed that there were other predictors of fatigue and impaired performance (unhealthy lifestyle; shift work; low control/support). When these were included in the analyses the effects of fatigue on performance were no longer significant. However, workload (job demands) remained a significant predictor of performance in these multi-variate analyses.

The results obtained in the survey show a different pattern of results to those obtained in the diary studies. There could be a number of different interpretations of these discrepancies. The first could be that the measures of workload and fatigue used in the survey were different from those used in the diary studies. However, job demands were correlated with fatigue in the survey which is similar to the observed relationship between workload and fatigue in the diary studies. What may be more important are the different measures of safety/performance used in the three studies. The first study used a mathematical calculation of the risk of being involved in an incident. The second study used an objective measure of reaction as the indicator of effects of the working day. The third study used a subjective assessment of performance efficiency which may not be correlated with the objective indicators of performance or safety.

5   Overall Discussion

The research described in this article has confirmed that workload is an important factor to consider in the operations of railways. Previous research on workload in the railways has largely focused on signallers. The present research has shown that it is highly relevant to the staff of passenger rail companies. The first two studies focused on safety critical staff, namely conductors/guards and engineers. The results from this research showed that workload increased fatigue, which in turn was associated with a greater risk of incidents and slower reaction times. Workload itself did not appear to have a direct influence on safety and performance outcomes. These findings are important for policy and practice. One of the problems faced by railway companies is where to place workload in terms of health and safety practice. The demonstrated strong link between workload and fatigue indicates that workload should come under the agenda of "fatigue". The company involved in the present research have a fatigue policy, and are also developing a scheme of fatigue awareness training. At the moment, fatigue is conceptualised in terms of working hours, and the HSE fatigue index is used as a tool to monitor and prevent fatigue. This suggests that future research should develop appropriate methods for assessing the workload of rail staff. One approach would be to develop the assessments of subjective workload used here. This needs to be supported by objective measurement of workload. Fundamental research is required to compare subjective and objective workload and also to distinguish between physical workload, mental workload and emotional workload. Approaches to these issues have already been developed in fatigue research. The link between workload and fatigue means that templates are already in place to help gain a better understanding of the area and make advances in policy and practice.

The last study used a survey methodology to collect data from a greater range of occupations. High job demands were one of the predictors of fatigue, and both of these were associated with perceptions of reduced performance. Multi-variate analyses showed that high workload remained a significant predictor of performance whereas the effects of fatigue could be accounted for by other factors. These discrepant results in the studies could reflect differences in the jobs represented or in the measures of performance used.

Further analyses are required to determine whether the overall results obtained are consistent when specific jobs are analysed. Again, a practical issue for the rail companies is where the workload should be addressed. The first two studies described here suggest that workload can affect levels of fatigue and as such should be treated as a safety issue. The areas covered by the survey in the third study fall more within the remit of the HR department. This is not to say that performance efficiency is not an issue, rather that different underlying mechanisms may be involved due to both outcomes and predictors being based on subjective perceptions. Validation of the results of the survey using objective measures is an important next step. This could be achieved for both the predictor variables (e.g. objective measurement of job demands) and the outcomes (objective measurement of performance). The results of the survey justify these future studies and suggest further fundamental research to inform practice and policy.

In conclusion, the results reported here show that workload influences the performance of rail staff, either directly or through its association with fatigue. An important feature of the research has been the use of single item measures of workload, fatigue and performance. These short measures were acceptable and could be administered in real-life contexts.

Appendix 1. Diary Questions

Before work diary:
a. How many hours sleep did you get last night?

b. How was the quality of your sleep?

Not at all good								Very good	
1	2	3	4	5	6	7	8	9	10

c. How long did it take you to travel to work? _____ minutes

d. How well are you feeling?

Not at all well								Very well	
1	2	3	4	5	6	7	8	9	10

e. How alert do you feel now?

Very tired									Very alert
1 2	3	4	5	6	7	8	9	10	

After work diary:
f. How was your workload today?

Very low								Very high	
1	2	3	4	5	6	7	8	9	10

g. How much effort did you have to put into your job today?

Very little								A great deal	
1	2	3	4	5	6	7	8	9	10

h. How fatigued do you feel now?

Not at all fatigued								Very fatigued	
1	2	3	4	5	6	7	8	9	10

i. How stressed do you feel now?

Not at all stressed							Very stressed		
1	2	3	4	5	6	7	8	9	10

j. What was the total length of your breaks today?
_____ minutes

Appendix 2: Questionnaire to Assess Wellbeing of Rail Staff (SWELL, [19])

1.   *Age (years):*
2.   *Gender: M/F*
3.   *Job description:*
4.   *Health-related behaviours*
A healthy lifestyle involves taking exercise, eating a balanced diet, not smoking, not drinking excessive amounts of alcohol, and not being overweight. To what extent do you have a healthy life style?

Not at all   Very much so
1   2   3   4   5   6   7   8   9   10

5.   *Personality*
People often describe themselves as being positive ("seeing" the glass as half full) or negative ("seeing the glass as half empty"). How would you describe yourself?

Very negative   Very positive
1   2   3   4   5   6   7   8   9   10

Thinking about the last 6 months:

6.   *Life satisfaction*
How satisfied are you with life in general?

Not at all   Very much so
1   2   3   4   5   6   7   8   9   10

7.   *Life stress*
How much stress have you had in your life in general?

Very little   A great deal
1   2   3   4   5   6   7   8   9   10

8.   *Happiness*
Would you say you are generally happy?

Not at all   Very much so
1   2   3   4   5   6   7   8   9   10

9.   *Anxious/Depressed*
Would you say that you generally feel anxious or depressed?

Not at all   Very much so
1   2   3   4   5   6   7   8   9   10

10.   *Musculo-skeletal problems*
Do you suffer from musculo-skeletal disorders (e.g. arthritis; back pain; sciatica; repetitive strain injury)?

Not at all   Very much so
1   2   3   4   5   6   7   8   9   10

11.   *Noise and vibration*
Are you exposed to noise or vibration at work?

Not at all   Very much so
1   2   3   4   5   6   7   8   9   10

12.   *Shift work/Night work*

Do you work shifts or work at night? Yes/No

13.   *Fumes*

Are you exposed to fumes, dust or solvents at work?

Not at all   Very much so

1   2   3   4   5   6   7   8   9   10

14.   *Job demands*

How demanding do you find your job (e.g. do you have constant pressure, have to work fast, have to put in great effort)?

Not at all demanding   Very demanding

1   2   3   4   5   6   7   8   9   10

15.   *Job control and support*

Do you feel you have control over your job and support from fellow workers?

Not at all   Very much so

1   2   3   4   5   6   7   8   9   10

16.   *Perceived stress at work*

How much stress do you have at work?

Very little   A great deal

1   2   3   4   5   6   7   8   9   10

17.   *Job satisfaction*

Are you satisfied with your job?

Not at all   Very much so

1   2   3   4   5   6   7   8   9   10

18.   *Physical and mental fatigue*

How physically or mentally tired do you get at work?

Not at all tired   Very tired

1   2   3   4   5   6   7   8   9   10

19.   *Illness caused or made worse by work*

Have you had an illness (either physical or mental) caused or made worse by work? Yes/No

20.   *Presenteeism*

Do you ever come to work when you are feeling ill and knowing you can't do your job as well as you would like to? Yes/No

21.   *Efficiency at work*

How efficiently do you carry out your work?

Not very efficiently   Very efficiently

1   2   3   4   5   6   7   8   9   10

22.   *Work-life balance*

Do you find your job interferes with your life outside work or your life outside of work interferes with your job?

Never   Very often

1   2   3   4   5   6   7   8   9   10

---

23.   *Happy at Work*
Are you happy at work?
Never   Very often
1   2   3   4   5   6   7   8   9   10

24.   *Anxious/Depressed because of work*
Are you anxious or depressed because of work?
Never   Very often
1   2   3   4   5   6   7   8   9   10

25.   *Absenteeism*
Approximately how many days sick leave have you had in the last 12 months?

___

26.   *Accidents at work*
How many accidents requiring medical attention have you had in the last 12 months?

___

References

1. Norris, B.J., Wilson, J.R., Clarke, T., Mills, A.: Rail Human Factors: Supporting the Integrated Railway. Ashgate, London (2004)
2. Krehl, C., Balfe, C.: Cognitive workload analysis in rail signalling environments. Cognit. Technol. Work **16**, 359–371 (2014). doi:10.1007/s10111-013-0266-7
3. Wilson, J.R., Cordiner, L.A., Nichols, S.C., Norton, L., Bristol, N., Clarke, T., Roberts, S.: On the right track: systematic implementation of ergonomics in railway network control. Cognit. Technol. Work **3**, 238–252 (2001). doi:10.1007/s10111-001-8005-x
4. Moray, N.: Mental Workload Its Theory and Measurement. Plenum Press, New York (1979)
5. Moray, N.: Subjective mental workload. Hum. Factors **24**, 25–40 (1982). doi:10.1177/001872088202400104
6. Wickens, C.D.: Engineering psychology and human performance, 2nd edn. HarperCollins Publishers Inc, New York (1992)
7. Pickup, L., Wilson, J., Sharples, S., Norris, B., Clarke, T., Youngs, M.S.: Fundamental examination of mental workload in the rail industry. Theoret. Issues Ergon. Sci. **6**(6), 463–482 (2005). doi:10.1080/14639220500078021
8. Hart, S.G., Staveland, L.E.: Development of NASA-TLX (task load index): results of experimental and theoretical research. In: Hancock, A., Meshkati, N. (eds.) PHuman Mental Workload 1988, pp. 139–178. North Holland, New York (1988)
9. Kirwan, B., Ainsworth, L.K.: A Guide to Task Analysis. Taylor & Francis, London (1992)
10. Hancock, P.A., Caird, J.K.: Experimental evaluation of a model of mental work load. Hum. Factors **35**, 413–429 (1993). doi:10.1177/001872089303500303
11. Kahneman, D.: Attention and Effort. Prentice Hall inc, New Jersey (1973)
12. Pickup, L., Wilson, J.: Workload Assessment Tools. Report IOE/RAIL/03/02, The University of Nottingham (2003)
13. RSSB T147: Mental workload assessment for train drivers (2005). https://www.rssb.co.uk/research-development-and-innovation/research-and.../t147
14. Cain, B.: A review of the mental workload literature. In: Defence Research and Development Canada Toronto, Human System Integration Section, Part II, vol. 4, pp. 1–34 (2007)

15. Young, M.S., Brookhuis, K.A., Wickens, C.D., Hancock, P.A.: State of science: mental workload in ergonomics. Ergonomics **58**(1), 1–17 (2015). doi:10.1080/00140139.2014. 956151

16. Eggemeier, F.T.: Properties of workload assessment techniques. Adv. Psychol. **52**, 41–62 (1988). doi:10.1016/S0166-4115(08)62382-1

17. Williams, G.M., Smith, A.P.: A holistic approach to stress and well-being. Part 6: The Wellbeing Process Questionnaire (WPQ Short Form). Occupational Health (At Work), 9/1. 29–31 (2012). ISSN 1744-2265

18. Williams, G.M., Smith, A.P.: Using single-item measures to examine the relationships between work, personality, and well-being in the workplace. Psychol. Special Ed. Positive Psychol. **7**, 753–767 (2016). doi:10.4236/psych.2016.76078

19. Smith, A.P., Smith, H.N.: An international survey of the wellbeing of employees in the business process outsourcing industry. Psychology **8**, 160–167 (2017). doi:10.4236/psych. 2017.81010

20. Mark, G.M., Smith, A.P.: Stress models: a review and suggested new direction. In: Houdmont, J., Leka, S. (eds.) Occupational Health Psychology: European Perspectives on Research, Education and Practice. EA-OHP Series, vol. 3, pp. 111–144. Nottingham University Press, Nottingham (2008)

21. Spencer, M.B., Robertson, K.A., Folkard, S.: The development of a fatigue/risk index for shiftworkers. Research Report 446. Sudbury: HSE Books (2006)

22. Broadbent, D.E.: Is a fatigue test possible? Ergonomics **22**(12), 1277–1290 (1979)

23. Smith A.P.: From the brain to the workplace: research on cognitive fatigue in the laboratory and onboard ship. In: Ackerman, P. (eds.) Cognitive Fatigue: Multidisciplinary perspectives on current research and future applications. American Psychological Association, chap. 14, pp. 291–305. ISBN: 978-1-4338-0839-5. 2011

24. Parkes, K.R.: The effects of objective workload on cognitive performance in a field setting: a two-period cross-over study. Appl. Cognit. Psychol. **9**(7), 153–171 (1995)

25. Fan, J., Smith, A.P.: The impact of workload and fatigue on performance. In: Longo, L., Leva, M.C. (eds.) Human Mental Workload: Models and Applications, H-WORKLOAD 2017. CCIS, vol. 726, pp. 1–16. Springer International Publishing (2017). doi:10.1007/978-3-319-61061-0_6

Author Index

Balfe, Nora   106, 239
Bienert, Nancy   120
Builes, Yilmar   225
Byrne, Aidan   187

Cahill, Joan   161
Callari, Tiziana C.   161
Chauvin, Christine   198
Correro II, Anthony N.   51
Crowley, Katie   106

Delamare, Lise   174
Delmonte, Emma   239

Edwards, Tamsyn   120

Fan, Jialin   90
Fortmann, Florian   161
Fowler, Camila   239

Gligorijević, Ivan   213
Golightly, David   174
Goswell, Graham   174
Guastello, Stephen J.   51

Hancock, P.A.   3
Hasselberg, Andreas   161
Helman, Shaun   239
Hutchins, R.   239

Javaux, Denis   161
Judas, Samantha   198

Ković, Vanja   213

Leva, M. Chiara   225
Longo, Luca   30, 106
Luz, Saturnino   30

Mačužić, Ivan   213
Marra, David E.   51
Martin, Lynne   120
Mercer, Joey   120
Michels, Maura   51
Mijović, Bogdan   213
Mijović, Pavle   213
Milovanović, Miloš   213
Moustafa, Karim   30

Nistico, Chiara   198

Rauffet, Philippe   198
Rypkema, Jouke   143

Schimmel, Henry   51
Smith, Andrew P.   90, 251
Smith, Brendan   106
Smith, Hugo N.   251
Smith, K. Tara   77
Stoeve, Sybert H.   161
Suck, Stefan   161

Tong, Simon   239
Toumelin, Norbert   198
Treble, Peter   174

van Doorn, Bas A.   161
van Wincoop, Alfred   143

Wickens, Christopher D.   18

Zeilstra, Melcher   143

Printed in the United States
By Bookmasters